The 4000-Footers of the White Mountains

The 4000-Footers of the White Mountains

Steven D. Smith

Mike Dickerman

Bondcliff Books · Littleton, New Hampshire

The 4000-Footers of the White Mountains

Library of Congress Card Number: 2001117768
ISBN 1–931271–01–1

Disclaimer: Every effort was made to ensure that the information in this book was accurate at press time. However, trail conditions are subject to change. We would appreciate hearing of any changes. Also, readers should note that hiking in the mountains is a potentially hazardous activity. Weather and trail conditions can change rapidly. Proper gear, clothing, conditioning, and knowledge are prerequisites for a safe journey. Readers are responsible for their own actions and safety, and are urged to exercise caution and sound judgment. Use of this guide is at the reader's own risk. The authors and publisher assume no responsibility.

Text composition by Passumpsic Publishing, St. Johnsbury, Vt.
Printed in the United States by Sherwin Dodge Printers, Littleton, N.H.

Photograph Credits
Ken Stampfer: pages 36, 45, 55, 74, 79, 102, 125, 130, 184, 208, 216
All other photographs by the authors

Cover Photo: Owl's Head Mountain and the Pemigewasset Wilderness as viewed from the summit of Mt. Garfield. Photograph by Ken Stampfer.

Additional copies of this book may be obtained directly from:
Bondcliff Books
P.O. Box 385
Littleton, NH 03561

To all past and present
stewards of the trails

Contents

Acknowledgments ix
Introduction xi
History of the Four Thousand Footer Club / xiii
Hiking Advice / xvii
WMNF Parking Passes / xx
Protecting the Mountain Environment / xx
Trail Stewardship / xxi
Trail Maintaining Organizations / xxii
White Mountains History in a Nutshell / xxiii
White Mountains Geology / xxv
Life on the Mountainsides / xxvi
Using This Guide / xxix
Abbreviations / xxxi

Presidential Range and Dry River

Mount Adams 1
Mount Eisenhower 13
Mount Isolation 20
Mount Jackson 26
Mount Jefferson 31
Mount Madison 41
Mount Monroe 51
Mount Pierce 59
Mount Washington 64

Wildcats-Carter Range

Carter Dome 85
Middle and South Carter 94
Mount Moriah 101
Wildcat Mountain 107

Zealand-Crawford Region

Mount Field 114
Mount Hale 119
Mount Tom 124
Mount Willey 128
Zealand Mountain 134

Pemigewasset Wilderness

The Bonds 139
Mount Carrigain 151

Galehead Mountain 160
Mount Garfield 164
North and South Hancock 169
Owl's Head Mountain 174
North and South Twin Mountain 179

Franconia Range

Mount Flume 187
Mount Lafayette 192
Mount Liberty 201
Mount Lincoln 207

Kinsman-Moosilauke Region

Cannon Mountain 212
North and South Kinsman 219
Mount Moosilauke 228

Sandwich Range and Waterville Valley

Mount Osceola and East Osceola 239
Mount Passaconaway 247
Mount Tecumseh 254
North and Middle Tripyramid 261
Mount Whiteface 269

North Country

Mount Cabot 274
Mount Waumbek 280

Appendixes

4000-Footer Feats and Oddities 287
How Many 4000-Footers Can You See? 289
4000-Footer Checklist 292
Bedrock Types of the 4000-Footers 294
Useful Websites and Phone Numbers 296

Selected Bibliography 297

Acknowledgments

The authors would like to thank the many fine companions, too numerous to list here, who have accompanied them on their treks to the 4000-footers over the last two decades. Steve would like to make special note of Bill Vecchio, with whom he did most of the 4000-footers, finishing on Owl's Head in 1981. Thanks also go to Gene Daniell, longtime recordkeeper of the Four Thousand Footer Club and the final authority on all matters concerning White Mountain peakbagging; Ken Stampfer, for contributing a number of fine photos; P. Thompson Davis, for reviewing and improving the geology notes; and Laura and the late Guy Waterman, for inspiration.

Scott Cahoon of Passumpsic Publishing performed his usual layout magic with an unwieldy manuscript, and the folks at Sherwin Dodge Printers have been great, as always.

Thanks also to National Geographic Maps for use of their excellent Topo! software to create the locator map for the peaks. For more information on their map CD products, call 415–558–8700 or visit www.topo.com.

We owe a great debt to our respective spouses, Jeanne Dickerman and Carol Smith, for their unending patience and unwavering support as we plodded through this time-consuming project.

And with deep appreciation, we thank all those who have been stewards of the trails we are so privileged to enjoy, from the early trailblazers of the 19th century to the legions of volunteers who wield hoe, saw and clippers to keep our paths in good health today.

Introduction

Do you enjoy hiking in the White Mountains?

Have you ever been a stamp collector?

If you answer "yes" to both of the above, you are a likely candidate to become a member of the Four Thousand Footer Club (FTFC) of the White Mountains, sponsored by the Appalachian Mountain Club (AMC). Perhaps you already are a member, officially or unofficially. In either case, this book is written for you.

Hikers who aspire to join this hardy group practice the art of "peakbagging," a form of goal-oriented hiking in which one climbs, on foot, a given set of mountains defined by location and elevation. In New Hampshire's White Mountains, peakbaggers set their course for the 48 summits that rise 4000 feet or more above sea level, from mighty Mt. Washington (6288 ft.) down to lowly Mt. Tecumseh and Mt. Isolation (4003 ft.). As defined by the AMC, to qualify as a 4000-footer a peak must rise at least 200 ft. above the low point of a ridge that connects it with a higher neighbor. The list appears on pages 501–502 of the current (1998) edition of the authoritative *AMC White Mountain Guide*, and on pages 292–293 of this guide.

A quick scan shows such time-honored White Mountain favorites as Washington, Lafayette and Moosilauke. But other names—Hancock, Cabot, Bond, Owl's Head, Isolation—may be unfamiliar even to seasoned White Mountain trampers. And that's exactly why some AMC members created the FTFC back in 1957. Their intent was to entice hikers away from the well-trampled trade routes on the Presidential and Franconia Ranges and out to these lesser-known peaks. (See below for more on the history of the FTFC.)

Over four decades later, the FTFC can rightfully be declared a hiking phenomenon. At the end of 2000 the club boasted 6,851 members, each of whom has received a nifty red, white and blue patch and illustrated scroll attesting to their extensive travels across the White Mountains. Probably thousands more have completed the list but not bothered to apply for official recognition.

As Gene Daniell, longtime Secretary of the FTFC and editor of the *AMC Guide* notes, climbing the 4000-footers is an extremely democratic activity. The White Mountains are small indeed (though feisty at times) when compared to the world's great ranges, and they are very accessible. You need bring only reasonably sturdy legs and lungs, some basic hiking gear, and a strong dash of persistence.

White Mountain peakbaggers come in all shapes and sizes. They can be as young as five or as old as seventy-five. There are even a number of trail-hardened canines who have climbed them all. It's a great family venture, and kids, especially, seem to take pride in the accomplishment.

There are many reasons to climb the 4000-footers aside from merely checking them off the list. Hikers who never venture away from the familiar destinations miss out on some exceptionally beautiful corners of the mountains, whether it be the wilderness panorama from the sharp peak of West Bond, the back-door view of Mt. Washington from lonely Mt. Isolation, the striking lake views from Mt. Whiteface, or the North Country feel of Mt. Cabot. Along the way you'll sample every flavor of White Mountain trail, from the smooth railroad grades in the Pemigewasset Wilderness to the breath-stealing scrambles up the steep flanks of East Osceola, the Hancocks and the Wildcats.

Of course, every club has its rites of passage, and many FTFC members will say that the ascent of Owl's Head is the true test of a peakbagger's devotion. This wooded hump rises deep in the Pemigewasset Wilderness and affords, after a nine-mile slog in, a wonderful fifty-foot view composed entirely of balsam firs. (Some hikers maintain that Owl's Head suffers from overly bad press, for there is a unique view from a rock slide below the summit, and the trek does take you through some lovely remote country.)

How does one get started on climbing the 4000-footers? If you're an experienced hiker who has already scaled some of the major peaks such as Washington, Lafayette or Moosilauke, you already have a good idea of the equipment, preparation and effort you'll need. If you haven't done much hiking, start small and start slow. Try some shorter and easier hikes such as Welch and Dickey Mtns. near Waterville Valley, Hedgehog Mtn. on the Kancamagus Highway, Mt. Pemigewasset in Franconia Notch, or Mt. Willard in Crawford Notch. Each of these hikes is in the 3–5-mile round trip range, with about 1000–1800 ft. of climbing—a good workout, but less demanding than a 4000-footer. For specifics on hiking gear and safety, look below to the section on "Hiking Advice."

If you find the above-mentioned moderate hikes to your liking, you're ready to graduate to some of the easier 4000-footers. Some of the best "starter" peaks, relatively short with good views, include Mt. Jackson, Mt. Hale, Mt. Pierce, Cannon Mtn., and Mt. Osceola from Tripoli Rd. Once you've cut a few notches on your hiking stick, you may find that you're hooked on this 4000-footer game. You can spend many pleasurable hours planning routes with this guide and the *AMC Guide* and its accompanying trail maps. For more information and an application for the FTFC, send a self-addressed stamped envelope to: Four Thousand Footer Committee, Appalachian Mountain Club, 5 Joy St., Boston, MA 02108.

If you're an energetic hiker with lots of free time, you could finish the 4000-footers in one or two busy summers. But most folks spread their peakbagging out over several years or even decades, leaving plenty of time for other hiking pursuits. Gene Daniell will tell you that in climbing the 4000-footers, the race does not go to the swift. "Most hikers find that it was the pursuit of the goal and not the accomplishment that was the real pleasure," he says.

And what happens when you finally bag all 48 peaks? It seems that very few hikers hang up their boots once they get their patch and scroll. Rather, they return to favorite peaks time and again, sometimes trying out new routes to the summits, or fan out and explore other corners of the mountains.

For those incurably afflicted with the peakbagging bug, there are more lists: the New England 4000-footers, the Northeast 111 4000-footers (including the Adirondacks and Catskills), the bushwhack challenges of the New England Hundred Highest, and so forth. Or one can indulge in any number of variations on the White Mountain list, such as climbing them in winter, in order of height, or in one continuous trip.

The end result is, hopefully, that a hiker who climbs the 4000-footers comes away with a deeper appreciation of the mountain world, a knowledge he or she can share with other hikers just starting out. That, in turn, may lead to a commitment to preserve and protect the fragile beauty of the mountains, be it through involvement in trail maintenance or some other avenue. The peakbagger then becomes not merely a collector of mountains, but a steward of the mountains as well. And that's a worthy goal in any hiker's book.

HISTORY OF THE FOUR THOUSAND FOOTER CLUB

Peakbagging in the Northeastern mountains got its start in New York's rugged Adirondacks in 1918, when two teen-age brothers, Bob and George Marshall, and the family's guide, Herb Clark, began climbing all the mountains in that region exceeding 4000 ft. The requirement was that a mountain must rise at least 300 ft. above its col with a higher neighbor, or be at least ¾ mile distant. In 1925 they stood on their forty-sixth and final summit, Mount Emmons. Of the 46 peaks, only 14 then had trails, and eight had apparently never been climbed before. (Bob Marshall went on to become a groundbreaking conservationist and founder of The Wilderness Society.)

In 1937 the first "Forty-Sixers" club was formed in Troy, N.Y., to be succeeded by today's "Adirondack Forty-Sixers" in 1948. Through 1999, over 4,600 hikers had followed in the footsteps of Clark and the Marshalls to bag all the Adirondack high peaks. Although more recent surveys showed that four of the original peaks actually failed to top the 4000-ft. mark, a reverence for tradition has kept these summits on the Adirondack 46er list.

The founder of peakbagging in the White Mountains was Nathaniel L. Goodrich, librarian at Dartmouth College, avid mountain explorer, and renowned AMC trailman in the "golden era" of trail building from about 1915–1930. (Goodrich and cohorts Charles W. Blood, Paul R. Jenks and Karl P. Harrington laid out such classic routes as Webster Cliff Trail, Garfield Ridge Trail, Kinsman Ridge Trail and Wildcat Ridge Trail. Their work on these "through trails" unified what had previously been several disconnected clusters of trails; see Laura and Guy Waterman's *Forest and Crag.*) In a December 1931 article in *Appalachia*, the journal of the AMC, Goodrich proposed a list of 36 White Mountain 4000-footers that he had climbed, stipulating that each peak must rise at least 300 ft. above any ridge connecting it with a higher 4000-ft. neighbor. He noted that his 300-ft. benchmark was arbitrary and could easily be changed to 200 ft. or 400 ft.

Original List of White Mountain 4000-Footers

Includes elevations as of 1931

Washington	6284	S. Carter	4645	Tripyramid, N	4140
Adams	5805	Garfield	4485	Passaconaway	4116
Jefferson	5725	Liberty	4460	Cannon	4077
Monroe	5390	Hancock	4430	Hale	4077
Madison	5380	Wildcat "A"	4415	Wildcat "E"	4070
Lafayette	5249	Kinsman, S.	4363	Moriah	4065
S. Twin	4926	Flume	4327	Tom	4040
Carter Dome	4860	Osceola	4326	Hancock, E.	4035
Moosilauke	4810	Zealand	4301	Owl's Head	4023
Pleasant	4775	Field	4300	Waumbek	4020
Bond	4714	Osecola, E	4185	Jackson	4012
Carrigain	4647	Cabot	4170	Tecumseh	4004

By 1934 AMC member Francis B. "Mully" Parsons had climbed Goodrich's original list of 36 peaks, getting inaccessible Hancock on his second try and climbing Owl's Head from Greenleaf Hut. Goodrich had since expanded his list to include 51 peaks with names and a total of 88 with stated elevations. Parsons went on to complete the list of 51, and also a list of New England 4000-footers, by 1949. He published his list and an account of his climbs in the December 1949 *Appalachia*.

In the summer of 1948 Mr. and Mrs. J. Daniel McKenzie climbed all the 4000-footers of Vermont, New Hampshire *and* New York, a remarkable feat described in the June 1958 *Appalachia*. Dana C. Backus, who started climbing the peaks as a member of the AMC trail crew in 1923, finished Goodrich's 36 peaks in 1953, including the required bushwhack ascents of Hancock and Owl's Head. Of the latter peak, he wrote in the December 1953 *Appalachia*, "My clothing was ripped to ribbons. Scarcely enough was left of my shirt to flag a wheelbarrow, but I had at last reached the top of Owl's Head." In the summer of 1956 AMC member Roderick Gould climbed Goodrich's 36 peaks, plus two more—Willey and West Bond—that he had determined were additional qualifiers under the 300-ft. rise rule.

Meanwhile, Walter C. "Gus" Merrill distributed Goodrich's expanded list of 51 named peaks, and several AMC climbers completed this group of mountains in the mid-1950s. At a meeting of the club's General Outings Committee, Edwin Scotcher suggested that a Four Thousand Footer Club (FTFC) be created, similar to the Adirondack Forty-Sixers. The committee saw it as a way to introduce climbers to new areas, away from the familiar

Presidential and Franconia Ranges, thereby boosting participation in the club's organized outings. In March 1957 a sub-committee composed of Parsons, Merrill, Barbara Richardson and Albert S. Robertson sent a letter to the governing AMC Council requesting approval for the idea. The letter included a design for a shoulder patch designed by artist Mark Fowler. The Council approved the idea but asked that the list of 51 peaks be modified using a specific benchmark, rather than selecting mountains merely on the basis of having a name.

After exchanging letters with officials of the Adirondack Forty-Sixers, the AMC Four Thousand Footer Club committee held a map party at Parsons' home, using the 1955 *AMC White Mountain Guide*, the latest U.S. Geological Survey topographic maps, and magnifying glasses. They decided to use a 200-ft. rule, and the list was accepted by the AMC Council. After adding South Hancock and dropping Old Speck in Maine, the committee ended up with a list of 46 peaks—the same number of 4000-footers as the Adirondacks.

In May 1957 an AMC trip placed about 40 climbers on the summit of then-trailless North Hancock. Roderick Gould became the first to complete the new "official" list on May 26. Thomas S. Lamb followed on September 2. The next to finish, on September 14, were the eminent mountaineers, Miriam Underhill and Robert L. M. Underhill. On September 21 forty-one trampers summitted on South Hancock, including seven more finishers, and by year's end, the total of "four-thousanders" was nineteen, counting Goodrich and Parsons from the 1930s.

The first FTFC awards meeting was held on April 26, 1958, including presentation of the aforementioned shoulder patch and a scroll designed by renowned cartographer Erwin Raisz. (This scroll is still in use today, and the awards gathering continues as an annual April event attended by hundreds.) The official list was published in the June 1958 issue of *Appalachia*, along with climbing directions for the summits without maintained trails—Cabot, Waumbek, Tom, Zealand, Owl's Head, West Bond and the Hancocks. In August of that year "Red Mac" MacGregor, who had climbed his first peak in 1911 and in the 1920s was the first manager of the AMC hut system, became the senior member of the FTFC at age 74.

"AMC 4000-Footer Club Spurs Climbers" read a *Boston Globe* headline in September 1958. A wave of peakbagging enthusiasm swept through the ranks of the AMC. There were sixteen finishers in 1958 and another dozen in 1959. New members were listed annually in *Appalachia*, and by 1962 the membership was at 129. A year-and-a-half later the roster had swelled to 199, including seven-year old Sarah Merrow and a mongrel named Friskie. "Herd paths" developed on the trailless peaks, and one-by-one these summits acquired official, maintained trails, though to this day the path up Owl's Head is technically not considered a trail.

Right after the FTFC became official, Miriam and Robert Underhill launched a new peakbagging venture—climbing the mountains in winter.

This, wrote Miriam, "would present an even more sporting challenge than ambling up the well-trodden trails in summer." As originators of the game, the Underhills could set the rules—climbs must be made during calendar winter, typically between December 22 and March 20. "'Snow on the ground' and other namby-pamby criteria definitely did not count." As described by Miriam in the December 1967 *Appalachia*, the treks to the more remote peaks in those days of unbroken trails were true winter epics, in some cases requiring several return trips.

On December 23, 1960, the Underhills became the first to complete the winter peaks by cramponing to the top of cloud-wreathed Mt. Jefferson in the company of several friends. The temperature was –8° F with a 72 mph wind. Remarkably, Miriam was 62 and Robert 71 at the time. In February 1962, atop Mt. Monroe, Merle Whitcomb became the third hiker (and second woman) to complete the "winter 4000." The feat was not repeated again until 1967, and through the winter of 2000–2001, just 254 trampers had done the 48 peaks in winter, less than 4 percent of those who had finished the list in summer.

Winter seems to inspire some peakbaggers. Among the more remarkable snow-season feats have been climbing the peaks by moonlight (Fred Hunt), standing atop each summit at midnight (Mike Bromberg) and making ascents of each peak from all four points of the compass (Guy Waterman). Equally astonishing is the scaling of each peak in every month of the year (Gene Daniell). See the Appendix for more on these and other unusual spins on peakbagging.

A dozen years after the creation of the FTFC, one of its founders, Al Robertson, looked back with satisfaction. "The response far exceeded our expectations," he wrote in the June 1969 *Appalachia*. "At times, Guyot Shelter looked like Times Square! Climbers of the 1910 to 1940 era dusted off their gear and reappeared upon the scene. . . . More importantly, the list was attractive to new climbers."

From 1966 through 2000, at least 100 hikers have finished the White Mountain 4000-footers each year, with notable surges in activity in the early 1970s and throughout the 1990s, with over 200 finishers per year. Famous peakbaggers have included the late Meldrim Thomson, governor of New Hampshire in the 1970s, and U.S. Supreme Court Justice David Souter.

As peakbagging caught on, new lists were developed—the New England 4000-footers in 1964 (adding 12 peaks in Maine and 5 in Vermont), the Northeast 111 in 1967 (adding the Adirondacks and Catskills), and the New England Hundred Highest, also in 1967 (including a dozen or so peaks accessible only by map-and-compass bushwhacks.) These lists are all officially recognized by the present AMC Four Thousand Footer Committee.

The publication of a new South Twin Mtn. quadrangle by the U.S. Geological Survey led to the addition of two new peaks to the White Mountain 4000-footer list. Galehead Mtn. was put on the roster in 1967, and in 1980 the magnificent Bondcliff became 4000-footer No. 48.

Over the years peakbaggers and the FTFC have not been without their critics. As a wave of new backpackers swept over the mountains in the early 1970s, some observers concluded that the club had done its job too well. In a June 1973 *Appalachia* article, then editor Phil Levin proposed the abolition of the FTFC. Heated correspondence, pro and con, followed in succeeding issues.

Critics have charged that peakbagging introduces, in Levin's words, "an undesirable artificiality into the natural scenery of the mountains." The peakbagger, it's said, is obsessed with a numbers game that demeans the mountain experience. Peakbaggers also have been taken to task for affecting use patterns and attracting more hikers to fragile trails and once-undisturbed summits. The results, critics say, are increased trail erosion and a loss of solitude in the mountains.

Supporters of peakbagging have countered that the way one enjoys the mountains is a matter of individual choice, as long as it does not detract from others' experiences, or degrade the mountains themselves. They add that most hikers who take up "the list" are already active hikers, and that many FTFC members are involved in trail maintenance and other stewardship activities. (For an excellent summary of the peakbagging debate, see Laura and Guy Waterman's *Forest and Crag* and *Backwoods Ethics*.)

Over the last three decades the FTFC has flourished under the guidance of leaders such as Dick Stevens, Paul Bernier, Bruce Brown, Gene Daniell, Deane Morrison and Tom Sawyer, ardent peakbaggers all. It seems likely that peakbagging is here to stay, and that for many it can be a magnificent obsession, opening new horizons and deepening one's commitment to cherish and protect the mountain world. Nathaniel Goodrich, the man who started it all in the White Mountains, spoke for generations of peakbaggers to follow when he wrote, "Yes, I have done the lot, and wish heartily there were more."

HIKING ADVICE

With some basic precautions, knowledge and common sense, hiking the 4000-footers can be a safe and enjoyable experience. An excellent resource is Dan H. Allen's *Don't Die on the Mountain*.

Season

The regular hiking season runs from about Memorial Day to Columbus Day. Earlier in the spring there is likely to be mud on the lower slopes and snow at higher elevations, in big snow years lasting even into June on the high, wooded ridges. Snow and ice may cloak the trails up high in late fall, and the days are considerably shorter. Special gear, clothing and knowledge are needed for winter hiking; see below.

Weather

Though fine, sunny summer days are common enough, at other times these mountains serve up some of the wildest weather on the continent. Be prepared for quick weather changes! Several storm tracks converge in this region, frequently lashing the upper slopes with wind, rain, snow and ice. The *average* wind speed at the summit of Mt. Washington is 35 mph. Snow has fallen in every month of the year and the top of Mt. Washington is in the clouds 55–60% of the time. These mountains deserve respect!

Hikers venturing to the high peaks should always check the forecast. It is likely to be 20 or more degrees colder at the summit than in the valley, and significantly windier and cloudier. Be especially cautious early or late in the season. Make alternate plans if the weatherman calls for a stormy day. Avoid stream crossings if heavy rain has occurred or is predicted. Even if good conditions are forecast, be prepared to head down if the weather takes an unfavorable turn. Many have died of exposure on these slopes, even in summer and fall. Thunderstorms are extremely dangerous to hikers on exposed ridges—keep a wary eye out for them. Recorded White Mountain local forecasts can be obtained by calling 603–447–5252 (Conway) or 603–444–2656 (Littleton), or check the Mt. Washington Observatory website (*www.mountwashington.org*) or AMC website (*www.outdoors.org*).

Choosing a Hike

When deciding where to go hiking, several factors should be considered—weather, the fitness, ability and ambition of your group, stream crossings, available daylight, and the length, steepness, elevation gain, exposure and roughness of the trail. A standard formula for estimating hiking times is two miles per hour, plus a half-hour for every 1000 ft. of elevation gain. If you're new to hiking the high peaks, start with easier trips before working your way up to the longer, more difficult hikes. Stay within your limits! Strenuous ascents of the high Presidentials and long trips like Owl's Head, the Bonds and Mt. Isolation are challenging treks that are not suited for beginners. Leave word of your itinerary with family or friends.

Clothing and Footwear

Dress for the season, elevation and weather. In cooler temperatures, layering is the key. Wool and synthetics are far better than cotton for warmth and insulating value, especially when wet. We always bring plenty of extra layers, even on hot days. When hiking to higher elevations, especially above treeline, bring rain and wind outerwear, an insulating jacket or sweater, extra shirts and socks, long pants, hat and gloves. 4000-footer trails are often rough, rocky and rooty, and are slippery when wet; wear sturdy, broken-in boots and wool/synthetic socks.

In Your Pack

In addition to the extra clothing mentioned above, we recommend bringing these items in a good-sized pack for a 4000-footer day hike: at least two quarts of water, lunch and high-energy snacks, map/guidebook, compass, watch, sunscreen, first aid kit, flashlight or headlamp, insect repellent (black flies and mosquitoes are worst in June), pocket knife, rope or cord, toilet paper, sunglasses, waterproof matches, camera, binoculars and bandanas (very useful). Lining your pack with a large plastic garbage bag will keep clothing dry. Trekking poles or a walking stick can be very helpful for balance on rugged trails and at stream crossings.

Maps

A good topographic trail map is essential. Highly recommended are the series of maps that come with the indispensable *AMC White Mountain Guide*; they may be purchased separately on waterproof tyvek. Another excellent choice is the waterproof Map Adventures map that comes with the *White Mountains Map Book*; it, too, can be purchased separately. The Randolph Mountain Club and Wonalancet Out Door Club have fine maps for the Northern Presidentials and Sandwich Range, respectively. Bradford Washburn's map of the Presidential Range (published by AMC) is highly detailed and accurate. The popular DeLorme trail map and guide is good for an overview of the Whites. U.S. Geological Survey maps are unmatched for showing topographic detail, though trail locations may be inaccurate on older maps. The National Geographic / Topo! CDs for New Hampshire contain all the relevant USGS maps and are great for laying out peakbagging routes with elevation profiles.

On the Trail

Start early and set a steady, moderate pace that is comfortable for all in your group. Establish a turn-around time and stick to it, leaving plenty of time to get out before dark. (Darkness comes earlier in late summer and fall.) Watch your footing carefully on rocky, rooty and steep sections, especially when wet, and at stream crossings. Follow trail markings (blazes and cairns) and signs carefully, particularly above treeline and at junctions and stream crossings. Keep your group together and always wait up at trail junctions so no one goes astray. Filter or treat all surface water before drinking.

Prevent Hypothermia

Stay as warm and dry as possible in cool, damp weather. Hypothermia, the lethal chilling of the body core, can occur in summer, especially in wet, windy weather above treeline. Early signs include shivering, clumsiness, slurred speech and apathy. Get the victim into warm, dry clothing ASAP, before the condition worsens.

Rescue

Hikers should be as self-reliant as possible, but accidents do occur. There are highly capable and dedicated groups of search-and-rescue professionals and volunteers in the White Mountains. In an emergency situation, one hiker should stay with the victim and others should hike out for help. (Hence the maxim that four persons make a safer hiking party.) A cell phone *can* be a lifesaver; a key number is the N.H. State Police emergency line, 1–800–852–3411. Note that under recent N.H. legislation rescue calls that are unnecessary or due to reckless actions may result in a hefty fine for the calling party.

Winter

The snowy months can be an exhilarating and exciting season for hiking the high peaks. However, the combination of cold, deep snow, ice, bitter winds and short days requires great caution and appropriate clothing and gear. Snowshoes and insulated boots are needed on the winter trails, and crampons and ice axe are necessities above treeline. Winter beginners should *not* start with a 4000-footer. Try shorter, easier trips first, preferably in the company of experienced winter trampers. The AMC offers many organized trips and workshops throughout the winter. Good books on winter hiking include *Winterwise*, by John M. Dunn; *AMC Guide to Winter Camping*, by Stephen Gorman; *Don't Die on the Mountain*, by Dan H. Allen; and *Snowshoe Hikes in the White Mountains*, by Steven D. Smith.

WMNF PARKING PASSES

In 1997 Congress directed the White Mountain National Forest (WMNF) and other National Forests to develop a parking permit program to provide recreation funding. Moneys raised are used for repair and maintenance of campgrounds, trails and shelters, for wildlife habitat enhancement, and for interpretive programs. You *must* have a parking pass to park at trailheads on WMNF land, which is shaded in green on the Appalachian Mountain Club's trail maps. There are four options for parking passes:

Daily Pass	$ 3.00	Purchased at trailhead; self-service tube
7-Day Pass	$ 5.00	Purchased at stores or ranger stations
Annual Pass	$20.00	Purchased at stores or ranger stations
Household Pass (two cars)	$25.00	Purchased at stores or ranger stations

If you plan on more than four hikes a year from WMNF trailheads, you're better off getting an annual pass.

PROTECTING THE MOUNTAIN ENVIRONMENT

As hikers we all have a responsibility to minimize our impact on the mountain environment. The objective is to Leave No Trace (LNT)—the name of a national organization dedicated to promoting outdoor ethics.

- Carry out what you carry in, and pick up any litter you find.
- Stay on the marked trails; please don't widen muddy spots, trample trailside vegetation or shortcut switchbacks, especially above treeline.
- Avoid hiking during "mud season," when trails are vulnerable to erosion.
- The call of nature should be answered at least 200 feet from any stream,

water source or trail, and waste should be buried in a cat hole 6 to 8 inches deep. LNT advocates packing out used toilet paper in double ziploc bags.

- Do not pick wildflowers or disturb wildlife.
- Limit your hiking group to 10 persons or less. Keep loud voices and noise to a minimum—other hikers will appreciate it.
- Keep dogs under control, or leave them at home. Don't let dogs wander off trail in the fragile alpine zone.
- If camping, use an established, legal site at least 200 feet off the trail. Some areas in the Whites are off-limits to camping, including the alpine zone, and within one quarter-mile of huts, shelters, and woods; the WMNF publishes an updated Backcountry Camping Rules brochure each year.
- Use a stove in preference to building fires; if you do build a fire, be extremely careful and erase all traces when you leave. Keep a clean campsite and hang your food so as not to tempt bears residing in the area.

TRAIL STEWARDSHIP

We strongly encourage all hikers climbing the 4000-footers to devote at least one day a year to trail maintenance. Over the last 30 years usage of trails in the White Mountains has greatly increased, while funds available for trail maintenance have declined, a victim of lean Forest Service budgets. The professional crews and dedicated core volunteers of the various maintaining organizations perform yeoman's work each year, but they can only do so much. Only with the help of additional volunteers can the 1200 miles of trails in the Whites be kept open for the enjoyment of hikers. Helping out with the trails gives you a sense of stewardship that goes beyond the bagging of peaks. Most volunteer trail work is not overly strenuous, and with a good group of people it can be a lot of fun.

There are numerous opportunities to participate in trail maintenance, from "adopting" your own trail to spending a day or even a week working on a specific project with an organized "crew."

Adopt-A-Trail Program

When you "adopt" a trail you agree to take over the basic maintenance of a section of trail, typically one to two miles in length. The most important work is the regular cleaning of drainages that divert water off the trail, essential to preventing trail erosion. Adopters also cut back brush, paint blazes, clear blowdown and pick up litter. Sponsoring organizations generally request that adopters make three trips per year to their chosen trail. The two largest Adopt-A-Trail programs are available through the WMNF and AMC. Similar programs are run by other groups. In most of these programs tools and training are provided for trail adopters. If you're interested in adopting a particular trail, look in the *AMC White Mountain Guide* to see what organization maintains it, and contact them to see if it or others are available; contact information is listed below.

Trail Work Days

If you don't want to take on the responsibility of adopting a trail, there are many work days sponsored by the various maintaining organizations (such as AMC and Trailwrights) throughout the hiking season. Two of the biggest single efforts are National Trails Day in early June and New Hampshire Trails Day in mid-July.

Donations

For hikers who truly do not have extra time to work on the trails, donations are always welcome. Funds are needed to purchase tools and supplies, and to hire highly skilled professional crews for major trail projects. The AMC Four Thousand Footer Committee maintains a trail fund supported by FTFC members who choose to contribute above the nominal basic dues cost. Such contributions can be mailed to: AMC Four Thousand Footer Committee, 5 Joy St., Boston, MA 02108. Donations may also be made to the organizations listed below; be sure to specify that the funds are to be used for trail maintenance.

TRAIL MAINTAINING ORGANIZATIONS

Appalachian Mountain Club: Maintains over 300 miles of trails in the Whites. In addition to the club's official trails program, based at Pinkham Notch, many chapters have their own volunteer crews. 603–466–2721; *www.outdoors.org*; AMC Trails, PO Box 298, Gorham, NH 03581

Chatham Trails Association: Oversees several trails in Evans Notch area.

Cohos Trail Association: Oversees the 160-mile Cohos Trail from Crawford Notch to the Canadian border. *www.cohostrail.org*

Dartmouth Outing Club: Responsible for many trails in Mt. Moosilauke area. *dartmouth.outing.club@dartmouth.edu*; 603–646–2834

New Hampshire Department of Parks: Responsible for trails in Franconia Notch and Crawford Notch State Parks. 603–271–3556; *www.nhparks.state.nh.us*; PO Box 1856, Concord, NH 03302

Randolph Mountain Club: Maintains over 100 miles on Northern Presidentials and Randolph valley. *www.randolphmountainclub.org*; Randolph Mountain Club, Randolph, NH 03570

Squam Lakes Association: Maintains 40 miles of trails in the Squam Range and on Sandwich Dome. 603–968–7336; *www.squamlakes.org*; PO Box 204, Holderness, NH 03245

Trailwrights: This dedicated group offers work trips and workshops on trails throughout the state. They also have their own list of 72 4000-footers, using different criteria than the AMC list. The Trailwrights list includes several bushwhack peaks. To qualify for membership, you must climb each peak individually, and must complete 72 hours of trail work. Contact them for more info. *www.Trailwrights.org*; PO Box 1945, Hillsboro, NH 03244

Waterville Valley Athletic and Improvement Association: Oversees many trails in the Waterville Valley area.

White Mountain National Forest: Maintains over 600 miles of trails in the Whites. 603–466–2713; *www.fs.fed.us/r9/white*; 300 Glen Rd., Gorham, NH 03581

Wonalancet Out Door Club: Works on 50 miles of trails in the Sandwich Range. *www.wodc.org*; HCR 64, Box 5, Wonalancet, NH 03897

WHITE MOUNTAINS HISTORY IN A NUTSHELL

The White Mountains are a range rich in history, adding great interest to climbs of the high peaks. In the individual chapters for the 4000-footers we list "Historical Highlights"—significant events that occurred on or around the mountains. The very brief historical summary presented here will provide a basic context for these events.

Native Americans inhabited parts of the White Mountain region, primarily in valleys around the fringes of the mountains. The Abenaki tribes who lived here seldom ventured high into the mountains, where powerful deities were thought to dwell. Abenaki place names are sprinkled around the White Mountains, and several peaks, including one 4000-footer, Mt. Passaconaway, were named after Abenaki chiefs.

Exploration of the mountains by colonists began with Darby Field's bold ascent of Mt. Washington in 1642, accompanied by two Indian guides. In the late 1700s and early 1800s numerous scientific explorations were conducted, especially in the Presidential Range. Among the more notable was the Belknap-Cutler expedition in 1784. Botanists poked into every nook and cranny in the 1820s and 1830s, and several Presidential Range features are named after them.

Meanwhile, white settlers began occupying valleys around the mountains in the late 1700s and early 1800s. The most famous pioneer clan was the Crawfords, who established inns at Crawford Notch and essentially founded the tourist industry in the White Mountains. Many of the first recreational hikers in the region were lured by the guide service offered by the Crawfords and the trails they established on the Presidential Range. Small hostelries were also established in other areas of the Whites.

The coming of the railroads and the construction of numerous hotels, many of the "grand" variety, launched the "golden era" of White Mountain tourism in the mid and late 1800s. Writers such as Thomas Starr King inspired visitors to get out and drink in the mountain scenery. Trails and bridle paths were built on several mountains, and in places like Waterville Valley entire networks of hiking paths were laid out.

The last three decades of the 1800s brought an era of intensive exploration and trail-building. Many mountain areas were visited for the first time during Charles H. Hitchcock's state geological survey from 1869–1871. The founding of the Appalachian Mountain Club in 1876 fostered additional probing into remote corners of the Whites, along with a flurry of trail-building. By century's end, hundreds of miles of paths had been cut, most notably on the Northern Presidentials, by such trail-blazers as J. Rayner Edmands (known for his comfortably graded paths), Eugene B. Cook, William H. Peek, and William G. Nowell. For many years hikers were guided by Moses Sweetser's comprehensive *The White Mountains: A Handbook for Travelers*, first published in 1876. In 1907 the AMC published its first guide to the trails of the Whites, and that has been the standard-bearer ever since.

The decades from the 1870s into the 1920s and 1930s saw intensive logging in the White Mountains. Timber barons such as Lincoln's infamous J. E. Henry laid logging railroads into remote corners of the mountains to haul out the timber; a number of these old grades serve as trails today. Clearcutting was the order of the day, and fires kindled in logging slash consumed vast acreages, the worst occurring in 1903.

In response to abusive logging and the destructive fires that followed, conservation groups led by the Society for the Protection of New Hampshire Forests successfully lobbied Congress to pass the Weeks Act in 1911, authorizing the creation of National Forests in the East. Several hundred thousand acres were soon acquired by the U.S. Forest Service for the White Mountain National Forest (WMNF). Today the WMNF spreads across some 780,000 acres. These lands are managed under the multiple use concept for recreation, water, timber, wildlife and other uses. Five Wilderness areas totaling 115,000 acres are left in an undisturbed state. About 40% of the WMNF is open to timber harvesting on a limited basis.

The years from about 1915 to the mid-1930s brought the expansion and unification of the White Mountains trail system and the development of the chain of AMC huts. Four AMC trail architects—Nathaniel L. Goodrich, Paul R. Jenks, Charles W. Blood, and Karl P. Harrington—were key figures in this era, along with the legendary hut system manager, Joe Dodge. The 1938 hurricane wrought havoc on many trails, and some were abandoned in its wake. The new mobility afforded to tourists and hikers with the coming of the automobile age made it easier than ever to get to—and around—the mountains. This spelled the end for most of the grand hotels.

A tremendous surge in hiking and backpacking in the late 1960s and early 1970s brought intensive pressure to bear on trails and backcountry facilities, forcing land managers to evolve new methods of coping with heavy use. The continued popularity of hiking into the 21st century has brought an increasing focus on trail maintenance. It has also fostered the development of a new "leave-no-trace" wilderness ethic, encouraging hikers to tread lightly on the land.

For a comprehensive and fascinating history of hiking in the White Mountains and the Northeast in general, we highly recommend Laura and Guy Waterman's *Forest and Crag*.

WHITE MOUNTAINS GEOLOGY

The geologic history of the Whites dates back some 500 million years, when the area was covered by a prehistoric ocean and the eastern edge of the North American continent was 100 miles or more to the west of New Hampshire. Over time sand, silt and mud were deposited on the floor of the sea and compressed into sedimentary rocks such as sandstones and shales. About 460 million years ago, a chain of volcanic islands resulted from the collision of the North American and Eurasian continental plates. Lofty peaks were thrust up to the west of New Hampshire. Intense heat and pressure transformed the sedimentary rocks into harder metamorphic ("changed") rocks.

Starting about 375 million years ago, after millions of years of erosion wore down the first mountain range, the continental plates of Europe and Africa collided with North America. Again, mountains were folded and thrust skyward, and sedimentary rocks were molded into tough, erosion-resistant metamorphic rocks. These rocks—primarily schist, quartzite and gneiss—make up most of the Presidential and Carter Ranges and Mt. Moosilauke. Thus, in the Granite State the very highest mountains are not composed of granite at all. Exposures of this metamorphic rock often show prominent foliation and folding, the latter indicating the tremendous pressures involved in their formation.

Most of the central and western White Mountains are made up of igneous ("firemade") rocks, which formed when magma (molten rock) welled up in the earth's crust. These are the granites and similar rocks for which New Hampshire is famous. The first such intrusion took place about 350 million years ago during the collision of the continents; a prominent rock of this time is Kinsman quartz monzonite, found in the Kinsman Range and in places on the lower slopes of the Franconia Range.

The largest intrusion of igneous rock, known as the "White Mountain Magma Series," occurred about 200 million years ago, as the continental plates were tearing apart. Some of this magma erupted above ground as lava, forming the Moat volcanics; these volcanic rocks were largely eroded away over the ages and are found in only a few places today. Some magma migrated into fractures in the crust and cooled into dikes or semi-circular ring-dikes (as seen with Mt. Waumbek and the Pliny Range). Other igneous rocks formed in large plutons far underground. Common rocks of this type include Conway granite and Mt. Osceola granite.

Millions of years of erosion have worn the White Mountains down from what may once have been far loftier heights, exposing the underlying metamorphic and igneous bedrock we see today. The most dramatic sculpting of the landscape in the last 2 million years has been accomplished by glaciers. Two types of glaciers carved the mountains of New Hampshire—the smaller valley glaciers that plucked out the steep headwalls and broad floors of cirques such as the Great Gulf and Tuckerman, Huntington and King

Ravines, and continental ice sheets that once covered even the top of Mt. Washington. Ice streams within the continental ice sheets carved U-shaped troughs from stream-eroded V-shaped valleys such as Pinkham, Crawford and Franconia Notches. Glaciers advanced and retreated several times; the last pullback took place about 12,000 years ago.

Evidence of continental glaciation can be viewed in many places on and around the 4000-footers. Besides the great scoops of the cirques and notches, individual ledges ("sheepbacks" or "roches moutonnées") and entire mountains (such as Mts. Monroe, Garfield and Galehead) were shaped by the ice flow, showing gentle slopes on the north side, where the glacier moved uphill, and steep faces on the south side, where the ice plucked rock away as it ground downslope. Other signs of glaciation include scratches and striations on exposed ledges, glacial "erratic" boulders that were deposited by the glacier far from their point of origin, and pond basins, such as the Lakes of the Clouds, that were scooped out of the bedrock. Most of the soil in the White Mountains is glacial till—a jumbled mix of rocks, sand and clay left when the last ice sheet receded.

After the demise of the glaciers, frost action continued to work on the bedrock. When water freezes to ice, it expands with a power sufficient to shatter rock. Countless freeze-thaw cycles have left desolate piles of boulders around the cones of the higher Presidential peaks. The same process created the Old Man of the Mountain on the side of Cannon Mtn., and will someday destroy it. Frost action working on smaller rocks above treeline has created visible patterns—circles and stripes—on the alpine lawns.

Minor modifications of the mountain landscape still take place today, largely in the form of landslides. These occur on steep slopes (25 to 35 degrees) when heavy rains saturate thin soil cover, sending a cascade of soil, vegetation and rock roaring down the mountainside. The deadly Willey Slide of 1826 is the most famous of these, though the scar has long since revegetated. Several new slides fell in the mid-1990s on Mt. Osceola, North Twin, Mt. Pierce and the west side of the Bond-Guyot-South Twin ridge.

For those interested in such things, we have included in the Appendix a list of basic bedrock types for the 4000-footers culled from a series of geological bulletins produced by the state of New Hampshire.

LIFE ON THE MOUNTAINSIDES

In terms of vegetation and climate, ascending a 4000-footer is like traveling to the northern reaches of Canada. Every 1000-foot rise in elevation has about the same effect as heading about 230 miles north—you lose three degrees in average temperature. You also gain eight inches in annual precipitation. The climate is colder, wetter and windier at higher elevations, making life harsher for plants, animals and hikers. Distinctive zones of vegetation have evolved in response to these altitudinal gradients. In one day you climb from the temperate world of the valley floor to the arctic-alpine world above treeline. Although there are many local variations, the zones listed below are typical of what you will encounter on your way up one of the higher peaks. For further reference consult the many excellent field guides available. Three guides published by AMC Books are especially pertinent to the Whites: *Field Guide to the New England Alpine Summits*, by Nancy G. Slack and Alison W. Bell; *At Timberline*, by Frederic L. Steele; and *North Woods*, by Peter J. Marchand.

Northern Hardwood Forest

Elevation: Up to 2000–2500 ft.

Trees: The dominant species of this light, airy, leafy forest—famous for its fall foliage displays—are sugar maple, yellow birch, and American beech. May also include paper birch, white ash, red maple, white pine, quaking aspen, Eastern hemlock, red spruce, black and pin cherry, and red oak. Hemlocks often dominate in cool, moist ravines. Paper birch forms lovely groves in burned areas, and also in the transition zone between the hardwoods below and the conifers above. Common shrubs in the hardwood zone are hobblebush, striped maple, and mountain maple.

Wildflowers: Spring: red and painted trilliums, trout lily, bellwort, violets. Late spring/early summer: pink lady's slipper, bluebead lily, wood sorrel, purple twisted stalk, wild sarsaparilla, bunchberry, goldthread, starflower, Canada mayflower.

Birds: Red-eyed and solitary vireos, scarlet tanager, rose-breasted grosbeak, veery, wood thrush, hermit thrush, black-throated blue, black-throated green, Canada and black-and-white warblers, ovenbird, redstart, wood pewee, least flycatcher, black-capped chickadee, blue jay, yellow-bellied sapsucker, pileated, downy and hairy woodpeckers, broad-winged and red-tailed hawks, barred owl, ruffed grouse.

Mammals: Eastern chipmunk, white-tailed deer, moose (look for large, cloven tracks, tooth scrapings on young trees, "cow pies" in summer and heaps of large pellets in colder seasons), black bear (look for claw marks on beech trunks), coyote, white-footed mouse, porcupine, short-tailed weasel, fisher, raccoon, bobcat, snowshoe hare.

Spruce-Fir Forest

Elevation: ca. 2500 ft.–4000 ft.

Trees: Red spruce and balsam fir dominate in the dark, shady conifer forests at these elevations. They are well adapted to the cold, wet climate and thin, acidic, nutrient-poor soil found here. To tell them apart: spruce needles can be easily rolled between thumb and forefinger, while the flat needles of the fir cannot. These woods may be wonderfully open or frightfully thick and tangled, and are often carpeted with mosses or ferns. Other trees common at this elevation include mountain ash and the pinkish-barked, heart-leaved variety of paper birch, with striped and mountain maple also hanging in.

Wildflowers: Bunchberry, wood sorrel, bluebead lily, Canada mayflower, starflower, goldthread, twinflower, wood aster, large-leaved goldenrod. Flowers that occur at all elevations will bloom later in the higher terrain.

Birds: Winter wren (loud, tinkling, trilling song), Swainson's thrush, boreal chickadee (with a brown cap, quite tame), spruce grouse (absurdly tame), white-throated sparrow (song is a sad, sweet whistle), yellow-bellied flycatcher, golden-crowned and ruby-crowned kinglets, yellow-rumped, magnolia, bay-breasted, blackpoll, Blackburnian (up to ca. 3000 ft.), and Nashville warblers, black-backed woodpecker, common junco, Canada or gray jay (the bold "whisky jack" or "camp robber" who will gladly take food from your hand), red-breasted nuthatch, purple finch, pine siskin, white-winged crossbill (irregular). Around ponds: rusty blackbird. Near cliffs: common raven.

Mammals: Red squirrel, moose (who even range above treeline on occasion), snowshoe hare, and others who venture up from the hardwoods.

Balsam Fir Forest

Elevation: ca. 4000 ft.–4500 ft.

Trees: Above 4000 ft. the adaptable and prolific balsam fir dominates until the low scrub at treeline is reached. These woods may be open and mature or wracked with blowdown and crammed with scrubby young growth. A remarkable phenomenon is the "fir wave," a band of dead and dying trees that slowly migrates up or down the slope in the direction of the prevailing wind, appearing as a gray band from a distance. These are thought to be caused by a combination of wind and icing. In places gnarled, scrubby heart-leaved paper birches and mountain ash hold their own with the firs. As elevation increases, the woods become more stunted.

Wildflowers: Similar to spruce-fir forest.

Birds: A number of the spruce-fir species range into this zone. An additional specialty at this elevation is the much sought-after Bicknell's thrush.

Mammals: Similar to spruce-fir forest.

Krummholz Zone

Elevation: ca. 4500 ft.–4800 ft.

Trees: At this elevation, a zone of tension between the forest and the alpine zone, the trees are stunted and twisted; krummholz means "crooked wood" in German. Balsam fir and black spruce are the dominant trees.

Birds: White-throated sparrow, common junco, blackpoll and yellow-rumped warblers, Bicknell's thrush. Other species may venture up from the lower conifer forests.

Alpine Zone

Elevation: Above ca. 4800 ft.; treeline is sometimes lower, sometimes higher depending on wind exposure and other factors.

Wildflowers: The hardy, low-lying plants that thrive in this harsh realm of cold, snow, fog, rain, ice, rock and relentless wind, where trees cannot survive, are famous for their colorful early summer blooms, especially on the "lawns" around Mt. Washington. There are dozens of plants to see up here, and several distinct communities have evolved in response to local microclimates. The AMC's *Field Guide to the Alpine Summits* is an excellent resource. Most conspicuous in June are the white blooms of diapensia, the magenta of Lapland rosebay and the pink of alpine azalea. Later in the summer the small white flowers of mountain sandwort bloom profusely. Another conspicuous plant is the grass-like Bigelow's sedge, which carpets the alpine meadows. Above treeline, hikers should be constantly aware of the fragility of this plant life—one careless step can crunch away years of hard-won growth. Please stay on marked trails, or bare rock, at all times.

Birds: Only a handful of birds nest in the alpine zone, mainly the species mentioned under the krummholz zone.

Mammals: Various mice, shrews and voles, even an occasional woodchuck.

USING THIS GUIDE

What started out as a simple almanac-type guide to the White Mountain 4000-footers soon evolved into the much lengthier tome you're reading now. As we "researched" the peaks, we came to appreciate the unique qualities of each mountain—its physical attributes, its history, its trail approaches, and the views afforded (or not) from its summit. This has greatly enhanced our enjoyment of the mountains. We hope it does the same for you.

The chapters for each peak, or pair or trio of summits (e.g. Kinsmans, Bonds), are broken down into seven sections:

Mountain Facts

- Elevation in feet and meters.
- Ranking of height among the 48 peaks.
- What mountain range and towns and/or townships the mountains are located in.
- Which United States Geological Survey (USGS) topographic quadrangles cover the mountains. These are either 7½′ (1:24,000 scale) or 7½′ × 15′ (1:25,000 scale) maps. (Note: At press time, several of the USGS 7½′ × 15′ quadrangles were being split into 7½′ maps with new names; we reference the original 7½′ × 15′ quad names.)

Geography

This presents a physical description of the mountains, including major ridges, spurs, streams, ravines and other outstanding features. We recommend having a trail or topographic map on hand as you read this section.

Nomenclature

The origins of the mountains' names are described here. In some cases the names of ravines or other features on the mountain are also included in the discussion. Readily available references on White Mountain nomenclature are *Place Names of the White Mountains*, by Robert and Mary Julyan, and *The White Mountains: Names, Places & Legends*, by John T. B. Mudge.

Historical Highlights

Presented in timeline fashion, this section lists major events occurring on or around the mountains, including first ascents (if known), interesting explorations, dates of trail and shelter construction and other noteworthy events. Invaluable references for compiling this information included many older editions of the *AMC White Mountain Guide* and the AMC's journal, *Appalachia*, and Laura and Guy Waterman's comprehensive history of Northeastern hiking, *Forest and Crag*.

Trail Approaches

In this section we present summaries and descriptions of the major trail approaches to each mountain. Many 4000-footers are blessed with a wonderful variety of trails, and rather than covering only the "standard" routes, we have included many more for those who wish to seek out less-traveled ways to the high peaks. For each approach there is a summary of round trip distance and elevation gain, brief trailhead directions, and a guidebook-style narrative of the trail route. A few of the steeper trails are not recommended for descent and are listed as one-way routes to the summit, with descent via an alternate trail. Loop and point-to-point traverse options are mentioned where appropriate.

No trail maps are included here; these trail descriptions are intended for use with a good White Mountain trail map. We suggest that every hiker aiming to climb the 4000-footers obtain a copy of the latest *AMC White Mountain Guide* (26th edition, 1998; 27th edition due out in 2003). This authoritative guide describes every maintained hiking trail in the mountains and comes with a complete set of trail maps that covers all the 4000-footers. Most mileages and elevation gains in our descriptions were obtained from the *AMC Guide*. Another excellent resource is the *White Mountains Map Book* by Map Adventures, which includes an easy-to-read, waterproof map that covers all the 4000-footers except Moosilauke, Waumbek and Cabot; these are covered by page maps in the accompanying book.

Winter

These are notes intended for experienced winter hikers who are considering snow-season ascents. Winter beginners should gain experience at lower elevations before attempting any of the higher peaks, especially those above treeline, where dangers are multiplied in winter.

View Guide

In days of old, meaning the mid-to-late 1800s, summit views were a bigger deal than they seem today. The guidebooks of that era, most notably Moses Sweetser's *The White Mountains: A Handbook for Travelers*, placed special emphasis on description and appreciation of summit views, extending into many pages of small print. Panoramic sketches were also provided for a few of the notable vistas. This latter art was resurrected in 1995 with the publication of *Scudder's White Mountain Viewing Guide*, a labor of love compiled over two decades by Brent E. Scudder. Among the 43 panoramas included in Scudder's book are 14 from White Mountain 4000-footers (listed below) and two more from close neighbors Mt. Hight and The Horn.

In this book we have included fairly detailed descriptions of the views from all the summits that grant you an outlook, plus a few other vantage points along popular trail approaches. If you're lucky enough to get a clear day, you can while away your summit stay with the appropriate View Guide, used in conjunction with a trail map and compass, and a Scudder's panorama if available.

At the end of the View Guide we list the number of other White Mountain 4000-footer summits that can be seen from the peak in question. On the wooded summits this is, of course, a somewhat theoretical notion. For a fuller discourse on this matter, refer to the Appendix item, "How Many 4000-Footers Can You See?"

Scudder's panoramas are available for these 4000-footers:

Mt. Adams
Mt. Bond
Cannon Mtn.
Mt. Carrigain
Mt. Eisenhower
Mt. Isolation
Mt. Jackson
South Kinsman Mtn.
Mt. Lafayette
Mt. Moosilauke
Mt. Osceola
South Twin Mtn.
Mt. Washington
Wildcat D

ABBREVIATIONS

AMC	Appalachian Mountain Club
ca.	circa (about, approximately)
DOC	Dartmouth Outing Club
E	east
FR	Forest Road (in WMNF)
ft.	feet, foot
L	left
m	meters
mi.	miles
N	north
R	right
RMC	Randolph Mountain Club
S	south
USFS	United States Forest Service
USGS	United States Geological Survey
W	west
WMNF	White Mountain National Forest
WODC	Wonalancet Out Door Club

The 4000-Footers of the White Mountains

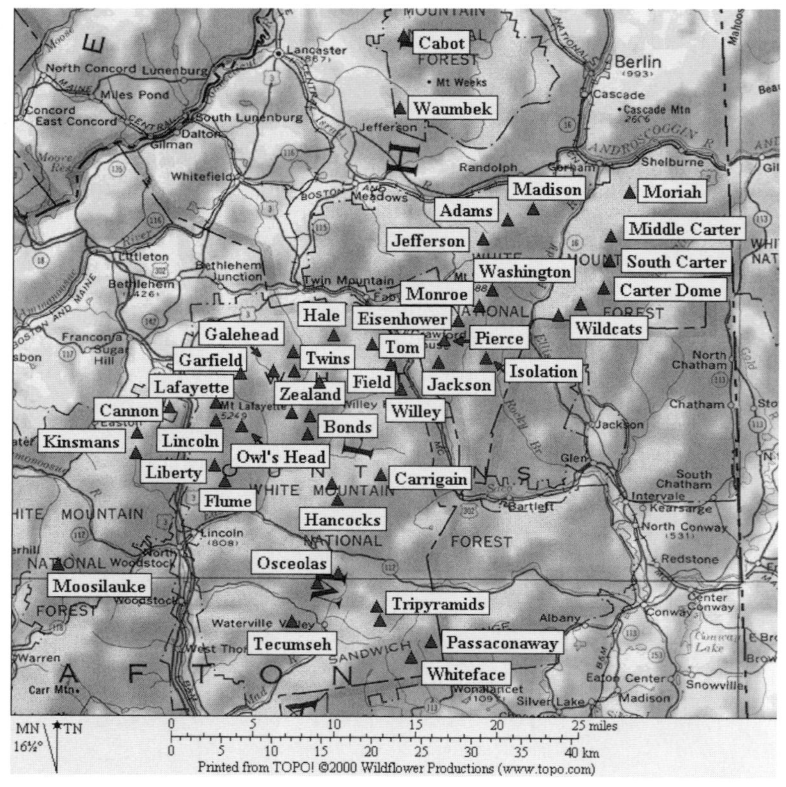

Locator map for the White Mountains 4000-footers.

Mount Adams

ELEVATION: 5799 ft./1768 m ORDER OF HEIGHT: 2
LOCATION: Northern Presidential Range, Town of Randolph, Townships of Low and Burbanks Grant and Thompson and Meserves Purchase
USGS MAP: 7½′ × 15′ Mt. Washington

GEOGRAPHY

With a summit elevation of 5799 ft., Mt. Adams is the second highest peak in New England, but there is nothing else second-rate about this ruggedly spectacular mountain. Some maintain that it's the most interesting of all the 4000-footers. Mt. Adams lies just a few miles N of Mt. Washington along the curving, barren ridgecrest of the Northern Presidential Range. It is flanked by two impressive neighbors—Mt. Madison on the NE and Mt. Jefferson to the SW. The upper part of the mountain is a pyramid of frost-riven rock thrusting 1000 ft. above timberline.

As seen from elsewhere in the mountains, the summit of Mt. Adams, "presents the appearance of a symmetrical pyramid," wrote 19th-century guidebook author Moses F. Sweetser. "It is exceeded by no other in picturesque grandeur and alpine character, on account of its sharp and slender peak and of the profound ravines which traverse its flanks."

The sharp peak of Adams is surrounded by several subsidiary peaks. Mt. John Quincy Adams (5410 ft.) is a rugged, rocky hump that towers above the Adams-Madison col. Mt. Sam Adams (5585 ft.) is a prominent peaklet W of the main summit, with a lesser knob, Adams 4 (5355 ft.) just to the N. In the col between Adams and Sam Adams is Thunderstorm Junction, a major trail intersection marked by a huge cairn. Gray Knob (4481 ft.) is a minor eminence on Nowell Ridge near the cabin of the same name maintained by the Randolph Mountain Club (RMC), caretaker of most of the many miles of trails on Adams.

Magnificent ravines, carved out thousands of years ago by alpine glaciers, ring the mountain on practically all sides. The most impressive of the ravines are the Great Gulf—the huge glacial cirque drained by the West Branch of the Peabody River and separating the mountain from nearby Mt. Washington—and rugged King Ravine, with its 1100-ft. headwall and boulder-strewn floor on the N side of the mountain. Mt. Adams shares three other cirques with its neighboring mountains: Castle Ravine to the W, Jefferson Ravine to the S, and Madison Gulf to the E; the latter two are tributary ravines to the Great Gulf.

Several prominent ridges run N and NW from the summit down towards the Moose River and US 2 in the Randolph valley. From summit to valley floor there is an elevation drop of nearly 4500 ft. Durand Ridge, the more northerly of the lot, is a steep, sharp ridge flanked by King Ravine to the W and Snyder Brook valley to E. The narrow, upper portion of the ridge running above treeline is known as the Knife Edge. Nowell Ridge is a broad ridge with several spurs NW of Mt. Adams, bordered by King Ravine on the E and Cascade Ravine on the SW. The lesser Israel Ridge is the next ridge to the W, between Cascade and Castle Ravines; its lower end is known as Emerald Tongue. Emerald Bluff (4025 ft.) is a fine viewpoint on the edge of Israel Ridge overlooking Castle Ravine. Several lesser defined, unnamed ridges, strewn with scrubby scree slopes, drop off steeply to the mountain's S and into the depths of the Great Gulf.

In the col between Mts. Adams and Madison, just a short distance from the Appalachian Mountain Club's Madison Spring Hut, lies Star Lake (4896 ft.), a tiny, shallow tarn in a bigger-than-life setting. Storm Lake, an even smaller year-round pool of water near the junction of the Israel Ridge and Gulfside Trails, is located on Adams's long, gently sloping SW ridge some 5200 feet above sea level. This bare SW ridge leads about a mile from the peak of Sam Adams down to Edmands Col (4938 ft.), named for J. Rayner Edmands, perhaps the best known of the early Randolph area trail builders. This wild, windswept saddle marks the low point on the ridge between the summits of Mt. Adams and Jefferson.

Numerous streams flow out of Mt. Adams's nothern ravines, and along these brooks are many scenic waterfalls accessed by the RMC's extensive trail network. Among the largest of these streams is Snyder Brook, which drains the long, twisting, non-glacial valley between Mt. Madison's Gordon Ridge and Mt. Adams's Durand Ridge. Cascades found along Snyder Brook include Duck, Salmacis, Tama, Salroc and Gordon Falls.

Out of King Ravine flow the icy waters of Coldbrook, which originates beneath the boulder field at the floor of the ravine and pours out over Mossy Fall. Probably its best known waterfall is Coldbrook Falls, which is easily accessed just 0.75 mi. from the Appalachia parking lot. Spur Brook, a western tributary of Coldbrook, features Chandler Fall, Canyon Fall and Spur Brook Falls.

Cascade Brook, rich in waterfalls, drains Cascade Ravine and joins Castle Brook from Castle Ravine at the Forks of the Israel to form the W-flowing Israel River. Mystic Stream, a tributary of the Israel, drains the NW slopes of Nowell Ridge. On the lower N slopes of Nowell Ridge are the headwaters of the Moose River, which flows E through Randolph valley.

An unusual note about Mt. Adams is that it is a sacred mountain to members of the Atherius Society, whose symbols are painted on rocks near the summit.

NOMENCLATURE

The mountain was named on July 31, 1820, by members of the Weeks-Brackett party of Lancaster, which that day was guided to the summit of Mt. Washington by legendary innkeeper and local pioneer Ethan Allen

The south slopes of Mt. Adams rise steeply out of the Great Gulf.

Crawford. The summit was named in honor of the nation's second President, John Adams (1735–1826). The Lancaster party, which included Adino N. Brackett, John W. Weeks, General John Wilson, Charles J. Stuart, N. S. Dennison, and Samuel A. Pearson (all of Lancaster) and mapmaker and NH Secretary of State, Philip Carrigain, also gave names to most of the other peaks in the Presidential Range. For many years, however, there was some confusion over the naming of the peaks, especially those of today's Mts. Adams and Jefferson. Several early maps of the White Mountain region mislabeled the summits, transposing the names of the two peaks.

Several of the mountain's sub-peaks have received their own Adams-related names. These include Mt. John Quincy Adams (5410 ft.), Mt. Sam Adams (5585 ft.), and Adams 4 (5355 ft.) and Adams 5. Collectively they are known as the "Adams Family" of peaks. John Q. Adams (1767–1848) was the son of John Adams and the nation's sixth president. Sam Adams (1722–1803) was a Revolutionary War hero and a signer of the Declaration of Independence. He was also a former governor of Massachusetts.

King Ravine, the great glacial cirque cut into Mt. Adams's northern flanks, is named for Rev. Thomas Starr King, author of the classic book, *The White Hills: Their Legends, Landscape and Poetry* (1859), and an early explorer of the ravine. Durand Ridge, the steep, rugged ridge running N from the summit, was named by frequent visitor and local trailbuilder William Peek in honor of the Town of Randolph's original grantees, the Durand family of London. Nowell Ridge, on the W side of King Ravine, is named for Dr. William Grey Nowell, a longtime summer resident of Randolph and an enthusiastic explorer and trailbuilder in the late 19th century.

HISTORICAL HIGHLIGHTS

First Ascent: One month after the Weeks-Brackett party climbed Mt. Washington and assigned names to the various Presidential Range summits, three of its members (Adino Brackett, John W. Weeks and Charles J. Stuart), along with Richard Eastman, returned to the range for six more days of exploration. During this trip they climbed to the summits of all the Northern Peaks, including Mt. Adams, and are credited with the first recorded ascents of Mts. Adams, Madison and Jefferson.

ca. 1829: Botanist J. W. Robbins explores Northern Presidentials and Great Gulf.

1854: Benjamin Osgood climbs mountain, places register, bottle at summit. By 1866, register contains 12 names, by 1876, 20 names.

1857: Thomas Starr King and Gorham guide James Gordon lead party on first ascent of King Ravine.

1865: Members of Alpine Club of Williamstown, Mass.—first organized hiking club in America—traverse Northern Peaks of Presidentials after spending previous night atop Mt. Washington.

1874: In survey report, state geologist Charles H. Hitchcock writes, "Any lover of mountain scenery must yearn to stand upon the top of Mt. Adams."

1875–76: Charles Lowe and William Nowell build Lowe's Path up Mt. Adams. Early users of path are required to pay nominal "toll."

1876: Lowe cuts new branch trail up King Ravine.

1877: Ravine House at northern base of mountain opens. Building, dating back to 1850s, was earlier known as Mt. Madison House.

1881: Lowe and Charles E. Fay ascend King Ravine headwall by course of Cold Brook. Account of climb appears in *Appalachia*. Benjamin F. Osgood cuts first trail into Great Gulf, but it is abandoned by turn of century.

1882–1884: Air Line Trail up Durand Ridge—shortest route up Mt. Adams from Randolph—is built. Upper portion above treeline is constructed by Laban Watson, E. B. Cook. Lower portion built by Cook, William Peek.

1883: Original Scar Trail is constructed by Cook and Peek.

1884: AMC builds first section of Gulfside Trail from Madison-Adams col to Air Line.

1886: Fire breaks out in King Ravine and sweeps up east wall over "Knife Edge" into Snyder Brook ravine.

1887: Charles Lowe makes first recorded winter ascent of summit.

1888: AMC constructs Madison Spring Hut in Madison-Adams col.

1890: William Nowell, others, build Log Cabin beside Lowe's Path. Cabin is first permanent camp established on Northern Peaks.

1892: J. Rayner Edmands begins work on Israel Ridge Path, linking valley with summit of Mt. Adams. Also constructs birchbark shelter (The Perch) at head of Castle Ravine and Cascade Camp on Cascade Brook. He builds network of pleasure paths in Cascade Ravine, accessing upper cascades, and another along Israel Ridge past viewpoints at "Tip o' the

Tongue" and Emerald Bluff. In this year he also starts extending Gulfside Trail (originally called Highland Path) SW from Air Line by Gateway of King Ravine; within several years this trail connects Northern Peaks with Mt. Washington.

1893: Edmands builds The Link as connecting trail along lower slopes of Adams.

1893–99: Randolph Path from Howker Ridge Trail to Jefferson-Adams col built by Edmands.

1895–1897: Edmands builds graded Valley Way from Appalachia to Madison Hut, using some sections of earlier trails up Snyder Brook valley.

1899–1901: Edmands builds Short Line, providing easier access to King Ravine.

1901: Spur Trail from Randolph Path to Lowe's Path (just below Thunderstorm Jct.) is cut by Charles C. Torrey.

ca. 1903–1907: Heavy logging disrupts many trails on Northern Peaks, extending 2 mi. up trails such as Israel Ridge, King Ravine and Air Line. Lower section of Israel Ridge Path is obliterated beyond restoration.

1906: E. Y. Hincks builds Gray Knob cabin just E of Gray Knob, a small hump on crest of Nowell Ridge.

1908: New trail from Star Lake (near Madison Hut) to summit is constructed.

1908–1910: Under direction of Warren Hart, series of audacious trails is built in Great Gulf: Great Gulf Trail up valley in 1908; Adams Slide Trail, one of steepest in mountains, and Buttress Trail, both on S face of Adams, in 1909; and Madison Gulf Trail in 1910.

1909: Crag Camp, situated on ridge at edge of King Ravine, is built as private camp by Nelson H. Smith.

1910: Randolph Mountain Club (RMC) is formed.

1927: Cascade Camp is destroyed by flood.

1932: RMC directors vote to adopt and maintain previously unoffiical Great Gully Trail up King Ravine. Upper section of trail is relocated in 1933 to complete direct link to Gulfside Trail, Lowe's Path. Chemin des Dames is built to connect King Ravine with Air Line.

1938: The Perch is blown away by September hurricane.

1939: RMC takes over maintenance of Crag Camp.

1940: October fire guts Madison Hut. By August of following year, AMC, under leadership of legendary hutmaster Joe Dodge, reopens hut to hikers.

1948: RMC builds new Perch as memorial to Louis Cutter, well-known mapmaker and tireless RMC trail builder and maintainer in early 1900s.

ca. 1950: Klaus Goetze of RMC oversees cutting of Emerald Trail up side of Castle Ravine to Emerald Bluff.

1962: Ravine House in Randolph closes.

1964: Great Gulf Wilderness created by Congress.

Early 1970s: Adams Slide Trail abandoned.

1985: Original Log Cabin razed, replaced by RMC with new open-door shelter.

1989: New insulated and closed Gray Knob cabin built by RMC.

1994: Original Crag Camp razed and is replaced by new camp accommodating 20 hikers.

1998: January ice storm shatters hardwood forest on lower N slopes of Adams; herculean effort by RMC clears thousands of fallen trees from trails.

TRAIL APPROACHES

Mt. Adams has a multitude of possible trail approaches, especially from US 2 to the N, for the northern slopes of the mountain have the densest network of footpaths in the White Mountains. This is one of the toughest ascents in the Whites, involving nearly 4500 ft. of elevation gain in 4½–5 mi. of relentless uphill. The upper cone of the mountain is a jumble of broken rock, devoid of trees and any protection from the elements. The climb should only be undertaken in favorable weather conditions, and all above-treeline precautions that apply to Mt. Washington are of equal importance when climbing Adams. Allow plenty of time for this very strenuous trip, which includes much tedious boulder-hopping in its upper reaches.

North Approaches from US 2

Many trail combinations can be used to climb Adams from the N. Six major routes, some with optional variations, are described here, from E to W.

From Appalachia

Trailhead (1306 ft.): The large parking area at Appalachia is one of the major trailheads in the Whites. It's located on the S side of US 2, 5.5 mi. W of NH 16 in Gorham and 2 mi. E of Lowe's Store in Randolph. Various loops can be fashioned from the routes described here.

Valley Way, Gulfside Trail, Air Line
9.4 mi. round trip, 4500-ft. elevation gain

This relatively moderate route follows the steady and sheltered Valley Way—a wide, rocky trade route in places—to AMC Madison Hut, from which the exposed boulder-climb up the summit cone is undertaken. If doing a loop, this is a preferred way to descend. From parking area, follow blue-blazed Valley Way across old RR grade and powerline (where Air Line forks R) and into woods. Climb moderately through hardwoods and then hemlocks, passing several trail junctions. (Parallel Fallsway offers chance to see several small waterfalls on Snyder Brook.) Just beyond jct. R with Beechwood Way at 0.8 mi., Valley Way bears R and climbs to jct. with Randolph Path at 0.9 mi./1953 ft.

Valley Way now climbs steadily along slope high above Snyder Brook, bearing L (E), then R (S) into fine birch glade. Pass jct. with Scar Trail on R at 2.1 mi./2811 ft. and crossing of Watson Path at 2.4 mi./3175 ft. Long, steady climb continues up lower E slope of Durand Ridge, passing jct. L with Lower Bruin at 2.8 mi./3584 ft., side trail R to Valley Way Campsite (2 tent platforms) at 3.1 mi., and jct. R with Upper Bruin at 3.3 mi./4150 ft. Valley Way now climbs more steeply up headwall of ravine, with brook mostly close by on L. Emerge from scrub and at 3.8 mi./4800 ft., just past jct. with Air Line Cutoff, reach jct. with Gulfside and Star Lake Trails, 100 ft. below Madison Hut.

Turn R here on Gulfside Trail and climb through scrub and in open to jct. with Air Line at 4.1 mi./5125 ft.; look back for imposing view of Mt. Madison's massive pyramid. (Short detour to R on Air Line provides spectacular view down into Gateway of King Ravine.) In 250 ft. turn L off Gulfside onto upper part of Air Line, which climbs SSW up open, boulder-strewn cone, passing to W of John Quincy Adams. Rocky climb steepens and continues to sharp, small summit at 4.7 mi./5799 ft.

Star Lake Trail Option

This trail offers a steep, rugged alternative route from Madison Hut to summit of Adams, with unusual views. From hut, Star Lake Trail climbs easily S to Madison-Adams col. At 0.2 mi. from hut Parapet Trail forks L. Bear R on Star Lake Trail, passing by W side of Star Lake, sprinkled with lichen-dotted rocks. Beyond jct. L with Buttress Trail at 0.3 mi., slab below John Quincy Adams through scrub, then begin brutal climb up E side of main summit—very steep and rocky, with large boulders and some ledge scrambling. Look back for interesting views of Mt. Madison rising above Star Lake. Near top swing R across rocky shoulder and reach summit at 1.0 mi. from hut.

Air Line

8.6 mi. round trip, 4500-ft. elevation gain

This is the shortest route to Adams, and provides maximum views with its traverse of the exposed Knife Edge on upper Durand Ridge. From Appalachia parking, follow Air Line/Valley Way across old RR grade and into powerline swath, where Air Line diverges R. Climb at easy to moderate grades through hardwoods, passing several trail junctions, including Randloph Path at 0.9 mi./2000 ft. Grade soon steepens, and trail becomes very steep at 2700 ft. as it struggles up NW end of Durand Ridge. Grade eases at 2.4 mi./3700 ft. where Scar Trail comes in from L. (Alternate approach of 3.1 mi. can be made to this point via Valley Way, Scar Trail and Scar Loop; along way there are good views up valley of Snyder Brook and out to N from Durand Scar, ca. 3200 ft.)

Climb is steady to treeline at 3.0 mi./4350 ft., where Air Line emerges from scrub onto exposed ledges. For next 0.5 mi. there are outstanding views W across King Ravine and N to Crescent, Pliny and Pilot Ranges and distant horizons. While ambling up open ledges among wild rock formations, pass jct. L with Upper Bruin at 3.1 mi. and jct. R with Chemin Des

Dames from King Ravine at 3.2 mi./4475 ft. Scenic climb continues up Knife Edge to jct. L with Air Line Cutoff at 3.5 mi./4800 ft. Air Line now climbs steeply to shelf above headwall of King Ravine. At 3.7 mi./5100 ft. King Ravine Trail departs R to descend through Gateway of cirque. In 200 ft. Air Line meets Gulfside Trail, turns R to follow it for 100 yards, then bears L to ascend boulder-heaped cone of Adams, reaching summit at 4.3 mi./5799 ft.

Lower Air Line, Short Line, King Ravine Trail, Upper Air Line
4.6 mi. one way, 4600-ft. elevation gain

Many hikers deem the ascent through King Ravine the most spectacular route to Adams, especially when combined with a return down Durand Ridge on Air Line (8.9 mi. loop). Traverse of King Ravine invloves rough scrambling over boulders and ledges and is not advisable in wet weather or for descent.

From Appalachia parking follow Air Line for 0.8 mi. and bear R onto Short Line, which ascends moderately. Randolph Path joins from L at 1.3 mi./2275 ft. and splits R at 1.7 mi./2500 ft. Becoming rockier and wilder, Short Line leads S up valley of Cold Brook into lower area of King Ravine, climbing at moderate grade. Reach jct. with King Ravine Trail at 2.7 mi./3150 ft. and follow it into ravine, quickly reaching Mossy Fall spilling between two boulders.

Ascent becomes steep and rugged up through floor of ravine amidst scrub growth and huge boulders. Large rock on R offers good view back down ravine. At 3.1 mi./3700 ft., on upper floor of cirque, Chemin Des Dames departs L for Air Line. Just beyond, King Ravine Trail splits; somewhat easier route, "Elevated," is to L and offers good views up to walls of ravine, while "Subway," to R, features difficult scrambling over and under boulders. The two routes soon rejoin, and very steep Great Gully Trail leaves on R at 3.2 mi./3775 ft. Then short loop path R diverges for Ice Caves. After it rejoins, King Ravine Trail commences very steep, rough ascent of headwall (1100 ft. in 0.5 mi.), with ledge and boulder scrambling. Steep grade calls for frequent pauses to admire stunning views back down ravine. Near top of headwall trail climbs up through cut known as "The Gateway," with smooth rock slabs up on R and rough crags on L, and emerges at jct. with Air Line at 4.0 mi./5100 ft., with fine view L to Mt. Madison. From here follow Air Line 0.6 mi. to summit of Adams.

Amphibrach, Spur Trail, Lowe's Path
10.2 mi. round trip, 4500-ft. elevation gain

A less-used, slightly longer approach with good views along W edge of King Ravine from Spur Trail. From Appalachia parking, follow Air Line/Valley Way across old RR grade and into powerline clearing. Bear R here on Air Line, and in 100 yards R again on combined Amphibrach/Link Trails. This path runs W at easy grade, then bears L to cross Coldbrook on Memorial Bridge at 0.7 mi./1425 ft.; good view of Coldbrook Fall upstream. Just past bridge swing L on Amphibrach (Link goes straight) and climb S at moderate grade on W side of Coldbrook. At 1.8 mi./2200 ft. pass jct. R with Monaway and cross Spur Brook just beyond. Cross Cliffway at 2.2 mi. and climb steadily to five-way jct., "The Pentadoi," at 2.6 mi./2925 ft.

Turn R on Randolph Path, cross Spur Brook, and quickly bear L onto Spur Trail for steep climb along cascades on brook. At 2.7 mi. side path L leads to Chandler Fall, and at 2.9 mi./3450 ft. Hincks Trail leaves on R. Spur Trail recrosses brook and continues steep, rough climb up E spur of Nowell Ridge. At 3.4 mi. short side path L leads to Lower Crag and good view into King Ravine, and RMC Crag Camp, perched on W rim of cirque, is reached at 3.5 mi./4247 ft.; Gray Knob Trail splits R just beyond. Spur Trail remains steep, passing 100-yard side path L to Knight's Castle, airy ledge perch above ravine, at 3.7 mi./4600 ft. Emerge from scrub at 3.9 mi. and climb steadily up E side of Nowell Ridge, with continuous views, to meet Lowe's Path at 4.7 mi./5425 ft. Turn L on Lowe's Path and reach Thunderstorm Jct. (5490 ft.) in less than 0.1 mi. Continue up Lowe's Path over broken rock to summit of Adams at 5.1 mi./5799 ft.

North Approach from Lowe's Store (US 2)

Lowe's Path
9.4 mi. round trip, 4450-ft. elevation gain

Trailhead (1375 ft.): Park at Lowe's Store on US 2 in Randolph (nominal parking fee, not covered by WMNF Parking Pass) and walk 100 yards W on US 2 to sign for Lowe's Path on S side of road.

This straightforward climb is generally considered the "easiest" route to Adams, with some steepness but mostly moderate grades on long climb up Nowell Ridge. Upper 1.5 mi. is above treeline.

From road, trail enters woods and passes sign giving history of route. Cross old RR grade and powerline and ascend moderately through hardwoods. Cross Link at 1.7 mi./2475 ft. King Ravine Trail forks L at 1.8 mi. Grade becomes steeper at ca. 3000 ft., leading to RMC's Log Cabin at 2.4 mi./3263 ft. Here Cabin-Cascades Trail splits R. Ascent remains steep, crossing Randolph Path at 2.7 mi./3600 ft. and rising to crest of Nowell Ridge at ca. 4300 ft. Grade eases to jct. L with short trail called "The Quay," and with Gray Knob Trail just beyond, at 3.2 mi./4400 ft. Outlook on R across from Quay provides good view W.

Lowe's Path soon breaks above treeline and climbs steadily up broad, open rocky ridge, with wide views and full exposure to NW winds. Cross minor peak of Adams 4 at 4.1 mi./5355 ft. and continue up to giant cairn at Thunderstorm Jct. at 4.4 mi./5490 ft. Cross Gulfside Trail and continue steady climb up rock-strewn summit cone on Lowe's Path, reaching top of Adams at 4.7 mi./5799 ft.

NORTH APPROACH from Bowman

Castle Trail, Israel Ridge Path, Lowe's Path
10.8 mi. round trip, 4300-ft. elevation gain

TRAILHEAD (1500 ft.): This route starts at parking area at Bowman, on S side of US 2, 1.0 mi. W of Lowe's Store.

This is a fine hike for Adams-baggers looking for wild scenery off the beaten track. Highlights include waterfalls and a short side trip to Emerald Bluff, a superb viewpoint. From parking area, cross old RR grade and follow signs up R-hand driveway 100 yards to where Castle Trail departs on R. Traverse open logged area and enter WMNF at 0.3 mi. At 0.4 mi. cross powerline and Israel River just beyond—tough at high water. On far bank turn L, then R and follow old logging road on easy climb through open hardwoods. At 1.3 mi./1900 ft. bear L on Israel Ridge Path and recross river at 1.4 mi. Castle Ravine Trail leaves R at 1.7 mi. as Israel Ridge Path climbs L up side of slope into Cascade Ravine, passing jcts. with Link and Cabin-Cascades Trails at 2.5 mi./2800 ft. (Short side trip R on Link leads to top of First Cascade, scenic spot with limited view.)

Path continues up E side of Cascade Brook, with waterfalls to R, crosses at top of Second Cascade at 2.7 mi. (view to Mt. Bowman and out to NW), and makes steep, rough climb up Israel Ridge through mossy virgin conifer forest, then slabs upward along E side of ridge. At 3.5 mi./4050 ft. Emerald Trail comes in on R; Emerald Bluff, spectacular viewpoint overlooking Castle Ravine and Mt. Jefferson's Castellated Ridge, can be visited with easy side trip of 0.1 mi. each way. Israel Ridge Path turns L at this jct., climbs to Perch Path at 3.7 mi., then turns R and climbs to jct. with Randolph Path and treeline at 4.1 mi./4825 ft. At 4.2 mi. Israel Ridge Path splits L off Randolph Path and rises to meet Gulfside Trail on SW ridge of Adams at 4.6 mi./5225 ft. (To R, Gulfside descends easily over open ridge 0.7 mi. to Edmands Col.) Turn L here as Israel Ridge Path and Gulfside Trail coincide, passing tiny pool known as Storm Lake. Climb steadily up open slope on SE side of ridgecrest. Israel Ridge Trail diverges R at 5.1 mi./5475 ft. and joins Lowe's Path at 5.2 mi. Continue up rocky cone to summit at 5.4 mi./5799 ft.

SOUTHWEST APPROACH from Edmands Col

For those traversing the Northern Presidential ridge from Mt. Jefferson towards Mt. Adams, the gentle climb up Adams' SW ridge from Edmands Col provides a scenic and relatively easy stretch of above-treeline walking. From the col (4938 ft.), Gulfside Trail ascends gradually up the ledgy ridgecrest, passing wild and impressive crags. There are excellent views R into Jefferson Ravine, with the Carters and Mt. Washington beyond, back to Mt. Jefferson, and L to the Castellated Ridge and North Country. Easy to moderate climbing continues to a 5200-ft. shoulder with more fine views.

Trail skirts to L of small 5274-ft. peak and meets Israel Ridge Path (5225 ft.) at 0.7 mi. from Edmands Col. These two trails coincide, passing tiny

Storm Lake on L and angling up along SE side of ridge, well below crest. At 1.2 mi./5745 ft. veer R on Israel Ridge Path, then R again on Lowe's Path at 1.3 mi., and hop rocks up to summit of Adams at 1.5 mi./5799 ft.

South Approaches from Great Gulf

Backpackers or very strong day hikers can approach Mt. Adams from the Great Gulf Trail in the Great Gulf Wilderness. Great Gulf Trail starts at parking area (1350 ft.) on NH 16, 4.1 mi. N of AMC Pinkham Notch Camp and 6.5 mi. S of US 2 in Gorham. As described in Mt. Washington chapter, Great Gulf Trail leads at easy to moderate grades up valley of West Branch of Peabody River. For approach to Adams-Madison col via steep Madison Gulf Trail, leaving 2.8 mi. from trailhead, see chapter on Mt. Madison. Another possible approach is Buttress Trail. From Great Gulf Trail, 4.5 mi. from trailhead, take Six Husbands Trail across West Branch and up to jct. with Buttress Trail at 5.0 mi./3350 ft. Buttress Trail crosses Jefferson Brook, climbs to extensive talus slope at 5.2 mi., and angles up it with excellent views of Great Gulf, Jefferson's Knee and Jefferson Ravine. Trail reenters woods and swings L at 5.5 mi/3925 ft. for long slabbing climb up SE shoulder of Adams at moderate and occasionally steep grades, with rough footing. Trail is at least partly sheltered by scrub much of way except for open section starting at ca. 6.5 mi. Reach Star Lake Trail in Adams-Madison col at 6.9 mi./4900 ft. Turn L for steep, rough climb up open rocks to summit of Adams at 7.6 mi./5799 ft.

WINTER

Being the second highest peak in the Whites, but at the top of the list in terms of total elevation gain from start to finish, a winter hike to Mt. Adams is a serious undertaking. As the upper reaches of the mountain are above treeline, hikers usually will be exposed to cold winds and treacherous footing featuring a mix of ice, snow and broken rock. Only strong and experienced hikers, fully equipped for extended above-treeline travel, should attempt this climb, and then, only in good weather. Full crampons are required. Lowe's Path and Valley Way are commonly used approach routes and are usually well packed-out through the winter.

The Randolph Mountain Club's Gray Knob Cabin, situated at the crest of Nowell Ridge just off Lowe's Path, operates on a year-round basis and is ideal as a base camp for hikers looking to ascend any of the northern peaks, but especially Mt. Adams. The insulated cabin accommodates up to 15 guests on a first come, first serve basis. An overnight fee is charged per person.

VIEW GUIDE

Many hikers have long considered Mt. Adams to possess the grandest view of all the White Mountain 4,000-Footers. "It rivals the magnificent sweep of being on Washington, without the foreground clutter, and with even more of a sense of the world dropping away on all sides," once wrote the late Guy Waterman, whose peakbagging credentials rival those of any hiker in the last 70 years.

The summits of more than 30 of New Hampshire's highest peaks can be seen from Adams's sharp crown, while many of Maine's highest peaks, including the jumble of 4000-Footers in the Rangeley Lakes region, are also seen from the summit far to the NE.

The most dramatic summit view is that looking S and SW across the gaping chasm of the Great Gulf and Jefferson Ravine toward Mts. Washington and Jefferson. Washington's summit, with its myriad of mountaintop buildings and towers, lies just to the W of due S, and towers 2000 feet above the remote inner recesses of the Great Gulf. Sloping down from Washington's summit to the E (L) one sees the auto road twisting its way up the mountain from Pinkham Notch, while above and to the R is Chandler Ridge, with its two notable knobs, Nelson Crag and Ball Crag, seen side-by-side due S.

To the R of Washington along its long connecting ridge with Jefferson is the sharp peak of Mt. Clay. Just above Clay and well in the distance is the round dome of Mt. Carrigain, while Sandwich Dome (near Waterville Valley) is spotted L of Carrigain. On clear days distant Mt. Kearsarge is visible between Sandwich Dome and Carrigain. Directly below Clay's summit spire, rising up out of the Great Gulf, is the wildly steep and narrow E ridge of Jefferson known as Jefferson's Knee. From Clay, off in the distance on the R can also be seen Mts. Tecumseh and Osceola, with the extended ridge of Hancock in front, while nearer at hand, more to the SW, lie Mts. Willey and Field in the Willey Range by Crawford Notch. Mt. Cardigan is over the peak of Willey, Mt. Hitchcock and Scar Ridge are seen over Willey's R shoulder, and Loon Mtn. peers over Field. To R of and beyond Field is Carr Mtn.

The barren summit of Mt. Jefferson, rising dramatically above the depths of Jefferson Ravine, is seen close by to the SW, with Mt. Bond's top just visible to the left of the 5716-ft. peak. Following Jefferson's W ridge down to Jefferson Notch, visible above (L-R) in the distance are Mt. Moosilauke, South Twin, and Mts. Lincoln and Lafayette. Liberty's sharp peak is to the L of Moosilauke. The tip of Cannon is seen over the R shoulder of Lafayette, and North Twin and Hale are in front, with the ski slopes of Mt. Rosebrook (Bretton Woods) just over the slope of Jefferson.

Looking in a more westerly direction, the twin peaks of Mts. Cleveland and Agassiz in Bethlehem are seen just above and to the R of the nearer peaks of Mts. Deception and Dartmouth on the opposite side of Jefferson Notch. Due W, some 80 miles away, is Vermont's Camel Hump, with Cherry Mt. and Owl's Head in nearby Jefferson just R of the Hump and L of Mt. Mansfield, Vermont's highest mountain.

Cherry Pond, just 11 miles distant, sparkles in the broad Jefferson Meadows seen above and to the R of Mt. Sam Adams. Jay Peak in northern Vermont looms on the horizon above US 2 and Jefferson village, with Adams 4 seen below the highway.

To the NW, rising out of the village of Jefferson to the R are the Pliny Range peaks of Mts. Starr King and Waumbek, with 3606-ft. Mt. Pliny seen under Waumbek's long, level ridgeline. Further to the R lies the Pilot Range and then Mt. Cabot, with its telltale talus field high on its south-facing slope. To Cabot's R are the Bulge and the Horn, two New England 100 Highest peaks. The rounded summits of Mt. Weeks are seen in front of Cabot, with Pond of Safety below.

Looking N, well beyond the Crescent Range peaks across US 2, are the Nash Stream mountains and more distant summits of New Hampshire's Great North Woods, plus Quebec's Mt. Megantic and western Maine's Rump Mtn. (both just R of Durand Lake in Randolph). The waters of Lake Umbagog on the Maine-N.H. border are visible to the NNW, with Mt. Aziscohos rising above its W shores and West Kennebago above its E shores.

Close by to the NE you look down on Mt. Madison's sharp summit, with tiny Star Lake nestled in the flat col at its base and the long, serrated Osgood Ridge stretching out to the R. The rocky hump of John Quincy Adams rises to the L of Star Lake. The city of Berlin is seen in the distance beyond J. Q. Adams, and just L of Madison's peak lie the many peaks of the twisting Mahoosuc Range. Old Speck, highest of the Mahoosucs, is at the far L end with Saddleback Mtn. on its L and Mt. Abraham on its R, both near Rangeley, Maine. The winding Androscoggin River is seen almost even with and R of Madison's summit, with the distant pyramid of Mt. Blue beyond the pool in the river known as Reflection Pond. The N end of the Carter-Moriah Range rises out of the valley to the three Moriah summits. Caribou Mtn. near Evans Notch is visible above the S ridge of Mt. Moriah. The high, wooded ridgecrest of the Carters dominates the E view, running across nearly to the SE, with giant Carter Dome standing guard over the Glen House clearing and NH 16 as it climbs toward Pinkham Notch. Wildcat A is to the SE on the S side of Carter Notch, with Wildcat Ski Area further R just below the Doubleheads and North Conway's Kearsarge North. Distant hills, including Effingham's Green Mtn., are seen to the SSE through Pinkham Notch, with North Moat to the R over the shoulder of Nelson Crag.

NO. OF 4000-FOOTERS VISIBLE: 31

Mount Eisenhower

ELEVATION: 4760 ft./1451 m ORDER OF HEIGHT: 12
LOCATION: Southern Presidential Range, Townships of Chandlers Purchase, Sargents Purchase, Beans Grant and Cutts Grant
USGS MAPS: 7½′ Stairs Mtn., 7½′ × 15′ Mt. Washington

GEOGRAPHY

The round, symmetrical dome of Mt. Eisenhower is, as one 19th-century guidebook author wrote, "the most conspicuous" peak in the southern reaches of the Presidential Range. Situated approximately halfway between the peaks at the N end of Crawford Notch and massive Mt. Washington, capstone of the Presidentials, Eisenhower is arguably the finest of the peaks along this portion of New Hampshire's greatest mountain range.

Mt. Eisenhower lies along the ridgeline between Mts. Pierce and Franklin, and its most striking features are its massive, bare, dome-shaped crown (seen especially well from the Bretton Woods–Crawford Notch region) and its expansive, nearly flat summit area, some six acres in size. A ledgy, knobby ridge extends to Mt. Pierce on the SW, while the barren bulge of Mt. Franklin rises abruptly to the NE.

As seen from the Bretton Woods side, huge landslides scar the mountain's W slopes. Several of these landslides crashed down the mountain in 1826, the year of the tragic Willey family slide in nearby Crawford Notch. Abenaki Ravine, out of which flows Abenaki Brook, cuts deep into the mountain slopes WSW of the summit dome. Spur ridges run NW and WNW from the summit, with Mt. Pleasant Brook flowing between them.

Just to the mountain's E lies Oakes Gulf, a large glacial cirque carved out of Mt. Washington's southern base. The Dry River (or Mt. Washington River, as it is sometimes called) drains to the S out of Oakes Gulf, converging with the Saco River at the S end of Crawford Notch. Much of the Dry River valley lies in the remote Presidential Range-Dry River Wilderness. The steep SE face of Eisenhower's dome overlooks a cirque-like basin that drains S, then E into the main valley of Dry River. A long ridge extends S from the Eisenhower-Franklin col, enclosing this basin and providing a route for the Mt. Eisenhower Trail.

Near the NE base of Eisenhower's summit cone is Red Pond, a tiny mountain tarn once described by guidebook author Moses Sweetser as "a dull puddle of bad water." Red Pond is unique in that in times of heavy rain, it purportedly drains into both the Ammonoosuc and Saco River valleys. Its name is culled from the red moss which is so prolific in the general vicinity of Mt. Eisenhower.

For years, a large pile of stones has marked the official summit of the peak, though this cairn is somewhat lower in elevation than in the past. On crystal clear days, with the aid of quality binoculars, it is possible to spot the summit cairn from as far as 15 miles away.

NOMENCLATURE

The peak, originally known as Mt. Pleasant or Pleasant Dome, was renamed in 1972 in honor of the nation's 34th president, Dwight D. Eisenhower. Until 1820, the mountain was a nameless, but prominent bump along the mountain ridge. It was first dubbed Mt. Pleasant by the Weeks-Brackett party, a group of mountain explorers from nearby Lancaster, led by Ethan Allen Crawford, who hiked up onto Mt. Washington to choose names for the peaks in the Presidentials. As there were not enough former presidents to go around for all the summits on the range, the group decided on the name "Pleasant" for the round, bald mountain. They may have been influenced by the toasts of a concoction called "O-be-joyful" that had been raised as each previous peak was christened. Other early names for the mountain were "Mt. Prospect," used by James Pierce in an 1824 article, "Dome Mountain," and "Pleasant Dome."

After President Eisenhower died in 1969, New Hampshire notable Sherman Adams, formerly Assistant to the President under Ike, led the effort to rename the mountain. The change was approved by the U.S. Board on Geographic Names, and the official dedication took place in 1972 at the Eisenhower Wayside Park by US 302. Many an observer has since noted the resemblance between the bare summit dome and Ike's bald pate.

HISTORICAL HIGHLIGHTS

First Ascent: Probably by Darby Field and his Indian companions back in June 1642, during Field's monumental first ascent of Mt. Washington. Recently uncovered material seems to indicate that Field's route up the mountain took him over several of the southern Presidential Range peaks (including Eisenhower), and not up and over Boott Spur, as previously thought.

1811: Capt. Alden Partridge, founder of Norwich University, traverses Southern Presidentials with guide Ethan Allen Crawford. Walk more or less follows route of soon-to-be-built Crawford Path.

1819: Crawfords construct footpath from top of Crawford Notch to Mt. Washington, following for most part ridgeline of Southern Presidentials. Trail runs over summit of mountain that one year later (1820) would be named Mt. Pleasant by group of Lancastrians guided onto Presidentials by Ethan Allen Crawford.

1840s: Second trail up Mt. Pleasant is established from Fabyan area at Bretton Woods. Trail served as bridle path, similar to many others developed throughout the White Mountains during this time period.

1867: *Eastman's White Mountain Guide* notes that even though Crawford Path now bypasses main summit of Mt. Pleasant, an unmarked path can still be followed to its top. Horses, however, "can very seldom be induced to take" this loop trail over the summit.

1890: Author Rev. Julius Ward says of view from mountaintop: "The ridge from the peak of Jefferson to that of Washington looks like the wall of a fortress laid close to the sky, and the whole range might bid defiance to the armaments of the world."

1892–1898: Saco Valley Lumber Company builds logging RR up Dry River

valley to SE of Mt. Eis
used for part of Dry R

1896: After lengthy perio
is restored. The trail,
Strike Spring" on asce
halfway up cone on S

1906: AMC Snow-Shoe S
tain.

1909: J. Rayner Edmands
Northern Peaks of th
trail from Fabyan's to
of his work is still quit
propriately named the

1916: AMC Guide notes
necting with loop trai
stone gateway half-mile from upper terminus of new path in Pleasant-Franklin col.

1918: Willard Helburn and Henry Chamberlain complete first single-day winter traverse of Presidential Range peaks, including Mt. Pleasant. Despite stormy weather, pair covers 22 miles in 14 hours and climbs over nine summits (including Monroe twice).

1919: AMC officially designates connecting trail from Crawford Path to summit as Mt. Pleasant Loop.

1928: Cut-off trail between Edmands Path, Mt. Pleasant Loop no longer warrants mention in AMC Guide.

1934: First mention in AMC guide of new Mt. Pleasant Trail, linking Dry River Valley to Crawford Path in Pleasant-Franklin col. Also, Edmands Path now listed as officially beginning on E side of Mt. Clinton Road, not at Bretton Woods, as previously described.

1972: Three years after N.H. legislature passes bill authorizing name change, ceremony is held near Bretton Woods to formally christen peak Mt. Eisenhower, in honor of WWII hero and former U. S. President Dwight D. Eisenhower. Representing Eisenhower clan at event is Julie Nixon Eisenhower, daughter of President Richard Nixon and wife of David Eisenhower, grandson of Ike.

TRAIL APPROACHES

WEST APPROACH from Mt. Clinton Road

Edmands Path, Mt. Eisenhower Loop
6.6 mi. round trip, 2750-ft. elevation gain

TRAILHEAD (2000 ft.): Parking area for Edmands Path is on E side of Mt. Clinton Road, 2.3 mi. N of US 302 at Crawford Notch and 1.5 mi. S of jct. of Base Road and Jefferson Notch Road.

If it's just Mt. Eisenhower that you're looking to climb, then the Edmands Path is the choice ascent route. This historic trail, sections of which date back more than 150 years, was masterfully reconstructed in 1909 by J. Rayner Edmands, one of the true pioneer White Mountain trail builders in the late 19th and early 20th centuries. Grades are moderate, with no really steep sections. The upper 0.5 mi. of this route is fully exposed to weather.

Blue-blazed trail starts off on level, easy grades, crosses two small brooks, and at 0.4 mi. crosses Abenaki Brook. After stream crossing, trail joins old woods road and in 10 minutes begins moderate ascent through forest of maple, beech and birch. Steady, uneventful climb continues up into deep fir forest. At 2.2 mi./4000 ft., trail swings L, passes through stone gateway, and climbs past small streams flowing over ledges (treacherous if icy). At 2.5 mi./4250 ft. climb eases as trail begins graded traverse across NW ridge. Occasional views down to Bretton Woods and vicinity are gained on L.

Trail swings around nose of ridge and runs nearly level through scrub firs and stunted birches, with views N to Mt. Jefferson; Mt. Franklin looms close by to NE. Cross open talus slope on carefully laid rocks and emerge above treeline, reaching jct. with Mt. Eisenhower Loop at 2.9 mi./4450 ft., a short distance above loop's N jct. with Crawford Path. This is just SW of Eisenhower-Franklin col. Loop trail to summit leads R, dips slightly with tiny Red Pond to L, then zigzags steeply in open up NE end of summit ridge. Ledges offer views down to Red Pond and out to Dry Diver valley. Grade eases along tundra-like crest with wide views. Summit, marked by 6-ft. high cairn, is attained at 3.3 mi./4760 ft. When walking above timberline, especially on Eisenhower's summit cone, be sure to stay on marked trail to protect fragile alpine plants found along Presidential Range.

Southwest Approach from US 302

Crawford Path, Mt. Eisenhower Loop
9.4 mi. round trip, 3200-ft. elevation gain

Trailhead (1900 ft.): This approach starts at parking area on L (W) side of Mt. Clinton Rd., 0.1 mi. N of its jct. with US 302 near the top of Crawford Notch.

Another popular, but significantly longer way to ascend Mt. Eisenhower is via the historic Crawford Path, constructed in 1819 by the pioneering Crawford family, from the top of Crawford Notch. Follow Crawford Connector to Crawford Path at 0.4 mi., then climb on steady grades (see Mt. Pierce chapter) and reach timberline at 3.1 mi./4250 ft., where Webster Cliff Trail from summits of Mt. Pierce and Jackson comes in on R. (Summit of Pierce is 01. mi. up this trail.) Crawford Path continues NE through patchy scrub, frequently passing over ledges with fine views in every direction. After passing over several minor humps along ridge, small stream is crossed in col at 3.8 mi./ca. 4060 ft., then grade steepens as ascent of Eisenhower begins. S end of Mt. Eisenhower Loop to summit is reached at

Round-domed Mt. Eisenhower and the peaks of the Southern Presidentials.

4.3 mi./4425 ft. Diverge L onto loop trail for 0.4 mi., 335 ft. climb to summit, ascending in open via switchbacks with continuous views.

South Approach from US 302 via Dry River

Dry River Trail, Mt. Eisenhower Trail, Crawford Path, Mt. Eisenhower Loop
8.5 mi. one way, 3850-ft. elevation gain

Trailhead (1205 ft.): This approach starts on Dry River Trail on E side of US 302 in Crawford Notch State Park, 0.3 mi. N of Dry River Campground.

Though seldom used by day hikers, this route provides an attractive hike up the remote Dry River valley and a spur ridge leading to the crest of the Southern Presidentials between Mts. Eisenhower and Franklin. With a car spot at Edmands Path trailhead, an interesting 11.8 mi. traverse is possible. Because of a potentially difficult crossing of Dry River, this route should not be attempted in high water.

From trailhead, Dry River Trail follows old road, then logging RR grade to 0.9 mi. Short climb leads to framed view of Mt. Washington at head of valley at 1.5 mi./1700 ft. Trail drops to cross suspension footbridge at 1.7 mi. and continues up valley, alternating rough ups-and-downs with easy walking on RR grade. Reach jct. L with Mt. Clinton Trail at 2.9 mi./1900 ft. Keep on Dry River Trail up valley, on and off RR grade, crossing brook at 3.6 mi. and making R turn up to higher bank at 4.2 mi. At 4.9 mi./2600 ft. cross Isolation Brook and reach jct. R with Isolation Trail. Stay on Dry River Trail along bank high above river, passing cleared outlook up to high boreal ridge of Mt. Pierce.

At 5.2 mi./2650 ft. turn sharp L on Mt. Eisenhower Trail and descend to crossing of Dry River on large rocks—difficult in high water. Trail heads downstream for 0.2 mi., then swings R (NW) and climbs easily to jct. L with Dry River Cutoff at 5.5 mi. Mt. Eisenhower Trail now climbs N up W side of ridge at varying grades. At ca. 6.5 mi./3300 ft. pass through blowdown areas with dense young growth and occasional views of Mts. Pierce and Jackson and Eisenhower's bald dome, and down into remote valley to W. Sharp R turn at 7.0 mi./3600 ft. leads to steeper, rocky ascent through thick woods. Partial views back to S and up to Eisenhower and Franklin begin at ca. 4000 ft., and trail attains crest of W ridge at 7.6 mi./4200 ft. Pass outlook on R with view SW and wind upward through high scrub to treeline and views back into Dry River valley. Continue in open across broad ridge between Franklin and Eisenhower and meet Crawford Path at 7.9 mi./4475 ft.

Turn L on Crawford Path, descend slightly, and rise to jct. R with Mt. Eisenhower Loop at 8.1 mi., with Red Pond to L. Turn R on Eisenhower Loop, quickly pass jct. R with Edmands Path, and climb 0.4 mi./300 ft. to summit at 8.5 mi./4760 ft.

WINTER

For a variety of reasons, the hike up Mt. Eisenhower is considerably tougher in winter than in any other season. For starters, the standard ascent route, the Edmands Path, is difficult to reach as the Mt. Clinton Road is not open to public vehicle traffic in the winter. This means anyone wishing to ascend via this trail will most likely have to walk the road for 2.2 mi. just to get to the trailhead. More often than not, winter hikers will approach the peak from Mt. Pierce via the Crawford Path, and either double back via their ascent route or take the Edmands Path down to Mt. Clinton Road, and then walk out via the road to the Crawford Path parking lot. From Mt. Pierce to Eisenhower's summit (and especially on the latter's bald, summit cone), the Crawford Path is at or above treeline and hikers are thus exposed to the elements. On the Presidentials, this can mean low or near zero visibilty, heavy snow, extreme cold temperatures and dangerous winds. Full winter regalia, including crampons, is required. If, upon reaching treeline just below Mt. Pierce's summit, conditions are less than ideal, by all means save the peak-bagging for another day and retreat back down the Crawford Path.

VIEW GUIDE

Perhaps no summit on the Presidential Range offers a better perspective on its southern peaks than Eisenhower. Though the broad, flat summit area lacks the dramatic flair of other White Mountain peaks, its 360-degree view more than makes up for its shortcomings. Better perspectives S and N can be gained from spots a bit down either end of the Eisenhower Loop Trail; please stay on the marked footway.

Mt. Washington's summit cone is the dominating feature to the NE, with the sharp crest of Mt. Monroe seen just below and to the R of its towering neighbor, with Mt. Franklin in front. The long flat ridge of Boott Spur extends E from Washington over deep Oakes Gulf. The jumbled peaks of Rocky Branch Ridge and the long, flat Montalban Ridge stretch S from Boott Spur, on the opposite side of the broad, remote Dry River Valley. A little further R and above Rocky Branch Ridge are Chandler Mtn. and the twin peaks of Doublehead Mtn., while Mt. Kearsarge North near North Conway is seen above and to the L of Mt. Isolation, high point on Montalban Ridge, with the Green Hills to the R. The Moats are seen above the S end of Mt. Davis. To the S, seen above and beyond the Dry River valley and lower Montalban summits, is the rocky crown of Chocorua, while the many peaks of the Sandwich Range (Passaconaway, Whiteface, Tripyramid and Sandwich Dome) extend further to the W.

Looking SW, the view includes the ledgy ridge extending to neighboring Mt. Pierce, with Mts. Jackson and Webster beyond to the L. Carrigain, Osceola and the Hancocks are in the distance. The Willey Range looms more to the R and closer. Bondcliff, Mt. Bond and the tips of Mts. Moosilauke and Liberty are to the R of Mt. Field. Behind Mt. Tom the Twin Range extends across to South and North Twin, with Mts. Lincoln and Lafayette peering over behind. Mt. Hale is to the R and in front of North Twin.

The Bretton Woods area and Twin Mountain village lie close at hand just N of W, with Vermont's Mt. Mansfield visible on clear days just above the Mt. Washington Hotel complex. Other Green Mountain peaks such as Abraham, Ellen, Camel's Hump, Jay Peak and Burke can be spotted across the horizon. The long, wooded Dartmouth Range is across the Bretton Woods plateau to the NW, with Cherry Mtn. behind to the L and Vermont's Burke Mtn. beyond. The N view takes in a wide range of distant summits. The long, level Pliny Range, including Mt. Waumbek, is just W of N, with Mt. Cabot peering over behind. North Country peaks such as Goback Mtn. (between Starr King and Waumbek) and Dixville Peak (to the R of the Plinys) can be seen further afield. Nearby to the NNE, towering above the Ammonoosuc Valley and the Cog Railway up Mt. Washington, are the Northern Presidential summits of Mts. Jefferson and Clay.

NO. OF 4000-FOOTERS VISIBLE: 32

Mount Isolation

ELEVATION: 4003 ft./1220 m ORDER OF HEIGHT: 47 (tie)
LOCATION: Montalban Ridge, Townships of Sargents Purchase and Cutts Grant
USGS MAP: 7½′ Stairs Mtn.

GEOGRAPHY

Those who climb the 4000-footers are often pleasantly surprised by this remote and attractive little peak beside the historic Davis Path on Montalban Ridge. Hidden from civilization deep in the Presidential Range–Dry River Wilderness, the open summit of Isolation offers a unique and captivating view of Mt. Washington and the Southern Presidentials and a wonderful sense of, well, isolation.

The bare knob of Mt. Isolation is one of many small summits on the elongated, densely wooded Montalban Ridge, which stretches nearly 20 miles S from Mt. Washington's Boott Spur, between the valleys of Dry River and Saco River on the W and the Rocky Branch of the Saco on the E. Isolation is towards the N end of this ridge, between a 4293-ft. knob sometimes called "North Isolation" on the N and Mt. Davis (3819 ft.), with a long series of minor peaks, on the S. Summits farther S along the main ridge include Stairs Mtn. (3463 ft.) and Mt. Resolution (3415 ft.).

On the E, Isolation overlooks the upper valley of the Rocky Branch, an area burned in forest fires from 1912–1914 and now supporting large areas of birch forest. A prominent bald crag juts E from the S end of Isolation's summit ridge. This spur and a ridge extending SE from a knob up the main ridge enclose a broad basin to the E of Isolation's summit. Across the valley to the E rises the mostly trailless Rocky Branch Ridge, a subsidiary ridge extending S from Mt. Washington's Slide Peak. On the W of Mt. Isolation is the broad, remote basin of Dry River (also known as Mt. Washington River), draining down from Oakes Gulf on the S side of Mt. Washington. A spur ridge runs SW from Isolation into this valley. The high ridge of the Southern Presidentials walls in the Dry River valley on the W.

The usual climbing route to Mt. Isolation is long—14.6 mi. round trip—but not overly strenuous. Because of its remoteness, many peakbaggers put this one off, and 4000-Footer Club records indicate that this is the most common "finishing peak" of the 48. It's well worth the wait.

NOMENCLATURE

Isolation is an entirely appropriate name for this remote peak. It was bestowed by William H. Pickering, one of the most active of the early AMC explorers, and first appeared on his 1882 Contour Map of the Mount Washington Range. Pickering named Mt. Davis, Isolation's near neighbor to the S, for Nathaniel T. P. Davis, a Crawford Notch innkeeper who completed the daunting task of constructing a bridle path along this ridge in 1845. The name "Montalban Ridge" was applied to the entire range by guidebook editor Moses Sweetser in 1876. This was a Latin version of "white mountain" and was originally rendered as "Mount Alban."

HISTORICAL HIGHLIGHTS

First Ascent: Unknown

1844–1845: Nathaniel T. P. Davis, son-in-law of Abel Crawford and manager of Mt. Crawford House in lower Crawford Notch, builds 16-mile bridle trail from Saco valley to Mt. Washington. Trail runs close by summit of Mt. Isolation. Because of length and comparatively monotonous wooded middle section, Davis Path is least popular of bridle paths to Mt. Washington and falls into disuse by 1853.

1871: Joshua H. Huntington, Assistant State Geologist, traverses Davis Path along Montalban Ridge.

1881: AMC party led by William H. Pickering traverses Montalban Ridge from Boott Spur down past Mt. Davis, noting that Davis Path "has now ceased to exist, and the forests form an unbroken wilderness." They admire Isolation's "superb" view of Mt. Washington and Southern Presidentials.

1892–1898: Saco Valley Lumber Company builds logging RR up Dry River to W base of Mt. Isolation and logs much of valley. RR grade is later used for part of Dry River Trail.

1907: First edition of *AMC White Mountain Guide* cautions that three long days should be allocated for trip over Montalban Ridge to Washington since "the path no longer exists, and the way is exceedingly difficult on account of scrub." The book notes that Mt. Isolation can be climbed by following logging road and bridle path up Rocky Branch valley (latter cut ca. 1904 by owners of land to examine spruce timber in upper valley), then climbing up slope through virgin spruce with little undergrowth.

1908–1914: Logging railroad constructed by Conway Lumber Company up Rocky Branch to E base of Mt. Isolation and valley heavily logged. RR bed is later resurrected as Rocky Branch Trail.

1910: Group from AMC Snow-Shoe section makes winter ascent of Mt. Isolation. Later in year Davis Path, then almost completely overgrown, is reopened as footpath by AMC. Party led by Warren W. Hart hires Maine woodsman Joe Bouchard to find route through the dense thickets, and spends twelve days cutting and blazing, including side paths to Mt. Isolation, Mt. Davis and Giant Stairs.

1912–1914: Fires sweep through upper valley of Rocky Branch in wake of logging, burning 10,000 acres.

1916: AMC Guide mentions view from ledge by Davis Path N of Mt. Isolation at edge of 1914 fire, giving "an impressive and desolate view." AMC has established Camp Isolation, shelter off Davis Path 1 mi. N of summit.

ca. 1930: WMNF opens Rocky Branch Trail, following RR grade up valley, then crossing Rocky Branch Ridge to NH 16.

Early 1930s: Dry River Trail opened up that valley by WMNF; 5 mi. in it climbs W side of Montalban Ridge to meet Davis Path at Isolation Shelter. (This upper branch is later incorporated as part of W section of Isolation Trail.) E section of Isolation Trail built, connecting Isolation Shelter with Rocky Branch Trail in valley.

ca. 1935: WMNF builds Rocky Branch Shelter #2 near jct. Rocky Branch and Isolation Trails.

1975: Presidential Range-Dry River Wilderness created by Congress, includes Mt. Isolation.

1980: Dilapidated Isolation Shelter removed.

TRAIL APPROACHES

East Approach from NH 16

Rocky Branch Trail, Isolation Trail, Davis Path
14.6 mi. round trip, 3600 ft. elevation gain

Trailhead (1200 ft.): Parking area for NE end of Rocky Branch Trail is at end of short spur road off W side of NH 16, 5.5 mi. N of covered bridge in Jackson.

This is the most commonly used approach to Isolation, involving a climb over a col in Rocky Branch Ridge and a roundabout trek up Rocky Branch valley to Montalban Ridge N of the summit. Grades are mostly easy after an initial steady climb. There are five crossings of Rocky Branch—difficult in high water.

From parking area, Rocky Branch Trail climbs by switchbacks through hardwoods and passes jcts. with Avalanche Brook Ski Trail on L at 0.5 mi. and on R at 0.7 mi. After approaching small brook on R at two L turns, trail makes steady, winding climb to W and SW up hardwood slope—stiffest climbing of trip. At 1.8 mi./2900 ft. make sharp L onto old logging road and proceed at easy grade, slightly downhill, through lovely glades of white birch. At 2.3 mi. trail sweeps R and climbs moderately to Wilderness boundary, soon cresting broad height-of-land on Rocky Branch Ridge at 2.8 mi./3100 ft., just N of 3244-ft. knoll known as Engine Hill. Follow short bypass L around boggy area and descend gradually, with glimpses of Montalban Ridge ahead. Farther down this gentle grade footing is wet with tedious rock-hopping in bushy terrain. At 3.5 mi. trail angles L and descends to cross Rocky Branch at 3.7 mi./2800 ft.

On far side is jct. R with Isolation Trail. (Rocky Branch Shelter #2 is short distance L down Rocky Branch Trail.) Turn R on Isolation Trail for easy stretch mostly on old RR grade, with occasional washouts. Cross river at 4.1 mi., and climb up off RR grade at 4.3 mi., gaining old logging road at higher level. Footing is muddy at times, though recent treadway work has alleviated problem. Next two crossings of brook are close together and can be avoided by short bushwhack. In this area trail passes through fine open woods of birch and fir regenerated after 1912–14 fires. Last crossing is at 5.4 mi./3423 ft., high up in valley.

Trail now swings L away from river and climbs gradually through deep, mossy, wet fir woods with primeval feel. Blowdowns and soggy footing may be encountered on this section. At 6.1 mi. follow yellow blazes carefully through confusing area of campsites and side paths. Climb to jct. with Davis Path at 6.3 mi. / 3850 ft. Turn L (S) on Davis Path for slight descent to wet sag, then follow trail at easy grades along thickly wooded ridge, with occasional peeks ahead at summit of Isolation and R to Southern Presidentials beyond Dry River valley. At 7.0 mi. trails veers L and steepens, climbing around NE side of summit. Reach jct. R with side path to summit of Isolation at 7.2 mi. Turn R and scramble up ledgy pitch—steepest of day—emerging on open ledges with striking panorama of Mt. Washington and Southern Presidentials at 7.3 mi. / 4003 ft. High point is at cairn a few yards S from best viewing area.

Return trip involves 300-ft. climb from Rocky Branch back over Rocky Branch Ridge—grade is gentle, but climb comes near end of long day!

NORTHEAST APPROACH from NH 16

Glen Boulder Trail, Davis Path
12.0 mi. round trip, 5050 ft. elevation gain

TRAILHEAD (1975 ft.): Glen Boulder Trail begins at S end of parking area for Glen Ellis Falls on W side of NH 16, 0.7 mi. S of Pinkham Notch Camp.

This is a shorter but considerably more strenuous approach to Isolation, with spectacular above-treeline views en route and much exposure to weather. The downside is the grueling 1500-ft. climb over the shoulder of Boott Spur on the return trip.

After 0.3 mi. of gradual ascent, Glen Boulder Trail begins steep, rocky climb, passing jcts. with Diretissima at 0.4 mi. and Avalanche Brook Ski Trail at 0.8 mi. / 2600 ft. Grade remains steep, reaching treeline with ledgy scramble at 1.4 mi. and immense Glen Boulder at 1.6 mi. / 3729 ft., with wide views E. Trail climbs in open up steep, rocky terrain, then enters high scrub at 2.0 mi. Grades are moderate as path tunnels through conifers, passing side trail R to spring at 2.3 mi. Emerge from trees and reach small Slide Peak at 2.6 mi. / 4806 ft. This small open nub provides fine view S down Rocky Branch valley and Montalban Ridge. The summit of Mt. Isolation is distinguishable as ledgy patch far below. Trail traverses open ridge with impressive views R into Gulf of Slides, then angles R (NW) for steady climb through scrub and alpine meadows to meet Davis Path at 3.2 mi. / 5175 ft.

Turn L and follow Davis Path on easy descent of broad, open S ridge of Boott Spur. Views are superb R into Dry River valley, L into Rocky Branch and ahead to Montalban Ridge and bare patch of Mt. Isolation. Pass fine rock perch on L and descend into scrub at 3.6 mi. / 4800 ft. Descent is steady through woods to col at 4.2 mi. / 4180 ft. Climb easily past knob of "North Isolation" and down through blowdown area. Pass jct. R with W branch of Isolation Trail at 4.8 mi. / 4150 ft. and drop to jct. with E branch of Isolation

Trail at 5.1 mi./3850 ft. Continue 0.9 mi. ahead on Davis Path to summit, as described above.

With car spot, this route can be combined with exit to NH 16 via Isolation Trail and Rocky Branch Trail for loop trip of 13.3 mi. with 3900-ft. elevation gain.

Other Approaches

Longer approaches, mainly used by backpackers, can also be made to Mt. Isolation. Consult AMC Guide for details.

Davis Path from US 302

9.8 mi. one-way, 4400-ft. elevation gain (plus 1400 ft. on reverse trip)

This is a long ridge walk through wild, varied forests with many ups and downs and little reliable water. Spectacular views can be enjoyed en route with short side trips to Mt. Crawford (at 2.2 mi.; 0.6 mi. round trip, 160-ft. elevation gain), Giant Stairs (at 4.4 mi.; 0.4 mi. round trip) and Mt. Davis (at 8.5 mi.; 0.4 mi. round trip, 100-ft. elevation gain), with best view on ridge, including stunning view across Dry River valley to Southern Presidentials and Mt. Washington.

Dry River Trail and Isolation Trail from US 302

8.5 mi. one-way, 3350-ft. elevation gain (plus 400 ft. on reverse trip).

This is an approach of 4.9 mi. over sometimes rough trail up deep, secluded Dry River valley, with view of Mt. Washington at 1.5 mi., followed by steady climb up rough, muddy Isolation Trail to Davis Path, 1.2 mi. N of summit of Isolation.

Rocky Branch Trail from Jericho Road

9.6 mi. one-way, 2900-ft. elevation gain.

This is a long, easy walk up S section of Rocky Branch Trail, mostly on old logging RR grade with four potentially difficult crossings of river. At 6.1 mi. meet Isolation Trail just N of Rocky Branch Shelter #2 and follow it and Davis Path to summit (including 4 more river crossings). Return loop can be made via southbound Davis Path and Stairs Col Trail; total for loop is 19.1 mi. with 3700-ft. elevation gain.

WINTER

Mt. Isolation can be one of the more difficult winter peaks to reach due to its remoteness, especially if you're breaking trail the whole way through this little-used area. The trailhead parking area is usually plowed. The Rocky Branch Trail can be difficult to follow in the open hardwoods as it ascends to Rocky Branch Ridge. Crossing the Rocky Branch is problematical if it's not well-frozen. Many winter peakbaggers shorten the trip by bushwhacking from the Rocky Branch up to Davis Path either N or S of

Mt. Isolation; this option is suitable only for veteran snowshoers skilled at navigating off-trail with map and compass. The sense of remoteness on Isolation's snow-crusted peak is even greater in winter!

VIEW GUIDE

The bare ledges atop the summit of Isolation offer spectacular views in several directions. The classic vista is looking N to Mt. Washington thrusting above the craggy cirque of Oakes Gulf, buttressed by Boott Spur and Slide Peak on the R and the sharp double peak of Monroe to the L. In the foreground are two wooded humps higher up on Montalban Ridge. Across the remote Dry River valley the long, high ridge of the Southern Presidentials extends L from Monroe to Franklin, Eisenhower, Pierce, Jackson and Webster, displaying their sharp E slopes, including two smaller cirques below Mts. Monroe and Franklin. Over Webster and Jackson, just S of W, are the three peaks of the Willey Range, with Mt. Bond to the R of Mt. Willey; Mts. Guyot, Lincoln and Lafayette above Jackson; the Twins between Mts. Field and Tom; and Mt. Hale to the R. Bondcliff, Mt. Flume and Mt. Moosilauke are to the L of Willey.

Mts. Carrigain and Hancock are prominent to the SW over the mouth of the Dry River valley, with the Nancy Range to the L of and in front of Carrigain. The view S is somewhat limited, but by standing on the highest ledge and looking over the scrubby trees you can see the Sandwich Range—Passaconaway, Whiteface, Tripyramid and Sandwich Dome—spread to the S beyond the many lower summits of Montalban Ridge. Mt. Tremont is below Passaconaway. Mt. Chocorua is just E of S, with North Moat to the L. To the SE there are views to Doublehead and Kearsarge North, with Maine's Pleasant Mtn. beyond and between them, and lower mountains in the Jackson area. To the E Black Mtn. and the Baldface Range rise beyond Rocky Branch Ridge. The high peaks of the Carters peer over to the NE, with the Wildcats beneath Carter Dome.

NO. OF 4000-FOOTERS VISIBLE: 29

Mount Jackson

ELEVATION: 4052 ft./1235 m ORDER OF HEIGHT: 39
LOCATION: Southern Presidential Range, Township of Beans Grant
USGS MAPS: 7½′ Crawford Notch, 7½′ Stairs Mtn.

GEOGRAPHY

Though it pokes only a couple hundred feet above the Southern Presidential ridgecrest, Mt. Jackson's small rocky cone is a distinctive and deservedly popular destination. The lowest 4000-footer among the Presidentials, it's flanked by Mt. Webster (3910 ft.) a mile away on the SW and Mt. Pierce (4312 ft.) two miles to the N along a broad ridge with an intermediate 3821-ft. hump. On the W it overlooks the upper portion of Crawford Notch, with the broad Bretton Woods valley to the NW. To the E is the wild valley of Dry River in the Presidential Range-Dry River Wilderness. A broad spur ridge extends SE from Jackson into this valley, along with another from the ridge between Jackson and Webster. To the NE is a deep valley between Jackson and Pierce, drained by a major tributary of Dry River.

Jackson's cone is girdled by steep ledges, and the view from its flat, rocky top is a fine reward for a short but rugged climb. Most of the mountain is cloaked in a beautiful coniferous forest, including old growth on the NW slopes along the Webster-Jackson Trail. On the lower NW slope are two prominent rock outcrops accessed by side trails—Bugle Cliff (2450 ft.) and the aptly-named Elephant Head (2050 ft.), which overlooks the "Gateway" at the top of Crawford Notch. Farther S are the long, thin waterfalls known as Flume Cascade and Silver Cascade, easily viewed from US 302 near the top of the Notch. Silver Cascade Brook extends far up on the W side of Mt. Jackson.

NOMENCLATURE

Though it's often assumed that this Presidential Range peak was named for President Andrew Jackson, the appellation was actually given in honor of Charles T. Jackson, a Bostonian who supervised the first geological survey of New Hampshire in 1839–1841. The name was bestowed in 1848 by the botanist William Oakes, who reportedly had his guide light a bonfire on the summit to celebrate the occasion. Historian Frederick Kilbourne noted that Jackson's work in New Hampshire—authorized by the legislature with an appropriation of $9,000—was "primitive" in its methods and "accomplished little of real scientific value." The bulk of the fieldwork was accomplished by assistants, among them Edward Everett Hale, whose name also lives on among the 4000-footers.

HISTORICAL HIGHLIGHTS

First Ascent: Unknown.

1771: Crawford Notch "discovered" by moose hunter Timothy Nash; he and friend Benjamin Sawyer maneuver horse down through pass and win land grant from governor. Within several years first crude road is built. Historians believe that before Nash's adventures, Native Americans had established their own rough path through Notch.

1803: Improved road through Notch, "Tenth New Hampshire Turnpike," is completed.

1828: Ethan and Abel Crawford build Notch House, a large inn, near base of Elephant Head. Henry D. Thoreau stays there in 1839.

1848: Botanist William Oakes names mountain after State Geologist Charles T. Jackson and sends his guide, Amasa Allen, to kindle bonfire atop summit.

1876: AMC stalwart William H. Pickering and friend ascend Webster via Silver Cascade Brook, then bushwhack across ridge to Jackson. He recounts trip in March 1877 *Appalachia* and in Moses Sweetser's guidebook, noting that the summit "has altogether a most lonely appearance." Sweetser himself recommends route along ridge from Mt. Clinton, though warning that "the transit is very laborious, the way being frequently obstructed by thickets of dwarf spruce."

Early 1890s: Rough trail is cut from top of Notch to summits of Jackson and Webster—forerunner of today's Webster-Jackson Trail.

1892–1898: Saco Valley Lumber Company builds logging RR up Dry River valley to E of Mt. Jackson and logs much of valley. RR grade is later used for part of Dry River Trail.

1895: Crawford House management cuts trail from Clinton (now Pierce) to Jackson, but it is soon abandoned.

1911–1912: Webster-to-Jackson section of Webster Cliff Trail located and cut by Paul R. Jenks and Mrs. Jenks.

1913: Paul R. Jenks and Charles W. Blood cut Webster Cliff Trail from Jackson to Clinton, mainly following route of 1895 path.

1917: Author Winthrop Packard pens chapter in his *White Mountain Trails* entitled "Up Mount Jackson—The Climb from Crawford's Through an Enchanting Forest."

TRAIL APPROACHES

NORTHWEST APPROACH from US 302 at top of Crawford Notch

Webster-Jackson Trail
5.2 mi. round trip, 2150-ft. elevation gain

TRAILHEAD (1900 ft.): Trail starts on E side of US 302 just N of Gateway of Crawford Notch, 0.1 mi. S of Crawford Depot. Parking is on W side of road.

This is a relatively short but rough-and-tumble climb with gnarly footing and a number of short, steep pitches. The lower section passes through old-growth spruce; the upper reaches traverse fine boreal forest.

Blue-blazed trail starts with moderate climb. At 0.1 mi. spur leads R 0.2 mi. to Elephant Head, open ledge with good view of Notch and area above Gateway. Main trail continues up bank above Elephant Head Brook, then turns R for section alternating easy traverses and steep, rocky pitches. At 0.6 mi./2450 ft., between second and third steep pitches, short side trail R leads over knoll to top of Bugle Cliff and good view down into Notch; use caution if wet or icy. Cross Flume Cascade Brook at 0.9 mi. and climb moderately, with occasional dips, to fork at 1.4 mi./2800 ft.

Bear L here on Mt. Jackson branch of trail (R fork leads to Mt. Webster) and climb steadily, with many twists and turns, crossing several small brooks. At 2.4 mi./3800 ft. swing L past Tisdale Spring (unreliable) and past open "fir wave" of dead trees, with partial views NW and of summit cone up ahead. Trail soon bears R and climbs steeply across and up W side of summit cone, ending with scramble up open slabs. Reach summit cairn and jct. with Webster Cliff Trail at 2.6 mi/4052 ft.; excellent views in all directions from ledgy, scrubby top of mountain.

Loop Options
Several loop hikes are possible using the ridgetop Webster Cliff Trail (white-blazed, part of Appalachian Trail).

Mt. Jackson and Mt. Webster
6.5 mi., 2400-ft. elevation gain

From summit of Mt. Jackson, follow Webster Cliff Trail S. Drop steeply off cone and meander along ridge, crossing several small, wet gullies. At 1.3 mi. from Jackson, Webster-Jackson Trail splits R; continue 0.1 mi. ahead on Webster Cliff Trail for easy climb to craggy summit of Mt. Webster, with awesome view into Crawford Notch. Retrace steps 0.1 mi. and turn L on Webster branch of Webster-Jackson Trail for rough, wet descent. Make steep down-and-up crossing of Silver Cascade Brook just before reaching jct. with Jackson branch, 1.1 mi. from summit of Webster. From here descend 1.4 mi. to trailhead.

Mt. Jackson and Mizpah Spring Hut
6.9 mi., 2350-ft. elevation gain

From summit of Jackson, follow Webster Cliff Trail N, negotiating steep ledgy pitch off cone. In 0.4 mi. trail winds through open alpine meadows with good views. Pass side path R to E outlook, then dip into woods and continue N along ridge. Climb over 3821-ft. hump and descend easily to jct. L with Mizpah Cutoff, 1.6 mi. from Jackson. To visit hut, continue 0.1 mi. ahead on Webster Cliff Trail. To descend, return to Mizpah Cutoff and follow it 0.6 mi. to Crawford Path. Turn L here and proceed 1.7 mi. down Crawford Path to its terminus on US 302. Turn L for 0.2 mi. road walk to Webster-Jackson trailhead.

To add loop over Mt. Pierce via Webster Cliff Trail and Crawford Path, totals are 8.3 mi./2900 ft. See Mt. Pierce chapter for details.

WINTER

Jackson is a popular winter peak with a snowshoe track much of the season. Snow-laden conifers make it an especially pretty climb. Steep pitches may be icy or crusty, and the final scramble up the ledges on the cone can be tricky and may require crampons. With deep, wind-drifted snow, the trail may be difficult and even impossible to follow in the open fir wave area near Tisdale Spring, even though the summit is in sight just above. Once past the steep pitches off the cone, the ridge walk along Webster Cliff Trail in either direction is winter wonderland material, although this trail, too, may be hard to follow.

VIEW GUIDE

With the exception of scrub on the E side, most of Jackson's summit is bare ledge with superb views all around. Jackson's placement on the southern extension of the ridge gives it an exceptionally fine perspective on the Southern Presidentials, Mt. Washington, Oakes Gulf and Dry River valley. From the NE side you gaze up the winding ridge at an array of taller Presidential peaks: nearby Pierce (with AMC Mizpah Spring Hut at its base), Jefferson, Eisenhower, Clay, Franklin, Monroe, Washington, and Boott Spur, with Carter Dome and Wildcat to the R of Slide Peak. Oakes Gulf is impressive under Washington, at the head of Dry River valley.

Across this valley to the E is the long Montalban Ridge, bristling with dark forests, and including Mts. Isolation, Davis, Stairs, Resolution (splotched with gravel slides), and rocky Crawford, anchoring the S (R) end. South Baldface (to the R of Isolation), Sable and Chandler (over Mt. Davis), the Doubleheads, Kearsarge North, North Moat (over Resolution) and Table Mtn. (over Crawford) rise beyond. To the S the winding Saco River valley leads out to Mts. Chocorua and Tremont, with Bartlett Haystack between them and Bear Mtn. under Chocorua. Mt. Paugus is between the Haystack and Tremont, with Mt. Shaw in the Ossipees beyond to its L. The high peaks of the Sandwich Range—Passaconaway, Whiteface, Tripyramid and Sandwich Dome—are to the R, above nearby Mts. Bemis and Nancy. Majestic Mt. Carrigain dominates to the SSW, with the far-flung ridges of Hancock to the R and the Osceolas and the tip of Tecumseh popping up between them. To the SW, beyond nearby Mt. Webster and the Pemigewasset Wilderness, are distant Loon, Carr, Kineo, Cushman and Smarts Mtns. The Willey Range looms large and close to the W across Crawford Notch, with Mt. Willey's talus slopes especially notable. The tops of Mts. Bond, Guyot, Lincoln, and Lafayette and the Twins (between Field and Tom) peer over the Willey Range, and Mt. Hale is to the R behind Tom. Vermont's Mt. Mansfield is seen to the R of Hale. To the NW is the spacious Bretton Woods valley and the Mt. Washington Hotel, and distant northern Vermont peaks beyond, including Burke Mtn. and Jay Peak. To the NNW is the long, dark line of the Dartmouth Range, with Cherry Mtn. behind on the L and the Pliny Range beyond on the R. Mt. Cabot peeks over the E ridge of Mt. Waumbek.

NO. OF 4000-FOOTERS VISIBLE: 30

Mount Jefferson

ELEVATION: 5716 ft./1742 m ORDER OF HEIGHT: 3
LOCATION: Northern Presidential Range, Townships of Thompson and Meserves Purchase and Low and Burbanks Grant
USGS MAP: 7½′ × 15′ Mt. Washington

GEOGRAPHY

Mt. Jefferson is, like its neighboring Northern Presidential giants, Adams and Madison, a pyramid of broken rock whose upper slopes (above ca. 4500 ft.) are devoid of trees. The actual summit of the mountain is a small plateau festooned with three rocky peaklets, the middle one being the highest.

Jefferson's nearest companions along the massive ridge of the Northern Presidentials are Mt. Clay (5533 ft.) to the S and Mt. Adams to the NE. On its S side Jefferson's summit cone descends to Monticello Lawn (ca. 5400 ft.), a gentle plateau carpeted with sedges. From here the ridgecrest narrows and descends to Sphinx Col (4959 ft.), the low point between Mts. Jefferson and Clay. On its NE side Jefferson's summit cone drops steadily to Edmands Col (4938 ft.), the wild, windswept saddle between Jefferson and Adams.

Several striking ridges and magnificent glacial cirques radiate from the summit mass of Mt. Jefferson; some of these are traversed by trails that are among the most rugged and exciting in the Whites. On the W is the Ridge of the Caps, marked by three rough, rocky knobs, "The Caps," at 4422 ft., 4691 ft. and 4830 ft. The lower, tree-clad part of this ridge rises from Jefferson Notch (3009 ft.), which divides Mt. Jefferson from the wooded, trailless Dartmouth Range to the W. Jefferson Notch is the highest point reached by a public road in New Hampshire. The slopes on the S side of the notch and the Ridge of the Caps are drained by one of the two Jefferson Brooks. Flowing from the N side of the notch and ridge is the South Branch of the Israel River.

Extending NW from the summit of Jefferson is the sharp, spectacular Castellated Ridge, which at ca. 4450 ft. narrows into wild, fin-like rock formations known as "The Castles." At the lower end of this ridge is a wooded spur known as Mt. Bowman (3449 ft.). On the NE side of the Castellated Ridge is Castle Ravine, "wild, steep, rocky and well-watered," (Sweetser), one of the least-visited glacial cirques in the Whites. The talus-strewn headwall of this NW-facing bowl tops out at Edmands Col. Israel Ridge of Mt. Adams forms the other wall of the ravine. Castle Brook flows down the valley, uniting with Cascade Brook at the base of the Castellated and Israel Ridges to form the Israel River.

The E side of Mt. Jefferson, facing into the glacier-scoured abyss of the Great Gulf, is perhaps even more spectacular. On the NE the mountain's barren slopes drop precipitously into Jefferson Ravine, a deep cirque that

Mt. Washington and the head of the Great Gulf, as seen from the summit of Mt. Jefferson.

opens E from Edmands Col, between Mts. Jefferson and Adams, and out to the main valley of the Great Gulf. This trailless basin is drained by another Jefferson Brook. Dropping E into the Great Gulf from the upper slopes of Mt. Jefferson are two sharp, truncated ridges known as "Jefferson's Knees." The northern of these ridges is a wildly steep and narrow arête, improbably traversed by the Six Husbands Trail.

On the SE side of Mt. Jefferson, opening E from Sphinx Col, is a smaller valley, sometimes called the "Ravine of the Sphinx," that drains into the Great Gulf. All of Mt. Jefferson's eastern slopes eventually drain into the West Branch of the Peabody River, which flows NE through the main valley of the Great Gulf at the base of the mountain.

NOMENCLATURE

Like several other Presidential summits, Mt. Jefferson was named by a group of explorers from nearby Lancaster who ascended Mt. Washington on July 31, 1820 under the guidance of the legendary Ethan Allen Crawford. The party, which included mapmaker Philip Carrigain, proceeded to name six of the surrounding peaks. This mountain was named for Thomas Jefferson (1743–1826), America's third President. Subsequently there was confusion among some mapmakers and guidebook writers, who transposed the names of Mts. Adams and Jefferson, but this was cleared up by the 1870s.

Jefferson's Knees and Jefferson Ravine were named by early AMC stalwart William H. Pickering in the late 1870s; a map which appeared in *Appa-*

lachia showed the names "North Knee" and "South Knee." Monticello Lawn was named in 1876 by guidebook editor Moses F. Sweetser in reference to Thomas Jefferson's Virginia home. The name "Castellated Ridge" appeared in 1859 in Thomas Starr King's *The White Hills: Their Legends, Landscape and Poetry*. Sphinx Col takes its name from a nearby rock formation. The name of Edmands Col commemorates the great trailbuilder J. Rayner Edmands, who laid many graded paths across the Presidential Range from 1891–1909. Mt. Bowman was named either for Hon. Selwyn Z. Bowman, who was a student assistant on a mountain survey, or for John Bowman, an early innkeeper in nearby Randolph.

HISTORICAL HIGHLIGHTS

First Ascent: A month after the Weeks-Brackett party climbed Mt. Washington and assigned names to the Presidential Range summits, three of its members (Adino Brackett, John W. Weeks and Charles J. Stuart), plus Richard Eastman, returned to the range for six more days of exploration. During this trip they climbed to the summits of all the Northern Peaks, including Mt. Jefferson, and are credited with the first recorded ascents of Mts. Adams, Madison and Jefferson.

1841: Boston minister and author Rev. Edward Everett Hale, on geological survey expedition, climbs to summits of Mts. Jefferson, Washington.

1852: First trail on Northern Peaks—Stillings Path—is built. Path begins at Jefferson Highlands and runs nine miles to point about one mile from Castellated Ridge. Trail, skirting side of Mt. Jefferson, is used to haul lumber up to Mt. Washington for building of first Summit House.

1883–84: Castle Path to summit from Bowman Station (Randolph) is built by E. B. Cook, Laban Watson, others. Trail ascends by way of craggy Castellated Ridge.

1892: J. Rayner Edmands begins multi-year project of extending Gulfside Trail from Airline on Mt. Adams to summit of Mt. Washington, including segment on Jefferson's E flank.

1902: New Jefferson Notch Road from Crawford's to Jefferson Highlands opens. State road reaches elevation in excess of 3000 feet in passing over height-of-land in Jefferson Notch.

1903: Lower section of Castellated Ridge Trail is blocked by ongoing lumbering operation.

1907: First edition of AMC guide makes note of trail running from Edmands Col to summit. So-called White Trail is approximately half-mile long and for most part follows series of white trail blazes painted onto rocks (1891) by Charles Lowe.

1909: One year after completing bushwhack descent over Jefferson's Knee into Great Gulf, trailmaster Warren Hart oversees construction of Six Husbands Trail following same basic route. This is part of three-year trail-building spree in Great Gulf from 1908–1910.

1910: Randolph Mountain Club (RMC) is formed.

1913: Sphinx Trail from Clay-Jefferson col down into Great Gulf is built. Path serves as emergency route off ridge during stormy weather.

1915–19: RMC members cut trail up Castle Ravine to Edmands Col.

1918: Maintenance of loop trail over summit from Gulfside Trail is taken over by AMC. Name of path is changed from New York University Trail to Mt. Jefferson Loop.

1920: Caps Ridge Trail from height-of-land at Jefferson Notch to summit is constructed by AMC crew.

1941: During October backpacking trip, Louis Haberland, 27, Roslindale, Mass., dies on mountain from exhaustion, exposure. Haberland is second fatality on mountain in five years, another hiker having died of heart attack while ascending Caps Ridge Trail in July 1937.

ca. 1948: Cornice Trail from Edmands Col and Randolph Path is extended around N and W sides of summit cone, linking with Gulfside Trail near Monticello Lawn.

1956: Forest Service erects Quonset-style survival shelter in Adams-Jefferson col, considered one of most potentially hazardous spots in White Mountains.

1960: Robert and Miriam Underhill make December 23 climb to summit and are first to complete Winter 4000-Footer list. Conditions at summit are less than ideal with temperature at –8 degrees and winds gusting over 70 mph.

1982: Citing misuse of shelter by backpackers and increasing damage to local alpine vegetation, Forest Service removes Edmands Col emergency shelter.

TRAIL APPROACHES

As with the other high Presidentials, an ascent of Mt. Jefferson via any route, even the relatively short Caps Ridge Trail, requires caution as there is extensive above-treeline exposure and much scrambling over ledges and boulders. For safety's sake, and to enjoy the wide views, pick a clear day for a climb of Jefferson.

West Approach from Jefferson Notch Road

Caps Ridge Trail
5.0 mi. round trip, 2700-ft. elevation gain

Trailhead (3008 ft.): Caps Ridge Trail starts from a parking area at the high point of Jefferson Notch Rd., 3.4 mi. N of the Cog Railway Base Rd. near Bretton Woods and 5.5 mi. S of Valley Rd. in Jefferson (off NH 115 or US 2). This gravel road is not plowed in winter and may be muddy, icy or snowy early or late in the hiking season.

Due to the high elevation of trailhead, Caps Ridge Trail provides the shortest route and least elevation gain to a high Presidential peak and is, by a wide margin, the most popular route to Mt. Jefferson. However, this trail is far from easy as the traverse of the rocky Caps involves some fairly difficult ledge scrambling, and the upper half of the climb is fully exposed to wind and weather. Ledges on the Caps are very slippery when wet. Despite moderate statistics, the difficulty of this hike should not be underestimated.

From parking area, trail enters fir woods, crosses wet area and climbs at easy grade for about 0.3 mi. Pitch is steeper to ca. 3500 ft., then eases again in beautiful boreal forest. At 1.0 mi./3791 ft. ledge on R provides view up to Caps and summit of Jefferson and out to Bretton Woods valley and Southern Presidentials; this outcrop is also notable for potholes scoured by glacial meltwater. At 1.1 mi. is jct. L with The Link.

Caps Ridge Trail continues up moderately, then becomes steeper and rougher up to treeline. Ahead loom the Caps, tortured heaps of lichen-covered rock. Steepest ledge scramble of trail leads to top of first Cap at 1.5 mi./4422 ft. Climb remains sporty and very steep up ledgy ridge, with ever-expanding views, leading past second Cap (4691 ft.) and up to highest Cap at 1.9 mi./4830 ft. Steep climb continues, with bouldery summit mass looming ahead, to jct. L with Cornice Trail at 2.1 mi./5025 ft. Now you slog steadily up summit cone over piles of broken rock, aiming for false summit, beyond which grade is easier to true summit several hundred yards beyond, reached at 2.5 mi./5716 ft.

Loop Options

For a scenic loop around S side of Jefferson's summit and back to Caps Ridge Trail, descend NE off summit on Mt. Jefferson Loop for 0.1 mi., then turn R on Six Husbands Trail and descend steadily E for 0.3 mi. over rocks to Gulfside Trail (5325 ft.). This side of summit opens striking views of Mt. Adams seen across depths of Jefferson Ravine. Turn R on Gulfside and slab along SE side of summit, with very slight climb, for 0.4 mi. to Monticello Lawn and jct. R with S end of Mt. Jefferson Loop (5375 ft.). Follow tall cairns of Gulfside across plateau, lushly grown with alpine sedges. In 0.1 mi. turn R on The Cornice and traverse SW side of summit cone, descending moderately over sedgy slopes and across fingers of talus. In 0.5 mi. reach Caps Ridge Trail (5025 ft.); turn L here for 2.1 mi. descent over Caps and down through woods to trailhead. Loop adds 1.0 mi. and 50 ft. of elevation gain to hike for total of 6.0 mi./2750 ft.

Other loops are possible around NW side of summit back to Caps Ridge Trail via 1) Castle Trail and Cornice (adds 0.8 mi. to hike, entirely above treeline) and 2) Castle Trail and The Link (adds 1.7 mi. and 150 ft. of elevation gain to hike, including traverse of spectacular Castles on Castellated Ridge). However, the 0.7 mi. section on Cornice or 1.7 mi. on Link are extremely rough and tiring, making for slow going, even though they involve little climbing. The Link, in particular, is noted for treacherous footing with rocks, roots and holes, and is in woods except for crossing of slide with good views.

From the depths of the Great Gulf to the summits of the Northern Presidentials (l–r), Mts. Jefferson, Adams and Madison.

North Approaches from US 2 at Bowman

Trailhead (1500 ft.): Two approach routes are possible from trailhead for Castle Trail, located on S side of US 2, 3 mi. W of Appalachia parking and 4.2 mi. E of jct. with NH 115. Park in area on N side of old RR grade.

Castle Trail

10.0 mi. round trip, 4200-ft. elevation gain

This is a long but highly rewarding approach up Castellated Ridge, with terrific views and some tough scrambling along the Castles, and the usual Northern Presidential rock-hop above treeline. The upper 1.2 mi. is fully exposed to weather and NW wind.

From parking area, cross RR grade and follow R-branching road (L is private) 0.1 mi. to trail sign on R. Traverse on level through logged area to WMNF boundary at 0.3 mi. Cross power line clearing and turn L to crossing of Israel River just beyond, at 0.4 mi.; not an easy crossing, and very tough at high water. Bear L on far side, then R up bank. Grades are easy on old logging road through hardwoods to jct. L with Israel Ridge Path at 1.3 mi./1900 ft. At 1.5 mi. Castle Trail swings R and begins climb out of valley, up NE side of Mt. Bowman. Ascend steadily through hardwoods to ca. 2400 ft., then into white birches. At 2.2 mi./2750 ft. grade becomes quite steep and remains so until crest of ridge between Mt. Bowman and Castellated Ridge is attained at 2.5 mi./3350 ft. Blowdown area here gives partial views into Castle Ravine and up to Castles ahead.

Grade is easy along level shoulder, then you climb moderately with good footing through fine, lichen-draped fir forest. Trail steepens again as ridge narrows, and steady climb leads to jct. with The Link at 3.5 mi./4025 ft. Castle Trail now becomes steep and rough, with several scrambles up ledges and boulders and first open views. Reach first Castle at 3.8 mi./4450 ft.—superb viewpoint looking E into Castle Ravine, S to Ridge of Caps and Southern Presidentials, SW to Carrigain and Willey, Twin and Franconia Ranges, and N to Pliny Range and many distant ridges. Trail struggles up through rearing rocky plates of The Castles, where ridge is breathtakingly sharp and narrow. Continue steady, exposed climb as ridge becomes less well-defined, enjoying continuous views, especially good to W and down into Castle Ravine. Pass jct. with The Cornice at 4.5 mi./5100 ft. and slog up boulder-strewn slope to summit of Jefferson (a few yards R on Mt. Jefferson Loop) at 5.0 mi./5716 ft.

Castle Trail, Israel Ridge Path, Castle Ravine Trail, Randolph Path, Gulfside Trail, Mt. Jefferson Loop

5.2 mi. one way, 4250-ft. elevation gain

The ascent through Castle Ravine is one of the wildest and most beautiful trips in the Presidentials, and sees little hiker traffic. Brook crossings can be difficult. The section up the headwall is a difficult scramble, and this route is not recommended for descent. With return to trailhead via Castle Trail, a spectacular 10.2 mi. loop is possible. Another option is to descend via Randolph Path and Israel Ridge Path on NE side of Castle Ravine, with short side trip to great views at Emerald Bluff. Including side trip, this is a 10.8 mi. loop.

From trailhead at Bowman, follow Castle Trail for gradual 1.3 mi. as described above. Bear L here onto Israel Ridge Trail and cross Israel River—may be tricky—at 1.4 mi. Proceed up along stream and turn R onto Castle Ravine Trail at 1.7 mi./2100 ft. Recross river at 1.9 mi. (again, not easy), pass the Forks of Israel (confluence of Castle and Cascade Brooks), and hop across Castle Brook at 2.1 mi. and 2.2 mi. Cross brook again at 2.5 mi./2600 ft. Trail now climbs up above brook through birches, with glimpses up to Castles. At 3.2 mi./3125 ft. The Link comes in from L. Continue gradually up valley through wild, lush fir forest, passing jct. L with Emerald Trail at 3.4 mi. Castle Ravine Trail crosses brook and just beyond Link splits R for steep, rough climb to Castle Trail below Castles.

Castle Ravine Trail proceeds up floor of valley, crossing brook several times on mossy rocks. Clamber around boulders where stream gurgles beneath and begin steep ascent up headwall on narrow, rough, winding path, passing overhanging Roof Rock at 3.8 mi./3600 ft. Work up rugged trail to open boulders at ca. 4000 ft., offering fine view back down ravine and out to NW (including Pliny Range), and up to Castles. Scree-strewn headwall looms ahead. Above here is long, difficult scramble up loose and very steep talus. Follow markings carefully to top of headwall, where trail issues forth through sedgy draw to meet Randolph Path at 4.5 mi./4900 ft.

Turn R on Randolph Path for short rise to Edmands Col, windswept saddle of glacier-scraped ledges, at 4.6 mi. Turn R here on Gulfside Trail and climb steep, rough section past Dingmaul Rock, with views L into Jefferson Ravine. At 4.8 mi./5125 ft. turn R onto Mt. Jefferson Loop and climb steeply up jumbled rocks to summit at 5.2 mi./5716 ft.

EAST APPROACH from Great Gulf

Great Gulf Trail, Six Husbands Trail, Mt. Jefferson Loop
6.9 mi. one way, 4450-ft. elevation gain

TRAILHEAD (1350 ft.): This route starts at the large parking area for the Great Gulf Wilderness on W side of NH 16, 6.5 mi. S of US 2 in Gorham, and 4.1 mi. N of AMC's Pinkham Notch Camp.

Hikers who enjoy a challenging trip through wild, remote country will relish the rugged approach to Jefferson via Six Husbands Trail. This audacious route scales the precipitous buttress of the northern Jefferson's Knee, with some difficult ledge scrambles and several nearly vertical ladders—not for the faint of heart! This trail is not recommended for descent. With a long car spot, a day trip can be made up Six Husbands with descent via Caps Ridge Trail to Jefferson Notch; total is 9.4 mi. Very strong day hikers, or, more reasonably, backpackers with a base camp in Great Gulf, can make a 14.5 mi. loop with ascent via Six Husbands and descent back to Great Gulf on the somewhat less difficult, but still very steep, Sphinx Trail from Sphinx Col.

From parking area, walk N along old road for 0.1 mi., turn L and cross Peabody River on suspension footbridge, then swing L and up to jct. with Great Gulf Link Trail (from Dolly Copp CG) at 0.3 mi. Bear L here at easy grade on wide trail through spruces along West Branch of Peabody. At 0.6 mi. Great Gulf Trail splits L off road (a ski trail in winter), then rejoins at 1.0 mi. Continue past more ski trail jcts. and over several brooks on bridges. At 1.6 mi. is jct. R with Hayes Copp Ski Trail. Enter Great Gulf Wilderness and reach jct. with Osgood Trail at 1.8 mi./1850 ft.

Continue ahead on Great Gulf Trail, following West Branch of Peabody. Pass scenic view of stream at 2.4 mi., then climb steeper pitch to gravelly opening atop high bank known as The Bluff, reached at 2.7 mi./2278 ft. Here there are good views up to N side of Mt. Washington, Mt. Jefferson and Mt. Adams. Just beyond, bear L on Great Gulf Trail where Osgood Cutoff veers R, and descend steep bank to cross Parapet Brook, then climb to hogback where Madison Gulf Trail splits R at 2.8 mi. Great Gulf Trail drops steeply to cross West Branch on suspension footbridge. Climb bank on far side and bear R on Great Gulf Trail as Madison Gulf Trail veers L towards Pinkham Notch. Great Gulf Trail now settles in for long, moderate stretch up along West Branch through deep fir forest, with rough, rocky footing in places. Pass Clam Rock on L at 3.1 mi. At 3.3 mi. rocks in riverbed provide view ahead to Jefferson's Knee and route of Six Husbands Trail. Cross Chandler Brook at 3.9 mi./2800 ft.; on far bank Chandler Brook Trail departs L. Continue moderate climb up valley to four-way jct. at 4.5 mi./3100 ft.

Turn R here on Six Husbands Trail and drop to cross West Branch (tricky in high water) and climb over low ridge to bank above Jefferson Brook. Buttress Trail departs R at 5.0 mi./3350 ft. Here Six Husbands Trail turns sharp L and starts working up lower slope of Knee, passing two boulder caves. Very steep climbing leads to pair of almost-vertical ladders at 5.5 mi., the second scaling a sheer mossy ledge. Steep going continues to second pair of ladders; at top of upper ladder is dicey scramble up smooth ledge with steep drop-off on L. The way remains steep, with several views back down Great Gulf to Carters and across Jefferson Ravine to Mt. Adams.

Grade eases as top of Knee is approached, and open crest of ridge is reached at 5.8 mi./ca. 4700 ft. Convenient crag provides well-deserved resting spot here, with stupendous broadside view of Mt. Adams. Traverse level shoulder, then wind up through scrub and bare patches to jct. R with Edmands Col Cutoff at 6.2 mi./4925 ft. Six Husbands Trail now climbs steeply over talus; snowfields may linger in this area into July. Cross Gulfside Trail at 6.5 mi./5325 ft. Continue climbing up broken rock to Mt. Jefferson Loop at 6.8 mi./5625 ft. Turn L for final short climb to summit at 6.9 mi./5716 ft.

SOUTH APPROACH via Gulfside Trail

Hikers traversing Presidential ridge from S approach Mt. Jefferson from Mt. Washington and Mt. Clay via Gulfside Trail, in midst of longest stretch of trail above treeline in the East. From Mt. Washington summit, Gulfside Trail descends N, then NW along rim of Great Gulf with awesome views down into valley. Mt. Clay Loop splits R near Washington-Clay col at 1.1 mi./5400 ft. (offering alternate route along ridge of Mt. Clay with dramatic views into Great Gulf). Jewell Trail diverges L at 1.4 mi. Gulfside Trail descends N along W side of ridge, passing N end of Mt. Clay Loop at 2.2 mi./5025 ft., and reaching Sphinx Col, a neat little corridor between rock walls, and jct. R with Sphinx Trail at 2.3 mi./4959 ft. (Sphinx Trail descends moderately at first, then very steeply down somewhat sheltered ravine between Mts. Clay and Jefferson. Lower half of trail follows stream closely with slippery footing, and meets Great Gulf Trail 1.1 mi. from Gulfside Trail, elevation 3625 ft. From here it is 5.6 mi. out to Great Gulf trailhead via Great Gulf Trail.)

From Sphinx Col, Gulfside Trail makes steady, rocky climb along E side of Jefferson's S shoulder. Cornice comes in on L at 2.8 mi./5325 ft. Gulfside now traverses plateau of Monticello Lawn. At 2.9 mi. bear L on Mt. Jefferson Loop and hop rocks up to summit of Mt. Jefferson at 3.2 mi. from Mt. Washington.

WINTER

Mt. Jefferson is among the toughest of the winter peaks. Because Jefferson Notch Rd. is not plowed, Caps Ridge Trail is not a practical approach. Thus a climb of at least 5 mi. is required to reach the summit—longer than Washington or Adams. A commonly used winter route follows Lowe's Path for

2.7 mi., then Randolph Path for 2.2 mi. to Edmands Col. The upper part of Randolph Path has great exposure to bitter NW winds. From Edmands Col winter peakbaggers must undertake a steep climb of 0.6 mi. up Gulfside Trail and Mt. Jefferson Loop, traversing a long, steeply sloping snowfield en route. The total for this route is 11.0-mi. round-trip, with 4350-ft. elevation gain. Full winter gear, including crampons and ice axe, is required. Only experienced and properly equipped hikers should attempt this climb, and then only on days with clear weather and relatively light winds.

VIEW GUIDE

While certainly offering a view that is far better than average, Mt. Jefferson's summit vista is generally rated inferior to that of several other Presidential Range peaks, such as Mts. Adams, Madison, or Washington. Some would argue, in fact, that the mountain's best views are found not on its summit, but along its many rugged ridges and their varied approach trails. Still, there are fine vistas of Mts. Adams and Washington close by and of many other peaks further afield.

Looking to the N across the Randolph Valley are the significantly lower peaks of the Crescent Range, while more to the L (NW) are the Pliny and Pilot Range summits, with Waumbek and Starr King rising out of Jefferson village and Cabot and the Horn further N and somewhat to the R.

Close by to the NE is the sharp rocky crest of Mt. Adams and its many subsidiary summits, with distant ridges seen to either side, including the Bear Mtn. group (E of the Mahoosucs) and symmetrical Mt. Blue to the R. Also to the R, part of Mt. Madison's Osgood Ridge is seen descending into the depths of the Great Gulf. (More dramatic views of Adams rising from the cavernous Jefferson Ravine are obtained from trails on the E side of Jefferson's summit.)

The E view out over the Great Gulf takes in the peaks of the Carter-Moriah Range with Moriah furthest N, followed on the right by North, Middle, and South Carter. Carter Dome and Mt. Hight are visible over a jumble of rocks more to the ESE. To the R of Carter Dome can be seen Carter Notch and Wildcat Mt., with Mts. Sable and Chandler over Wildcat.

Mt. Washington's gray, bouldery mass rises out of the Great Gulf to the SE, blocking out everything in that direction. Portions of the auto road, clinging to the ridge on the lip of the Great Gulf, are visible below and L of Washington's summit, while the Cog Railway is seen attacking Washington's on its W slopes. The headwall of the Great Gulf appears as a striking gouge in the side of the mountain.

Turning to the S, Mt. Clay and Monticello Lawn are close at hand in the foreground, with Mt. Monroe and Lakes of the Clouds Hut visible R of Mt. Clay. A beautiful sweep of the southern Presidentials (Little Monroe, Franklin, Eisenhower, Jackson, Pierce, Webster) extends L–R from Monroe, blending in somewhat with the peaks of the Crawford Notch area, including Mts.

Willey, Field and Tom descending to the N. Far beyond and just over Little Monroe are the Sandwich Range summits, with Passaconaway anchoring the range to the L, and Whiteface, Tripyramid and Sandwich Dome to its R. Mt. Carrigain in the Pemi Wilderness is visible to the SSW over the lower end of the southern Presidentials; on its R is the broad spread of Mt. Hancock, with the Osceolas and Tecumseh beyond. On very clear days Mt. Monadnock can be seen over Carrigain's Signal Ridge. Scar Ridge is to the R of Hancock, over the col between Willey and Field.

WSW over the broad Bretton Woods plain and the comparatively low Rosebrook Range are Mt. Hale, the Twins, and the Bond Range. The Twins are directly above Mt. Hale, with Mts. Lafayette and Lincoln of the Franconia Range seen above and behind the Twins. Mts. Bond and Guyot are over Mt. Tom, with the tips of Mts. Flume and Liberty seen over Guyot. Mt. Moosilauke, meanwhile, is visible between Liberty and Lafayette, over the ridge connecting Guyot and So. Twin. To the R of Lafayette can be seen the tips of North Kinsman, Cannon and Garfield.

Looking W, the low, wooded Dartmouth Range summits of Mts. Dartmouth and Deception are close by on the opposite side of Jefferson Notch, with a vast view out towards Vermont beyond. Cherry Mtn. in Carroll is R of the Dartmouth Range. The little twin summits of Mts. Agassiz and Cleveland in Bethlehem are almost due W, with Vermont's Camel's Hump far on the horizon, also due W.

To the NW over the flat Jefferson Meadows and L of US 2 is Mt. Prospect in Lancaster. L of Prospect and R of the Dalton Range Mountains near the Connecticut River are Burke and Umpire Mts. in Vermont, with Mt. Mansfield in the Green Mountain Range more to the S (L) of Burke. Other Vermont peaks seen to the NW include the two sharp summits of Jay Peak and the lower mountains around U-shaped gap that holds Willoughby Lake.

NO. OF 4000-FOOTERS VISIBLE: 40

Mount Madison

ELEVATION: 5366 ft./1636 m ORDER OF HEIGHT: 5
LOCATION: Northern Presidential Range, Townships of Thompson and Meserves Purchase and Low and Burbanks Grant, Town of Randolph
USGS MAPS: 7½′ × 15′ Mt. Washington, 7½′ Carter Dome

GEOGRAPHY

The rocky pyramid of Mt. Madison anchors the NE end of the Presidential Range, soaring 4000 ft. above the valleys of the Moose River to the N and the Peabody River to the E. Like its Northern Presidential neighbors, the upper cone of Madison is bare of trees and heaped with fragments of frost-broken rock. The summit itself is a narrow, rocky, wind-beaten crest. Thomas Starr King was enamored of Madison, calling it "beautiful, clear, symmetrical, proud, charming, gigantic."

Close by to the SW is Mt. Adams, which towers more than 400 ft. above Madison. In the flat, barren 4890-ft. col between the two peaks is tiny, rock-bound Star Lake. To the S of Mt. Madison, with its headwall just below this col, is Madison Gulf, a wild glacial cirque that opens out into the lower valley of the Great Gulf. At the top of the headwall, just E of Star Lake, is a crag called The Parapet, which offers a magnificent view over Madison Gulf, the Great Gulf and the mountains beyond. Madison Gulf is drained by Parapet Brook.

Extending SE from Madison's summit cone is Osgood Ridge, which stretches more than a mile above treeline over a series of small rocky peaks before broadening and descending to the West Branch of the Peabody River. This ridge encloses Madison Gulf on the E. Partway down, an eastern spur ridge drops over a 2586-ft. knob and down to the main branch of the Peabody River. On the NE side of Osgood Ridge is a broad basin drained by E-flowing Culhane Brook.

Extending NE from Madison's summit is the wild Howker Ridge, which runs over a series of steep knobs known as "The Howks" (4315 ft. down to 3915 ft.) in its upper reaches. Below the Howks the ridge splits into two spurs, one dropping NE and the other N, then NW, with Town Line Brook draining the valley between them. (This stream runs across the town line between Randolph and Gorham, and drops over a trio of cascades known as Triple Falls.) At the base of the NE spur is the 1650-ft. col with Pine Mtn. (2405 ft.), a low, ledgy summit to the NE that offers outstanding views of Madison and Adams. To the W of Howker Ridge is Bumpus Basin, a trailless, wooded north-facing glacial cirque drained by Bumpus Brook. Hitchcock Fall and Coosauk Fall are found on this stream's lower reaches.

Running N from Madison's summit is Gordon Ridge, which separates Bumpus Basin on the E from the long valley of Snyder Brook, flowing N from the Madison-Adams col, on the W. The lower NW spur of Gordon Ridge was burned in a 1921 fire, leaving bare ledges such as Dome Rock and Upper Inlook; this scenic ridgelet is traversed by the Inlook Trail.

NOMENCLATURE

Like several of its Presidential Range neighbors, Mt. Madison was named on July 31, 1820, by the Weeks-Brackett party from Lancaster, which was guided by Ethan Allen Crawford. James Madison (1751–1836), for whom the mountain is named, was the nation's fourth President.

Osgood Ridge was named for Benjamin F. Osgood, a well-known guide at the Glen House in the valley SE of the Northern Peaks; he opened a trail along his namesake ridge in 1878. Howker Ridge was named for James

Howker, who had a farm in the valley at the base of the ridge. Gordon Ridge honors another guide, James Gordon of Gorham, who led Thomas Starr King on several adventures in the 1850s. Bumpus Basin and Brook were named for Silas Bumpus, an early settler in Randolph, while Culhane Brook commemorates another pioneer family in the Peabody valley to the E.

HISTORICAL HIGHLIGHTS

First Ascent: One month after the Weeks-Brackett climbed Mt. Washington and assigned names to the various Presidential Range summits, three of its members (Adino Brackett, John W. Weeks and Charles J. Stuart), along with Richard Eastman, returned to the range for six more days of exploration. During this trip they climbed to the summits of all the Northern Peaks, including Mt. Madison, and are credited with the first recorded ascents of Mts. Adams, Madison and Jefferson.

ca. 1860: Gorham guide James Gordon builds short-lived trail to Mt. Madison.

1862: Inspired by writings of Rev. Thomas Starr King, group of trampers attempts ridge walk over Northern Presidentials to Mt. Washington. Clergyman Phillips Brooks of Philadelphia barely survives ordeal.

1877: Ravine House at northern base of mountain opens. Building, dating back to 1850s, was earlier known as Mt. Madison House.

1878: Benjamin Osgood opens path to summit from Glen House up what is today called Osgood Ridge.

1882: Laban Watson completes work on Watson Path from Ravine House to Mt. Madison summit.

1888–89: Stone hut (Madison Spring Hut) is built by AMC in Madison-Adams col.

1889: Watson, Rosewell Lawrence make first recorded winter ascent of peak. On previous day, pair had climbed up Mt. Adams, only second to do so.

1895–97: J. R. Edmands builds Valley Way trail to hut, utilizing sections of existing trails previously built by E. B. Cook, Watson.

1901: Trail up Howker Ridge from Randolph (near train station) is finished, more than 20 years after first section was constructed. Lower part of path is subsequently relocated several times.

1903–07: Lower N slopes of Northern Peaks are ravaged by lumbering operations.

1906: Addition is built onto Madison Hut, doubling its overnight capacity.

1909: First of two steep, rough trails from Great Gulf to Adams-Madison col is built. Buttress Trail is laid out, maintained by E. H. Blood. The following year, Madison Gulf Trail from Great Gulf is blazed by W. O. Crosby.

1910: Randolph Mountain Club is formed.

1911: A separate stone hut (known as "Number 2") is built by AMC as cookhouse for nearby Madison Hut.

1918: Willard Helburn, Henry Chamberlain ascend Madison early on morning of Feb. 22 at start of first-ever winter traverse of Presidentials.

1921: Gordon Ridge scene of forest fire. Local historian George Cross later writes: "It seemed as though all Madison . . . was on fire."

1922: Third building ("Number 3") is added to growing Madison Hut complex. New building serves as bunkhouse for up 60 guests.

1924–1926: Pine Link Trail connecting village of Gorham with Madison Spring Hut is constructed. Total length of trail, 8.1 miles.

1928: Southern terminus of Madison Gulf Trail relocated to Mt. Washington Auto Road.

1929: Hut operation is consolidated under one roof with addition built on to Madison "Number 3" and razing of original hut. Madison "2" is converted to storage building.

1931: First winter ski traverse of Northern Presidentials is achieved by Fritz Weissner, Milana Jank. Pair spend second night of three-day journey in Madison Hut.

1932: Inlook Trail to Dome Rock at lower end of Gordon Ridge cut by RMC. Trail follows course of former Inlook and Outlook Trail ravaged first by lumbering, then by 1921 forest fire.

1933: Daniel Webster-Scout Trail is constructed by New Hampshire Boy Scouts. It links Dolly Copp Campground with Osgood Trail at Osgood Jct., half-mile below summit.

1938: Heavy rains from fall hurricane cause landslide to fall across portion of Daniel Webster Scout Trail.

1940: Accidental fire guts Madison Hut. Madison "Number 2" is pressed into service until replacement hut is finished in 1941.

1948: Parapet Trail, linking Osgood Jct. with Madison Spring Hut, opens. Path provides more sheltered route to hut by contouring along S side of summit cone.

1957: 21-year-old hiker Thomas Flint dies from fall, exposure halfway up to summit from hut.

1964: Congress creates Great Gulf Wilderness, including S slopes of Mt. Madison.

1998: January ice storm devastates hardwood forest on lower N slopes of Madison; yeoman effort by RMC clears fallen trees from trails.

TRAIL APPROACHES

Mt. Madison has a variety of possible trail approaches from several directions. This climb is only slightly less difficult than an ascent of Mt. Adams or Mt. Washington, with 4000 ft. of elevation gain in about 4 mi. of steady climbing. The upper cone of the mountain is a jumble of broken rock, devoid of trees and any protection from the elements. The climb should only be undertaken in favorable weather conditions, and all above-treeline precautions that apply to Mt. Washington come into play when scaling Madison. Allow a full day for this very strenuous trip, which includes difficult boulder-hopping on the upper ridges.

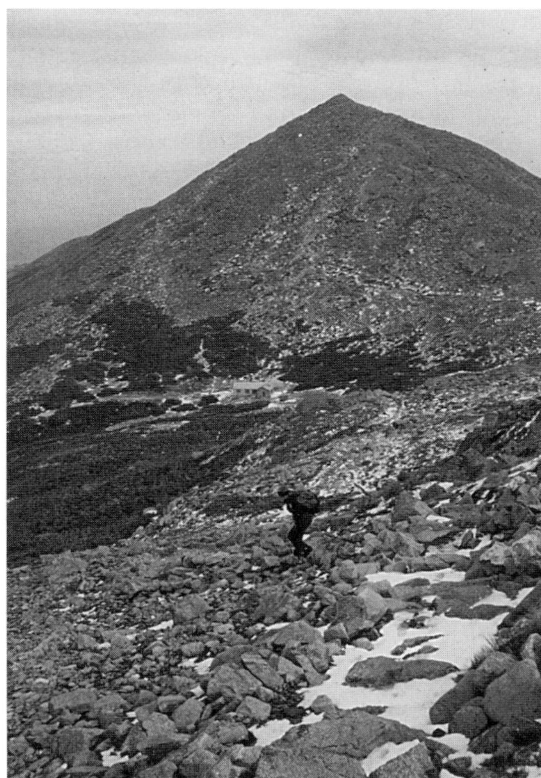

The sharp crest of Mt. Madison as seen from the lower slopes of neighboring Mt. Adams.

NORTH APPROACHES from US 2

From Appalachia

TRAILHEAD (1306 ft.): The large parking area at Appalachia is one of the major trailheads in the Whites. It's located on the S side of US 2, 5.5 mi. W of NH 16 in Gorham and 2 mi. E of Lowe's Store in Randolph.

Valley Way, Osgood Trail
8.6 mi. round trip, 4100-ft. elevation gain

This straightforward, relatively moderate route follows steady and sheltered Valley Way—a popular trail, wide and rocky in places—to AMC Madison Hut, from which exposed rock-hop leads up summit cone. From parking area, follow blue-blazed Valley Way across old RR grade and powerline (where Air Line forks R) and into woods. Climb moderately through hardwoods and then hemlocks, passing several trail junctions. (Parallel Fallsway offers chance to see several small waterfalls on Snyder Brook.) Just beyond jct. R with Beechwood Way at 0.8 mi., Valley Way bears R and climbs to jct. with Randolph Path at 0.9 mi./1953 ft.

Valley Way now climbs steadily along slope high above Snyder Brook and swings E, then S, entering nice stand of white birch. Pass jct. R. with Scar Trail at 2.1 mi./2811 ft. and crossing of Watson Path at 2.4 mi./3175 ft. Long, steady climb continues up lower E slope of Durand Ridge, passing jct. L with Lower Bruin at 2.8 mi./3584 ft., side trail R to Valley Way Campsite (2 tent platforms) at 3.1 mi., and jct. R with Upper Bruin at 3.3 mi./4150 ft. Valley Way now climbs more steeply up headwall of ravine, with brook mostly close by on L. Emerge from scrub and at 3.8 mi./4800 ft., just past jct. with Air Line Cutoff, reach jct. with Gulfside and Star Lake Trails, 100 ft. below Madison Hut.

Continue up to hut (refreshments available in summer) and turn L on Osgood Trail. After passing jct. L with Pine Link, Osgood Trail quickly begins steep climb up exposed W ridge of Madison, with scrambling over boulders and ledges. Views back to rock stack of Adams are impressive. At top of steep scramble, trail eases on narrow, rocky crest. Follow large cairns E to summit at 4.3 mi./5366 ft.

Valley Way, Watson Path
7.8 mi. round trip, 4050-ft. elevation gain

This is one of the shortest routes to Madison, but it is steep and rough for its upper 1.5 mi. with a long stretch of exposure to weather. The trail may be hard to follow with low visibility.

Follow Valley Way for 2.4 mi. as described above. Turn L here (3175 ft.) on Watson Path, which runs along W bank of Snyder Brook past large Bruin Rock. Pass jcts. with Brookside (L) and Lower Bruin (R) and cross brook at base of Duck Fall; follow signs and blazes carefully. Watson Path quickly commences relentlessly steep and rough climb up W side of Gordon Ridge through wild conifer forest. At 3.2 mi./4400 ft. trail emerges from scrub and continues climb in open with long stretch of rock-hopping. Cross Pine Link at 3.6 mi./4950 ft. Boulder-strewn ascent continues up N side of cone, attaining summit at 3.9 mi./5366 ft.

Options for climbing Madison and Adams together from Appalachia
Numerous possibilities exist using the extensive trail system on these peaks. These are two of many options:

1. Valley Way to Madison Hut; Gulfside Trail and Air Line to Mt. Adams, up-and-back; Osgood Trail to Mt. Madison, up-and-back; return from hut via Valley Way. Total: 10.4 mi., 5050-ft. elevation gain

2. Air Line to Mt. Adams; Air Line and Gulfside Trail to Madison Hut; Osgood Trail up-and-back to Mt. Madison; return from hut via Valley Way. Total: 10.0 mi., 5050-ft. elevation gain

NORTH APPROACH from Randolph East

Howker Ridge Trail, Osgood Trail
9.0 mi. round trip, 4550-ft. elevation gain (including 200 ft. on return)

TRAILHEAD (1225 ft.): Howker Ridge Trail begins at the Randolph East parking area on the Dolly Copp (Pinkham B) Road, 0.2 mi. S of US 2. Dolly Copp Rd. leaves US 2 about 1 mi. E of Appalachia parking area, at the foot of the steep climb up Gorham Hill.

Howker Ridge Trail is one of the wildest, least-used and most scenic routes to Madison, with waterfalls down low and several views from "The Howks" along the ridge. From parking area, trail crosses old RR grade, bears L where Randolph Path splits R, and rises gradually through logged areas—follow markings closely. At 0.4 mi. begin pleasant section alongside Bumpus Brook, passing Stairs Fall, Devil's Kitchen (small rock chasm) and Coosauk Fall. Sylvan Way splits R at 0.7 mi, and at 0.8 mi. Howker Ridge Trail bears L as Kelton Trail continues straight. Cross Bumpus Brook at base of tumbling Hitchcock Fall at 1.0 mi. / 1875 ft.

Trail now ascends at much more serious grade through deep softwood forest up NW spur of Howker Ridge. This long pull continues, with occasional breathers, to sharp, narrow crest of first Howk, with limited view up to Mt. Madison. Short ridge traverse leads to summit of this Howk at 2.3 mi. / 3425 ft. Descend 100 ft. and meander across level shoulder, then tackle stiff climb to second Howk at 3.0 mi. / 3951 ft.; open ledge provides view up to Mt. Madison beyond jumble of scrubby knobs, with Carters and Wildcats to E and Bumpus Basin to W. Drop steeply to col where Pine Link comes in from L at 3.1 mi., then climb to bare knob on next Howk and more views. Make short, steep drop to col and resume climb towards highest Howk. Pine Link splits R at 3.5 mi., and top of highest Howk is reached at 3.6 mi. / 4315 ft. This bare peak has sweeping views of Madison, Carters, Mahoosucs and Pliny / Pilot Ranges. Slight drop is followed by more steep climbing through scrub and then completely in open, angling SW to top of Osgood Ridge. At 4.2 mi. / 5100 ft. reach Osgood Trail at crest of ridge. Turn R for rocky, exposed climb to attain summit of Madison at 4.5 mi. / 5366 ft.

Various loops are possible for descent back to Randolph East, e.g. Watson Path, Brookside, Kelton Trail and lower Howker Ridge Trail (4.8 mi.) or Osgood Trail, Valley Way and Randolph Path (4.9 mi.). Consult AMC or RMC guides for details.

NORTHEAST APPROACH from Dolly Copp Rd.

Pine Link, Watson Path

7.6 mi. round trip, 4150-ft. elevation gain (including 200 ft. on return)

TRAILHEAD (1650 ft.): Pine Link starts at height-of-land on Dolly Copp (Pinkham B) Road, 1.9 mi. from NH 16 and 2.4 mi. from US 2.

This is the shortest route to the summit, though footing is often rough, and offers several views at mid-elevations. From road, trail ascends NE spur of Howker Ridge at varying grades. Cross swampy flat at 1.0 mi., then climb more steeply to top of ridge and ascend along crest. Pass outlook on L at 1.7 mi. At 1.9 mi. / 3650 ft. side path leads L to ledge with view up to

Madison and out to Carters. After slight dip, grades are easy/moderate to jct. with Howker Ridge Trail at 2.4 mi./3850 ft.

Bear L here as the trails coincide, climbing over a small, semi-bare Howk with good view. At 2.8 mi. Pine Link branches R at base of highest Howk and traverses wet area, then climbs steadily to treeline at 3.3 mi./4750 ft. Turn L on Watson Path at 3.5 mi./4950 ft. and climb steeply in open to summit of Madison at 3.8 mi./5366 ft.

Upper part of descent can be varied by looping back via Osgood Trail and Howker Ridge Trail; distance is same.

East Approach from Dolly Copp Campground

Daniel Webster-Scout Trail, Osgood Trail
8.0 mi. round trip, 4100-ft. elevation gain

Trailhead (1250 ft.): From NH 16 S of Gorham, take Dolly Copp (Pinkham B) Rd. to W for 0.3 mi., then turn L (S) on entrance road to Dolly Copp Campground. Scout Trail leaves on R 0.9 mi. down this road.

This approach is relatively moderate for first half, then quite steep and rough in upper half, with last mile fully exposed to weather. From campground, trail begins easy to moderate climb through hardwoods, crossing Hayes Copp Ski Trail at 0.2 mi. Trail angles SW, then NW, working up basin of Culhane Brook at reasonable grades. At 2.0 mi./2800 ft. enter conifer forest and climb more steeply to top of 3175-ft. shoulder, then angle up NE side of Osgood Ridge. Ascent becomes very steep and rocky at 2.9 mi., with first views popping out.

Break out above treeline at 3.2 mi. and continue relentless climb up talus, swinging L and up to crest of ridge and Osgood Jct. at 3.5 mi./4822 ft. Turn R here on Osgood Trail and scramble up to small rocky peak (5086 ft.), dip slightly, then boulder-hop up E end of summit ridge, past jct. R with Howker Ridge Trail, to top of Madison at 4.0 mi./5366 ft.

Southeast Approaches from Great Gulf Parking Area

Trailhead (1350 ft.): These routes start at large parking area for Great Gulf Wilderness on W side of NH 16, 6.5 mi. S of US 2 in Gorham, and 4.1 mi. N of AMC's Pinkham Notch Camp.

Great Gulf Trail, Osgood Trail
10.2 mi. round trip, 4050-ft. elevation gain

This is a long but scenic approach with an easy valley warm-up and the final 1.2 mi. along exposed Osgood Ridge. From parking area, walk N along old road for 0.1 mi., turn L and cross Peabody River on suspension footbridge, then swing L and up to jct. with Great Gulf Link Trail (from Dolly Copp CG) at 0.3 mi. Bear L here at easy grade on wide trail through spruces along West Branch of Peabody. At 0.6 mi. Great Gulf Trail splits L off road (a ski trail in winter), then rejoins at 1.0 mi. Continue past more ski trail jcts. and over several brooks on bridges. At 1.6 mi. is jct. R with Hayes Copp Ski Trail. Enter Great Gulf Wilderness and reach jct. with Osgood Trail at 1.8 mi./1850 ft.

Turn R on Osgood Trail and ascend moderately through hardwoods. Osgood Cutoff comes in on L at 2.6 mi./2486 ft.; Osgood Tentsite is on side trail R. From here up, Osgood Trail is part of Appalachian Trail. At 3.2 mi. grade becomes very steep through deep conifer forest. After several hundred ft. of climbing, pitch begins to ease off. Reach treeline at 3.9 mi./4300 ft. and traverse open rocky crest of curving ridge. Trail humps over long series of rocky nubbles, with rough footing. Views are magnificent, especially SW into Great Gulf surrounded by Mts. Washington, Clay, Jefferson and Adams.

Reach Osgood Jct. at 4.6 mi./4822 ft., where Parapet Trail goes L to slab S side of summit and Scout Trail comes in from R. Continue up ridge over 5086-ft. knob. Howker Ridge Trail enters on R at 4.9 mi./5100 ft. Osgood Trail clambers up E end of summit ridge to crest of Madison at 5.1 mi./5366 ft.

Great Gulf Trail, Madison Gulf Trail, Parapet Trail, Star Lake Trail, Osgood Trail

6.4 mi. one way, 4150-ft. elevation gain

This is perhaps the most challenging and interesting route to Madison. The climb up the headwall of Madison Gulf is one of the steepest trail sections in the Whites and should not be attempted by hikers uncomfortable with ledge scrambling. It should be avoided in wet weather and is not recommended for descent. For a long, strenuous and very scenic loop of 11.5 mi. from the Great Gulf trailhead, one could ascend via Madison Gulf Trail route and descend Osgood Trail.

Route begins on Great Gulf Trail as described above. At 1.8 mi., where Osgood Trail branches R, continue ahead on Great Gulf Trail, following West Branch of Peabody. Pass scenic view of stream at 2.4 mi., then climb steeper pitch to gravelly opening atop high bank known as The Bluff, reached at 2.7 mi./2278 ft. Here there are good views up to N side of Mt. Washington, Mt. Jefferson and Mt. Adams. Just beyond, bear L on Great Gulf Trail where Osgood Cutoff veers R, and descend steep bank to cross Parapet Brook, then climb to hogback where Madison Gulf Trail splits R at 2.8 mi. Follow this trail up little ridge between Parapet Brook and West Branch and rejoin older route of trail at 3.2 mi. Rocky, rooty trail now climbs up wild valley of Parapet Brook through fir forest, crossing two forks of stream at 3.5 mi. and 3.6 mi. Route veers away from brook, then returns to cross tributary brook.

Ascending higher into Madison Gulf, trail crosses main brook three times starting at 4.2 mi./3500 ft. Reach Sylvan Cascade, split waterfall dropping over mossy ledge, at 4.8 mi./3900 ft. Briefly traverse gentle upper floor of Gulf through wet, mossy fir forest, with walls looming above, then reach Mossy Slide and commence steep, rugged climb up headwall. This entails scrambles up boulders, several steep ledges, and a rock chimney; use of hands is required in places. A couple of spots are fairly difficult. After long pull, trail breaks above treeline and soon meets Parapet Trail atop headwall at 5.5 mi./4850 ft.

Turn L on Parapet Trail and climb to sharp R turn at 5.6 mi; side trail leads L to rocky battlement of The Parapet with dramatic view back down Madison Gulf and out to Mt. Washington and Carter Range. Parapet Trail runs across Adams-Madison col past rock-dotted Star Lake on L and meets Star Lake Trail at 5.7 mi. Turn R on Star Lake Trail and descend gently to AMC Madison Hut at 5.9 mi. Turn R here on Osgood Trail for steep, bouldery climb up W side of Madison summit cone. Level out on narrow crest and traverse to summit at 6.4 mi./5366 ft.

WINTER

As with all the higher Presidentials, this is a serious undertaking in winter with great exposure to wind and weather, though less so than on Adams, Jefferson or Washington. It should only be attempted on fine winter days by experienced winter trampers fully equipped for above-treeline travel. By far the most popular route is up via Valley Way, which is sheltered almost to Madison Hut. This trail is well packed out for much of the winter. Crampons and caution are required on the steep climb from the hut (closed in winter) up the boulder-strewn summit cone.

VIEW GUIDE

The open, rocky crest of Madison combines nearby views of Mts. Washington and Adams, the Great Gulf and the Carter Range with distant prospects to the N and NE.

The huge rocky bulk of Mt. Washington closes in the view to the S, beyond the lower Great Gulf. The Auto Road winds up the mountain's broad flank and past the little peak of Ball Crag to the L of the summit. To the R of Washington's summit is the gaping gouge of the upper Great Gulf, with Mt. Clay's double summit closing it in on the R. Close by to the SW is the giant rock-strewn pyramid of Adams, with the lesser peaks of Sam Adams and Adams 4 trailing out to the R. Below the creased crags of John Quincy Adams is Star Lake, sparkling on the flat col at the base of Adams' cone. On the L of the pond is the rocky battlement of The Parapet. Scar Ridge can be seen in the distance over the low point between Clay and Adams. (Mt. Jefferson is completely hidden by Adams.)

To the W and NW, beyond the great N ridges of Adams, there are distant views out to Vermont, including Camel's Hump, Mt. Mansfield and Jay Peak. The ridgecrest of Cherry Mtn. and Owl's Head is to the W. Closer in to the NW is the broad plain of the Israel River valley in the Jefferson-Whitefield area, with Cherry Pond visible to the R of Mt. Mansfield. To the NNW, beyond the Randolph valley at the foot of the mountain, are the wooded peaks of the Pliny Range—Starr King, Waumbek and the three rounded Weeks summits. Mt. Cabot is behind North Weeks, with The Bulge and The Horn jutting out to the R. Farther R and beyond are the mountains of the Nash Stream region, including the bare Percy Peaks. To the N, above the nearby Crescent Range, ridges roll out endlessly across New Hampshire's North Country.

The city of Berlin is prominent to the NNE in the Androscoggin valley. To the NE you look down on the jumbled knobs of Howker Ridge and the low, cliffy face of Pine Mtn. Beyond are the ledge-dotted ridges of the Mahoosucs, piled one upon another out to Old Speck, highest peak in the range, set back in the center. Baldpate is to the R of Old Speck. On the horizon are the high summits of the Rangeley, Maine area, including Saddleback, Crocker, Bigelow, Sugarloaf and Abraham. Farther to the R is the distant pyramid of Mt. Blue near Weld, Maine.

To the E and SE, across the valley of the Peabody River, is an impressive broadside vista of the Carter-Moriah Range, sweeping across Mt. Moriah, Imp Mtn., North, Middle and South Carter, Mt. Hight and Carter Dome, with its NW slide well-displayed. The tip of North Baldface is seen through Zeta Pass, and the lowlands of Maine sprawl beyond the Carters. The Wildcats carry the ridgeline on the R (W) side of Carter Notch, with the ski slopes in full view. The Glen House clearing is seen at the L base of Wildcat, and Kearsarge North rises beyond the Wildcats to the R of "C" Peak, with Maine's Pleasant Mtn. on the horizon.

Between Wildcat and the shoulder of Washington a view opens S through Pinkham Notch to the Moats and Mt. Chocorua, with distant Mt. Shaw in the Ossipee Range just to the R of Chocorua's pointed peak.

NO. OF 4000-FOOTERS VISIBLE: 10

Mount Monroe

ELEVATION: 5372 ft./1637 m   ORDER OF HEIGHT: 4
LOCATION: Southern Presidential Range, Township of Sargents Purchase
USGS MAPS: 7½′ × 15′ Mt. Washington, 7½′ Stairs Mtn.

GEOGRAPHY

Though overshadowed by Mt. Washington, its giant neighbor to the NE, craggy, treeless Mt. Monroe is one of the most distinctive peaks in the Whites. It is the northernmost and tallest of the chain of peaks that poke up from the ridgeline of the Southern Presidentials along the historic Crawford Path. The bare, rocky mass of Monroe rises abruptly from its 5108-ft. col with Mt. Washington to a short, level crest, with the high point on the S end.

Monroe is a classic example of a glacially eroded peak known as a "sheepback" or "roche moutonée," with a moderate slope on the NW, where the continental ice sheet flowed uphill, and a steep, craggy face on the SE, where the glacier plucked rocks away as it moved downhill. This profile is easily seen from vantages on the slopes of Mt. Washington to the NE.

Just to the W of the summit is a small subsidiary peak known as Little Monroe (5207 ft.), from which the open ridgecrest descends gently towards the slight rounded swell on the ridge called Mt. Franklin (5020 ft.). Below the main summit on the SSE is an open, level shoulder traversed by the Crawford Path. This area is noted for its profusion of alpine flowers blooming in June. From here a ridge descends S into the remote upper valley of the Dry River, forming the boundary between two steep glacial cirques. The main bowl of Oakes Gulf is to the E of this ridge, extending across to the high ridge of Boott Spur. To the W of Monroe's S ridge is a smaller cirque, enclosed by Monroe and Franklin, that has been called "Monroe Gulf." The wild area around Oakes Gulf contains some of the finest scenery in the mountains. The steep headwall between Monroe and Franklin is especially impressive.

Among the famous features of the Mt. Monroe area are the Lakes of the Clouds, two tiny alpine tarns that lie NE of the summit below the Monroe-Washington col. The Upper Lake (5050 ft.) is 0.4 acre in area and 6.5 ft. deep, while the Lower Lake (5025 ft.) measures in at 1.2 acres in area and 8.5 ft. deep. They are the ultimate sources of the Ammonoosuc River. The scenery around these glacially scooped basins is a striking mosaic of water, tundra and rock, with Monroe's summit presiding above. Nearby is the AMC Lakes of the Clouds Hut. To the N of the Lakes is the broad Ammonoosuc Ravine on the W side of Mt. Washington.

The less dramatic NW side of Monroe is marked by a broad ridge descending to the Cog Railway Base Station and the upper part of the Ammonoosuc River. Monroe Brook drains the basin to the E of this ridge, while Franklin Brook flows down through the ravine to the W.

NOMENCLATURE

In 1820 the Weeks-Brackett party, including mapmaker Philip Carrigain and guided by Ethan Allen Crawford, ascended Mt. Washington and bestowed names on the surrounding Presidential peaks. This summit was named for James Monroe, our fifth President, who was in office at the time. Oakes Gulf to the E was named for William Oakes, a botanist who explored the White Mountains from 1825 until his untimely death in 1848, the same year in which his book, *Scenery of the White Mountains*, was published.

The Lakes of the Clouds were called the "Blue Ponds" by the Weeks-Brackett party, who drank the ice-cold water "until some of us became quite blue . . ." In earlier days they were also known as "Washington's Punch Bowl."

HISTORICAL HIGHLIGHTS

First Ascent: It is generally thought that Darby Field and his Indian companions were the first persons to ascend Mt. Monroe during their epic journey up Mt. Washington in 1642. By all accounts, it is believed that Field at the very least passed by the two Lakes of the Clouds. A recently (1984) uncovered letter dating back to June 29, 1642, seems to indicate as well that Field and his party climbed over the summits of Mts. Eisenhower, Franklin and Monroe while on their way to Mt. Washington.

1811: Norwich University founder Capt. Alden Partridge traverses Southern Presidentials with guide Ethan Allen Crawford. Walk more or less follows route of soon-to-be-built Crawford Path and includes ascent of then unnamed Mt. Monroe.

1819: Crawford Path over Southern Presidentials is constructed by E. A. Crawford, Abel Crawford. Path probably passed over summit of Monroe at first, but was later rerouted around and below cone.

1820: Summit is christened Mt. Monroe by Lancastrian hikers guided to Mt. Washington by E. A. Crawford.

1837: Nathaniel Hawthorne pens short story, *The Great Carbuncle*. Tale is based on legend that great gem is hidden under remote cliff, supposedly at head of Dry River (probably in Oakes Gulf).

1891: Guidebook author M. F. Sweetser writes of mountain: "On account of its sharp and massive crags Monroe presents a fine alpine appearance to the distant observer. From points near at hand . . . Monroe has a formidable aspect, and the noble symmetry of its craggy walls excites the most lively interest."

1900: AMC members William B. Curtis and Allen Ormsbee perish on exposed Presidential Range when caught in fierce late June storm. Curtis dies near Crawford Path at base of Mt. Monroe; Ormsbee dies on summit cone of Mt. Washington.

1901: In aftermath of Curtis-Ormsbee deaths, AMC constructs small wood frame shelter in vicinity of Lakes of the Clouds.

1915: New stone refuge—Lakes of the Clouds Hut—is added to AMC hut chain and sees 272 visitors in first season of operation. Also, path to Lakes of the Clouds from Cog Railway base station (Ammonoosuc Ravine Trail) is opened.

1916: Account of hikers snow-bound at Lakes of the Clouds Hut during Sept. 1915 snowstorm appears in *Appalachia*.

1919: New loop path over summits of Monroe is "cairned" by AMC crews.

1922: Addition built on N side of Lakes of the Clouds hut for larger sleeping, kitchen facilities.

1927: Second addition to hut includes new women's bunkroom, kitchen and crew quarters.

1968: Hut at Lakes of the Clouds enlarged again. New dining room accommodating 90 guests added.

1972: Trail crews reconstruct path from hut to summit in effort to "harden" treadway.

ca. 1980: In effort to protect dwarf cinquefoil, rare alpine plant growing NE of Mt. Monroe, section of Crawford Path is rerouted away from fragile vegetation, as is upper portion of Dry River Trail.

TRAIL APPROACHES

North Approach from Cog Railway Base Road

Ammonoosuc Ravine Trail, Crawford Path, Mt. Monroe Loop
7.0 mi. round trip, 2900-ft. elevation gain

Trailhead (2500 ft.): The Ammonoosuc Ravine Trail leaves from a large parking area on the S side of the Cog Railway Base Road, 1.0 mi. E of its jct. with Mt. Clinton Rd. and Jefferson Notch Rd.

The shortest and most often used route to Mt. Monroe follows the steep and scenic Ammonoosuc Ravine Trail up to Lakes of the Clouds Hut. In addition to an out-and-back journey to Monroe, this route can be used to create loops over Mt. Washington to the NE or other peaks of the Southern Presidentials to the SW (see below). The upper portion of this route is fully exposed to weather, though in-season (June to mid-September) shelter is available at the hut. Heed the usual above-treeline precautions. Note that the Ammonoosuc Ravine Trail holds snow late into the spring, and in late fall it can be very icy where water runs over the ledges. Even when merely wet the upper ledges are slippery, especially coming down.

From parking area, follow blue-blazed trail E at easy grades through open fir and birch woods, crossing Franklin Brook at 0.3 mi. Old route from Base Station (0.3 mi. long) comes in on L at 1.0 mi. Trail now climbs easily alongside Ammonoosuc River (on L) through fir forest, with rocky footing in places, passing memorial plaque for Herbert J. Young, Dartmouth student who perished here in December 1928. Cross Monroe Brook at 1.7 mi./3225 ft. Woods get scrubbier, with evidence of landslides. At 2.1 mi./3450 ft. cross tributary stream by Gem Pool, clear basin of water below small mossy cascade.

Trail turns R (SE) here and begins long, steep ascent up section of rock steps. At 2.3 mi./3750 ft. sign marks side trail R to the Gorge, where high perch provides great view of two long waterslides. Steep rocky climb continues to brook crossing and first view W over Bretton Woods valley at 2.5 mi./4175 ft. Ledgy scrambling leads up past series of cascades with more brook crossings. Trees shrink to scrub and views open out to NW, and L up to scree-splotched slopes of Mt. Washington. Ascent continues up rock slabs and through intermittent patches of scrub. Grade eases higher up, and near top of climb rocky pile of Monroe appears up to R. Reach AMC hut and jct. with Crawford Path at 3.1 mi./5012 ft. During season, refreshments are available at hut.

Mt. Monroe provides the dramatic backdrop for Lakes of the Clouds and their namesake hut.

Now above treeline, follow Crawford Path S (R), climbing to jct. R with N end of Mt. Monroe Loop at 3.2 mi./5075 ft. Turn R on Monroe Loop and make winding climb up stone steps and over ledge scrambles to level ridgecrest. Proceed S 0.1 mi. and up to exposed summit outcrop at 3.5 mi. Views are excellent in all directions, especially down Southern Presidential ridge, out over Dry River valley, and up to Mt. Washington.

Summit Loop Option

If climbing Monroe only, a short loop extension on Mt. Monroe Loop over Little Monroe and back via Crawford Path is rewarding. From main summit, follow Monroe Loop W on short, steep descent with rocky footing akin to that on Northern Presidentials. Cross small flat col and hop over small peak of Little Monroe, then swing S over boulders and descend to Crawford Path, 0.4 mi. from main summit. Turn L here for beautiful walk along barren slopes on S side of Monroe, with impressive views down into Dry River basin and back to steep E slopes of Mt. Franklin. On level shoulder, Crawford Path swings L (N) and leads back to jct. with N end of Monroe Loop; take extra care to remain on marked trail through this section to protect endangered dwarf cinquefoil. Loop from main summit of Monroe around to this jct. is 1.0 mi., compared to 0.3 mi. via direct return down Monroe Loop.

Loop Option with Mt. Washington

Because it is a relatively short side trip, Monroe is often combined with the classic loop over the W side of Mt. Washington, using the Ammonoosuc Ravine Trail, Crawford Path, Gulfside Trail and Jewell Trail. Including both summits, loop total is 10.4 mi. with 4200-ft. elevation gain. This is a long, tiring day with great exposure to weather; for details see chapter on Mt. Washington.

Southern Presidential Loop Options

With car spot, ascent of Monroe can be combined with Mt. Eisenhower and Mt. Pierce, using connecting link along Crawford Path.

Mt. Monroe and Mt. Eisenhower

9.1 mi., 3300-ft. elevation gain

Ascend Monroe via Ammonoosuc Ravine Trail, Crawford Path and Mt. Monroe Loop (3.5 mi.). Descend S on Monroe Loop over Little Monroe to Crawford Path at 3.9 mi. Turn R for beautiful open walk along gentle ridge, passing short loop side path L to summit of Mt. Franklin at 4.2 mi.; this small peak offers fine view down into depths of Dry River basin. At 4.7 mi. Crawford Path begins descent down steep, ledgy shoulder to Franklin-Eisenhower col, then rises to meet N end of Mt. Eisenhower Loop at 5.4 mi./4475 ft. Climb up Eisenhower Loop to summit at 5.8 mi., then retrace steps 0.4 mi. off peak and turn L on Edmands Path (just before reaching Crawford Path) and descend 2.9 mi. to trailhead on Mt. Clinton Rd.

Mt. Monroe, Mt. Eisenhower and Mt. Pierce

10.7 mi., 3525-ft. elevation gain

Ascend Monroe and Eisenhower as described above. From summit of Eisenhower (5.8 mi.), continue S on Eisenhower Loop, descending to Crawford Path at 6.2 mi./4425 ft. Follow Crawford Path S through Eisenhower-Clinton col at 6.7 mi./4060 ft. and up to jct. L with Webster Cliff Trail at 7.4 mi./4250 ft. Make side trip up to summit of Mt. Pierce (0.2 mi. round trip), then turn L on Crawford Path and descend 3.1 mi. to trailhead on Mt. Clinton Rd. via that trail and Crawford Connector.

Ascent via Dry River Trail

Backpackers and strong day hikers with a taste for remote country can make a long trek through Dry River valley and up the headwall of Oakes Gulf, emerging at Lakes of the Clouds Hut. One-way trip to Monroe via this route, which cuts through heart of Presidential Range-Dry River Wilderness, is 10.0 mi. with 4400-ft. elevation gain. Dry River Trail starts on US 302 in lower Crawford Notch. Trail partly follows old logging RR grade in first 5 mi., with many looks at rock-bound river. Highlights include vista up valley to Mt. Washington at 1.5 mi.; view up to Mt. Pierce at 5.0 mi; Dry River Falls at 5.4 mi.; Dry River Shelter #3 at 6.3 mi.; long, gradual meander through mossy fir forest with primeval feel in upper valley; and spectacular views back down valley during steep climb up headwall of Oakes Gulf. A couple of stream crossings in valley can be quite difficult in high water. With car spot, descent can be made via Ammonoosuc Ravine Trail or other access off Southern Presidential ridge.

East Approaches

Various approaches can be made to Monroe from Pinkham Notch to the E, but they are longer, more exposed, and involve much more elevation gain than the route from the Cog Base Road. From Tuckerman Jct. above headwall of Tuckerman Ravine (accessed by Tuckerman Ravine Trail or by Tuckerman Ravine, Lion Head and Alpine Garden Trails), Tuckerman Crossover leads across broad, open expanse of Bigelow Lawn to Crawford Path in 0.8 mi. with 100-ft. elevation gain. Turn L on Crawford Path to reach Lakes of Clouds Hut in another 0.2 mi. From here it is 0.4 mi. to Monroe with 400-ft. elevation gain. There is 450-ft. elevation gain on return over Tuckerman Crossover. Round trip to Monroe from AMC Pinkham Notch Camp using Tuckerman Ravine Trail approach is 10.0 mi. with 4300-ft. elevation gain. Using Lion Head option adds 0.3 mi. each way.

WINTER

Difficult access, steep climbing and great exposure to weather make Monroe a very challenging winter peak that should only be attempted in good weather, by strong and experienced parties fully equipped for extended above-treeline travel. Full crampons are required. The Cog Railway Base Road is not open to public vehicular traffic, making the Ammonoosuc Ravine Trail an impractical winter approach. With favorable weather and long enough daylight (e.g. late winter), it might be plausible to approach Monroe from Pierce and/or Eisenhower as an out-and-back trip along Crawford Path. Most winter climbers attack Monroe from Pinkham Notch, doing it as a climb by itself or combining it with an ascent of Mt. Washington. In this case the Lion Head Trail winter route or the Boott Spur Trail might be used as approach or descent routes; the traverse of Bigelow Lawn is very exposed and dangerously confusing in cloud, as there are few terrain features to navigate by. The scramble up Monroe Loop on the NE side can be challenging in icy conditions.

VIEW GUIDE

Monroe's craggy peak is a superb viewpoint with especially fine views of the Southern Presidentials, the Dry River valley and its looming neighbor, Mt. Washington.

Washington is seen to the NE, beyond the level crest of Monroe's narrow summit ridge, with Lakes of the Clouds gleaming down to the R. Mts. Clay and Jefferson extend to the L of Washington, and to the R (E) is Boott Spur beyond the sweeping headwall of Oakes Gulf. Farther R, beyond these close-in vistas, the view expands out to the SE, with Maine's Pleasant Mtn. seen beyond the Doubleheads. More to the R, beyond the wooded shoulder of Slide Peak, is Kearsarge North, with the rounded upper peaks of Rocky

Branch Ridge closer in to the R. Right below to the SSE is the broad, barren shoulder of Monroe, with a long view to the horizon beyond the valley of North Conway. A bit farther R are the upper knobs of Montalban Ridge, the lower Rocky Branch Ridge and the pointed peaks of the Moats. To the S you gaze over the broad upper reaches of Dry River valley, clad in unbroken spruce forest, to the long, gentle, wooded Montalban Ridge, including Mt. Isolation, Mt. Davis, Stairs Mtn. and Mt. Resolution, with Mt. Parker on the L and Mt. Crawford on the R. Chocorua's sharp cone is over Parker, with Bear and the distant Mt. Shaw in the Ossipee Range over Resolution. The Belknap Range is seen over Crawford, and farther R Passaconaway towers over Tremont, with Whiteface to its R.

The view now sweeps down through the sharp, winding cut of the lower Dry River valley to Tripyramid and Sandwich Dome on the horizon. Mt. Kancamagus lies low to the R of Sandwich, above Mt. Nancy, and on clear days Mt. Kearsarge can be picked out beyond, with Monadnock just to its L. To the R of the valley, looking SSW, are majestic Carrigain and wide-spreading Hancock, with the Osceolas and Tecumseh peering over between them.

To the SW you look down the long, twisting, partly bare ridge of the Southern Presidentials, taking in Little Monroe, Franklin, Eisenhower, Pierce, Jackson and Webster. Beyond, across Crawford Notch, is the Willey Range, with Willey over Pierce. Field is seen over Eisenhower, with Bond, Liberty and Moosilauke beyond. Smarts Mtn. can be seen in the distance over the Willey-Field col. Farther R, to the WSW, the South Twin-Guyot ridge and Mts. Lincoln and Lafayette are seen over Mt. Tom, with North Twin, the lower Mt. Hale and the gentle Rosebrook Range to the R, over Little Monroe. The tip of Mt. Garfield is just visible over the shoulder of North Twin. Due W is the broad Bretton Woods valley and the prominent Mt. Washington Hotel, with a long view out to Vermont and the Green Mountains beyond, including Mts. Abraham and Ellen, Camel's Hump and Mt. Mansfield.

To the NW are the heavily wooded Dartmouth Range and its neighbor, Cherry Mtn. Farther R, looking NNW, is the long, level ridge of Mt. Waumbek, with the rounded Weeks summits, Mt. Cabot, The Bulge and the sharp-peaked Horn (the latter over North Weeks) behind and to the R. The bare Percy Peaks are just to the R of The Horn, with the massive ridge of Long Mtn. farther R. Many other North Country mountains span the horizon. Farther R the distant view is cut off by the rugged Ridge of the Caps leading up to Mt. Jefferson.

NO. OF 4000-FOOTERS VISIBLE: 32

Mount Pierce

ELEVATION: 4312 ft./1314 m ORDER OF HEIGHT: 27
LOCATION: Presidential Range, Townships of Beans Grant and Cutts Grant
USGS MAPS: 7½′ Stairs Mtn., 7½′ Crawford Notch

GEOGRAPHY

The rounded crest of Mt. Pierce rests less than 5.5 mi. from Mt. Washington, midway along the long ridgeline of the Southern Presidentials. It's flanked by the reddish-brown dome of Mt. Eisenhower to the N and the pointed crown of Mt. Jackson to the S. To the uninitiated Presidential Range tramper, the mostly open summit of Pierce affords a first close-up glimpse of life above the trees. For that reason, the mountain is perfect for hikers wishing to get a taste of above-treeline conditions without facing the perils of extensive exposure to the elements.

The mountain's long ridgeline, stretching NE to SW, is best viewed from the vicinity of Bretton Woods and the Mount Washington Hotel. From this vantage point, Pierce rises gradually to the L (E) out of the narrow Crawford Notch. On closer inspection you will find that two separate ridges, split by tumbling Gibbs Brook, extend from the Notch and US 302 to a point near the summit ridge. Crawford Cliff is a small crag, accessible by a side trail, at the lower W end of the northerly of these ridges.

Deep Abenaki Ravine lies just to the N of the summit and separates the mountain from Mt. Eisenhower's western ridges. The NW slopes of Pierce are drained by Sebosis and Assaquam Brooks. The Gibbs Brook valley, on the W slope of the mountain, is noteworthy as the home to the Gibbs Brook Scenic Area. This 1,500 acre tract, through which the Crawford Path passes on its way up the mountain, is an old growth forest of unharvested red spruce and yellow birch. This dramatic section of forest is littered with ancient, moss-covered blowdowns which drape over both the trail and the brook valley.

To the E and some 1500 ft. below the summit is the Dry River (or Mt. Washington River) valley, which drains out of Mt. Washington's Oakes Gulf and flows S to meet up with the Saco River at the southern end of Crawford Notch. A nameless tributary of the Dry River flows SE down a long valley between spur ridges of Pierce and Jackson, while another stream drains a broad basin on the E between Pierce and Eisenhower.

Beyond Pierce's subsidiary, semi-open SW summit (4185 ft.), the ridge dips to a large, fairly level depression extending all the way to Mt. Jackson's sharp summit cone a mile and a half away. The summit of Jackson provides an excellent vantage point for seeing the layout of Mt. Pierce from the S. Particularly noteworthy is AMC's Mizpah Spring Hut, seen here tucked well below and to the S of the main summit.

NOMENCLATURE

The mountain has long endured an identity crisis of sorts as it has commonly been known as both Mt. Pierce and Mt. Clinton. As a result of an act of the New Hampshire legislature on April 13, 1913, the mountain's official name is Mt. Pierce, in honor of the nation's 14th President, New Hampshire native Franklin Pierce. The peak's original name—in honor of former New York governor and senator DeWitt Clinton (1769–1828)—has continued to live on, however, thanks in great part to the Appalachian Mountain Club, which for more than 70 years insisted on sticking with the Mt. Clinton name on its trail maps. It wasn't until the mid-1970s that AMC finally relented and tagged the summit with both names (with Mt. Clinton appearing in parentheses under Mt. Pierce). For the record, AMC maps now identify the mountain solely as Pierce. Other mapmakers haven't been as accommodating, though, and still insist on using just the mountain's original name.

Although it's been close to 90 years since the mountain's name was changed, the Mt. Clinton name continues to live on elsewhere in the vicinity. The Mt. Clinton Road connects US 302 with the Cog Railway Base Road, while the Mt. Clinton Trail leads hikers from the Dry River valley up to AMC's Mizpah Spring Hut at the southern base of the mountain's summit ridge.

Gibbs Brook is named after Joseph Gibb, onetime landlord of the Crawford House.

HISTORICAL HIGHLIGHTS

First Ascent: Unknown

1819: Crawford family members establish footpath from top of Crawford Notch to summit of Mt. Washington. The trail, known as the Crawford Path, passes near summit of Pierce.

1828: Notch House built by Crawford family on E side of Crawford's plateau; opens in 1829 under management of Thomas Crawford.

1839: Crawfords begin conversion of Crawford Path to bridle path.

1840: Abel Crawford, now 75 years old, is first to ride horse entire length of trail to Mt. Washington. He's accompanied by son, Tom, and state geologist Charles T. Jackson.

1852: Crawford House opens near base of Crawford Path.

1859: Original Crawford House burns in April, but new and larger hotel is quickly built and opens in time for summer tourist season.

1892–1898: Saco Valley Lumber Company builds logging RR up Dry River to SE of Mt. Pierce and logs much of valley. RR grade is later used for part of Dry River Trail.

1895: Crawford House management cuts hiking trail from Clinton to Jackson, but path is soon abandoned.

1913: Second access route to summit is established with completion of trail from summit of Mt. Webster (to the S) to jct. with Crawford Path. This section of trail becomes, a year later, a link in newly-cut Webster Cliff Trail from Willey House Station (at S end of Notch) to Mt. Pierce.

1913: New Hampshire legislature passes law renaming mountain in honor of 14th president, New Hampshire native Franklin Pierce (1804–1869).

1915: Mizpah Cut-off Trail, linking Crawford Path with recently established open log shelter at Mizpah Spring, is cut by AMC members. Shelter is situated approximately ¾ mi. from summit of Mt. Pierce.

1934: AMC guide includes first mention of new path (Mt. Clinton Trail) connecting Dry River Trail with Mizpah Spring Shelter, providing approach from SE.

1965: AMC dedicates Mizpah Spring Hut, newest addition to its chain of backcountry huts. It's first new hut to be built by club since completion of Zealand Falls Hut in 1932.

late 1960s: Dry River Cutoff opened, connecting middle of Dry River valley with Mt. Clinton Trail.

1976: Beset by financial problems attributed to energy crisis, Crawford House is shut down, contents are auctioned off.

1977: November fire levels Crawford House.

TRAIL APPROACHES

West Approach from Mt. Clinton Rd. near Crawford's

Crawford Connector, Crawford Path, Webster Cliff Trail
6.4 mi. round trip, 2400-ft. elevation gain.

Trailhead (1920 ft.): Crawford Path begins on E side of US 302 across from site of former Crawford House, 0.2 mi. N of Gateway of Notch, but no parking is available here. Trail parking area is now found on Mt. Clinton Rd. (signed), just a few hundred yards from road's intersection with US 302. Mileages below are from Mt. Clinton Rd. parking area.

The Crawford Path, believed to be the longest continuously maintained hiking trail in America, provides the most direct route to the summit of Mt. Pierce. Crawford Connector, built in 1991, leaves parking lot and crosses Mt. Clinton Rd. It climbs gradually and at 0.4 mi. crosses bridge over Gibbs Brook, joining Crawford Path 0.2 mi. from its start at the highway. In its lower reaches, Crawford Path climbs above and to R of Gibbs Brook. At 0.6 mi., short side path L leads to nice viewpoint overlooking Gibbs Falls. Trail soon enters expansive old growth forest (Gibbs Brook Scenic Area), while ascending at steady, moderate grade. After about one mile of climbing, trail rises well above and to S of Gibbs Brook, and at 1.9 mi./3380 ft. reaches jct. with Mizpah Cut-off leading R to AMC's Mizpah Spring Hut.

Ascending now at gentler grade, Crawford Path continues for another 1.2 mi. along NW shoulder of Mt. Pierce through fine boreal forest. Higher up trees are considerably smaller, soon giving way to openings as summit area is approached. First glimpses are to NE, where Mt. Eisenhower and Mt.

Washington dominate scene. Trail levels and emerges from scrub, reaching jct. R with Webster Cliff Trail at 3.1 mi./4250 ft. Crawford Path continues ahead to Mt. Washington; turn R here on Webster Cliff Trail and climb through alpine zone to Pierce's mostly open summit at 3.2 mi./4312 ft. Please stay on marked trail to protect fragile alpine vegetation.

Mizpah Hut Loop Option

There are several possible loop hikes available to Mt. Pierce-bound hikers, with the most popular including a visit to AMC's Mizpah Spring Hut via the Webster Cliff and Mizpah Cut-off Trails. From summit of Pierce, continue S along Webster Cliff Trail, passing first over summit of SW knob of Pierce, with view back to Mt. Washington, then at 0.6 mi. reach open ledge with nice view S. After short, steep descent, Mizpah Hut is reached at 0.8 mi./3800 ft. Beyond hut, take Mizpah Cut-off (W) for easy 0.7 mi. descent back to Crawford Path. Loop total is 6.6 mi. with little additional climbing.

More ambitious hikers can continue from hut S along Webster Cliff Trail to Mt. Jackson, which is reached in 1.7 mi. From Jackson's summit, follow Webster-Jackson Trail 2.6 mi. back to US 302. From here it's a 0.3 mi. walk back to trailhead parking on Mt. Clinton Rd. Loop total is 8.6 mi. with 2850-ft. elevation gain.

Mt. Eisenhower Loop Options

Many peakbagging hikers choose to "bag" both Pierce and Mt. Eisenhower in a single day. This is usually accomplished by taking Crawford Path and Webster Cliff Trail to summit of Pierce, then returning to Crawford Path and following it N through scrub and over open ledge, descending to 4060-ft. col in 0.7 mi. At 1.2 mi./4425 ft. is jct. L with Mt. Eisenhower Loop. This trail climbs up bare dome, paralleling Crawford Path, and at 1.6 mi./4760 ft. reaches Eisenhower's bare, exposed summit. Hikers can retrace steps from here for 9.6 mi. round trip with 3200-ft. elevation gain. Or, follow Eisenhower Loop to its northern terminus, then bear L (W) on Edmands Path for 2.9 mi. descent to its trailhead on Mt. Clinton Rd., 2.3 mi. from US 302. Total loop distance (including road walk back to Crawford Path parking area) is 10.4 mi. with 3050-ft. elevation gain.

Southeast Approach from Dry River

Another alternate approach to Mt. Pierce is via Dry River and Mt. Clinton Trails from SE. This is least used and least crowded of Pierce approaches, and longest, at 6.7 mi. *one way*. This approach begins on Dry River Trail on E side of US 302, 0.3 mi. N. of Dry River Campground in Crawford Notch State Park; trailhead elevation 1205 ft. Dry River Trail roughly follows old logging railroad grade that once cut deep into valley. After entering Presidential Range-Dry River Wilderness at 0.7 mi., trail leaves and re-enters railroad grade several times, climbs to framed viewpoint up valley to Mt. Washington at 1.5 mi., then descends steeply to cross river on suspension bridge at 1.7 mi. Trail proceeds up E side of river, with several ups and downs, at times on old RR grade. At 2.9 mi./1900 ft. reach jct. L with Mt. Clinton Trail to Mizpah Hut. Bear L here onto Mt. Clinton Trail, cross river (very difficult at high water), and climb at easy to moderate grades along tributary through hardwoods and mixed woods. At 3.4 mi. make first of seven crossings of brook. Trail is wet and eroded in places. Last crossing is at 4.7 mi. Above here walking becomes smoother through beautiful, remote boreal forest. Pass jct. R with Dry River Cutoff at 5.4 mi./3425 ft. and continue to Mizpah Hut at 5.9 mi./3800 ft. To reach Mt. Pierce, turn R on Webster Cliff Trail and climb 0.8 mi. to summit.

WINTER

The Crawford Path is one of the most heavily used trails in winter, thus it's usually broken out soon after even the fiercest of winter storms. As the summit of Mt. Pierce lies on the fringe of the alpine zone, there's plenty of exposure, so all visitors to the mountain this time of year should be equipped with appropriate winter clothing and gear. Frequently, the upper section of the trail (near its jct. with the Webster Cliff Trail) is obscured by drifting snow and can be very difficult, if not impossible, to follow. When in doubt, especially in foul weather, retrace your steps and return the way you came. You can always make another attempt under more favorable conditions.

VIEW GUIDE

Though views to the S and W are limited by high scrub, ledges just below the main summit area provide a spectacular close-up view of neighboring Presidential Range peaks, and ranges to the N and E. Caps Ridge, rising out of Jefferson Notch, runs L to R up to the summit of Mt. Jefferson to the NNE. To Jefferson's R is the craggy spire of Mt. Clay. Round-domed Mt. Eisenhower, Pierce's near neighbor to the NE, is flanked on the R by the massive summit cone of Mt. Washington. Just to the R of Eisenhower, with its E face sliced off as if with by a knife, is Mt. Monroe. More to the E is seen Oakes Gulf just under Boott Spur, while long, flat Montalban Ridge runs to the S. To the E, over Montalban Ridge, are the Baldfaces, Sable and Chandler near Evans Notch, and to the SE are the Doubleheads (over Mt. Isolation) and Mt. Kearsarge North (over Mt. Davis) near Conway-Jackson. Maine's Pleasant Mtn. is seen between the Doubleheads and Kearsarge North.

To the NW, Mt. Rosebrook and Bretton Woods Ski Area are close at hand, with Vermont's Mt. Mansfield seen above the ski slopes on the horizon. The limited W view includes nearby Mt. Hale and more distant Camel's Hump in the Green Mountains. By poking around you can find partial views W over the scrub to the Twin-Bond Range, with Mts. Lafayette and Lincoln poking up to the L of South Twin. Down near the jct. of Webster Cliff Trail and Crawford Path there are wider views NW down into the Bretton

Woods valley, and N to the Dartmouth Range and the Pliny and Pilot Ranges beyond.

Good views S and SW are obtained from several vantage points along the Webster Cliff Trail a short distance S of the main summit. Seen from here are nearby Mts. Jackson and Webster and the scarred face of Mt. Willey across Crawford Notch, the Pemi Wilderness peaks of Mt. Carrigain and Mt. Hancock, and further S Passaconaway, Whiteface, Tripyramid and Sandwich Dome in the Sandwich Range, and Mt. Osceola near Waterville Valley.

NO. OF 4000-FOOTERS VISIBLE: 30

Mount Washington

ELEVATION: 6288 ft./1636 m ORDER OF HEIGHT: 1

LOCATION: Presidential Range, Townships of Sargents Purchase, Thompson and Meserves Purchase, Pinkhams Grant

USGS MAPS: 7½′ × 15′ Mt. Washington, 7½′ Carter Dome, 7½′ Stairs Mtn.

GEOGRAPHY

At 6288 ft., Mt. Washington is the tallest of the New Hampshire 4000-Footers and the highest peak in all of New England and the Northeast. Though its summit elevation is puny compared to other great mountain ranges of the world, Mt. Washington is renowned worldwide for its fierce weather and frequent fatalities.

Lying as it does at the center of three storm tracks, the mountain is a magnet for severe weather at any time of the year. Typically, the mountain receives more than 250 inches of snow in a year, and snow has been known to fall in every calendar month, even July and August. One of the mountain's long-held claims to fame is that the highest land wind speed ever documented (231 mph) was recorded at the summit on April 12, 1934.

Mt. Washington's nearest 4000-ft. neighbors along the Presidential Range are Mt. Monroe to the SW and Mt. Jefferson to the N. In between Washington and Jefferson is the 5533-ft. summit of Mt. Clay, essentially a NW shoulder of Washington.

The vast upper slopes of the mountain lie completely above timberline and are home to an abundance of rare and fragile alpine plants. Depending on the amount of exposure to the prevailing NW winds, timberline on Mt. Washington varies from 4500 to 5000 ft. above sea level. As the summit cone is also littered with large boulders and loose rocks, for years the mountain has been appropriately dubbed "The Rock Pile." The mountain is composed of metamorphic rock, primarily mica schist and quartzite.

The massive bulk of Mt. Washington is flanked on practically all sides by deep and dramatic ravines carved by ancient alpine glaciers. The best known of these cirques is Tuckerman Ravine, on the mountain's SE side. With its steep headwall and bowl-shaped rim, Tuckerman Ravine is probably the best example of a glacial cirque in all the White Mountains. The ravine is an especially busy place each spring as snow blown off the mountain's exposed ridges and into the bowl provides for exceptional backcountry ski possibilities. Generally, the spring ski season runs through at least the month of May, and oftentimes well into June.

Looming high above Tuckerman Ravine to the N is the craggy 5033-ft. spur of Lion Head, while to the S lies 5500-ft. Boott Spur, the high point along Washington's rugged SE shoulder, with its picturesque Hanging Cliffs poised above the cirque. At the base of the ravine is delightful Hermit Lake, a 0.3-acre tarn with as dramatic a backdrop as any pond in the region. Close by is Hermit Lake Shelter (AMC/WMNF), with ten open-front shelters and three tent platforms.

Two other spectacular glacial ravines scarring the mountain's E face are Huntington Ravine and the Gulf of Slides. Huntington Ravine is NE of Tuckerman's and Lion Head, and its sheer face has long provided a challenging climb for summit-bound hikers and nimble rock climbers. For many winters it has also been a mecca for ice climbers. The less frequented Gulf of Slides lies to the S of Boott Spur, with Slide Peak (4806 ft.) and a ridge just N of the spur holding the massive Glen Boulder (a glacial erratic perched above the Ellis River valley S of Pinkham Notch) forming its S wall. Although no officially maintained hiking trails lead up to its floor, a well defined ski trail starting at AMC's Pinkham Notch Visitor Center can be followed 2.6 mi. to the base of the ravine's slide-raked headwall.

Another lesser-known ravine on the Pinkham Notch side of the mountain is the Ravine of Raymond Cataract. This high, scalloped basin is sandwiched between Huntington and Tuckerman Ravines and is home to Raymond Cataract, a beautiful waterfall that, unfortunately, is no longer accessible by trail.

These great ravines on the E side of Washington are well-displayed in the views from Wildcat Ridge Trail and Wildcat Ski Area to the E.

The White Mountains' largest glacial cirque, the Great Gulf, cuts into Mt. Washington's slopes on the N, culminating in an impressive 1600-ft. headwall. The huge gouge of the Great Gulf, several miles long, separates Mt. Washington and its massive NE shoulder, Chandler Ridge, from the various peaks of the Northern Presidentials and provides a dramatic foreground for camera-toting hikers and tourists aiming their lenses at the likes of Mts. Adams or Madison. At the head of the Great Gulf lies scenic Spaulding Lake (4228 ft.), a tiny, half-acre tarn deep in the federally-designated Great Gulf Wilderness.

On the mountain's W side are Ammonoosuc Ravine and Burt Ravine. The former is a broad basin cut into the mountainside nearly due W from the summit, while Burt Ravine lies more to the NW, between Mt. Washington and Mt. Clay. At the head of Ammonoosuc Ravine, at an elevation of just over 5000 ft., are the two Lakes of the Clouds and AMC's namesake Lakes of the Clouds Hut. The tiny alpine ponds are situated in the rocky, windswept, saddle between Mts. Washington and Monroe. The Upper Lake (5050 ft.) is 0.4 acre in size, while the Lower Lake (5025 ft.) is 1.2 acres. The hut, largest in the string of AMC's backcountry hut system, can accommodate 90 overnight guests, and is open from June to mid-September.

Between Ammonoosuc and Burt Ravines runs a narrow ridgeline on which the Mt. Washington Cog Railway ascends the mountain from Marshfield Station. Pioneer settler and trailbuilder Ethan Allen Crawford cut an early footpath to the summit up this same ridge nearly 200 years ago.

Directly S of the summit cone lies Oakes Gulf, a remote and little-visited glacial ravine bordered by Boott Spur to the E and Mts. Monroe and Franklin in the southern Presidential Range to the W. This gaping cirque is a trademark feature of Mt. Washington when viewed from points to the S.

As rocky, steep, and craggy as Mt. Washington is, the mountain boasts several relatively "flat," but interesting areas at an elevation over 5000 ft. South of the summit cone on the divide between Tuckerman Ravine and Ammonoosuc Ravine is Bigelow Lawn, a broad alpine meadow featuring arctic grasses and a variety of flowering plants, best viewed in June and early July. Similarly, the Alpine Garden, E of the summit and upslope from Huntington Ravine and Ravine of Raymond Cataract, is a unique upland meadow best known for its assortment of alpine wildflowers.

The mountain's slopes are drained by several notable streams and rivers, the principal ones being the Ammonoosuc River, Dry River, Rocky Branch, New River, Cutler River, and Peabody River.

The Ammonoosuc River originates from the Lakes of the Clouds, flows in a westerly direction, and is eventually joined by Clay Brook (out of Burt Ravine), about a mile W of the Cog Railway base station. Dry River flows S out of Oakes Gulf for nearly 10 mi. down the wilderness valley between the Southern Presidentials on the W and Montalban Ridge on the E, joining the Saco River near the southern boundary of Crawford Notch State Park. To the S of Boott Spur and Slide Peak the Rocky Branch flows S towards the Saco down another long valley, between Montalban Ridge to the W and the Rocky Branch Ridge on the E. These two subsidiary ridges split from the main ridge S of Boott Spur.

New River, on the mountain's SE slopes, drains out of the Gulf of Slides and merges with the Cutler River (out of Tuckerman and Huntington Ravines) in Pinkham Notch to form the Ellis River.

The main stem of Peabody River originates on the mountain's eastern slopes and flows N out of Pinkham Notch toward the Androscoggin River. The headwaters of the West Branch of Peabody River flow out of the Great Gulf and remote Spaulding Lake. The West Branch joins the main stem approximately 2 mi. N of the base of the Mt. Washington Auto Road.

Being the tallest of the peaks, it's no surprise that the mountain is among the most visited summits in New England. Besides attracting huge crowds of hikers each year, the summit is also frequented by swarms of tourists accessing it by either the Cog Railway or the Mt. Washington Auto Road. The Cog climbs 3.25 mi. up the mountain from the W via tracks first laid more than 130 years ago. The average grade of the railway is 25 percent (1320 ft. per mile), with a maximum grade of 37.5 percent along Jacob's Ladder, the curving, 300-ft trestle approximately two-thirds of the way up the mountain.

From the E, tourists can attain the summit by driving up the winding 7.6-mi. Auto Road from a location at the NE base of the mountain known as the Glen (by NH 16). The average grade of the road, which is part paved, part hard-packed gravel, is 12 percent. The upper part of the auto road traverses Chandler Ridge—the huge NE shoulder of the mountain—and skirts the rim of the Great Gulf to the N. Two notable landmarks along Chandler Ridge, both a little bit S of the auto road, are Nelson Crag (5635 ft.) and Ball Crag (6112 ft.). Both are accessible on foot by way of the Nelson Crag Trail.

The summit of Mt. Washington is like no other in the Whites, with a half dozen or more structures occupying most of the mountaintop terrain. The Sherman Adams Summit Building serves as headquarters for Mt. Washington State Park, and is occupied year-round by staffers with the Mt. Washington Observatory.

NOMENCLATURE

This peak, the highest in the Northeast, was named for Revolutionary War general and our nation's first president, George Washington, probably in 1784, during the so-called Belknap-Cutler expedition, the first scientific foray up the mountain. The old Indian name for the mountain was "Agiochook," which has been translated to mean "Home of the Great Spirit," "The Place of the Spirit of the Forest," and "The Place of the Storm Spirit." The natives did not climb the mountain for fear of the Great Spirit which dwelled upon its summit. Another Indian name was "Waumbeket Methna," or "Mountain of the Snowy Forehead."

Tuckerman Ravine, the mountain's famous glacial cirque SE of the summit cone, is named for Dr. Edward Tuckerman, a botanist and longtime professor at Amherst College. Tuckerman was a frequent visitor to the White Mountains in the first half of the 19th century, devoting much of his time to studying and collecting area plants, particularly along the Presidential Range.

Huntington Ravine, another of the mountain's well-known cirques, is named for Joshua Huntington, who was part of the team of observers to spend the winter of 1870–71 atop the mountain. Nelson Crag, the 5635-ft. sub-peak at the head of Huntington Ravine, is named for one of Joshua Huntington's fellow summit occupants, S. A. Nelson of Georgetown, Mass.

Boott Spur, a subsidiary peak SE of the main summit, is named for

Dr. Francis Boott, an early 19th-century physician and botanist who was a member of Jacob Bigelow's 1816 scientific expedition on the mountain. Bigelow's name has been attached to the broad alpine meadow S of the summit and W of Tuckerman Ravine.

Mt. Washington's NE ridge, called Chandler Ridge, is named for Benjamin Chandler, the third person to die on the mountain. The 75-year-old Chandler disappeared on August 7, 1856 while ascending the peak. His body was found almost a year later under a ledge which he had crawled beneath, presumably to seek shelter.

Ball Crag, a sharp knob a short distance NE of the summit along the Nelson Crag Trail, is named for Dr. Benjamin Lincoln Ball, who in October 1855 got lost on the mountain during a winter-like storm, yet managed to survive the ordeal despite a lack of water, food, or sleep. Dr. Ball recounted his story in the book, *Three Days on the White Mountains.*

The Great Gulf, a huge glacier-carved cirque north of the mountain, was originally called Gulf of Mexico, for reasons that have never been understood. It was first referred to by its present-day name by Ethan Allen Crawford, who made note of a "great gulf" which he and others stumbled upon while wandering around the mountain's fogged-in upper reaches.

Spaulding Lake, the remote half-acre tarn at the head of the Great Gulf, is named for John H. Spaulding, early manager of the hotels situated atop the mountain. Spaulding, who also authored the book, *Historical Relics of the White Mountains* (1855), first visited the lake named in his honor in 1853.

HISTORICAL HIGHLIGHTS

First Ascent: Darby Field and two Indian guides are credited with the first recorded ascent of the mountain back in 1642. It has long been speculated that Field climbed the mountain from the SE, ascending by way of Boott Spur and Lakes of the Clouds. Documents uncovered within the last 20 years, however, seem to indicate that Field's route may actually have been over the peaks of the Southern Presidentials.

1725: Visitors to mountain in late April report snow depth of four feet on NW slope and pond near top "frozen hard."

1774: June climbers find 13 feet of snow in deep gully on S side of mountain.

1784: Cutler-Belknap expedition conducts first scientific research on Presidentials, taking various measurements and collecting rare alpine plants.

1792: Name "Mt. Washington" appears in print for first time in Vol. 3 of Jeremy Belknap's *History of New Hampshire.*

1816: Dr. Jacob Bigelow and party (including Dr. Francis Boott) tour mountains. Barometric measurements made by party determine summit elevation to be close to 6250 ft.

1819: Abel and Ethan Allen Crawford construct footpath to summit over Southern Presidentials. Crawford Path is nation's longest continuously maintained hiking trail.

1820: Walking path from Jackson to the Glen and up mountain is established.

1821: First women climbers, the Misses Austin of Portsmouth, N.H., guided by Ethan Crawford, attain summit.

1821: Crawfords cut second route to summit; trail mostly follows route of today's Cog Railway.

1823: Ethan Crawford builds three crude overnight shelters on summit; all fall victim to mountain weather within year or so.

1823: John A. Lowell and John Lowell Jr. conduct first known exploration of Ammonoosuc Ravine on W side of mountain.

1840: Abel Crawford, 75, is first to ride horse to summit over converted Crawford Path.

1845: Nathaniel Davis, son-in-law of Abel Crawford, opens new 15-mile bridle path, the Davis Path, from lower Crawford Notch along Montalban Ridge to summit.

1849: Englishman Frederick Strickland is first person to die on Presidentials after losing his way in October snowstorm.

1850: First Glen House built in clearing E of mountain near Pinkham Notch; hotel burns to ground in 1884.

1852: First Summit House hotel built atop mountain by Lancaster, Jefferson entrepreneurs.

1853: Second summit hotel, Tip-Top House, opens for business.

1853: Mt. Washington Road Co. chartered; plans to build carriage road to summit from Glen House.

1854: 40-ft. observatory erected on summit; proves to be economic failure and is demolished two years later.

1855: Lizzie Bourne, first woman to perish on mountain, succumbs to fatigue, weather just a few hundred yards from summit.

1858: Deputy sheriff Lucius Hartshorn and local guide Benjamin Osgood make first winter ascent of summit. Purpose of trip is to make attachment of summit property in connection with ongoing litigation to title.

1858: Henry D. Thoreau makes second visit to Mt. Washington, camping in Tuckerman Ravine. His guide starts accidental fire in scrub.

1861: Following failure of previous company to finish job, Mt. Washington Summit Road Co. completes construction of carriage road.

1862: First overnight winter stay atop mountain is made by John Spaulding, Chapin Brooks, Franklin White.

1869: Cog Railway, world's first mountain-climbing train, begins summer, fall passenger service to summit.

1870–71: Scientific team occupies summit for duration of winter. Team of four includes Joshua Huntington and photographer Amos Clough.

1871: U.S. Signal Service establishes year-round summit weather station; operates continuously until 1877, then summers only until 1892.

1872–73: Second Summit House built. Construction financed by Cog Railway, Boston and Maine RR interests.

1876: Sweetser's White Mountain guidebook devotes 11 pages to description of summit view.

1877: *Among the Clouds*, unique mountaintop newspaper, publishes first issue.

1879: Raymond Path from auto road to snow arch in Tuckerman's opened by Major Curtis B. Raymond, Boston.

1881: F. H. Burt, others, lay out path from snow arch to summit. Benjamin F. Osgood builds trail up Great Gulf to Spaulding Lake.

1893: Second Glen House, built in 1885, succumbs to nighttime fire.

mid-1890s: J. Rayner Edmands completes construction of Gulfside Trail, graded ridgecrest path connecting Mt. Washington with the Northern Peaks.

1895: AMC climber Herschel C. Parker makes first winter ascent of Tuckerman Ravine headwall.

1899: First engine-powered vehicle ascends mountain's carriage road. Locomobile is driven by Freelan Stanley, with his wife, Flora, a passenger. Vehicle makes climb to summit in a little more than two hours.

1900: AMC cuts original Boott Spur Trail, leading up N side of ridge from Hermit Lake area.

1902: Two AMC climbers make first winter ascent through Huntington Ravine.

1902: Mount Washington Hotel, greatest of grand hotels on W side of mountain, opens in July.

1905: Three AMC climbers, including trail-builder Warren W. Hart, make first winter ascent of Great Gulf headwall.

1906: Glen Boulder Trail to summit is completed.

1908: Devastating fire sweeps over summit, destroying majority of buildings.

1908–1910: Under direction of Warren W. Hart, AMC builds series of bold, steep trails up from Great Gulf, including Great Gulf Trail up valley and headwall, and Wamsutta Trail and Chandler Brook Trail up N slope of Chandler Ridge.

1910: AMC rock climbers led by George Flagg make first ascent of exposed, difficult route up Pinnacle in Huntington Ravine. Flagg documents feat with series of sketches.

1912: Grand plans for new summit hotel, new electric train around mountain (including tunnel through Mt. Jefferson's Castellated Ridge), are announced; by year's end, plans are scrapped due to financial difficulties.

1913: First ski ascent of mountain is made via Carriage Road by three members of Dartmouth Outing Club.

1915: Lakes of the Clouds hut built by AMC at SW base of summit cone near Mt. Monroe. Ammonoosuc Ravine Trail cut to provide access.

1915: Third Summit House opens; week later, old Tip-Top House gutted by fire.

1920: Lion Head Trail constructed; AMC builds Pinkham Notch Camp at E base of mountain.

1926: With help from friends, Arthur T. Walden, famed breeder of sled dogs, drives team of huskies to summit and back in 15 hours via Carriage Road.

1928–1930: Leading climbers of day, including Robert Underhill, Julian Whittlesey and Britain's Noel Odell, inaugurate ice climbing in Huntington Ravine with several notable first ascents.

1929: Peppersass, original Cog Railway engine, returns to mountain for one final ascent; on return trip, engine crashes; Boston photographer Daniel Rossiter is killed.

1930s: Works Progress Administration proposes scenic highway across Presidentials, but project is abandoned in face of strong opposition.

1932: Mrs. Florence Clark is first to drive dog sled team to summit unassisted.

1932–33: Winter reoccupation of summit takes place by fledgling Mt. Washington Observatory.

1934: Highest land wind speed ever recorded (231 mph) occurs on summit, April 12.

1934: WMNF and CCC cut Jewell Trail up W ridge of Mt. Clay; path is named for Sgt. Jewell, observer for Army Signal Corps on Mt. Washington.

1937: Yankee Network establishes summit FM radio broadcasting facility.

1938: September hurricane blows across mountain, ripping up 2400 feet of track on Cog Railway and heavily damaging two buildings at base station. Miraculously, Cog is back in operation by end of October.

1939: Tony Matt wins Inferno ski race down Tuckerman Ravine with legendary run, finishing in record time of 6:29.4.

1942: Military begins icing research, experiments on summit, to aid ongoing war effort.

1947: August forest fire burns 30–40 acres of hurricane-damaged timber one mile south of Cog base station.

1951: Longtime Cog owner Col. Henry Teague dies; wills railroad, summit holdings to Dartmouth College.

1952: New trail up long E ridge of Boott Spur opens. Path leaves from Tuckerman Ravine Trail less than half-mile from NH 16 and AMC Pinkham Notch Camp.

1954: WMTW broadcasts first television programming via summit transmitter.

1959: Dept. of Agriculture designates 5552 acres in Great Gulf as "wild" area to be preserved for future generations. Five years later, under Wilderness Act of 1964, Great Gulf is among tracts included in Wilderness Preservation system.

1962: Arthur Teague purchases Cog RR from Dartmouth.

1964: State of New Hampshire buys summit property, buildings from Dartmouth.

1967: Cog engine, passenger car crash near summit, eight are killed in worst ever mountain disaster.

1971: Mt. Washington State Park established at summit.

1980: Sherman Adams Summit Building, built by state, opens. Serves as year-round home to Mt. Washington Observatory crews. To make room for new building, old Summit House is razed.

1987: Forest Service denies guiding permit to Cog Railway, which had hoped to ferry spring skiers up to summit, then lead them down to Tuckerman Ravine. Preserving traditional walk-in experience of skiers is cited by USFS as major reason for its decision.

1993: Forest Service completes purchase of 857 acres of land at eastern base of mountain. Land is purchased from Mt. Washington Summit Road Company, which retains minimal holdings in Glen House for eventual development of cross-country ski center.

TRAIL APPROACHES

As befits the Northeast's tallest mountain, there are a variety of trail approaches to Mt. Washington, some meandering across high, barren ridges, others shooting up through spectacular ravines. The scenery on these routes is among the finest in New England, though arrival at the top can be anti-climactic when, after several hours of exertion, you are greeted with an array of buildings and antennas and the noise and tourist bustle of the Auto Road and Cog Railway. Nevertheless, the summit of Washington is a fascinating place to visit, for its long and storied history as well as its horizon-stretching views. The best viewing spot may be the deck of the Sherman Adams Summit Building, the centerpiece of the Mt. Washington State Park. Food and souvenirs are available for purchase here during the season from Memorial Day to Columbus Day. The Mt. Washington Observatory's summit museum is well worth a visit. NOTE: No summit buildings are available for shelter from Columbus Day through Memorial Day.

Because every route involves extensive hiking above treeline, attention to safety and the mountain's notoriously fickle weather is of paramount importance in considering a climb of Washington. Only clear, mild days in summer and fall with relatively light wind are suitable. It is likely to be 20 to 30 degrees colder and much windier at the summit than at the trailhead, and the summit is in the clouds about 60 percent of the time. Be prepared to turn back if the weather deteriorates. Rain, fog, snow, icing, thunderstorms, high winds and other weather factors can make for extremely dangerous conditions above treeline, and the weather can change very quickly. Though this is a puny mountain compared to the giants out West or around the globe, it is one of the most dangerous of all peaks; as has been well documented, most notably in Nicholas Howe's book *Not Without Peril*, over 100 lives have been lost on the slopes of Mt. Washington and the Presidentials, many due to exposure.

In addition to safety precautions, hikers should note that the climb of Mt. Washington is an arduous trip, involving 3800–4300 ft. of elevation gain. Almost every approach has some steep, rough sections, and the jumbled rocks of the upper cone require a long stretch of tedious rock-hopping.

Once at the top, the hiker must have enough energy and "legs" left for the long, knee-rattling descent.

West Approaches from Cog Railway Base Road

Trailhead (2500 ft.): A large hiker's parking lot is located on the R (S) side of the Cog Railway Base Rd., 1 mi. above the jct. with Mt. Clinton Rd. and Jefferson Notch Rd., and 5.3 mi. from US 302. This trailhead is nearly 500 ft. higher than Pinkham Notch on the E side of the mountain.

Ammonoosuc Ravine Trail, Crawford Path
9.2 mi. round trip, 3800-ft. elevation gain

This scenic and very popular route up the broad ravine SW of the summit passes by several waterfalls, the rock-rimmed Lakes of the Clouds, and the AMC hut of the same name. It is steep as it ascends to treeline and the hut. Note that the Ammonoosuc Ravine Trail holds snow late into the spring, and in late fall it can be very icy where water runs over the ledges. Even when merely wet the upper ledges are slippery, especially coming down.

From parking area, follow blue-blazed trail E at easy grades through open fir and birch woods, crossing Franklin Brook at 0.3 mi. Old route from Base Station (0.3 mi. long) comes in on L at 1.0 mi. Trail now climbs easily alongside Ammonoosuc River (on L) through fir forest, with rocky footing in places, passing memorial plaque for Herbert J. Young, Dartmouth student who perished here in December 1928. Cross Monroe Brook at 1.7 mi./3225 ft. Woods get scrubbier, with evidence of landslides. At 2.1 mi./3450 ft. cross tributary stream by Gem Pool, clear basin of water below small mossy cascade.

Trail turns R (SE) here and begins long, steep ascent up section of rock steps. At 2.3 mi./3750 ft. sign marks side trail R to The Gorge, where high perch provides great view of two long waterslides. Steep rocky climb continues to brook crossing and first view W over Bretton Woods valley at 2.5 mi./4175 ft. Ledgy scrambling leads up past series of cascades with more brook crossings. Trees shrink to scrub and views open out to NW, and L up to scree-strewn slopes of Mt. Washington. Ascent continues up rock slabs and through intermittent patches of scrub. Grade eases higher up, and near top of climb rocky pile of Monroe appears up to R. Reach AMC Lakes of the Clouds Hut and jct. with Crawford Path at 3.1 mi./5012 ft.

Turn L on Crawford Path and walk by hut, where water and toilets are available and refreshments may be purchased (in season, early June through mid-September). From here to summit route is completely above treeline, and is also part of Appalachian Trail. Dry River Trail splits R just past hut. Crawford Path passes between the two Lakes of the Clouds, with the larger Lower Lake on R and smaller Upper Lake on L. Climb to jct. just beyond at 3.3 mi./5125 ft., where Tuckerman Crossover continues straight and Camel Trail diverges R. Bear L on Crawford Path and begin moderate slabbing climb up rocky treadway, heading NE on L side of ridgecrest, with ever-

The bare and rocky summit come of Mt. Washington, as viewed from the top of Mt. Monroe.

expanding views back down to Lakes of Clouds, Southern Presidentials and horizons beyond.

At 4.0 mi./5625 ft. Davis Path comes in on R and in a few yards Westside Trail branches L. Crawford Path now zigzags more steeply up W side of Washington's summit cone. At flat spot at 4.4 mi./6150 ft., Gulfside Trail joins from L. Crawford Path swings R and climbs last pitch up to summit area, passing by buildings en route to highest outcrop, marked by sign, at 4.6 mi./6288 ft.

Jewell Trail, Gulfside Trail, Trinity Heights Connector
10.0 mi. round trip, 3900-ft. elevation gain

This western route is slightly longer and has less steep climbing than the Ammonoosuc Ravine approach, but is fully exposed to weather in the upper 2 mi. It ascends a westerly ridge of Mt. Clay, then follows the main ridge to Mt. Washington, with some spectacular views into the Great Gulf. Grades are mostly moderate with generally decent footing, though the upper section of Jewell Trail is rough and rocky.

From trailhead parking, cross Cog Railway Base Rd., enter woods, and cross Ammonoosuc River (here a mountain stream) at 0.1 mi. Climb at easy grades, passing jct. L with Boundary Line Trail at 0.4 mi. Climb moderately up small ridge, past jct. R with old trail route from Cog RR Base Station at 1.0 mi., then dip L to cross Clay Brook on footbridge at 1.1 mi. / 2850 ft. Trail now starts to ascend W ridge of Mt. Clay via several switchbacks, with partial view S into Burt Ravine from blowdown area at 2.0 mi. / 3600 ft. Route now swings over to N side of ridge, climbing steadily and keeping below crest. Ascent continues through high scrub until treeline is reached at 3.0 mi. / 4600 ft. Above here route is completely exposed rest of way to summit.

Trail now zigzags up slope of broken rock, with rough footing and wide views to W. Follow cairns and blazes carefully. At 3.5 mi. / 5150 ft. swing R and angle up to Gulfside Trail on W side of Mt. Clay summit ridge at 3.7 mi. / 5400 ft. Turn R here and head S along open ridge, with nearly level going to jct. L with Mt. Clay Loop at 4.0 mi. Gulfside Trail now begins climb up NW ridge of Mt. Washington, passing jct. R with Westside Trail at 4.1 mi. / 5500 ft. Route follows along rim of Great Gulf, with spectacular views down into that huge cirque and across to Mts. Jefferson, Adams and Madison. Cog Railway tracks are not far to R in this section. Higher up are more views into Great Gulf, with tiny Spaulding Lake nestled over 1500 ft. below on floor. These are some of finest views in White Mountains.

At 4.6 mi. / 5925 ft. Great Gulf Trail enters on L. Gulfside Trail turns right here and ascends S up summit cone over broken rock, soon crossing Cog Railway tracks. At 4.8 mi. / 6100 ft. turn L on Trinity Heights Connector (part of Appalachian Trail loop over summit) and scramble up to summit at 5.0 mi. / 6288 ft.

Loop Option

Many hikers ascending Mt. Washington from the W go up via Ammonoosuc Ravine / Crawford Path approach and return by Gulfside / Jewell route, which is easier to descend (weather permitting). Total for loop is 9.6 mi. with 3900-ft. elevation gain.

East Approaches from NH 16 at Pinkham Notch

Trailhead (2032 ft.): Several approaches to Mt. Washington begin at the AMC Pinkham Notch Visitor Center, located on the W side of NH 16 at the height-of-land in Pinkham Notch, 11 mi. S of US 2 in Gorham and 12 mi. N of US 302 in Glen. This is the busiest trailhead in the White Mountains. There is ample parking here, though at peak times you may have to use the overflow lots at Wildcat Ski Area, 0.7 mi. N along Rt. 16.

Tuckerman Ravine Trail

8.4 mi. round trip, 4250-ft. elevation gain

The trade route through Tuckerman Ravine is probably the most popular of all trails to Mt. Washington. On nice summer and fall weekend days there will be a steady parade of hikers ascending this way. Grades are relatively moderate and the scenery as you ascend through Tuckerman Ravine and up the headwall is magnificent. Snow and ice may linger in the famous bowl of Tuckerman well into spring and early summer, and at such times the portion of the trail up the headwall may be closed for safety reasons. Under ordinary conditions the ascent up the headwall is strenuous but not especially difficult; however, hikers should pay close attention to footing as fatal falls have occurred. From the bowl to the summit the trail is above treeline, though until you emerge above the headwall there is some protection from west winds.

From Pinkham Notch Visitor Center, follow footway to R behind Trading Post, passing avalanche warning signs (winter and spring only). In short distance bear L on Tuckerman Ravine Trail as Old Jackson Road splits R. Trail is wide and rocky tractor road in first 2.4 mi. to Hermit Lake area, with steady, moderate grade. After gentle start, at 0.3 mi. it swings L over bridge across Cutler River and climbs to viewpoint overlooking Crystal Cascade. Swing L to jct. L with Boott Spur Trail at 0.4 mi./2275 ft. After three more switchbacks, trail climbs steadily up rock-filled footway. Huntington Ravine Trail leaves on R at 1.3 mi./3031 ft. Tuckerman trail continues straight and steady, crossing brooks at 1.5 and 1.6 mi. Bear L at 1.7 mi./3425 ft. as Huntington Ravine Fire Road continues ahead. Catch occasional glimpses of Boott Spur as climb proceeds to jct. R with Raymond Path at 2.1 mi./3675 ft. Lion Head Trail (see below) leaves on R at 2.3 mi., and at 2.4 mi./3875 ft. Tuckerman trail reaches Hermit Lake complex on floor of ravine. Hermit Lake, a tiny pond, and 10 shelters plus 3 tent platforms are to R; tickets for camping must be purchased at Pinkham Notch Visitor Center. Here also Boott Spur Link leaves on L. Views from clearing are magnificent: crags of Boott Spur up to L, Lion Head up to R, the great gray and green bowl of Tuckerman yawning ahead.

The Tuckerman trail continues W toward the upper ravine, passing a tiny pond L and ascending fairly steeply via stone steps up the Little Headwall. Look back for views to Wildcats and Carters. Beyond, you enter broad, open, upper floor of ravine at ca. 2.8 mi./4300 ft., with impressive views up to headwall. Grades are easier across floor to foot of headwall. You angle steeply up to R; in early summer the Snow Arch, carved by running water, might be seen on L at 3.1 mi./4525 ft.; it is dangerous to approach too closely. Higher up trail swings L to traverse beneath cliffs high on headwall; watch footing carefully. At top of headwall climb straight up slope to jct. R with Alpine Garden Trail at 3.4 mi./5125 ft. and on to multi-trail Tuckerman Jct. at 3.6 mi./5383 ft.

Turn sharp R here on Tuckerman Ravine Trail for tough slog up summit cone over broken rock. Lion Head Trail joins from R at 3.8 mi./5675 ft. Tuckerman trail continues steep, bouldery ascent to Auto Road by lower parking lot; from here, ascend wooden stairways to summit buildings and high point, marked by sign, at 4.2 mi./6288 ft.

Lion Head Trail Option

Hikers who enjoy steep climbing can opt to ascend crag of Lion Head to N of Tuckerman Ravine and enjoy dramatic views down into bowl. This can also be used as alternate route if section of trail on Tuckerman headwall is closed. From Pinkham Notch, take Tuckerman Ravine Trail for 2.3 mi as described below. Turn R on Lion Head Trail (3825 ft.) and after brief traverse, begin very steep, switchbacking climb up side of ridge, with some ledge scrambles. At 2.7 mi./4350 ft. reach treeline and turn sharp L as winter Lion Head route joins from R. Trail now climbs steadily W up open ridge, reaching top of Lion Head at 3.2 mi./5033 ft. To L are stunning views into Tuckerman Ravine bowl and across to Boott Spur.

Grade is now nearly level across upper ridge of Lion Head. Cross Alpine Garden Trail at 3.4 mi./5175 ft. Lion Head Trail soon begins to work steeply W up rocks of summit cone and reaches Tuckerman Ravine Trail at 3.9 mi./5675 ft. Turn R on Tuckerman trail and ascend to summit at 4.3 mi./6288 ft.

Tuckerman Ravine Trail, Boott Spur Trail, Davis Path, Crawford Path
10.6 mi. round trip, 4300-ft. elevation gain

This longer route over the great shoulder of Boott Spur is very scenic, with miles of above-treeline walking (and exposure to weather), and sees far less hiking traffic than Tuckerman Ravine. It can be combined with the Tuckerman Ravine or Lion Head route to make a very attractive loop of 9.5 mi.

From Pinkham Notch, follow Tuckerman Ravine Trail for 0.4 mi. and bear L onto Boott Spur Trail. Cross Sherburne Ski Trail and soon tackle short, steep scramble, then begin long, steady climb up lower E ridge of Boott Spur. At 0.9 mi. trail turns sharp R where short spur L leads to partial view E. Continue up ridge, passing side trail L to spring, and reach minor crest at 1.4 mi./3275 ft., where side path R leads to stand-up view of Huntington Ravine. Steady ascent lifts you to short spur R to Harvard Rock at 2.1 mi./4046 ft. Open rocky area here offers fine view into Tuckerman Ravine and out to Wildcats, Carters and Mahoosucs. Trail angles SW and up through high scrub, breaks above treeline at 2.3 mi., and runs at easy grade to Split Rock at 2.4 mi./4337 ft.

Turn R and ascend along S side of ridge, with views into Gulf of Slides. Boott Spur Link joins from R on flat shoulder at 2.6 mi./4650 ft.; here there is impressive view of Tuckerman headwall. Boott Spur Trail proceeds up middle of open ridge, climbing steeply to short level terrace at 3.0 mi./5075 ft. Uphill march resumes over broken rock; near top of ridge swing L below shattered wall of rock, work up through it, and emerge by summit of Boott Spur, which is short distance to L. This satellite peak provides excellent views of Wildcats, Carters, Mahoosucs to E and NE, Nelson Crag and Mt. Washington's cone to N and NW, and many other White Mountain peaks to W. Boott Spur Trail dips to meet Davis Path just beyond at 3.3 mi./5450 ft.

Turn R on Davis Path for long, gently graded walk in open across ridge of Boott Spur and Bigelow Lawn beyond. This is grand stretch of hiking, with views of Carters and Maine mountains to R, Washington's great cone ahead, and Southern Presidentials and western Whites to L, all seen across expanses of alpine tundra. At 3.9 mi., where Lawn Cutoff diverges R, Davis Path begins traverse of broad plateau of Bigelow Lawn, following line of tall cairns. Camel Trail goes L at 4.0 mi., and Davis Path crosses Tuckerman Crossover at 4.3 mi. Southside Trail enters on R at 4.6 mi./5575 ft., and at 4.7 mi. Davis Path ends at Crawford Path. Turn R on Crawford Path for fairly steep climb up W side of summit cone, quickly passing jct. L with Westside Trail. Reach jct. L with Gulfside Trail at 5.1 mi./6150 ft. Turn R for final climb on Crawford Path to summit at 5.3 mi./6288 ft.

Old Jackson Road, Nelson Crag Trail
10.6 mi. round trip, 4350-ft. elevation gain

This longer and less-used approach from Pinkham begins with a pleasant warmup on Old Jackson Road followed by a sustained steep climb up Nelson Crag Trail. The upper 2.5 mi. is above treeline with excellent views, especially into Huntington Ravine, and great exposure to weather.

Find start of Tuckerman Ravine Trail behind Trading Post at Pinkham; in 100 ft. or so Old Jackson Road diverges R at a sign. First 0.4 mi. is nearly level, passing several ski trail jcts. At jct. R with Crew Cut Trail, OJR begins steady climb through nice hardwood forest. Grade eases as you cross low divide, passing jct. R with George's Gorge Trail at 0.9 mi./2525 ft. Trail remains nearly level or slightly downhill until sharp L at 1.6 mi. After short, steep pitch, pass jct. L with Raymond Path and reach Nelson Crag Trail at 1.7 mi./2625 ft.

Turn L on Nelson Crag Trail and begin climbing through woods, moderate at first, then becoming steep, rough and relentless. Break above treeline at 2.8 mi./4350 ft. Trail is in open from here to summit, with inspiring views E, N and S. Climb at less steep grade to Cragway Spring beside curve on Auto Road at 3.4 mi./4825 ft. Trail bears L here and struggles up steep rocky terrain on upper Chandler Ridge. Grade eases as you approach Nelson Crag, which is reached at 4.1 mi./5635 ft. To L are eye-popping views into Huntington Ravine. Trail is nearly level to crossing of Alpine Garden Trail at 4.3 mi., then rises and swings L to cross Huntington Ravine Trail at 4.5 mi./5725 ft. Steady climb over rocks leads to top of Ball Crag at 4.9 mi./6112 ft. After slight dip, cross Auto Road and Cog Railway tracks and clamber up to summit at 5.3 mi./6288 ft.

Huntington Ravine Trail

The route up the headwall of Huntington Ravine is notorious as the most difficult section of trail in the White Mountains, requiring exposed rock scrambling that will be uncomfortable for many hikers. In a few spots falls could result in serious injury. As neither of the authors has any experience with this trail, we are not including it as a regular approach in this book. We

Snow-capped Mt. Washington and the Presidentials adorned in their usual winter garb.

have heard varied reports on Huntington—some hiking friends were terrified by it, others were exhilarated. Those who are up to the challenge should attempt it only on a clear, dry day, and it should not be used for a descent route. For details, see the description and extensive cautionary notes in the AMC guide. It is accessed via the lower Tuckerman Ravine Trail.

SOUTHEAST APPROACH from NH 16

Glen Boulder Trail, Davis Path, Crawford Path
11.4 mi. round trip, 4400-ft. elevation gain

TRAILHEAD (1975 ft.): Glen Boulder Trail starts at parking area for Glen Ellis Falls, on W side of NH 16, 0.7 mi. S of AMC Pinkham Notch Camp. This route climbs past the landmark Glen Boulder and lofty Boott Spur, with views starting at just 1.4 mi. and nearly continuous vistas (and exposure) along the upper 3 mi.

Glen Boulder Trail leaves S edge of Glen Ellis Falls parking area and ascends past restrooms into woods. After moderate start, climb steeply to R around cliff to meet Diretissima (1.0 mi. connecting route from NH 16 just S of Pinkham Notch Visitor Center) at 0.4 mi./2300 ft. Turn L here and traverse slope, then climb steadily, crossing Avalanche Brook Ski Trail at 0.8 mi./2600 ft. Cross two branches of brook, then commence stiff climb up rocky footway through dense conifers. After a couple of teaser views, break above trees with fairly difficult ledge scramble at 1.4 mi. and climb steadily in open to immense Glen Boulder, glacial erratic perched at edge of ridge, at 1.6 mi./3729 ft. Enjoy wide views N and S down valley and across to Wildcats and Carters.

Trail turns sharp R here and climbs steeply in open over rough ledges. Grade eases and trail re-enters scrub at top of ridge at 2.0 mi./4300 ft. Trail now climbs at mellow grade through high scrub, passing side trail R to spring at 2.3 mi/4550 ft. Moderate ascent continues to small nub of Slide Peak at 2.6 mi./4806 ft., where trail emerges in open again. Here there is fine view S down Rocky Branch valley and Montalban Ridge and out to western and southern White Mountains, with Southern Presidentials to R. Trail now runs easily along rim of Gulf of Slides, with good views R into that cirque, then swings R and rises steadily through alpine terrain and patches of scrub to meet Davis Path at 3.2 mi./5175 ft.

Turn R on Davis Path and climb moderately past craggy knob on L and up broad, open S ridge of Boott Spur. Look back for views down Rocky Branch and Dry River valleys. Pass just to L of summit of Boott Spur to jct. R with Boott Spur Trail at 3.7 mi./5450 ft. Continue on Davis Path across open, level ridge of Boott Spur and Bigelow Lawn, up to Crawford Path and on to summit of Washington as described above for Boott Spur Trail route. Reach summit at 5.7 mi./6288 ft.

Northeast Approach from Great Gulf

Great Gulf Trail, Gulfside Trail, Trinity Heights Connector
7.9 mi. one way, 5000-ft. elevation gain

Trailhead (1350 ft.): This route starts at large parking area for Great Gulf Wilderness on W side of NH 16, 6.5 mi. S of US 2 in Gorham, and 4.1 mi. N of AMC's Pinkham Notch Camp.

One of the most dramatic ways to approach Washington is through the deep, secluded valley of the Great Gulf and up the great, rock-strewn headwall, emerging from the abyss just 0.4 mi. below the summit. This is a long, strenuous route recommended for ascent only, with descent via another, shorter route down the E side of the mountain to a car spotted at the base. The headwall can also be ascended by backpackers from a base camp in the gulf, but note that camping is prohibited above the Sphinx Trail jct. There are a number of marked, designated campsites along the Great Gulf Trail below this point.

From parking area, walk N along old road for 0.1 mi., turn L and cross Peabody River on suspension footbridge, then swing L and up to jct. with Great Gulf Link Trail (from Dolly Copp CG) at 0.3 mi. Bear L here at easy grade on wide trail through spruces along West Branch of Peabody. At 0.6 mi. Great Gulf Trail splits L off road (a ski trail in winter), then rejoins at 1.0 mi. Continue past more ski trail jcts. and over several brooks on bridges. At 1.6 mi. is jct. R with Hayes Copp Ski Trail. Enter Great Gulf Wilderness and reach jct. with Osgood Trail at 1.8 mi./1850 ft.

Continue ahead on Great Gulf Trail, following West Branch of Peabody. Pass scenic view of stream at 2.4 mi., then climb steeper pitch to gravelly opening atop high bank known as The Bluff, reached at 2.7 mi./2278 ft. Here there are good views up to N side of Mt. Washington, Mt. Jefferson and Mt. Adams.

Just beyond, bear L on Great Gulf Trail where Osgood Cutoff veers R, and descend steep bank to cross Parapet Brook, then climb to hogback where Madison Gulf Trail splits R at 2.8 mi. Great Gulf Trail drops steeply to cross West Branch on suspension footbridge. Climb bank on far side and bear R on Great Gulf Trail as Madison Gulf Trail veers L towards Pinkham Notch. Great Gulf Trail now settles in for long, moderate stretch up along West Branch through deep fir forest, with rough, rocky footing in places. Pass Clam Rock on L at 3.1 mi. At 3.3 mi. rocks in riverbed provide view ahead to Jefferson's Knee. Cross Chandler Brook at 3.9 mi./2800 ft.; on far bank Chandler Brook Trail departs L. Continue moderate climb up valley to jct. with Six Husbands and Wamsutta Trails at 4.5 mi./3100 ft.

Beyond jct., Great Gulf Trail continues moderate climb up valley, with glimpses of Jefferson's Knees up to R. Pass by many fine cascades and pools, starting at 5.2 mi. and continuing for 0.2 mi. Look back for views of Mts. Adams and Madison. Cross West Branch and tributary and in wet, mossy fir forest reach jct. R with Sphinx Trail, steep route up to Sphinx Col between Mts. Clay and Jefferson, at 5.6 mi./3625 ft. Recross West Branch and pass picturesque Weetamoo Falls at 5.7 mi./3675 ft. Continue up bouldery footway into upper gulf, obtaining occasional glimpses up to headwall. Last pitch up through stunted birch and fir lifts you to Spaulding Lake at 6.5 mi./ 4228 ft. Bordered by rock slides, this tiny tarn rests in one of most picturesque settings in East. Headwall of gulf is overpowering sight to S. Trail runs along E shore. From tall boulder at S end of lake, enjoy views N over water to Adams and Madison.

Beyond lake, Great Gulf Trail soon tackles arduous climb up 1600-ft. headwall. Scramble over huge boulders and along gurgling stream. Views open as you ascend—first back down gulf past Jefferson's Knees to Adams and Madison and Mahoosucs beyond. Continue clambering up broken rock; distant vistas start to appear over various cols and saddles on surrounding ridges. Look carefully for blazes and cairns as steep ascent continues in SE direction. Watch footing on loose rocks. At top of headwall trail bears R and emerges to meet Gulfside Trail at 7.5 mi./5925 ft. Continue straight on Gulfside Trail, easing up to jct. with Trinity Heights Connector at 7.7 mi./6100 ft. Turn L here for final 0.2 mi. climb over rocks to summit, reached at 7.9 mi./6288 ft.

Backpackers can make 3.1-mi. loop back to Great Gulf via Nelson Crag, Alpine Garden and Wamsutta Trails; descent on lower Wamsutta Trail is very steep. This loop brings you back to Great Gulf Trail 4.5 mi. from trailhead.

WINTER

Even though Mt. Washington experiences some of the worst weather in the world, especially during the winter months, the mountain is by no means off limits to winter climbing enthusiasts. Provided you are fully experienced in winter mountain travel and equipped with proper outerwear and appropriate gear, on the right day a winter ascent of the mountain can be a safe, enjoyable, and exhilarating experience.

Because much of the climb is above treeline, exposing hikers to cold winds and treacherous footing (featuring a mix of ice, snow and broken rock), only strong and experienced winter hikers, fully equipped for extended above-treeline travel, should attempt this climb. Even then, it should only be undertaken in clear weather with relatively light winds. The *average* wind speed on Mt. Washington's summit is 45 mph during the winter months, and the average temperature in February is 5.6 degrees. Preventing frostbite and hypothermia is of critical concern on any winter venture on the mountain.

Among the essential items you'll need for a successful and safe climb are full crampons, snowshoes, ice axe, plenty of gloves and mittens, gaiters, map and compass, bivouac sack/space blanket, sunglasses, abundant warm clothing layers and windproof outer garments.

Another potential hazard of any winter ascent of the mountain is the threat of avalanches, especially in Tuckerman and Huntington Ravines. Throughout winter and for much of the spring backcountry ski season, the U.S. Forest Service issues daily advisories concerning the threat of avalanches on the mountain. These bulletins are posted at the Pinkham Notch Visitor Center, at Hermit Lake Shelter, and on the Internet at www.mountwashington.org/avalanche.

The most popular winter route up the mountain utilizes the Tuckerman Ravine and Lion Head Trails from Pinkham Notch (NH 16). The winter route up Lion Head varies significantly from the Lion Head summer route in that it begins off the Huntington Ravine Fire Road, about 0.1 mi. from its junction with Tuckerman Ravine Trail (and 1.8 mi. from AMC's Pinkham Notch Visitor Center.) The winter route, which is closed to hikers during the summer and fall months, joins the summer Lion Head route at treeline.

Because there is no road access to the Cog Railway base area during the winter, an ascent of the mountain from the W is a long and difficult undertaking, and is thus rarely made. The best winter approach from the Bretton Woods-Crawford Notch side is via the historic Crawford Path, but since this route involves more than five miles (one-way) of above treeline travel, it should only be attempted in good weather and by persons in excellent physical condition.

Take note that none of the summit buildings are open to the public during the winter months and cannot be relied on as places to seek shelter in times of poor weather. If you have any doubts about the weather, especially above timberline, do not hesitate to retrace your steps and save the climb for another, better day.

VIEW GUIDE

The view from Mt. Washington has been celebrated for centuries. In his 1876 guidebook, Moses Sweetser devoted eleven pages of very small print to describing its intricacies. Over the years several panoramic sketches identifying visible features have been produced, most recently by Brent Scudder in *Scudder's White Mountain Viewing Guide.* As the highest peak in the entire region, Mt. Washington naturally commands the most comprehensive view, in clear weather covering points in four states (N.H., Maine, Vt., N.Y.) and the province of Quebec, plus the Atlantic Ocean. If you're lucky enough to have a clear day on top—and the summit is in cloud, on average, 60 percent of the time—you could spend hours scanning the horizons.

Over the years some observers have opined that Mt. Washington's superior height actually produces an inferior view, because everything around it is diminished in stature and effect. One 19th-century visitor deemed the Mt. Washington view "vast, but vague," preferring somewhat lower viewpoints such as Moosilauke or Lafayette. Inveterate peakbagger Gene Daniell places Washington 31st in his rankings of 4000-footer views, noting that "you can see forever, but forever's just too damn flat—Washington makes all the other peaks insignificant." Nevertheless, from Washington you can run your eye over a great deal of country, including the tops of 43 other New Hampshire 4000-footers—tying it with Mt. Carrigain in that regard. The observation deck of the Sherman Adams Summit Building is probably the best single place to take in the views. By scrambling around to various sides of the summit you can gain some better perspectives in several directions.

Perhaps the most dramatic view from Washington is that to the N, where the rocky peaks of the Northern Presidentials—Clay, Jefferson, Adams and Madison, L to R—rise in an orderly line from the abyss of the Great Gulf. Farther afield, Mts. Starr King and Waumbek loom above Jefferson village between Clay and Jefferson. Mt. Cabot, The Bulge and The Horn are over Jefferson, with the Pilot Ridge to the L and the bare Percy Peaks behind to the R. Countless North Country ridges can be seen in the distance, and several peaks in Quebec can be spotted across the northern horizon.

Close by to the NE is the broad upper shoulder of Chandler Ridge, including the rock nubbles of Ball Crag (L) and Nelson Crag (R). In this direction, to the R of Mt. Madison, are the many summits of the Mahoosuc Range, piled one upon another with Old Speck, the highest, back to the L. A portion of the Androscoggin River is seen in front of the Mahoosucs. Several of the 4000-footers in the Rangeley, Maine, region can be seen beyond the Mahoosucs, 60 to 75 miles away, including Saddleback, Bigelow, Sugarloaf and Abraham. To the L of the Mahoosucs part of the city of Berlin, with its smoke-belching mills, can be seen, with the glimmer of Umbagog

Lake beyond. To the R of the Mahoosucs, above Nelson Crag, is the pyramidal Mt. Blue near Weld, Maine.

Swinging to the ENE, the view now sweeps over the nearby Carter-Moriah Range across the Peabody River valley, starting on the L with Mt. Moriah and running across North, Middle and South Carter, dipping to Zeta Pass, then rising again to Mt. Hight and Carter Dome, seen due E. Beyond the Carters are the mountains around Evans Notch: Caribou between Middle and South Carter, and the Royces (L) and Speckled (R) between South Carter and Hight. Vast horizons open out into Maine in the distance, including prominent Streaked Mtn. over Carter Dome.

To the R of Carter Dome is the long spread of Wildcat Ridge with its five lettered summits and ski trails in front. The twin bare cones of the Baldfaces are over the highest Wildcat summits (A, B and C). Jackson's Black Mtn. and the Baldface neighbors Sable and Chandler are beyond the lower D and E summits of Wildcat. In this direction, at mid-morning in summer, the glimmer of the Atlantic Ocean may be seen 75 miles away on the Maine coast. A bit farther to the R is the low, long profile of Maine's Pleasant Mtn. with the nearer, twin Doubleheads to the R. Another matched pair, the Gemini, are just above the Doubleheads, with parts of Sebago Lake beyond. Immediately to the R, looking SE, is the unmistakable pyramid of Kearsarge North near North Conway, with the Green Hills trailing off to the R. The broad valley of the Saco River at North Conway is at the base of the Green Hills.

Close by and down to the SSE is the great craggy side of Boott Spur, forming the S wall of Tuckerman Ravine. Over Boott Spur is darkly wooded Iron Mtn. near Jackson, with the Moats behind to the R. The ski slopes of Attitash are in front of the Moats, and Ossipee Lake is beyond. Farther R, almost due S, the rocky spire of Mt. Chocorua is seen over the lower Montalban Ridge peaks of Mts. Langdon and Parker. Bear Mtn. is just R of Chocorua, and Mt. Shaw in the distant Ossipee Range is between them.

Just W of S you look down the long, flattish Montalban Ridge, including Mts. Isolation, Davis, Stairs, Resolution and Crawford. Mt. Paugus is over Resolution, with the distant Belknap Range behind and a part of Lake Winnipesaukee seen through a low point to the R, over Bartlett Haystack. To the R of Haystack is Mt. Tremont, with Mts. Passaconaway and Whiteface looming behind. To the R of Montalban Ridge is a nice view down the remote Dry River valley to Tripyramid (L) and Sandwich Dome (R). Mts. Monadnock and Kearsarge in southern New Hampshire can be spotted just to the R of the Dome, with the peaks of the Nancy Range in closer and a bit R. Next to the R is the trademark profile of Mt. Carrigain with its Signal Ridge on the L. The Osceolas peer over Carrigain's R shoulder, and farther R is North Hancock's broad dome and sprawling ridges. Mt. Cardigan is seen in the distance to the L of North Hancock, while Scar Ridge is to the R of Hancock's long N ridge.

Next to the R is one of Washington's most striking vistas, looking SW down the barren, twisting ridge of the Southern Presidentials, with Monroe's crags (L) and Eisenhower's dome (R) especially notable. Pierce is seen between these two peaks, and Jackson and Webster are to the L of Monroe, under the N ridge of Hancock. Beyond the Southern Presidentials is the Willey Range, with talus-scarred Willey over Pierce, Field just R of Eisenhower, and rounded Tom farther to the R. Behind and between Field and Tom are Mts. Bond and Guyot, with Mts. Flume and Liberty peering over and Mt. Moosilauke rising beyond. More distant peaks include Smarts Mtn. (to the L of Moosilauke, in line with Eisenhower) and Vermont's sharp Killington Peak (over the R shoulder of Moosilauke). Looking to the R of the Willey Range, South Twin and slide-marked North Twin stand out, with Mts. Lincoln and Lafayette behind on either side of South Twin. Mt. Hale is to the R of the Twins, beyond the nearer Rosebrook Range and the Bretton Woods valley.

To the W the view extends out the Ammonoosuc River valley and far into Vermont, with distinctive Camel's Hump just N of W. On exceptionally clear days Mt. Marcy, the highest of New York's Adirondacks, can be spotted slightly R of the red-and-white Mt. Washington Hotel down in the valley. New York's Mt. Whiteface may also appear just to the R of Camel's Hump.

To the WNW are the long wooded ridges of the nearby Dartmouth Range, including Mt. Deception on the L and Mt. Dartmouth on the R. A bit farther away are Cherry Mtn. and Owl's Head. On the horizon is Vermont's Mt. Mansfield, in line with Deception, while Burke Mtn. and Jay Peak are seen to the R of Dartmouth, beyond sparkling Cherry Pond. From here the view swings around to the NW over more lowlands, coming back to Mt. Clay.

NO. OF 4000-FOOTERS VISIBLE: 43

Carter Dome

ELEVATION: 4832 ft./ 1473 m ORDER OF HEIGHT: 9
LOCATION: Carter Range, Township of Beans Purchase
USGS MAP: 7½′ Carter Dome

GEOGRAPHY

Carter Dome is the highest peak in the string of mountains which run more or less north-to-south on the E side of Pinkham Notch, which includes the Carter-Moriah Range and the peaks of Wildcat Ridge. This massive mountain is known for its round, symmetrical shape and its unique persepctive on Mt. Washington, which lies directly across the way on the W side of Pinkham Notch.

The mountain's NW-facing slope is scarred by a huge landslide which stripped the mountain to its bedrock during a drenching October 1869 rainstorm. A major portion of the mountain, including the summit, has also never fully recovered from a devastating 1903 forest fire which severely scoured Carter Dome's broad, flat crest and denuded neighboring Mt. Hight of its vegetation.

On the SW side of the mountain is Carter Notch—the deep glacier-carved pass separating Carter Dome from Wildcat Ridge to the W. The U-shaped notch, with the rounded mass of the Dome towering on its E side, is a noted landmark visible from many distant points. Among the features of the notch are the Carter Lakes, two tiny tarns situated just S of the 3388-ft. height-of-land, and the nearby AMC Carter Notch Hut. On the SW flank of Carter Dome, overlooking the notch, is a remarkably steep and craggy face, with rocks strewn across the bowl beneath the cliffs. Pulpit Rock, an immense boulder jutting out above the notch high up on the Dome's side, is particularly prominent when viewed from the vicinity of the lakes and hut. Over the centuries, falling rocks and ledges from both Carter Dome and Wildcat Mtn. have amassed into one gigantic boulder field S of Carter Lakes. This barrier of rocks, known as the Rampart, is visited frequently by adventure seekers staying at the hut.

The main summit of Carter Dome is flanked by two major spur peaks. Bare-topped Mt. Hight (4675 ft.) is less than a mile NNE along the ridgecrest beyond a shallow col. This has probably the best view of any summit on the E side of Pinkham Notch. Just to the N of Hight, Zeta Pass (3890 ft.) separates the Carter Dome group from South Carter and the other Carter peaks.

The SE spur of Carter Dome, also bare on top, is known as Rainbow Ridge (4274 ft.). To the SE its slopes descend gently to Perkins Notch (2590 ft.), the broad, gentle gap between Carter Dome and Black Mtn. to the S. The Wild River takes its rise on the E side of Perkins Notch at tiny No-Ketchum Pond and surrounding bogs.

From the broad E side of the Carter Dome massif several ridges and valleys sprawl down to the upper Wild River valley. The lower slopes are largely cloaked in a paper birch forest that grew up after the great 1903 fire. Red Brook drains the slopes on the E side of Rainbow Ridge; several beaver ponds dot the plateau at the base of the ridge. The several branches of Spruce Brook drain the E side of Carter Dome itself and Mt. Hight. The main branch of the stream originates in a high cirque-like basin between the two peaks and flows down a long, curving valley. The ridge that borders this valley on the S sweeps down to a low but prominent rock peak (2930 ft.) that was bared by the fire. On the N side of the main Spruce Brook valley, Mt. Hight's E ridge splits into two massive wooded shoulders. This interesting E side of Carter Dome and its spurs can be studied from the barren Baldface summits across the Wild River valley.

The SW slopes of Carter Dome and Rainbow Ridge drain into the valley of Wildcat River. The NW slopes of the Dome and the W side of Mt. Hight are drained by tributaries of Nineteen-Mile Brook.

NOMENCLATURE

The entire ridge from North Carter to Carter Dome was once known simply as "Mt. Carter," presumably for Dr. Ezra Carter, a physician who explored the Whites in the 1800s looking for medicinal herbs and roots. The name "Carter's Mt." appeared as early as 1823. Arnold Guyot's 1860 map listed "Carter, S. Peak and N. Peak." In 1876 the AMC adopted the name "Carter Dome" for the highest and southernmost peak. Mt. Hight, a 4675-foot peak less than a mile N of the Dome, is supposedly named for a frequent hiking companion of Dr. Carter, a Mr. Hight of Jefferson.

Other accounts, however, say the peaks were named for two local hunters (named Carter and Hight) who while passing through Carter Notch became separated, with each ascending the ridges on either side of the notch. As a result, one ridge was named Carter and the other Hight. Guidebook author Moses F. Sweetser wrote that it was uncertain which of the mountains assumed either of the names, but that the mountain W of Carter Notch was usually referred to as Mt. Hight, and the peak E of the notch, Mt. Carter. The western peak Sweetser refers to is today known as Wildcat Mt., while Mt. Hight was eventually assigned to Carter Dome's northern neighbor.

HISTORICAL HIGHLIGHTS

First Ascent: Unknown.

1852: First Glen House hotel built at western base of Carters.

1869: Heavy rains result in Oct. 4 landslide on Carter Dome that strips N and W slopes of mountain to its bedrock ledges for nearly a mile.

1876: William Nowell, Charles Lowe, and Dr. F.I.R. Stafford explore Carter Notch–Carter Dome area. Descent route is via steep NW slide. Jackson resident Jonathan "Jock" Davis builds path from Jackson to Carter Notch.

1877: Nowell and Lowe build Nineteen-Mile Brook Trail to Carter Notch.

1879: Jonathan Davis cuts trail from Carter Notch to summit of Carter Dome.

1881: AMC founders William Fenollosa and William Pickering climb to summit by way of Carter Notch and erect four-foot cairn atop mountain. In reporting on trip in *Appalachia*, Pickering writes of summit vista: "It may safely be said that there are few finer view-points for Mt. Washington than this."

1883: AMC group, including Eugene Cook, Charles Lowe and George Sargent, makes two-day trailless traverse of Carter Range from Gorham to Carter Notch. Also, trail from Carter Notch to Dome is extended to the "grand-viewing" N summit (Mt. Hight). Tripod observatory is erected on Dome.

1885: Under Nowell's direction, work is completed on extending ridge trail northward from Carter Dome—today's Carter-Moriah Trail. Crude overnight camp is also established in Carter Notch.

1889: After failing in effort the previous year, group of AMC Snow-Shoe Section hikers make successful winter ascent of summit.

1893: *Among the Clouds*, published atop Mt. Washington, reports, "The fire in the forests on Carter Dome Mountain, only a short distance to the rear of the Glen House site, loomed up with renewed brilliancy last evening and was a grand sight when viewed from the Summit."

1891–1903: Major logging railroad operation in Wild River valley on E side of Carters.

1903: Fire sweeps over portion of Carter Range, destroying viewing tripod at Carter Dome summit and forcing partial relocation of Jackson-Carter Notch path.

1904: N.H. Forestry Commission reports: "The forests of the Carter Range have been heavily lumbered. . . . The cutting on this range now extends up as far as there is merchantable growth, to 3,500 feet elevation on the average."

1904: AMC constructs log cabin in Carter Notch, on E shore of larger of two Carter Lakes; replaces previously built open shelter.

1907: Fire lookout tower erected on summit.

1914: Second hut, this one of stone, is built in Carter Notch. Original log cabin is given to Forest Service for use by fire lookouts working atop Carter Dome; it is evenutally demolished in 1924.

ca. 1915: WMNF acquires 35,000 acres in Wild River valley.

1921: Wildcat River Trail from Jackson is cut; replaces former Jackson-Carter Notch Path.

ca. 1925: USFS builds Carter Dome Trail up to Zeta Pass; new steel fire tower replaces older structure.

ca. 1931: Black Angel Trail from Wild River valley to ridge between Carter Dome, Mt. Hight, is built by USFS.

1933: Rainbow Trail from Wild River Trail (near No-Ketchum Pond) to Carter Dome is built by USFS.

1947: Summit fire lookout tower is removed.

1962: Lavatory building, bunkhouse added to Carter Notch facilities by AMC.

1972: Carter Notch Hut opens for first time in winter on caretaker basis.

TRAIL APPROACHES

West Approaches from NH 16

Trailhead (1487 ft.): All approaches from W start at parking area for Nineteen-Mile Brook Trail, on E side of NH 16, 1.0 mi. N of Mt. Washington Auto Road and 2.3 mi. S of entrance to Dolly Copp Campground.

There are several ways to attack Carter Dome from Rt. 16 and Pinkham Notch, including a rugged, but rewarding loop hike through spectacular Carter Notch and up and over the summit ridge. All involve elevation gain of ca. 3500 ft. The easiest route up the mountain is via the Carter Dome Trail, which leaves Nineteen-Mile Brook 1.9 mi. from its start. A series of switchbacks have tamed the steepest sections of the trail as it approaches the main ridge. This route is also convenient if you wish to loop over Mt. Hight via the Carter-Moriah Trail. The approach by way of Carter Notch is very scenic, but you pay for it with a very steep climb out of the Notch from Carter Lakes.

Carter Dome only out and back

Nineteen-Mile Brook Trail (to Carter Notch), Carter-Moriah Trail
10.0 mi. round trip, 3550-ft. elevation gain

Nineteen-Mile Brook Trail provides scenic brookside approach to Carter Notch. From parking area, trail follows old road at easy grades through hemlocks, then hardwoods, following Nineteen-Mile Brook (on R). At about 1.0 mi. traverse rough spot along bank (tricky if icy). At 1.2 mi. pass small dam and pool in brook. Continue rolling, easy ascent through yellow birches to jct. L with Carter Dome Trail at 1.9 mi./2322 ft. Continue ahead on Nineteen-Mile Brook Trail, crossing two tributaries on footbridges and traversing more birch forest. Grade steepens through fir woods after small brook crossing at 3.1 mi. Stiff climb leads to height-of-land in Carter Notch and jct. R with Wildcat Ridge Trail at 3.6 mi./3388 ft. Continue ahead on Nineteen-Mile Brook Trail, descending L to shore of Upper Carter Lake, with view up to cliffs of Wildcat Mtn. At 3.8 mi./3300 ft. turn L on Carter-Moriah Trail by edge of pond.

Trail soon begins very steep climb out of Notch on rock steps. At 4.1 mi./3900 ft. (0.3 mi. from Notch), look for side path on R to ledge with stunning vista overlooking Carter Notch and Hut, with Wildcat behind, and distant view S down valley of Wildcat River. Pulpit Rock juts out close by on L. From ledge path, trail continues to climb, but on more moderate grades. At 4.5 mi. side path drops L to spring. Higher up grade eases and as you approach gravelly clearing atop broad, scrubby summit at 5.0 mi./4832 ft., ledgy spot on L provides stand-up view to S. View to W and N is found on other side of clearing. Rainbow Trail comes in on R.

Nineteen-Mile Brook Trail, Carter Dome Trail
10.0 mi. round trip, 3450-ft. elevation gain (add 0.2 mi., 150-ft. elevation gain for loop over Mt. Hight)

For approach via Carter Dome Trail, first 1.9 mi. is on Nineteen-Mile Brook Trail as described above. Turn L here (elevation 2322 ft.) on Carter Dome Trail and begin moderately-graded ascent E up valley. Cross brook at 2.4 mi. and again at 2.7 mi./2800 ft. Trail now climbs by series of switchbacks on

N side of valley, with glimpses up to Carter Dome. Swing R at ca. 3400 ft. for steady climb through firs to deep woods of Zeta Pass at 3.8 mi./3890 ft. Turn R on combined Carter Dome and Carter-Moriah Trails and climb easily to where Carter-Moriah Trail splits L for Mt. Hight at 4.0 mi./4000 ft. Continue straight on Carter Dome Trail, which slabs up and across W slope of Hight. At 4.6 mi./4600 ft., just S of Hight-Carter Dome col, Carter-Moriah Trail re-enters from L. Black Angel Trail comes in on L just beyond. Carter Dome/Carter-Moriah Trails now climb at easy grades through high scrub, with occasional vistas, to clearing at flat summit of Carter Dome at 5.0 mi./4832 ft.

Loop Hike over Carter Dome

Nineteen-Mile Brook Trail (to Carter Notch), Carter-Moriah Trail, Carter Dome Trail
10.0 mi. round-trip, 3450-ft. elevation gain (add 0.2 mi., 150-ft. elevation gain for loop over Mt. Hight)

Loop Option over Mt. Hight: If descending Carter Dome via Zeta Pass on either out-and-back via Carter Dome Trail, or loop up from Carter Notch, the short detour over Mt. Hight is highly recommended; for extra 0.2 mi. with just 150 additional ft. of climbing you can enjoy the best views on the Carter-Moriah Range. From summit of Carter Dome, descend gently N on combined Carter-Moriah/Carter Dome Trail. In 0.4 mi. Black Angel Trail diverges R for Wild River valley. In a few yards keep straight on Carter-Moriah Trail where Carter Dome Trail splits L for Zeta Pass. Continue easy descent to Carter Dome-Hight col (4530 ft.). Mostly gradual climb lifts you to bare, rocky summit of Hight at 0.8 mi. from summit of Carter Dome. Panoramic view include great looks W to Presidentials, N and S along Carter Range, and E over Wild River valley to Baldface Range.

Atop summit, Carter-Moriah Trail makes sharp turn to L (NW) and drops into trees for very steep and rough descent for 0.4 mi., then more gradual as trail swings L to meet Carter Dome Trail at 1.2 mi. from Carter Dome summit. Turn R to reach Zeta Pass in 0.2 mi.

SOUTHEAST APPROACH from Carter Notch Rd.

Bog Brook Trail, Wild River Trail, Rainbow Trail
12.0 mi. round trip, 3200-ft. elevation gain

TRAILHEAD (1810 ft.): Bog Brook Trail starts at a small, rough parking area on Carter Notch Rd. near its end, about 5.2 mi. from NH 16A in Jackson (the jct. is by Wentworth Hotel; road is paved until last 0.8 mi.)

This is a remote, little-used, but very scenic approach to Carter Dome. Brook crossings can be difficult in high water. From road, follow Bog Brook Trail slightly downhill to cross Wildcat Brook, a nameless brook, and Wildcat River within short distance. On far side, at 0.7 mi., bear R on Bog Brook Trail as Wildcat River Trail goes L. Ascend gradually and cross gravel log-

Carter Dome, Wildcat Mtn., and Carter Notch line the eastern side of Pinkham Notch.

ging road at 1.0 mi. (This provides approach from end of Carter Notch Rd. that avoids previous three brook crossings, but is at least 0.5 mi. longer.) Easy ascent continues N up valley through varied forests. Footing is wet in places. At about 1.8 mi. make first of four crossings of Bog Brook. Just after last crossing reach jct. with Wild River Trail at 2.8 mi./2417 ft. Turn R here and soon break out into beautiful birch glades. Re-enter conifers and reach jct. with Rainbow Trail at 3.5 mi./2590 ft. in Perkins Notch.

Turn L on Rainbow Trail and ascend gradually, then begin long, steady climb through white birch forest. Attain open summit knob of Rainbow Ridge at 5.0 mi./4274 ft. Views are excellent from this unheralded vantage point: S to great spread of southern and western White Mts., W to Wildcat Ridge and Mt. Washington, E to Wild River valley and Baldface Range, N to Carter Dome and Mt. Hight near at hand. From open area trail descends slightly to saddle, then climbs fairly steeply to 4600-ft. shoulder, with restricted view back down to knob. Route now climbs at moderate grade through open fir forest, then swings L for steeper pitch to summit of Carter Dome at 6.0 mi.

Loop Option

Descent can be made via Carter-Moriah Trail to Carter Notch, then back to Carter Notch Rd. via Wildcat River Trail and Bog Brook Trail (see Wildcat Mtn. chapter for details). This creates 11.5 mi. loop with great variety of scenery and much less hiker traffic than Nineteen-Mile Brook Trail approaches.

East Approach from Wild River Road

Wild River Trail, Black Angel Trail, Carter-Moriah Trail
8.0 mi. one way, 3700-ft. elevation gain

Trailhead (1150 ft.): Wild River Trail begins at end of USFS Wild River Rd. (FR 12), 5.7 mi. from NH/ME 113 in Evans Notch.

Backpackers and strong day hikers sometimes use this remote approach to climb Carter Dome from the beautiful Wild River valley. This route can be combined with other trails from Wild River (e.g. Rainbow Trail, Moriah Brook Trail, Shelburne Trail) and ridgecrest trails to create multi-day backpacks over Carter-Moriah Range. There are few views on Black Angel Trail route, but much fine forest walking.

From parking area and campground at end of road, follow Wild River Trail for easy 2.7 mi. cruise on old RR grade to Spider Bridge, where E end of Black Angel Trail enters on L. Cross bridge over Wild River and turn L, then in 0.1 mi. bear R on W leg of Black Angel Trail. From here it is over 5 mi. to summit of Carter Dome. Trail climbs gradually through open hardwoods for about 2 mi., then climbs more steeply up across broad E shoulder of Mt. Hight, crossing several branches of Spruce Brook. Higher up trail slabs through firs on S side of E ridge, then swings L for rough traverse below summit of Hight, passing partial views SE over valley. Trail bears SW and angles up to meet Carter-Moriah Trail at 7.6 mi./4600 ft. Turn L for gradual 0.4 mi. climb to summit of Carter Dome.

WINTER

The western approaches from NH 16 are used almost exclusively for winter ascents of Carter Dome. Certainly the easiest route to the summit is via the Carter Dome Trail, but that's provided the trail is already broken out. Grades are moderate all the way, but the long sidehill along the W slope of Mt. Hight can be difficult in crusty conditions. The route over Hight involves a section of steep, difficult snowshoeing and a crossing of the exposed and possibly icy summit, where crampons may be needed. The approach along the scrubby N ridge of Carter Dome becomes a scenic open ridge walk in winter, with the small trees buried in snow. Since AMC Carter Notch Hut operates on a year-round caretaker basis, you'll almost always find Nineteen-Mile Brook Trail broken out to Carter Notch. The steep climb out of the notch by way of the Carter-Moriah Trail makes for a difficult, but not impossible ascent of the peak. Crampons may be needed if hikers have glissaded the steep pitch above the Notch.

VIEW GUIDE

Carter Dome: From the various outlooks in the vicinity of the flat, scrubby summit, extensive views are obtained in most directions, though none are better than those directed across the Peabody River valley and Pinkham Notch toward Mt. Washington and the peaks of the Northern Presidential Range. "The most impressive part of the view is the tremendous panorama of the Mt. Washington Range, and in particular, the prospect into three of the great glacial ravines that lead toward the summit of the mountain. From no viewpoint can you gain a more comprehensive idea of the vast extent of the ravines," once wrote 19th-century author Rev. Julius Ward.

The glacial ravines Ward refers to—the Gulf of Slides, Tuckerman Ravine and Huntington Ravine—are best viewed from the main summit's N outlook, situated a short distance from the mountaintop cairn. More to the W, and just to the R of Mt. Washington, are seen (L–R) the craggy peaks of Jefferson, Adams and Madison, with the cirques of Jefferson Ravine and Madison Gulf in full view. From the same N outlook, looking N and NE, one sees the curving ridgeline of the Carter-Moriah range connecting the sharp, open summit of Mt. Hight with that of South and Middle Carter Mtns. Beyond them lies Mt. Moriah with its bare, rocky south-facing slope, while the peaks of the Mahoosuc Range extend onwards behind and to the NE of Moriah's summit. Shelburne Moriah is just to the L of Hight, and several 4000-footers in the Rangeley, Maine, area (e.g. Saddleback, Crockers, Sugarloaf, Spaulding, Abraham) can be spotted in the distance. The isolated pyramid of Mt. Blue is far to the NE. Meanwhile, the Androscoggin River valley and northern New Hampshire's lone city, Berlin, are unmistakably seen to the N; low, ledgy Pine Mtn. is seen closer in to the L. The low-spreading peaks of the Crescent Range and the higher peaks of the Kilkenny area (including the three peaks of Mt. Weeks, Mt. Cabot, The Bulge and The Horn) are seen to the NW, with many North Country ridges beyond.

Carter Dome's S view spot is decreasing in splendor with each growing season as the summit's trees are annually blocking out more and more of the horizon. To catch a glimpse of the many peaks lying to the S and SW, one must now climb to the top of a jumble of boulders 50 yards S of the summit cairn.

For those tall enough to see over the trees, the view S is quite impressive as wave after wave of blue ridges extend to the horizon, with many 4000-footers visible. Kearsarge North and Doublehead are to the SSE, with the Moats to the S. Looking more to the R, the view sweeps across the Sandwich Range peaks of Chocorua, Paugus, Passaconaway, Whiteface, and Tripyramid. Farther R are Kancamagus, Tecumseh and the Osceolas over Resolution and the Giant Stairs. Next to the R are majestic Carrigain and wide-spreading Hancock, seen over nearby Wildcat C. To the SW, beyond the swell of Mt. Isolation, is distant Moosilauke on the horizon. To the R of Moosilauke are Mts. Flume, Willey and Bond. In front of Bond are nearby Wildcat Ridge and the bare ridge above Glen Boulder, on the W side of Pinkham Notch. Lafayette and Lincoln peer over the ridge of Slide Peak, then the view swings around to massive Boott Spur, Washington and the Northern Presidentials to the W.

At one time decent views were also gained from an outlook just off the summit to the E. This is no longer the case, however, as the viewpoint is entirely grown up, denying visitors what was undoubtedly once a splendid vista into the Wild River valley.

Mt. Hight: The 360-degree panorama from this rocky peak takes in many of the peaks mentioned above, and then some. Its perspective on Carter Dome's eastern slope is particularly impressive in autumn when the mountain's birch-covered landscape is transformed into a sea of yellows and golds.

The view W from Hight's summit includes Mt. Washington and the Northern Peaks, with the curving auto road to Washington's top seen for nearly its entire eight-mile length. Several of the range's impressive glacial cirques are seen to great advantage.

To the NW, beyond the Crescent Range and Madison's Howker Ridge, are seen the Pliny and Pilot Range mountains, culminating in 4170-foot Mt. Cabot, the tallest mountain in New Hampshire N of the Presidentials.

To the N there's a good perspective on South and Middle Carter and rocky Mt. Moriah. Numerous peaks in New Hampshire's North Country and in western Maine are also visible. On the clearest days, Maine summits visible far to the NE include Sugarloaf and Spaulding, Abraham, Saddleback, and the Bigelows in the Rangeley area.

The view down into and across the broad Wild River valley to the E and SE is especially fine. No-Ketchum Pond and other bogs can be seen on the floor of the valley. Beyond are the peaks of the Evans Notch area, including Caribou Mtn., the Royces and Speckled Mtn. (almost due E), North and South Baldface to the SE, and Sable and Chandler a bit further S. Carter Dome's impressive bulk unfortunately blocks out any distant views to the S and SW.

NO. OF 4000-FOOTERS VISIBLE: 29 (from Carter Dome)

Middle and South Carter

MIDDLE CARTER

ELEVATION: 4610 ft./1405 m ORDER OF HEIGHT: 15
LOCATION: Carter Range, Township of Beans Purchase
USGS MAP: 7½′ Carter Dome

SOUTH CARTER

ELEVATION: 4430 ft./1350 ft. ORDER OF HEIGHT: 19
LOCATION: Carter Range, Township of Beans Purchase
USGS MAP: 7½′ Carter Dome

GEOGRAPHY

The high, massive ridge that forms the heart of the Carter Range—from the Moriah-Imp col on the N to Zeta Pass on the S—rises to a pair of 4000-footers and several lesser summits in its four-mile expanse. The summits along the crest include cliff-faced Imp Mtn. (3730 ft.), North Carter (4530 ft.), Mt. Lethe (4584 ft.), Middle Carter (4610 ft.) and South Carter (4430 ft.). Only the latter two peaks show enough lift to be "official" 4000-footers. The entire ridge is densely wooded, but ledgy outcrops N and S of Middle Carter provide excellent views. The summit of Middle Carter is narrow and scrubby, appearing as a small triangular peak jutting up from the ridge. South Carter is a symmetrical wooded peak rising to the N of Zeta Pass (called "North Notch" by early AMC trail-builder William G. Nowell), across which looms rocky Mt. Hight.

The Carter ridge makes a steep 800-ft. drop on the N slope of North Carter, a characteristic profile when seen from afar. The Imp Face (3165 ft.) is a western spur of North Carter featuring a sheer cliff with spectacular views above the deep ravine of Imp Brook. Cowboy Brook and branches of Nineteen-Mile Brook also drain the broad western slopes of the Carters into the Peabody River, which flows N along the W base of the ridge. The E side of the ridge is rugged and dramatic, presenting cirque-like headwalls and long valleys running out to the remote Wild River drainage. Four of these bowl-shaped basins can be seen. Two are drained by SW branches of Moriah Brook—one E of North Carter and the other E of Middle Carter. The twin cirques at the head of Cypress Brook are especially striking; one is between Middle and South Carter, the other is below Zeta Pass. This aspect of the range can be studied from viewpoints on the Baldface-Royce Range to the E. A long dividing ridge extends four miles E from Middle Carter, dividing the drainages of Moriah Brook and Cypress Brook.

NOMENCLATURE

The entire ridge from North Carter to Carter Dome was once known simply as "Mt. Carter," presumably named for Dr. Ezra Carter, a physician who explored the Whites in the 1800s looking for medicinal herbs and roots. The name "Carter's Mt." appeared as early as 1823. Arnold Guyot's 1860 map listed "Carter, S. Peak and N. Peak." In 1876 the AMC adopted the name "Carter Dome" for the highest and southernmost peak. William G. Nowell applied the names North, Middle and South Carter to the rest of the range, but in a different order than is used now. For many years today's Middle Carter was called South Carter, and what is now known as South Carter was dubbed Middle Carter. Not until the late 1950s was the order reversed to its more sensible present arrangement.

The Carter Range peaks, including Middle and North Carter, as seen from the southern ledges of Mt. Moriah.

HISTORICAL HIGHLIGHTS

First Ascent: Unknown.

1827: Hayes Copp establishes homestead in Peabody River valley at W base of Carter Range. In 1831 he marries Dolly Copp and they operate farm, inn and tourist stand for many years. In 1881 they agree to go their separate ways. Says Dolly, "Hayes is well enough. But fifty years is long enough for a woman to live with any man."

1852: First Glen House hotel built at western base of Carters. Famous hotel is rebuilt several times after fires; last building burns in 1967.

1876: Moses Sweetser's guidebook notes that the Carter Range "has been but partially explored," possibly by the Hitchcock geological survey.

1877: Charles Lowe and William Nowell build Nineteen-Mile Brook Trail; lower section is cut in 1894, replacing original access from Glen House.

1883: AMC group, including Eugene Cook, Charles Lowe and George Sargent, makes two-day trailless traverse of Carter Range from Gorham to Carter Notch.

1884: Under Nowell's direction, work begins on extending ridge trail northward from Carter Dome—today's Carter-Moriah Trail. Section from Mt. Hight to North Carter is completed in 1884, and that from Moriah to North Carter in 1885. Sweetser pronounces it a "magnificent mid-air promenade." Cost of building trail is $102. Imp Camp is also built in 1885.

1891–1903: Major logging railroad operation in Wild River valley on E side of Carters.

1906: Imp Shelter built on ridge near Imp Mtn.

ca. 1915: WMNF acquires 35,000 acres in Wild River valley. "Scout Trail" is built N-S along lower slopes of Mt. Moriah and Carters—trail persists into 1930s.
ca. 1925: USFS builds Carter Dome Trail up to Zeta Pass.
1929: Imp Trail built to Imp Face; Imp Trail loop soon completed.
1933: North Carter Trail built to connect Imp Trail with Carter-Moriah Trail.

TRAIL APPROACHES

WEST APPROACHES from NH 16

Middle and South Carter loop hike

Imp Trail, North Carter Trail, Carter-Moriah Trail, Carter Dome Trail, Nineteen-Mile Brook Trail, road walk on NH 16
12.4 mi. round trip, 3750-ft. elevation gain (subtract 1.6 miles if car spotted at Nineteen-Mile Brook trailhead)

Middle Carter only

Imp Trail, North Carter Trail, Carter-Moriah Trail
9.8 mi. round trip, 3600-ft. elevation gain

Middle and South Carter out and back

Imp Trail, North Carter Trail, Carter-Moriah Trail
12.4 mi. round trip, 4300-ft. elevation gain

South Carter only

Nineteen-Mile Brook Trail, Carter Dome Trail, Carter-Moriah Trail
9.2 mi. round trip, 2950-ft. elevation gain

South and Middle Carter out and back

Nineteen-Mile Brook Trail, Carter Dome Trail, Carter-Moriah Trail
11.8 mi. round trip, 3650-ft. elevation gain

TRAILHEAD (1270 ft.): Start at the N end of Imp Trail on the E side of NH 16, 5.4 mi. S of US 2 in Gorham.

Most peakbaggers climb Middle and South Carter via the loop from NH 16 to the W—a long day with plenty of elevation gain. The loop can be done in either direction, and as noted above out-and-back options are also possible. The description below follows the loop over both summits from N to S.

Starting on N leg of Imp Trail, climb gradually through hemlocks along

S side of Imp Brook. Pass cascade and cross brook at 0.8 mi./1610 ft. Climb steadily through hardwoods, level on 1900-ft. plateau, then begin rather steep ascent through conifers and birch with deep ravine to L. At 1.8 mi./2600 ft. bear R and wind upward to open ledges atop Imp Face cliff at 2.2 mi./3165 ft., with spectacular view of Presidentials to SW. From cliff, Imp Trail dips and passes vista over Imp Brook ravine, then contours roughly across slope. Gentle descent leads to jct. with North Carter Trail and S branch of Imp Trail at 3.1 mi./3270 ft. (S branch provides alternate 3.2 mi. approach to this point at moderate grades with no views. Trailhead is on NH 16, 0.3 mi. S of N branch.)

Turn L on North Carter Trail for steady climb through fir forest, reaching ridgecrest and Carter-Moriah Trail at 4.3 mi./4470 ft. From this jct., short, easy side trip L (N) along Carter-Moriah Trail to ledge on North Carter with view E into Wild River valley is highly recommended in clear weather; add 0.4 mi. for round trip with 100-ft. elevation gain. From jct., route to Middle and South Carter follows Carter-Moriah Trail S along high ridge. Hump over two ledgy knolls, then wind up to third knob, Mt. Lethe, with glimpse of Middle Carter ahead. Two more rocky bumps provide views E, W and S. Short climb to actual summit of Middle Carter leads past several outlooks from SW through N to NE. Ascend easily through high scrub to wooded summit, marked by sign, at 4.9 mi./4610 ft. Limited views E are available over trees.

Carter-Moriah Trail descends gradually to open area of ledge and scrub with fine view W to Presidentials and S to Wildcat, South Carter, Hight and Carter Dome. Going is nearly level along scrubby ridge with plank walkways and one short scramble to ledge with good view E to Baldface Range and S down ridge. After passing outlook on R, descend through woods to Middle/South Carter col at 5.8 mi./4190 ft. Climb up towards South Carter is occasionally steep, with one narrow look back at Middle Carter, then eases through beautiful boreal forest. Reach viewless summit of South Carter at 6.2 mi/4430 ft.

Continuing S, drop steeply to shoulder, then descend easily to Zeta Pass at 7.0 mi./3890 ft. (No camping within 1/4 mi.) Here joint Carter-Moriah/Carter Dome Trail continues ahead (S) to Mt. Hight and Carter Dome. (For strong hikers, out-and-back to Carter Dome from this point via Carter Dome Trail adds 2.4 mi. with 950-ft. elevation gain. Loop over Carter Dome and Mt. Hight via Carter Dome and Carter-Moriah Trails is 2.6 mi./1100 ft.) To descend to NH 16, turn R (W) on Carter Dome Trail. Moderate grades lead down N side of valley with glimpses up to Carter Dome. Descend switchbacks to brook crossing at 8.1 mi./2800 ft., recrossing at 8.4 mi. Reach Nineteen-Mile Brook Trail at 8.9 mi./2322 ft. Turn R for easy, rolling walk down along scenic stream, passing dam and pool at 9.6 mi. Reach trailhead for Nineteen-Mile Brook Trail at 10.8 mi./1487 ft. If no car spotted here, turn R for 1.6 mi. road walk, mostly downhill, to N trailhead for Imp Trail.

Other Approaches

Backpackers often approach the Carters via the Carter-Moriah Trail from S or N. For S approach see chapter on Carter Dome. The N approach comes up from the 3127-ft. col between Mt. Moriah and Imp Mtn. (For routes to col, see Mt. Moriah chapter.) Heading S, Carter-Moriah Trail meanders across ledges with views of Moriah Brook area. In 0.7 mi. side trail R leads 0.2 mi. to Imp Shelter and Campsite. Main trail skirts E side of Imp Mtn. and traverses flat shoulder of North Carter. At 1.8 mi. from col begin steep climb with ledgy scrambles and occasional views N. Reach summit of North Carter at 2.3 mi/4530 ft. and E outlook 0.1 mi. beyond. Elevation gain from col is 1400 ft. From viewpoint Middle Carter is 0.8 mi. S along Carter-Moriah Trail, as described above.

WINTER

If the snow is deep and unbroken, the trek over the Carters is a long slog. The loop route over the summits is good for snowshoeing with just an occasional ledgy scramble. (S branch of Imp Trail is easier snowshoeing than N branch, which has some sidehilling.) The ledgy knolls N of Middle Carter are exposed to weather and may be icy in places. With deep snow, views are improved along the scrubby ridgecrest on either side of Middle Carter, but even in the snowiest winters South Carter remains viewless.

VIEW GUIDE

Imp Face: The clifftop ledges open a huge vista SW across the Peabody River valley to Mt. Washington and an array of the Northern Presidentials, including a deep look into the Great Gulf. To the S is Pinkham Notch with Wildcat on the L. The upper Carter Range looms close by on the SE. The distant NW view takes in the Pliny and Pilot Ranges. The precipitous drop into Imp Brook ravine in front creates a dramatic effect.

North Carter Viewpoint: This flat SE-facing ledge has a magnificent outlook over the broad, remote valleys of Moriah Brook and Wild River, with the Baldface-Royce range and southern Maine lowlands to the E; occasionally the Atlantic Ocean is visible. The Moriahs and distant Maine mountains can be seen to the N, Caribou Mtn. to the ENE, and Speckled Mtn. to the ESE. Kearsarge North can be spotted to the S, and to the SSW are the distant Tripyramids, Mt. Tecumseh, and Mt. Osceola.

Middle Carter Viewpoints: The best views from Middle Carter are found on several ledges along the Carter-Moriah Trail just N of the summit. Taken together, these offer views from SSW around to ESE; some of the panorama can be seen only if you stand. The best sitting perch is the lower of these ledges, on the E side, with a view from NW through NE. The views of the Northern Presidentials are especially good from Middle Carter.

To the SSW is the distant Sandwich Range over the nearer summit of Wildcat A: Mts. Passaconaway and Whiteface on the L, the Sleepers over Wildcat A, and the Tripyramids to the R. The Lower Wildcats D and E are to the right of A, with Mt. Kancamagus above them and ski trails visible on their slopes. Mt. Resolution and the Giant Stairs are between Wildcats A and D. To the R of Kancamagus are Mt. Tecumseh; the Osceolas, with a deep gap between them; the dominant peak of Mt. Carrigain; and the long ridge of the Hancocks. Mt. Nancy is directly under Carrigain. To the R of the Wildcat ski trails, under Carrigain and Hancock, is the upper Rocky Branch Ridge with Mt. Isolation behind.

To the SW the great rocky sprawl of Mt. Washington dominates. On the L of the summit are the bare Glen Boulder Ridge, Slide Peak, the Gulf of Slides, Boott Spur, Tuckerman Ravine and the shallow ravine of Raymond Cataract. The craggy headwall of Huntington Ravine is below the summit.

To the R of and behind Washington is Mt. Clay, at the head of the Great Gulf. Farther R, to the W, is the great trio of pyramidal Northern Presidentials: Jefferson, Adams and Madison. You look into the lower Great Gulf, which curves to the L below Jefferson. The headwall of Jefferson Ravine is between Jefferson and Adams, and part of Madison Gulf is below Adams. Madison's Howker Ridge runs out to the R, with Vermont's Burke and Umpire Mtn. beyond.

To the NW is the long ridgeline of the Pliny and Pilot Ranges—L to R, Starr King, Waumbek, the three rounded knobs of Weeks, Cabot, The Bulge, The Horn, and Unknown Pond Ridge. Jay Peak in Vermont is in the distance to the L of Starr King. The Crescent Range is arrayed in front below the Pliny-Pilot ridge. Over the R end of the Crescents are the Percy Peaks and other mountains in the Nash Stream region. The view due N is blocked by the knobs just N of Middle Carter. To the NNE is the ledgy mass of Mt. Moriah, with the higher Mahoosucs, including Old Speck and Goose Eye, beyond to the L. Baldpate Mtn. is behind and to the R of Goose Eye. On clear days the 4000-footers of the Rangeley, Maine region can be picked out to the R of the Mahoosucs and Baldpate, including Saddleback, Sugarloaf, Crocker and Abraham. The ledgy hump of Shelburne Moriah rises over Mt. Moriah's ridgecrest, with the little-known peaks E of the Mahoosucs beyond. Farther R, over a prominent rock knob on Moriah's SE ridge, is the pyramidal Mt. Blue on the horizon.

More to the R, looking from NE through E, the view takes in Howe Peak, Caribou Mtn., Haystack Mtn., the Royces, the lower Wild River valley, Mt. Meader and Eagle Crag.

NO. OF 4000-FOOTERS VISIBLE: from Middle Carter, 22; from South Carter: 19 (theoretical, through the trees).

Mount Moriah

ELEVATION: 4049 ft./1234 m   ORDER OF HEIGHT: 41
LOCATION: Carter-Moriah Range, Town of Shelburne, Township of Beans Purchase
USGS MAPS: 7½′ Carter Dome, 7½′ Wild River

GEOGRAPHY

Ledgy Mt. Moriah is the northeastern outpost of the White Mountain high peaks, towering 3200 ft. above the town of Gorham at the N end of the Carter-Moriah Range. Major rivers enclose the mountain on three sides—the Peabody to the W, the Androscoggin to the N, and the Wild to the E. Moriah is a sprawling mass of ledgy ridges with a small, knobby rock peak in the center. Its proximity to town made it a popular destination—complete with bridle path and log shelter at the summit—as early as the mid-1800s. No horse has set foot on Moriah's summit in many years, but today hikers will find scenic trail approaches from several directions, with abundant views from open ledges and a 360-degree panorama at the top.

From the summit one ridge descends NW between Stony Brook and Pea Brook towards Gorham, passing over the low, rocky spur of Mt. Surprise (2194 ft.); this provides the route for the N end of Carter-Moriah Trail. Another ridge extends NE over Middle Moriah Mtn. (3755 ft.) and then E to the beautiful, ledgy Shelburne Moriah Mtn. (3735 ft.). This ridge is traversed by the Kenduskeag Trail. On the E the three Moriah summits enclose the long, trailless valley of Bull Brook, draining into the remote Wild River.

The main ridgecrest of the range runs S, then SW from Mt. Moriah, descending 900 ft. to its col with Imp Mtn. and the Carters. On the lower part of this ridge is a line of S-facing cliffs overlooking the upper valley of the long, twisting Moriah Brook, another tributary of Wild River; these ledges are traversed by the Carter-Moriah Trail. A remarkable feature of Mt. Moriah is the striking patches of bare rock on its long SE ridge, rising above Moriah Brook. This area was seared by a great forest fire in the 1890s; though much of the basin is revegetated with beautiful stands of paper birch, large areas of open rock persist. A bare rock peak (3550 ft.) crowns the upper part of this broad SE ridge.

NOMENCLATURE

It's believed that an early settler in the Androscoggin valley named Mt. Moriah after the hill of the same name in Jerusalem. Moriah in Hebrew means "provided by Jehovah." The name of the White Mountain Moriah appeared on Philip Carrigain's 1816 map of New Hampshire, and later on George P. Bond's 1853 map of the White Mountains. Arnold Guyot spelled it "Mori-

Looking south towards the Carter Range from the summit of Mount Moriah.

jah" on his 1860 map. Over time the name was extended to other local features such as Middle Moriah and Shelburne Moriah Mtns., Moriah Brook and Moriah Gorge.

HISTORICAL HIGHLIGHTS

First Ascent: Unknown

1805: Stephen Messer establishes first homestead in Gorham, then part of Shelburne.

1852: Atlantic and St. Lawrence Railroad completed to nearby town of Gorham, spurring interest in tourism in region.

1854–1855: Bridle path built from Gorham to summit by John Hitchcock, proprietor of the Alpine House in Gorham. Log house, 13 × 16 feet, is built at top. Guests at Alpine House can rent ponies for ascent of mountain. Interest declines and path and house fall into disuse when Carriage Road opens on nearby Mt. Washington in 1861.

1859: Thomas Starr King rhapsodizes about the beauty of Mt. Surprise and Mt. Moriah in his classic *The White Hills: Their Legends, Landscape and Poetry*.

1860s: Samuel Eastman's guidebook recommends ascent of Mt. Surprise for ease of access and superb views, and touts Moriah as "a very charming excursion for those who care to undergo the fatigue . . . suddenly you are on the desolate and jagged peak. What a view! The whole region seems thrown into wildest confusion." Height of Moriah is given as 4700 ft.

1879: Old bridle path to summit cleared by Prof. E. T. Quimby, who occupies peak as station of U.S. Coast and Geodetic Survey. Moses Sweetser's guidebook makes note of large boulder ¾ mile below summit, dubbed "Quimby's Pillow."

1885: Carter-Moriah Trail built from Moriah S to North Carter under direction of AMC's William G. Nowell.

1890s: Heavy logging via railroad in Wild River, Bull Brook, and Moriah Brook valleys to E. Fire burns over much of Moriah Brook valley and SE ridge of Moriah.

1899: Irving E. Vernon and Warren W. Hart build section of Carter-Moriah Trail from Gorham to Mt. Surprise; from there to Mt. Moriah old bridle path is used.

ca. 1915: WMNF acquires 35,000 acres in Wild River valley to E. Trail built up Moriah Brook valley to Moriah-Imp col, following old logging RR in lower part; this is precursor to present Moriah Brook Trail. Cross trail runs N-S along lower E slopes of Moriah and Carters, connecting Bull, Moriah and Cypress Brooks. This is dubbed the "Scout Trail" and maintained into the 1930s.

1920s: Trail built from Pinkham Notch Rd. to Moriah-Imp col, is included under name of Moriah Brook Trail. AMC guidebooks describe arduous bushwhack route from Shelburne Moriah to Mt. Moriah.

mid-1930s: Kenduskeag Trail opened from Wild River across Shelburne Moriah and Middle Moriah to Mt. Moriah, and on to Pinkham Notch Rd. (W section of this trail abandoned mid-1940s; maintenance on E end over Howe Peak suspended mid-1950s.) Rattle River Trail opened from Androscoggin valley to col between Shelburne Moriah and Middle Moriah.

1960: W half of Moriah Brook Trail has been renamed Stony Brook Trail.

1979: Section of Carter-Moriah Trail N of Moriah-Imp col relocated to run along top of S cliffs.

TRAIL APPROACHES

Northwest Approach from Gorham

Carter-Moriah Trail
9.0 mi. round trip, 3400-ft. elevation gain

Trailhead (800 ft.): From eastern jct. of US 2 and NH 16 in Gorham, drive 0.5 mi. E on US 2, turn R on Bangor Rd. and follow it 0.5 mi. to parking on L side at its end.

Carter-Moriah Trail provides long, steady approach with views in middle section from Mt. Surprise and ledges above. From trailhead, trail climbs steadily past logged areas and up through hardwood forest. At 2.0 mi. / 2190 ft., near minor summit of Mt. Surprise, ledges offer good views R (SW) to Presidentials. By summit there is small flume beside trail. Beyond slight dip, ascent is gradual, then steeper across series of open ledges with good views

W and N, and blueberries in season. From here trail makes meandering climb up Moriah's NW ridge through deep fir woods, with many little ups and downs and several disheartening false summits. At 4.2 mi./3700 ft., in fairly level section, summit is in view ahead. Final climb, fairly steep, leads to summit side path on R at 4.5 mi.; at this jct. is outlook on L with view N. Side path leads to uplifted rock knob that is actual summit of mountain, with panoramic views.

Southwest Approach from NH 16

Stony Brook Trail, Carter-Moriah Trail
10.0 mi. round trip, 3150-ft. elevation gain

Trailhead (930 ft.): From eastern jct. of US 2 and NH 16 in Gorham, drive 1.8 mi. S on 16 to parking area on L, just S of bridge over Peabody River.

This is a highly scenic approach up an attractive brook valley and across many open ledges on the ridge. From parking area, Stony Brook Trail crosses bridge over brook and ascends gently along its E side. Drop R to cross brook at 1.0 mi. and turn L onto old logging road for long, gradual climb up valley. Dip L to recross Stony Brook at 2.3 mi./1850 ft. Climb is now steadier up into birch and conifers, with NW ridge of Moriah visible off to L. Bear R at 3.4 mi., then quickly L for steeper pitch to Moriah-Imp col and jct. with Carter-Moriah Trail at 3.6 mi./3127 ft.

Turn L on Carter-Moriah Trail (part of Appalachian Trail), quickly passing jct. R with Moriah Brook Trail, and climb to ledge with view R into upper Moriah Brook valley and second viewpoint looking ahead to upper cliffs. Climb moderately through stunted woods to several tiers of ledge atop cliffs at 4.1 mi./3500 ft. Perches to R offer stunning views SE of Moriah Brook valley enclosed by bare spur ridge of Moriah, with Meader-Baldface ridge beyond; S to Carter Range; SW to Presidentials; and NW to Pliny/Pilot Ranges. Beyond cliffs grade is easier through pretty ridgetop firs, with occasional ledges opening views N to Mahoosucs and other Maine mountains. Cross open rocky knob and reach jct. with Kenduskeag Trail at 5.0 mi./4000 ft. Turn L with Carter-Moriah Trail for short, fairly difficult scramble up steep ledge. Side trail to summit of Moriah is short distance beyond on L.

Southeast Approach from Wild River Rd.

Wild River Trail, Moriah Brook Trail, Carter-Moriah Trail
14.4 mi. round trip, 2900-ft. elevation gain

Trailhead (1150 ft.): From NH/ME 113 N of Evans Notch and 3.1 mi. S of US 2, follow USFS gravel Wild River Rd. (FR 12) 5.7 mi. SW along Wild River to parking area at end on L, just before Wild River Campground.

Strong hikers will enjoy this long, rewarding route that combines an approach up the secluded, beautiful Moriah Brook valley, rich in hardwood and birch forest, with views from the S cliffs along the ridge. From parking area an easy 0.3 mi. on Wild River Trail leads to jct. with Moriah Brook Trail. Turn R here and cross Wild River on suspension footbridge, then bear L upstream along W side of river. At 0.7 mi. bear R on Moriah Brook Trail as Highwater Trail stays L. Follow old logging RR grade through birch and hardwood. At 1.7 mi. / 1521 ft. cross Moriah Brook at head of Moriah Gorge, scenic rocky chasm; difficult in high water. Easy RR grade walking through hardwoods leads to second crossing at 3.1 mi. / 1750 ft. Now on N bank of brook, pass series of attractive cascades and pools. Cross tributary at 3.5 mi. / 1950 ft. and continue up past more cascades into lovely white birch forest. Grades continue easy to moderate with four more crossings of dwindling brook, last at 5.3 mi., high in winding upper valley. Continue through birches, with S cliffs of Moriah looming ahead, and make short, steep climb to Moriah-Imp col and Carter-Moriah Trail at 5.8 mi. / 3127 ft. Turn R to follow Carter-Moriah Trail to summit, as described above.

NORTH APPROACH from US 2

Rattle River Trail, Kenduskeag Trail, Carter-Moriah Trail
11.4 mi. round trip, 3400-ft. elevation gain

TRAILHEAD (760 ft.): Parking area for Rattle River Trail (part of Appalachian Trail) is on S side of US 2, 3.5 mi. E of its eastern jct. with NH 16 in Gorham.

This is a little-used, wooded approach, most often traversed as part of a backpacking route. From parking area Rattle River Trail runs at easy grades to Rattle River Shelter at 1.7 mi. / 1250 ft., then crosses Rattle River (difficult in high water) and a tributary and climbs moderately. Recross river at 3.2 mi. / 2000 ft. and ascend steeply up head of valley to jct. with Kenduskeag Trail at 4.3 mi. / 3300 ft. (To L, or E, it is 1.3 mi. / 650 ft. climb to open, ledgy summit of Shelburne Moriah Mtn., with excellent views from ledges along way.) Turn R on Kenduskeag Trail and climb along S side of Middle Moriah Mtn. Descend slightly, then climb steeply past view towards Shelburne Moriah to meet Carter-Moriah Trail just below summit of Mt. Moriah at 5.7 mi. / 4000 ft. Turn R for short, steep scramble, then L on side path to summit ledge.

WINTER

Choose from two approaches—Carter-Moriah Trail from NW or Stony Brook Trail / Carter-Moriah Trail from SW. Both have plowed parking, moderate grades good for snowshoeing, and fine views from snowy ledges. In crusty or icy conditions good snowshoe crampons or boot crampons are required for the ledges, especially those atop the S cliffs. On the SW approach the ledge scramble just below the summit can be a challenge. The ledgy areas and summit knob are fully exposed to the wintry elements. The views from Moriah's ledges are especially dramatic in winter.

VIEW GUIDE

The small rock knob at the summit provides a good panorama of mountains around the horizon. To the N and NNE, on the L of nearby Middle Moriah, are the sprawling ridges of the Mahoosuc Range, with Old Speck the highest and most distant. Between Middle Moriah and the ledge-dotted Shelburne Moriah to its R is the trailless range to the E of the Mahoosucs. On clear days some of the 4000-footers in the Rangeley, Maine region stand out. To the R of Shelburne Moriah, beyond its ledgy spurs, are many distant hills in western Maine. Farther R, to the E and ESE, are Caribou Mtn., the Royces, and Speckled Mtn. (between the Royces) around Evans Notch. To the SSE and S, beyond a nearby shoulder of Moriah, are (L to R) the bare cones of the Baldfaces, Sable and Chandler, Kearsarge North, Doublehead, and the low ridge of Black Mtn. The long, flat ridge of Maine's Pleasant Mtn. is to the L of the Baldfaces. The Moats are beyond Black Mtn. and farther still is Mt. Shaw in the Ossipee Range. Most of the Wild River valley itself is obscured by the broad SE spread of Moriah; this area is better seen from the ledges atop the S cliffs.

Just W of S are the high, wooded peaks of the Carter Range, including Mt. Hight, Carter Dome, Middle Carter and North Carter, with the lower ridges of Imp Mtn. in front of North Carter. To the SW is an impressive spread of the barren Presidentials; L to R are Mts. Washington, Clay, Jefferson, Adams and Madison. Under Clay and Jefferson you can peer into the depths of the Great Gulf. The great walls of the Carters and the Presidentials block out any views of the southern and western Whites, giving Moriah the lowest count of 4000-footers visible among the 48 high peaks. On clear days, Vermont's Mt. Mansfield can also be seen in the distance to the R of Madison.

To the NW, beyond the low, ledgy Pine Mtn. and the sweeping Crescent Range, is the long chain of peaks in the Pliny and Pilot Ranges. (From the main summit ledge, the view in this direction is a stand-up, over the trees.) Just W of N, down in the Androscoggin River valley, is the town of Gorham, at the base of the mountain, with the Percy Peaks and other mountains in the Nash Stream region in the distance. Farther up the valley is Berlin with its smoke-puffing mills. The towns are bordered on the R by Mt. Hayes and other low summits at the SW end of the Mahoosuc Range.

NO. OF 4000-FOOTERS VISIBLE: 8

Wildcat Mountain (A Peak) and Wildcat D

WILDCAT MOUNTAIN (A PEAK)

ELEVATION: 4422 ft./1348 m ORDER OF HEIGHT: 20
LOCATION: Wildcat Ridge, Township of Beans Purchase, Town of Jackson
USGS MAPS: 7½′ Carter Dome, 7½′ Jackson, 7½′ Stairs Mtn.

WILDCAT D

ELEVATION: 4062 ft./1238 m ORDER OF HEIGHT: 37
LOCATION: Wildcat Ridge, Township of Beans Purchase, Town of Jackson
USGS MAPS: 7½′ Carter Dome, 7½′ Jackson, 7½′ Stairs Mtn.

GEOGRAPHY

Wildcat Ridge is a rugged mini-range extending about five miles from Pinkham Notch on the west to Carter Notch on the east. It bears a number of small peaks along its crest, five of which are lettered from "A" to "E", in order from east to west. Only two of these summits—D Peak and A Peak (the highest)—qualify for the 4000-footer list. D Peak replaced E Peak on the list only in the late 1980s, when Bradford Washburn's precise map of the Presidential Range established definitive elevations for the summits and showed D to be 16 ft. higher than E. The tough Wildcat Ridge Trail, with very steep climbing at either end, crosses all five peaks, with excellent views of Mt. Washington and Carter Notch from various ledges along the way.

Wildcat is renowned as a classic New England skiing mecca, with a skiing history dating back to the 1930s and a major ski area on its NW slopes. A gondola lift runs in both winter and summer/fall to the col between E Peak and D Peak.

At its east end the ridge rises very steeply out of Pinkham Notch, across from Mt. Washington and above the watery sliver of Lost Pond. (This great gap in the mountains is the divide between the Ellis River drainage on the south and the Peabody River drainage to the north.) Rough, ledgy terrain, with stunning views of the east side of Mt. Washington, swells up from the notch to wooded, viewless Wildcat E (4046 ft.). A shallow col separates E Peak from Wildcat D (4062 ft.), which sports an observation platform on top offering wide views to hikers and gondola-riding tourists. From here the ridge drops to deep Wildcat Col (3775 ft.), then rises to Wildcat C (4298 ft.), which offers a partial view east. Here the crest dips to another col and swings north over Wildcat B (4330 ft.) and up to the highest summit, Wildcat A (4422 ft.), where a ledge grants an excellent eastern outlook.

On its east side, A Peak drops off precipitously into spectacular Carter Notch, which harbors the two tiny Carter Ponds just S of its 3388-ft. height-of-land. This craggy gap, with its opposite wall formed by massive Carter Dome, shows a classic glacier-carved U-shape when viewed from afar. Nineteen-Mile Brook flows north from the notch, while Wildcat River drains south from the pass and the ponds. Over time a wild tumult of boulders has fallen from the cliffs of both Wildcat and Carter Dome, forming a rock barrier known as The Rampart on the floor of the notch a short distance S of the ponds and the AMC Carter Notch Hut.

A spur ridge runs north from A Peak to trailless Little Wildcat Mtn. (3350 ft.), forming the west side of the valley of Nineteen-Mile Brook. Ridges also extend south from C Peak and E Peak, enclosing the deep valley of Wildcat Brook. The upper part of this basin was once known as "The Hopper." At the south end of the ridge off E Peak is Hall's Ledge (2500 ft.), a spot once famous for its view of Mt. Washington but now largely overgrown, though still accessible by trail.

Two waterfalls are found along the western base of Wildcat Ridge—the famous Glen Ellis Falls and lesser-known Thompson Falls. Both are accessed by short trails.

NOMENCLATURE

On Jeremy Belknap's 1791 map this ridge was named East Mountain, as it is east of Pinkham Notch. For a time it was also called Mt. Hight, though the origin of the latter name is uncertain. Some accounts maintained that Hight was an early settler who accompanied Dr. Ezra Carter (for whom Carter Notch and the Carter Range were named) on his White Mountain explorations in search of medicinal plants in the early 1800s. Moses Sweetser's guidebook reported that Hight and Carter were two hunters who became lost around Carter Notch. Supposedly Hight climbed the mountain to the W (today's Wildcat) and Carter the peak to the E (now called Carter Dome). In any case, the "Wildcat" name was applied to the mountain in 1860 on geographer Arnold Guyot's map and it stuck. The name "Hight" was moved to the northern spur peak of Carter Dome. For some years the twin knobs of Wildcat E and Wildcat D were referred to as "The Wild Kittens."

HISTORICAL HIGHLIGHTS

First Ascent: Unknown

1774: A Captain Evans starts building first road through Pinkham Notch.

1852: First Glen House is built at NW base of Little Wildcat. Over years it gains renown as one of classic hotels in White Mountains. It is rebuilt several times after fires; last building burns in 1967.

1853: Famed intellectual Thomas Wentworth Higginson, an active mountain explorer, visits Carter Notch; meets local woodsman Bill Perkins, who recounts winter ascent of Wildcat on snowshoes. In *Forest and Crag*, Laura and Guy Waterman note that if true, this is first recorded winter ascent of 4000-ft. mountain in Northeast. Carter Ponds are called "Lakes of the Winds." Higginson's visit is described in article in *Putnam's Magazine*.

mid-1800s: Sometime during his extensive explorations in the White Mtns., geographer Arnold Guyot probably climbs Wildcat. His 1860 map is the first to use the name "Wildcat Mt.," giving it elevation of 4350 ft.

1876: Moses Sweetser's guidebook notes that clearing has been made high on west side of Wildcat with "best view attainable of Mt. Washington and the great ravines on the E." Viewspot is reached by good 1½-mi. path from Glen House.

1876–1877: Path from Jackson to Carter Notch is built by Jonathan G. Davis. First crude shelter is soon built in notch, then rebuilt in 1893.

1877: Charles E. Lowe cuts Nineteen-Mile Brook Trail for AMC. Lower part of trail built in 1894, replacing access from Glen House.

1883: Eugene B. Cook, Marian M. Pychowska and four other AMC members bushwhack up Wildcat from Carter Notch. They find viewpoint overlooking Carter Notch and another ledge (probably on C Peak) with view to Washington and western Whites. After making detailed view notes, they descend directly to Jackson-Carter Notch path. Trip is recounted in Dec. 1883 *Appalachia*.

1901: Trail is cut from Carter Notch to main summit (A Peak) by AMC's Louis F. Cutter. Also, platform is erected to provide view east to Mt. Washington.

1903: Fire burns Wild River valley, Carter Dome, and area south of Carter Notch.

1903: Group from AMC Snow-Shoe Section makes winter ascent of Wildcat A. In 1904 E Peak is snowshoed, and both peaks are traversed in winter of 1905.

1904: AMC builds small log cabin in Carter Notch.

1914: Stone hut, still in use today as part of Carter Notch Hut, is constructed by AMC in notch.

1919: Wildcat Ridge Trail is built by AMC, connecting Pinkham Notch with Wildcat A; replaces very obscure footway described in 1916 AMC guide. Path is laid out by Charles Blood, Paul Jenks and Nathaniel Goodrich. Blood observes that "considering its length, the route is much harder than would be expected."

1920: AMC builds first log cabins at Pinkham Notch Camp, opposite west base of Wildcat. The legendary Joe Dodge arrives in 1922 and expands camp over succeeding years.

1921: Wildcat River Trail built to replace original Jackson-Carter Notch path.

1924: Lost Pond Trail opened.

1920s: AMC guides describe bushwhack route up south ridge of E Peak, passing over a 3655-ft. "F Peak" en route.

Early 1930s: Trail built up valley of Wildcat Brook to Wildcat E, named Wildcat Brook Trail. Trail is abandoned in mid-1950s.

1933–1934: Several ski trails built by CCC on NW slope of Wildcat. Katzensteig Ski Trail extends 1⅓ mi. from behind Glen House to summit of Little Wildcat. Wildcat E Ski Trail runs from NH 16 to top of Wildcat Ridge, with 2000-ft. elevation gain in 1½ mi.; rated for experts only with maximum grade of 33 degrees. Wildcat Col and Hopper Trails traverse lower slopes. Wildcat High Country Cabin, just over crest of ridge from top of Wildcat E Ski Trail, is built for day use by skiers, offering wood stove and benches.

1958: Wildcat Ski Area opens in January with first gondola lift in the country.

1972: Wildcat Valley Ski Trail is cut by Jackson Ski Touring Foundation, leading from top of gondola between E and D Peaks south to Jackson. In upper part trail traverses south ridge of E Peak, somewhat close to route of former Wildcat Brook Trail.

TRAIL APPROACHES

The rugged Wildcat Ridge Trail, a link in the Appalachian Trail, provides the only hiking trail access to the Wildcat peaks. Approaches can be made from west, north, and south. A traverse combining the west and north approaches, both from NH 16, can be made with a car spot. The section climbing up the ridge from Pinkham Notch is very steep, with several ledge scrambles and traverses that can be dangerous if wet or icy. No matter what route you choose, you will sleep well after hiking the Wildcats. For those disinclined to negotiating steep trails, the ski trails of Wildcat offer an attractive option.

WEST APPROACH from NH 16 in Pinkham Notch

Wildcat D only

Wildcat Ridge Trail
4.4 mi. round trip, 2450-ft. elevation gain

Wildcat D and Wildcat Mtn. (A Peak), out-and-back

Wildcat Ridge Trail
8.4 mi. round trip, 3850-ft. elevation gain

Wildcat D and Wildcat Mtn. (A Peak), point-to-point with car spot and descent to NH 16 via north approach

Wildcat Ridge Trail; Nineteen-Mile Brook Trail
8.5 mi. traverse, 3150-ft. elevation gain (For Optional Approach via Lost Pond Trail, add 1.6 mi. round trip and 200 ft. to above totals.)

TRAILHEAD (1960 ft.): Wildcat Ridge Trail starts on east side of NH 16 opposite parking area for Glen Ellis Falls (where hikers should park), 0.7 mi. south of AMC Pinkham Notch Camp.

Cross highway to trail sign and immediately cross Ellis River, which can be very difficult in high water. (Note: This crossing can be avoided by starting hike at AMC Pinkham Notch Camp, on west side of NH 16 at height-of-land; ample parking; elevation 2030 ft. Cross highway to sign for Lost Pond Trail and cross infant Ellis River on bridge. Follow Lost Pond Trail S along river, then climb easily to Lost Pond at 0.5 mi. Trail runs along east shore with fine views across water to Mt. Washington, then passes through area of large boulders and descends to Wildcat Ridge Trail at 0.9 mi. This point is 0.1 mi. from start of Wildcat Ridge Trail.)

From jct. with Lost Pond Trail at 0.1 mi., Wildcat Ridge Trail quickly begins exceptionally steep, rugged climb up W end of ridge. In first 0.5 mi. you cross two open ledges with good views across Pinkham Notch to east side of Mt. Washington. Above second ledge, trail continues steeply a short way, then grade is easier along ridge to another ledge with good view south down Ellis River valley at 0.9 mi./3100 ft. Several minor ups and downs are followed by rocky, winding climb to very steep, windswept ledge area at 1.5 mi./3800 ft. Here is spectacular view east to glacial cirques on Washington, plus view S to Moats, Sandwich Range and other peaks.

Grade eases considerably beyond here. Trail dips through three small cols, then one last climb leads to densely wooded summit of Wildcat E, a former 4000-footer, at 1.9 mi./4046 ft. Descend to col and top of gondola station at 2.1 mi./3971 ft., then make short, steep climb to summit of Wildcat D at 2.2 mi./4062 ft. Observation platform provides panoramic views. (*AMC White Mountain Guide* notes that easiest descent via ski trails is 2.6 mi. from top of gondola, following trails on N side of area. Base of ski area is on NH 16 about one mile N of Pinkham Notch Camp.)

Continuing along ridge, trail makes fairly steep descent to Wildcat Col at 2.5 mi./3775 ft. Climb briefly to second, small col, then tackle steep, rough climb, with occasional breathers on level terraces, to Wildcat C, reached at 3.3 mi./4298 ft. Here there is partial view east towards Baldfaces. Descend to narrow 4150-ft. col, swing to N and traverse level shoulder, then hop up to Wildcat B (4330 ft.). Short descent leads to final col on ridge (4270 ft.), then make moderate ascent to summit of Wildcat A at 4.2 mi./4422 ft. Actual high point is rock just to R of trail; short spur path leads R to ledge with terrific view down into Carter Notch and across to Carter Range. For out-and-back option, retrace steps; for point-to-point traverse, descend steeply 0.7 mi. on Wildcat Ridge Trail to height-of-land in Carter Notch, then turn L on Nineteen-Mile Brook Trail for 3.6 mi. descent to NH 16.

North Approach from NH 16

Wildcat Mtn. (A Peak) only

Nineteen-Mile Brook Trail, Wildcat Ridge Trail
8.6 mi. round trip, 2950-ft. elevation gain

Wildcat Mtn. (A Peak) and Wildcat D, out-and-back

Nineteen-Mile Brook Trail, Wildcat Ridge Trail
12.6 mi. round trip, 4450-ft. elevation gain

Wildcat Mtn. (A Peak) and Wildcat D point-to-point with car spot and descent to NH 16 via west approach

Nineteen-Mile Brook Trail, Wildcat Ridge Trail
8.5 mi. traverse, 3650-ft. elevation gain

TRAILHEAD (1487 ft.): This route starts at parking area for Nineteen-Mile Brook Trail, on east side of NH 16, 1 mi. N of Mt. Washington Auto Road and 2.3 mi. S of entrance to Dolly Copp Campground.

Nineteen-Mile Brook Trail provides scenic brookside approach to Carter Notch. From parking area, trail follows old road at easy grades through hemlocks, then hardwoods, following Nineteen-Mile Brook (on R). At about 1 mi. traverse rough spot along bank (tricky if icy). At 1.2 mi. pass small dam and pool in brook. Continue rolling, easy ascent through yellow birches to jct. L with Carter Dome Trail at 1.9 mi./2322 ft. Continue ahead on Nineteen-Mile Brook Trail, crossing two tributaries on footbridges and traversing more birch forest. Grade steepens through fir woods after small brook crossing at 3.1 mi. Stiff climb leads to height-of-land in Carter Notch at 3.6 mi./3388 ft. (Carter Notch Hut is 0.2 mi. farther S and 100 ft. below via Nineteen-Mile Brook Trail.)

Turn R here on Wildcat Ridge Trail for steep ascent up side of Wildcat A via two long switchbacks (NW, then south), with many rock steps. About halfway up, trail crosses track of recent slide—use caution, dangerous if icy. Reach summit at 4.3 mi./4422 ft.; East view is on short side path L. For shorter out-and-back option, retrace steps. For Wildcat D, continue S, then W on Wildcat Ridge Trail.

SOUTH APPROACH from Carter Notch Rd. in Jackson.

Wildcat Mtn. (A Peak) only

Bog Brook Trail, Wildcat River Trail, Nineteen-Mile Brook Trail, Wildcat Ridge Trail
10.4 mi. round trip, 2750-ft. elevation gain

Wildcat Mtn. (A Peak) and Wildcat D, out-and-back

Bog Brook Trail, Wildcat River Trail, Nineteen-Mile Brook Trail, Wildcat Ridge Trail
14.4 mi. round trip, 4250-ft. elevation gain

TRAILHEAD (1810 ft.): This route starts at small parking area for Bog Brook Trail on Carter Notch Rd., about 5.2 mi. up from its start on NH 16A in Jackson (jct. is by Wentworth Hotel). Parking is rough and limited.

This route provides an attractive, less-used approach to Carter Notch up the valley of Wildcat River. Brook crossings are tough in high water. From trailhead, descend gently on Bog Brook Trail to crossings of Wildcat Brook, a nameless brook and Wildcat River in quick succession. After last crossing, at 0.7 mi., turn L on Wildcat River Trail and follow east side of Wildcat River at gentle grade. At 1.1 mi. cross gravel logging road (FR 233) that provides slightly longer approach from end of Carter Notch Rd. that avoids the three brook crossings. Cross Bog Brook at 1.7 mi. At 2.6 mi./2320 ft. reach jct. R with Wild River Trail. Continue ahead on Wildcat River Trail, soon crossing to W side of stream and climb moderately through fine hardwood and birch, with glimpses of Carter Dome. High up in valley grade steepens through conifers, leading to S end of Carter Notch at 4.2 mi.; here side trail R leads out to wild boulders of Rampart, with views up to crags on Carter Dome and Wildcat and S down valley. Carter Notch Hut is reached at 4.3 mi./3288 ft. Continue ahead on Nineteen-Mile Brook Trail, skirting small Lower Carter Pond on R and Upper Carter Pond on L; here is jct. R with Carter-Moriah Trail for Carter Dome. Shores of ponds provide wild views up to walls of notch. From Upper Pond, Nineteen-Mile Brook Trail climbs to height-of-land in notch at 4.5 mi./3388 ft. Turn L here on Wildcat Ridge Trail to access Wildcat A in 0.7 mi. and Wildcat D 2.0 mi. beyond, as described above.

WINTER

The W approach up Wildcat Ridge Trail from Pinkham Notch is not recommended—some of the ledges can be very dangerous. The Nineteen-Mile Brook Trail is a good approach, but the climb up from Carter Notch is difficult and the crossing of the slide halfway up is hazardous in icy conditions; crampons are essential for safety. The ridge walk between the peaks is a delight in winter, though there are some steep pitches in places. Winter peakbaggers often ascend or descend via the ski trails; hikers should stay along the edge and be alert for fast-moving skiers and snowboarders.

VIEW GUIDE

Wildcat D: The viewing platform provides a complete panorama. The centerpiece is the spectacular view of the east side of Mt. Washington, with great looks into the Gulf of Slides (below Boott Spur on the L) and Tuckerman and Huntington Ravines (L and R of the main summit). This is Washington's most impressive aspect. Looking NW, the sharp, rocky peaks of Adams and the slightly lower Madison are seen in back, to the R of Washington, with a fine look into Madison Gulf. To the N, down the Peabody River valley, distant peaks are seen in northern New Hampshire and NW Maine beyond low, ledgy Pine Mtn. To the NNE the lower Mahoosucs and Imp Face are seen over nearby Little Wildcat.

The rounded crest of Wildcat A is seen close by to the NE, with Carter Dome peeking over, Wildcats B and C to the R, and South and Middle Carter to the L. To the ESE are South Baldface, Sable, Black Mtn., Chandler, and Maine's Pleasant Mtn. The Doubleheads and Kearsarge North are to the SE. Waves of peaks and ridges are seen to the S and SW. Looking S you see Iron Mtn. with the Moats and Chocorua beyond. To the SSW are the lower Montalban Ridge summits of Langdon, Parker and Resolution with Bear Mtn., Bartlett Haystack below Passaconaway, Whiteface, Tremont and Tripyramid arrayed beyond. Giant Stairs are seen to the R of Resolution, with Mt. Kancamagus above. To the SW are Tecumseh, the Osceolas, Carrigain and wide-spreading Hancock, with neighboring Wildcat E just to the R. Peering over to the R of Wildcat E are Mt. Isolation, distant Moosilauke, Flume and Bondcliff, Willey, and Bond.

Wildcat Mtn. (A Peak): A small ledge on the east edge of the summit provides a startling view into Carter Notch, looking down on Carter Ponds and the roofs of the hut buildings and across to the massive Carter Dome with a huge rocky bowl gouged into its R flank. Mt. Hight is just to the L of the Dome, with South and Middle Carter (a pointed wooded peak) farther L. Shelburne Moriah and distant Maine peaks are seen through Zeta Pass between the Carters. On the far L are the lower Mahoosucs, Imp Face and the city of Berlin. To the R of the bouldery bowl on Carter Dome are Rainbow Ridge (a spur of the Dome), the bare cone of South Baldface, and the long ridge of Black Mtn, with Sable, Chandler, the Doubleheads, and Kearsarge North beyond. South and Middle Moat are seen to the far R, in the distance to the S.

NO. OF 4000-FOOTERS VISIBLE: Wildcat D, 24; Wildcat Mtn. (A Peak), 26 (largely through the trees).

Mount Field

ELEVATION: 4340 ft./1323 m ORDER OF HEIGHT: 23 (tie)
LOCATION: Willey Range, Towns of Bethlehem and Hart's Location
USGS MAP: 7½′ Crawford Notch

GEOGRAPHY

The central and tallest of the three 4000-ft. summits comprising the Willey Range, Mt. Field towers high above the floor of Crawford Notch and is flanked by imposing Mt. Willey to the SE and wooded Mt. Tom to the NW. The Willey Range parallels US 302 to the S and E as it passes through Crawford Notch. Field's summit is best seen from the highway as one approaches the Notch from the N (Bretton Woods). The high point is a small, sharp wooded knob that rises from the main mass of the mountain. Because of its heavy tree cover, Field's summit offers only limited views.

To the NE of the main summit lies Mt. Avalon, a 3442-ft. spur peak well known for its craggy summit and excellent vista. A little to the E, and 600 feet lower, is Mt. Willard (2850 ft.), one of the best known and most visited peaks in the Whites, with a sheer cliff on its S face and a stunning view down Crawford Notch.

The W face of Mt. Field is very steep, with small cliffs and slides overlooking a high, hidden basin to the SW, which empties into the North Fork of the Pemigewasset River's East Branch. Beyond the sharp drop off, a long, broad, trailless ridge extends two miles W over West Field (3691 ft., one of New Hampshire's 100 Highest peaks) and a nameless 3526-ft. knob before ending at Whitewall Mtn. (3405 ft.), whose ragged cliffs form the E wall of Zealand Notch. Two tiny ponds are hidden at the W base of West Field.

Willey Brook, which flows into the Saco River in Crawford Notch, drains the SE slopes of Field. A 140-foot-long railroad trestle, seen high above US 302 when passing through the Notch, was built over Willey Brook in 1875. To the NE, Field shares the deep, cirque-like valley of Crawford Brook with Mt. Tom.

NOMENCLATURE

State geologist Charles H. Hitchcock is credited with naming this mountain in honor of Darby Field, the Englishman who led the first recorded ascent of Mt. Washington. For an untold number of years prior to Hitchcock's naming of the peak (in 1874), early stereoscopic views of the Crawford Notch region identified the mountain as Mt. Lincoln, for assassinated Civil War–era president Abraham Lincoln. As Hitchcock noted in his *Geology of New Hampshire*, however, that name already existed on the 5089-ft. summit S of Mt. Lafayette on the Franconia Range. "I propose, therefore, the name of Mt. Field for the eminence near the Crawford House, in honor of the worthy gentleman (Darby Field) who first ascended Mt. Washington in 1642, and will use it upon the map and in the descriptions of this report," wrote Hitchcock.

HISTORICAL HIGHLIGHTS

First Ascent: Unknown

1828: Notch House built by Crawford family on E side of Crawford's plateau; opens in 1829 under management of Thomas Crawford.

1852: Crawford House opens at NE base of Mt. Tom.

1859: Crawford House burns in early spring, but new and larger hotel accommodating 400 guests is quickly built and opens in July. It becomes one of most fashionable grand hotels in White Mountains; over years guests include five U.S. Presidents.

1874: Hitchcock names mountain for Darby Field; peak previously known as Mt. Lincoln.

1876: Guidebook author M. F. Sweetser says of mountain: "It is 4,400 ft. high, but possesses no interest for tourists, the top being covered with dense thickets which shut out the view."

1882: A. E. Scott, AMC Councilor of Improvements, leads groups of six mountain explorers over trailless peaks of Twin-Bond Range in epic week-long sojourn. On seventh day, Scott and two women members of group bushwhack up and over Mt. Field from W to E, and conclude journey atop Mt. Willard.

Early 1880s: AMC proposal to build trail over mountain, linking Crawford's to Thoreau Falls region, is rejected by Crawford House management, owners of land on E side of mountain.

1907: AMC Snow-Shoe Section hikers reach "bleak summit of Mt. Field" after arduous climb in "below zero" temperatures.

1909: First trail to Field's wooded summit is established by Mr. and Mrs. J. A. Cruickshank. Trail leads from mountain's lower subsidiary summit, Mt. Avalon (to which trail had been built some years earlier), up to crest of Willey Range, over Field's summit, and S to Mt. Willey, where it connects with existing trail up that peak from the S.

1919: Trail from Willey House Station in Crawford Notch, up and over Mts. Willey and Field, and down to Avalon Trail, is designated as Willey Range Trail.

1933: A-Z Trail over Field-Tom col, linking Crawford's with AMC's newly built Zealand Falls Hut, is constructed. Willey Range Trail is extended at N end from Mt. Field to Field-Tom col, while at S end, first 1.5 mi. from Willey House Station are designated as part of Ethan Pond Trail.

1938: September hurricane levels stand of virgin spruce on Crawford side of height-of-land between Mts. Field and Tom.

1941: Following outbreak of spruce bark beetle infestation, CCC crews, under direction of Forest Service, level affected trees near jct. of A-Z and Avalon Trails.

1950: November windstorm wreaks havoc on Willey Range Trail, closed until 1952.

1952: Crawford Notch State Park created.

1969: W slopes of Field are included by Forest Service in new Lincoln Woods Scenic Area.

1976: Crawford House closes doors, contents auctioned off.

1977: Crawford House destroyed in November fire.

1979: AMC acquires land around Crawford House site and develops hostel.

TRAIL APPROACHES

Northeast Approach from US 302 at Crawford's

Avalon Trail, Willey Range Trail
5.6 mi. round trip, 2400-ft. elevation gain

Trailhead (1900 ft.): This approach starts at parking area by AMC Crawford Notch Hostel on W side of US 302, 8.5 mi. E of stoplight in Twin Mountain and 0.1 mi. N of Gateway of Crawford Notch.

The most direct ascent up Mt. Field is via the Avalon Trail, which climbs from the top of Crawford Notch to the summit in 2.8 mi. There are good views from Mt. Avalon en route. From parking area, cross field and RR tracks by AMC information center (located in restored Victorian train station) and enter woods on Avalon Trail. At 0.1 mi. Mt. Willard Trail splits L. Continue straight and climb gently to crossing of Crawford Brook at 0.2 mi. Just beyond, loop trail to Beecher and Pearl Cascades diverges L and rejoins at 0.4 mi. Avalon Trail ascends moderately, crossing brook again at 0.8 mi. Climbing is easy, then steeper to jct. with A-Z Trail to Zealand Falls Hut at 1.3 mi. / 2700 ft.

From here, Avalon Trail swings L, and in short distance begins sustained steep, rocky climb through deep fir woods to col just W of Mt. Avalon's summit at 1.8 mi. / 3350 ft. This open spur, reached by steep 100-yard side trail on L, offers excellent views of Presidentials, Bretton Woods area, Crawford Notch and upper Willey Range. From col, trail runs through open flat area with views of surrounding mountains, then begins mile-long climb through fir forest up NE slope of Mt. Field. Grade is steep in lower section, with limited views back to NE, then moderates up higher, reaching Willey Range Trail at 2.8 mi. / 4280 ft. From jct., turn L for summit, which is reached in less than 100 yards.

Loop Options
Several loop hikes from Crawford's over the Willey Range, with out-and-back jaunts to Tom and Willey, are popular with many peakbaggers. The loop over Tom and Field via Avalon Trail, A-Z Trail, Mt. Tom Spur, Willey Range Trail, and descent via Avalon Trail is 7.2 mi. round trip, with a 2800-ft. elevation gain.

For description of ascent to Mt. Tom via Avalon Trail, A-Z Trail and Mt. Tom Spur, see chapter on Mt. Tom. To continue to Mt. Field from jct. of A-Z Trail and Mt. Tom Spur at Field-Tom col (3700 ft.), continue 100 yards W on A-Z Trail and turn L on Willey Range Trail for easy-graded climb up N ridge of Field. In 0.9 mi. Avalon Trail comes in on L, and summit of Field is reached 100 yards beyond.

To reach Mt. Willey, continue S on Willey Range Trail, reaching Field-Willey col in 0.5 mi. Begin gradual ascent of Willey, passing over several knobs. Summit of Willey is reached in 1.4 mi. Return to Crawford's by way of Mts. Field and Avalon. For out-and-back hike from Crawford's to all three Willey Range summits, distance is 10.0 mi. round-trip, with a 3450-ft. elevation gain.

South Approach from US 302 at Willey House Station

Ethan Pond Trail, Willey Range Trail
8.2 mi. round trip, 3500-ft. elevation gain

This approach includes ascent of Mt. Willey along the way, and on return trip. For description of 2.7 mi./2850-ft. climb to Mt. Willey via Ethan Pond and Willey Range Trails, see Mt. Willey chapter. From summit of Mt. Willey, Willey Range Trail circles around past W outlooks, then descends gradually N, meandering along broad wooded ridgecrest over several small knobs. Field-Willey col (3980 ft.) is reached 0.9 mi. from Willey, then trail climbs S side of Mt. Field with three short, steep pitches, attaining summit at 1.4 mi. from Willey.

WINTER

A majority of winter hikers attack the summit from the N or NE from Crawford's, therefore avoiding the steep ascent of Mt. Willey from the S. If ascending by way of the Avalon Trail, take note that last half-mile of climbing up to spur trail to Mt. Avalon's summit is steep and sometimes icy. It is generally easier to ascend this stretch of trail then to descend it. Views around the summit of Mt. Field are improved by deep snow.

VIEW GUIDE

Mt. Field's summit vista is increasingly being obscured by trees. Still, with a little work, a generous number of distant peaks can be seen from various points around the summit. Looking S, Mt. Carrigain and the peaks around Carrigain Notch are visible, as are the Sandwich Range summits of Passaconaway, Whiteface, The Sleepers and Tripyramid. More to the SW are seen the Hancocks and Scar Ridge near Lincoln, while Sandwich Dome is spotted just R of Carrigain.

Looking W through the trees, one can make out most of the Twin-Bond Range, with the Franconias seen over and beyond the ridgeline from Guyot to the Twins. From a point along the Willey Range Trail just N of the true summit, Mt. Tom's fir wave-striped summit is seen to the N, while to its L are Mt. Hale and the Little River peaks. To the WNW are the Twins, easily identified by the long slide scarring North Twin's E-facing slope, while Zealand Ridge and the Zeacliffs are nearly due W, under the Guyot-Twin ridge.

From the end of a short side trail found off the summit to the E is a nice viewpoint looking N and E toward Bretton Woods and the Presidentials. The red-roofed Mt. Washington Hotel serves as the centerpiece of this vista, with neighboring Mt. Tom spotted to the L of the hotel, and Cherry Mtn. and Mt. Deception more to the NNE. Also seen from here are the more distant North Country peaks of Waumbek, Starr King, and Cabot. To the E are the Presidentials, with Mts. Jefferson, Washington and Monroe all visible.

NO. OF 4000-FOOTERS VISIBLE: 28

Mount Hale

ELEVATION: 4054 ft./1236 m ORDER OF HEIGHT: 38
LOCATION: Little River Range, Town of Bethlehem
USGS MAPS: 7½′ South Twin Mtn., 7½′ Crawford Notch

GEOGRAPHY

At just over 4000 ft. in elevation, Mt. Hale is the highest of the peaks comprising the Little River Range, which extends N from the neighboring Zealand Ridge to the three low Sugarloaves rising out of the Ammonoosuc River valley. The Little River valley separates this range from the Twin Range to the W. Hale's sprawling mass features several subsidiary summits, none, however, accessible by trail. From the rounded main summit, these peaks extend to the N, E, and S, along with lesser ridges extending NW and W.

The ridge connecting the three Sugarloaves—North (2310 ft.), Middle (2539 ft.) and South (3024 ft.)—leads progressively up to Hale's main summit ridge. North and Middle Sugarloaf are accessible by the Sugarloaf Trail and offer fine views, including Mt. Hale's N ridges, from their bare tops. Trailless South Sugarloaf is occasionally explored by trampers and its partially open summit offers unique views into the Zealand River and Mt. Tom Brook valleys.

Hale's 3740-ft. North Peak sports several sets of small cliffs extending down towards South Sugarloaf. A massive, steep-sided E spur of Hale (3460 ft.) juts out toward the broad Zealand valley and features a bald, burned crown and talus slopes along its base. To the S, the mountain's ridge extends gradually downward to the heavily wooded valley at the northern base of Zealand Mtn. A flat S shoulder of Mt. Hale is crossed by the Lend-A-Hand Trail, a footpath connecting the main summit to the AMC's Zealand Falls Hut. Farther S a separate 3700-ft. spur rises to the W of this trail. This flat-topped summit, one of New Hampshire's 100 Highest peaks, is commonly known as Zeale—a hybrid of Mts. Zealand and Hale.

Mt. Hale is surrounded on three sides by deep river valleys, including the Ammonoosuc River to the N, the Zealand River to the E and the Little River to the W. Both the Zealand and Little Rivers flow northward into the larger Ammonoosuc. Smaller streams draining the slopes of Hale include Tuttle Brook on the N, Hale Brook on the NE, and Hoxie Brook on the SE.

In the aftermath of two great forest fires that struck the Zealand area in 1886 and 1903, vast stands of white birch trees sprouted up on all flanks of the mountain. Today these mature birches constitute one of the largest and most spectacular such stands in all the Whites, and are particularly notable when ascending the mountain on either the Hale Brook Trail or the former firewarden's road.

As is the case with several 4000-footers, Hale's summit vista has deteriorated over the years. Where once the wide clearing at the summit offered nearly unobstructed views towards the majestic peaks of the Presidential Range and perfectly aligned Zealand and Carrigain Notches, trees now block much of the view, even from atop the five-foot high summit cairn.

In lieu of spectacular views, the summit does possess one unique feature among White Mountain peaks. Many of the volcanic rocks which litter the mountaintop are magnetic. A compass placed next to one of these stones will go haywire and no longer point N.

NOMENCLATURE

The mountain is named for Rev. Edward Everett Hale (1822–1909), a Boston Congregational minister, avid White Mountain explorer, writer, and author of the classic American short story, *A Man Without a Country*. Hale, who late in his life was a member of the fledgling conservation organization, the Society for the Protection of New Hampshire Forests, undertook many of his ventures into the White Mountains in the company of state geologist Dr. Charles T. Jackson. It was one of Jackson's successors, geologist Charles Hitchcock, who in 1874 chose to name the mountain after Rev. Hale.

HISTORICAL HIGHLIGHTS

First Ascent: Unknown

1874: State Geologist Charles Hitchcock, in Vol. 1 of his massive three-volume *Geology of New Hampshire*, notes that the peak he has named Mt. Hale "is sometimes confounded with the Twin Mountains, because only one of the Twins is seen from the hotel named after them."

1881: Moses Sweetser's guidebook describes Hale as "fine wooded peak . . . usually called . . . one of the Twins."

1883: Eugene B. Cook, described by authors Laura and Guy Waterman as "one of the most indefatigable explorers of the 1870–1880s," visits mountain in July 1883 and estimates summit to be in excess of 4,000 feet.

1885: Lumber baron J. E. Henry begins construction of logging rail line into Zealand River valley E of mountain. Operation continues into mid-1890s.

1886: Sparks from passing train engine touch off devastating Zealand Valley forest fire that sweeps over Sugarloaves and nearby summits of Rosebrook Range.

1893: 19th-century timber king George Van Dyke begins logging railroad operations in Little River valley, W of Mt. Hale.

1903: Second forest fire in Zealand area burns over 10,000 acres of forestland.

1907: AMC guidebook describes Mt. Hale as "a desolate, burned wilderness."

1925: Though no description is provided, map in AMC Guide indicates existence of path from Little River to summit. Subsequent edition of guide says route is via old lumber road, and that "outlook from peak is unobstructed and includes remarkable view of Zealand Notch, and in line directly beyond, Carrigain Notch."

1928: U.S. Forest Service erects fire lookout tower on main summit. Becomes operational the following year, and remains in use through 1948. Tower is accessed by Mt. Hale Trail (a.k.a Firewarden's Trail) from Little River valley to NW.

1936: Mountain now accessible by four routes. These include Mt. Hale Trail from Little River, Lend-A-Hand Trail from Zealand Falls Hut (built in 1934), Hale Brook Trail from Zealand valley, and Tuttle Brook Trail from Twin Mountain village.

1940: AMC guide notes that tractor road (Mt. Hale Trail) from Little River affords "excellent ski run" for intermediate skiers.

Early 1960s: Tuttle Brook Trail and Mt. Hale Trail are now abandoned.

1972: Fire tower atop summit is dismantled by Forest Service. All that remains are concrete support piers, including one inscribed with the date 10-17-28.

TRAIL APPROACHES

NORTHEAST APPROACH from Zealand Road (FR 16)

Hale Brook Trail
4.4 mi. round trip, 2300-ft. elevation gain

TRAILHEAD (1770 ft.): Hale Brook Trail begins at small parking area on R (W) side of Zealand Road, 2.5 mi. from US 302 E of Twin Mountain.

This trail provides the quickest and easiest ascent of Hale, which is considered one of the least difficult of the 4000-footers. Ascending on mostly moderate grades, trail climbs the mountain's NE ridge. Shortly after starting out, an intersecting cross country ski trail is passed, then recently clearcut section of forest is noticeable through woods on R. Steady uphill grade leads in 0.6 mi. to within earshot of Hale Brook. At 0.8 mi. stream is crossed just above smooth water chute, also on R.

Yellow-blazed trail steepens for short distance, climbing up and away from stream. Passing through glade of white birches, grade lessens, and at 1.1 mi./2460 ft. trail recrosses Hale Brook. Following sharp L turn at stream crossing, trail snakes its way up via series of switchbacks leading to broad, flat plateau connecting main and east ridges. Trail is rockier and footing trickier for next 0.2 mi., then grade steepens for final 0.3 mi. march to summit through nice fir forest, reaching top at 2.2 mi./4054 ft.

South Approach from Zealand Falls Hut

Twinway, Lend-A-Hand Trail
5.6 mi. round trip, 1300-ft elevation gain

Mt. Hale's alternative ascent route is the Lend-A-Hand Trail, which starts 0.1 mi. above AMC's Zealand Falls Hut and leads 2.7 mi. NW to summit. This trail, in conjunction with the Hale Brook, Twinway, and Zealand Trails, and Zealand Road, provides a comfortable loop hike over Mt. Hale and through the scenic Zealand River valley. Trail takes its name from journal for charitable organizations that Rev. Hale (the mountain's namesake) once edited.

Lend-A-Hand Trail begins 0.1 mi. above hut, branching off from Twinway (link in Appalachian Trail) at 2730 ft. Though never steep, lower sections of footway tend to be wet and slippery, especially through extensive section of bog bridges beginning about 0.5 mi. from trail's start. There are also nice birch glades along the way.

At 1.6 mi./3400 ft., a scrubby, ledgy area is passed as grade steepens. Through and over the trees are limited views SE to Willey Range, S to Zealand Notch, and SW to Zealand Mtn. Far off to L, and well off marked trail, is an inviting crag on Hale's southernmost spur ridge.

Following more strenuous climb, second, higher set of ledges is reached at 2.0 mi./3700 ft. Short side path R leads to interesting view of Zealand and Carrigain Notches, as well as Zealand Ridge. Next 0.5 mi. is on gentler grade across flat shoulder before trail steepens for final 0.3 mi. push to summit, through deep, mossy fir forest.

Loop Option

An alternative to the out-and-back approach to Mt. Hale is a loop hike via Hale Brook Trail, Lend-a-Hand Trail, Twinway, Zealand Trail and Zealand Road (8.6 mi. round trip, 2300-ft. elevation gain).

The Hale Brook/Lend-A-Hand loop hike usually begins with ascent of the mountain via Hale Brook Trail. From the summit, it's 2.8 mi. down to AMC Zealand Falls hut (2630 ft.), then a steep 0.2 mile descent from the hut to the jct. of the Ethan Pond and Zealand Trails (2460 ft.). Turn L onto Zealand Trail and follow it past a series of beaver ponds and along former Zealand Valley RR grade. In 2.5 easy mi., trail ends at Zealand Trail parking lot. Follow unpaved Zealand Road 1.0 mi. downhill back to Hale Brook Trail parking area.

WINTER

While the hike up Hale is considered among the easiest in summer and fall, it is a different story in winter. Because Zealand Road is closed to motor vehicle traffic in winter, any effort to reach the mountain by the popular Hale Brook Trail means an additional 2.8 mi. of road walking each way. The cushy 2.2 mi. one-way summer jaunt is stretched to 5.0 mi. The round trip hike is suddenly an epic 10.0-mi. battle.

Snowshoers can also expect some difficulty traversing the birch-lined quarter-mile section of the Hale Brook Trail approaching the second crossing of the stream. This side-sloping stretch is particularly hazardous when the snow cover is crusty or hard-packed. Care must be taken not to lose one's footing and slide precariously down the steep slope into the brook valley.

Winter trampers who reach the summit do enjoy one advantage over summer trekkers. In a good snow year, a hiker on the mountaintop is elevated several feet higher than normal and is able to see over and above the growing trees which surround the summit area.

VIEW GUIDE

Not many years ago Hale was considered an excellent open viewpoint, but over the last few decades tree growth around the fringes of the flat summit has been slowly choking off the views. Now you have to stand partway up the summit cairn to obtain a decent panorama.

Presently the predominant view is W, toward the nearby and higher peaks of the Twin Range. North Twin is easy to identify with an impressive slide scarring its upper reaches. The lower Nubble Peak, fronted with cliffs, is to the R, and to its R is a long view out towards Vermont. To the L of North Twin is massive South Twin, crowned with a tiny rock peak, and beyond that its connecting ridge with Mt. Guyot. Mt. Bond is behind and L of Guyot, and to Bond's L is the summit of Zealand Mtn. and upper Zealand Ridge. Mt. Hancock is seen farther L, over the lower Zealand Ridge, with a long ridge extending L to Mt. Carrigain. Mts. Tripyramid and Whiteface poke above this ridge.

Barely seen above the trees to the S are perfectly aligned Zealand and Carrigain Notches. Zealand Notch, the nearer of the two, is flanked by Whitewall Mtn. on the L and Zealand Ridge on the R. (This entire area is now better viewed from ledge 0.8 mi. down from the summit along Lend-A-Hand Trail.) The R side of Carrigain Notch is formed by massive Mt. Carrigain and Vose Spur, with the dark spires of Mts. Lowell and Anderson on the L side. To their L are seen Mts. Bemis and Nancy. Mts. Tremont and Chocorua are seen through the saddle between Anderson and Nancy. To the L the Moat Range is seen far to the SE.

To the ESE the three peaks of the Willey Range are prominent, with Mt. Webster poking up between Mts. Field and Tom, and Mt. Jackson to the L of Tom. From Jackson the long ridge of the Southern Presidentials leads L up over Mts. Pierce, Eisenhower, and Monroe to Mt. Washington, with Boott Spur behind on the R. Mt. Isolation is seen in the back just to the R of Pierce.

On the far L are Mts. Clay, Jefferson and Adams. Enjoy what views there are now—in 20 years they may be gone.

NO. OF 4000-FOOTERS VISIBLE: 23

Mount Tom

ELEVATION: 4051 ft./1235 m ORDER OF HEIGHT: 40
LOCATION: Willey Range, Town of Bethlehem
USGS MAP: 7½′ Crawford Notch

GEOGRAPHY

Rounded and wooded to the top, Mt. Tom is the northernmost and lowest of the three high peaks of the Willey Range. It's one of the easier 4000-footers to climb, and its limited views into the Zealand and Pemigewasset Wilderness areas have been expanded dramatically in recent years by a summit blowdown patch. To the S a high col separates Tom from neighboring Mt. Field. To the N the ridgecrest descends over two wooded humps, then continues several miles NW as the rather level Rosebrook Range, which includes Mt. Echo (3084 ft.), Mt. Stickney (3043 ft.), Mt. Rosebrook (3004 ft.) and Mt. Oscar (2746 ft.). Other ridges run NW and NE from the summit.

To the W the mountain's slopes descend rather gently into the valley of Zealand River. Mt. Tom Brook drains the area N of the summit, between Tom's NW ridge and the Rosebrook Range, while Mt. Field Brook flows from the broad basin on the W side of the mountain. On the E is Crawford's, the small plateau just N of the gateway of Crawford Notch. From Crawford's Tom looms as a fairly impressive mountain, displaying a wooded cirque-like valley with a steep headwall beneath the Tom-Field col; this E-facing valley is drained by Crawford Brook.

NOMENCLATURE

The mountain was named for Thomas J. Crawford, one of the legendary family that opened up the Crawford Notch region to visitors in the early and mid 1800s. Thomas was one of Abel Crawford's six sons, and among his brothers was the famed "giant of the mountains," Ethan Allen Crawford. From 1829–1852 Thomas ran the Notch House, a hostelry on the plateau beneath his namesake mountain. Here he entertained famous guests such as Henry David Thoreau and Francis Parkman. He also improved the Crawford Path (originally built by Abel and Ethan in 1819) to a bridle path in 1840, and in 1846 he built a carriage road up Mt. Willard, a low spur of Mt. Field with a dramatic view of Crawford Notch. Thomas' name had actually

The Willey Range, including Mts. Willey, Field, and Tom, form the western wall of well-known Crawford Notch.

been given to this mountain by Professor Edward Tuckerman, but Thomas himself renamed the lower peak after one of his guests. Thomas died in 1865, and in 1876 state geologist Charles H. Hitchcock bestowed Crawford's name on the 4000-footer in the Willey Range.

HISTORICAL HIGHLIGHTS

First Ascent: Unknown.

1828: Notch House built by Crawford family on E side of Crawford's plateau; opens in 1829 under management of Thomas Crawford.

1852: Crawford House opens at NE base of Mt. Tom.

1859: Crawford House burns in April, but new and larger hotel accommodating 400 guests is quickly built and opens in July. It becomes one of most fashionable grand hotels in White Mtns.; over years guests include five U.S. Presidents.

Early 1870s: Charles H. Hitchcock ascends Mt. Tom three times during field work for state geological survey. Applies name "Mt. Anadalusite" to a NE knob of mountain, after a rock found there by two Dartmouth student assistants. Names main peak "Mt. Tom" in final report.

1876: Moses Sweetser's guidebook describes route to summit of Tom roughly equivalent to today's trail route, and laments lack of view from top.

1880s: Path is marked from Crawford House to summit, first following trail to Mt. Avalon, then climbing up Tom's NE ridge.

1890: Rev. Julius Ward's book, *The White Mountains: A Guide to Their Interpretation*, describes ascent of Mt. Tom. "It is here," writes Ward, "that one feels the richness of the touches of nature."

1890s: Trail network is developed on Rosebrook Range to NW, including connector trail leaving NE ridge of Tom, skirting slope at 3000-ft. level and passing Stump Spring, a col called Hunter's Hollow, and a knob known as San Juan Hill.

1907: First AMC trail guide describes Mt. Tom trail as "much neglected" above jct. with Rosebrook Range trail. By 1928 upper portion is deemed too obscure to follow.

1933: A-Z Trail built over Field-Tom col to connect Crawford's with AMC's newly built Zealand Falls Hut. Willey Range Trail is extended N from Mt. Field to Field-Tom col. 1934 AMC guide notes that Tom can be climbed without trail from col.

1938: Hurricane devastates trails on Rosebrook Range; they are soon abandoned. Stand of virgin spruce on E side of Field-Tom col is also leveled by hurricane.

Late 1950s: After creation of 4000-Footer Club, increased interest in climbing Tom leads to development of rough blazed trail to summit.

Late 1960s: Mt. Tom Spur is officially adopted as AMC trail.

ca. 1970: Owners of Crawford House contemplate developing ski area on slopes of Tom, inviting Olympic skier Tom Corcoran (developer of Waterville Valley Ski Area) to look over site. Project never advances beyond speculative stage.

1976: Crawford House closes doors, contents auctioned off.

1977: Crawford House destroyed in November fire.

1979: AMC acquires land around Crawford House site and develops hostel.

TRAIL APPROACHES

East Approach from US 302 at Crawford's

Avalon Trail, A-Z Trail, Mt. Tom Spur
5.8 mi. round trip, 2150-ft. elevation gain

Trailhead (1900 ft.): This approach starts at parking area by AMC Crawford Notch Hostel on W side of US 302, 8.5 mi. E of stoplight in Twin Mountain and 0.1 mi. N of Gateway of Crawford Notch.

The usual approach to Mt. Tom is a moderate climb, much of it through open, attractive woods. From parking area, cross field and RR tracks by AMC information center (located in restored Victorian train station) and enter woods on Avalon Trail. At 0.1 mi. Mt. Willard Trail splits L. Continue straight and climb gently to crossing of Crawford Brook at 0.2 mi. Just beyond, loop to Beecher and Pearl Cascades diverges L and rejoins at 0.4 mi. Yellow-blazed Avalon Trail ascends moderately, crossing brook again at 0.8 mi. Climbing is easy, with a look L up to Mt. Avalon, then steeper to jct. with A-Z Trail at 1.3 mi./2700 ft.

Stay straight on yellow-blazed A-Z (Avalon-Zealand) Trail as Avalon Trail branches L. Cross down-and-up through steep gully and climb steadily, high up on S side of beautiful cirque-like valley through open forest with large yellow birches. Mt. Tom's NE ridge is seen across valley to R. At 1.9 mi./ 3200 ft. trail recrosses brook, now quite small, and bears R to slab rather steeply up headwall of valley, with glimpses of Mt. Washington out through trees. Swing L for final climb to Field-Tom col and jct. with Mt. Tom Spur, reached at 2.3 mi./3700 ft.

Turn R on Mt. Tom Spur. (A-Z Trail continues a few yards ahead to Willey Range Trail, then begins descent to Zealand valley.) Climb is easy, then moderate along narrow, wild ridgecrest trail, with occasional views from open blowdown patches towards Crawford Notch, Mt. Field and Pemi Wilderness. Cross small false summit, then reach clearing at true summit at 2.9 mi./4051 ft. Good view W and S from open blowdown area in front.

West Approach from Zealand Trail

A-Z Trail
3.3 mi. one-way, 1600-ft. elevation gain

Mt. Tom can be climbed from the W via the A-Z Trail from its jct. with Zealand Trail, 2.2 mi. from end of Zealand Rd. This point is 0.5 mi. below AMC Zealand Falls Hut via Twinway and Zealand Trail. See chapter on Zealand Mtn. for details on Zealand Trail. From A-Z/Zealand jct. (2450 ft.), follow A-Z Trail E on gradual to moderate climb through hardwoods, then white birches, crossing many small brooks and passing area logged in 1970s. Much of timber here was devastated by 1938 hurricane. At 2.1 mi. from Zealand Trail cross Mt. Field Brook and ascend more steeply with rocky footing. Reach Field-Tom col and jct. R with Willey Range Trail at 2.7 mi./ 3700 ft. Mt. Tom Spur is on L a few yards ahead on A-Z Trail; proceed to summit at 3.3 mi./4051 ft.

From end of Zealand Rd., round trip to Mt. Tom is 11.0 mi. with 2050-ft. elevation gain. From Zealand Falls Hut, round trip to Mt. Tom is 7.6 mi. with 1800-ft. elevation gain (including 200 ft. on return trip).

Loop hikes from Crawford's over the Willey Range, with out-and-back jaunts to Tom and Willey, are also popular with many peakbaggers. These include: a loop over Tom and Field via Avalon Trail, A-Z Trail, Mt. Tom Spur, Willey Range Trail, and descent via Avalon Trail, 7.2 mi. round trip, 2800-ft. elevation gain; a loop over Tom and Field with side trip to Willey on Willey Range Trail, 10.0 mi. round trip, 3450-ft. elevation gain.

WINTER

Mt. Tom is a fine winter climb with mostly moderate snowshoeing grades and little exposure to weather. Plenty of plowed parking is available at the AMC hostel. The most difficult spots are the steep gully above Avalon/A-Z junction, the sharp sidehill approaching the upper crossing of Crawford Brook, and the climb up the headwall of the valley. In deep unbroken snow both A-Z Trail and Mt. Tom Spur may be difficult to follow; the latter may require much branch-banging, but is a winter wonderland setting. With a deep snow platform the views from the blowdown areas along Mt. Tom Spur and the summit fir wave are even better.

VIEW GUIDE

Tom has never been noted as an outstanding viewpoint, but in recent years the blowdown/fir wave area at the summit has been expanding, and the view W and S over the high peaks of Zealand and Pemi Wilderness areas has blossomed with it. On the far L nearby Mt. Field is seen through the trees. To the S, beyond Field's lower W spurs and the rolling uplands of the eastern Pemi, are the Nancy Range (with Mt. Shaw of the Ossipee Range in the distance), majestic Mt. Carrigain, and the long ridges of Mt. Hancock, with its hidden N valleys well displayed. Mts. Passaconaway and Whiteface are seen through Carrigain Notch, and Sandwich Dome peers over between Carrigain and Hancock. Mts. Osceola and Hitchcock, Scar Ridge and Loon Mtn. are to the R of Hancock.

To the SW, beyond the backside of Whitewall Mtn., is the great bulk of Mt. Bond, showing a bare E shoulder, with Mt. Guyot to the R above the Zeacliffs and Zealand Ridge. A long, high ridge runs from Guyot across to the small peak of South Twin and slide-scarred North Twin. On clear days Camel's Hump in Vermont can be spotted to the R of North Twin. The upper Zealand valley, including Zealand Falls and the nearby AMC hut, is seen below, and Mt. Hale is to the far R. An obscure side path to the E off Mt. Tom Spur just below the summit leads to a partial view towards Crawford Notch, especially the Webster Cliffs. With deep firm snow additional views can be found towards the Presidentials along the Spur.

NO. OF 4000-FOOTERS VISIBLE: 21 (12 from fir wave viewpoint, 9 looking E).

Mount Willey

ELEVATION: 4285 ft./1306 m ORDER OF HEIGHT: 29
LOCATION: Willey Range, Towns of Bethlehem and Hart's Location
USGS MAP: 7½′ Crawford Notch

GEOGRAPHY

Forming the W wall of Crawford Notch, Mt. Willey is the southernmost and dominant peak of the Willey Range, though not quite the highest. A brooding hulk of a mountain, it's especially impressive when viewed from the depths of the Notch. Its steep sides are scarred by cliffs and rock slides, giving it a savage, ominous look. This aura was enhanced early on by the Willey Slide of 1826, which wiped out nine lives and captured the public imagination like no other episode in White Mountain history.

On the N Mt. Willey is separated from the slightly higher Mt. Field by a shallow col. From Willey's small conical summit at the S end of its crest the mountain's slopes drop off steeply on three sides. On the E is a mile-long wall of scrub and broken rock that plummets nearly 3000 ft. to the floor of the Notch. This slope was steepened by the continental ice sheets; Crawford Notch is a textbook example of glacial geology, best viewed from the nearby summit of Mt. Willard. Well down on this face is the naked slab known as the Willey Slide, a favorite haunt of ice climbers (not to be confused with the 1826 slide, which has long since grown up).

On the S side the ridgeline plunges to a broad height-of-land, once called Willey Notch, dividing Mt. Willey from a low trailless ridge that extends S to the Nancy Range. On the SW side of the mountain, facing the Pemigewasset Wilderness, is another precipitous slope, marked with rock slabs, overlooking beautiful Ethan Pond (sometimes called Willey Pond) and an expansive spruce-wooded plateau. A long cliff-faced ridge runs SW from the main ridge, enclosing Ethan Pond's basin on the N.

Hikers will find a steep and challenging climb up Willey from the S or a longer but easier ridgecrest approach from the N. Two outlooks near the summit offer dramatic views E and W.

NOMENCLATURE

For many years Mt. Willey was either nameless, or assigned some name lost to history. The name "Willey" was bestowed on the steep-faced peak in 1845 by the botanist Edward Tuckerman, who reportedly made the first ascent. It commemorates the notorious Willey Slide of 1826, which wiped out the family of settler Samuel Willey, Jr.

HISTORICAL HIGHLIGHTS

First Ascent: It's believed that the first recorded ascent was made by the botanist Edward Tuckerman in 1845.

1771: Moose hunter Timothy Nash reportedly discovers Crawford Notch, spotting gap from tree on Cherry Mtn. to N. Nash and pal Benjamin Sawyer bring horse through Notch and receive land grant from governor. Soon Notch is established as part of trade route between coast and mountains.

ca. 1792: First house built on floor of Notch below Mt. Willey by a Mr. Davis. Modest structure, known as "Notch House," serves as way station for those travelling through pass and is occupied by various tenants.

Looking south down the Saco River valley from the summit of Mt. Willey.

1803: Road through Notch improved and becomes part of Tenth NH Turnpike.

1825: Samuel Willey, Jr. settles in Notch House with wife, five children and two hired hands.

1826: After hot, dry summer, tremendous deluge on August 28 triggers massive landslide on E side of Mt. Willey. Willey family flees house for nearby shelter, but all are buried by slide and killed. Ironically, slide splits on rock upslope and house is unscathed. Three of nine bodies are never found. Storm leaves wake of flood and destruction through Saco valley. Slide tragedy is later immortalized in Nathaniel Hawthorne short story, "The Ambitious Guest": *Down came the whole side of the mountain in a cataract of ruin.*

1829: Ethan Allen Crawford discovers Willey Pond, later named Ethan Pond. In following years he guides inn guests there on fishing trips.

1844: Hotelier Horace Fabyan repairs Notch House and builds Willey Hotel next to it.

1845: Botanist Edward Tuckerman ascends and names Mt. Willey.

1871: Party from Charles H. Hitchcock's geological survey traverses Willey Range.

1874–1875: Portland & Ogdensburg Railroad constructs line through Crawford Notch along lower E slope of Willey, including high trestle over ravine of Willey Brook.

1876: On August 28, 50th anniversary of Willey Slide, group of AMC climbers makes trailless ascent of mountain from Willey House site via Kedron Brook and S slope.

1878: Charles E. Lowe builds first trail up mountain, following same route.
1881: Moses Sweetser's guidebook touts bushwhack route to Willey via Mts. Avalon and Field.
1906: AMC opens new trail from Willey House RR station—route of today's Ethan Pond Trail.
1909: Mr. and Mrs. J. A. Cruickshank blaze new trail from Mt. Avalon over Mt. Field to Mt. Willey.
1911–1916: J. E. Henry's crews are cutting timber in North Fork basin on W side of Mt. Willey.
1913: State of N.H. buys 5,975 acres in Crawford Notch for $62,000.
1918: AMC adopts ridgecrest path and names it Willey Range Trail.
1936: Kedron Flume Trail opened from Willey House site to S of original AMC route (now abandoned).
1950: Hurricane wreaks havoc on Willey Range Trail, closed until 1952. Crawford Notch State Park created.
1969: Forest Service designates W slopes of Willey as part of Lincoln Woods Scenic Area.
1984: Crawford Notch railroad line closed.
1995: Rail line reopened by Conway Scenic Railroad for tourist excursions.

TRAIL APPROACHES

Southeast Approach off US 302 in Crawford Notch

Ethan Pond Trail, Willey Range Trail
5.4 mi. round trip, 2850-ft. elevation gain

Trailhead (1440 ft.): Take US 302 to Appalachian Trail crossing in Crawford Notch, 1 mi. S of Willey House site. At sign for Ripley Falls (summer only), drive 0.3 mi. S up paved side road to kiosk and parking area at end.

This is the shorter and steeper of the two day-hike approaches to Willey; the upper climb is very steep. From parking area follow Ethan Pond Trail (part of Appalachian Trail) across RR tracks and climb 0.2 mi. to jct. where Arethusa-Ripley Falls Trail bears L. Bear R for stiff climb on Ethan Pond Trail. Grade eases at 0.5 mi./1900 ft. and trail makes pleasant traverse through hardwood forest to jct. R with Kedron Flume Trail at 1.3 mi./2400 ft. Rougher climbing leads to jct. with Willey Range Trail at 1.6 mi./2600 ft.

Continue ahead on Willey Range Trail, cross Kedron Brook, and ascend at moderate grade. At 2.0 mi./3000 ft. climb becomes very steep, with two sets of ladders at ca. 3400–3500 ft. and occasional limited views back to S. Steep ascent continues to superb E outlook on short side path R at 2.7 mi.; outstanding view of Presidentials and Crawford Notch. Trail bends L and climbs slightly to true summit, marked by cairn in scrubby firs. Descend slightly along trail to W outlook just beyond, with panorama over eastern Pemigewasset Wilderness; here trail swings R past one more view W and enters woods for ridge traverse to Mt. Field.

Kedron Flume Trail Option
Steep Kedron Flume Trail is alternate approach for lower half of this hike. Beginning at Willey House site (1300 ft.) on US 302, it climbs by switchbacks to RR tracks at 0.4 mi. and continues at moderate grade to Kedron Flume, long, thin cascade, at 1.0 mi./1900 ft.; limited view across Notch. Above here steep, rough climb leads to Ethan Pond Trail at 1.3 mi./2400 ft. Distance is same as lower approach via Ethan Pond Trail with additional 150 ft. of elevation gain.

North Approach from US 302 at Crawford's

Avalon Trail, Willey Range Trail
8.4 mi. round trip, 3100-ft. elevation gain

This approach includes an ascent of Mt. Field along the way, and on the return trip. For description of 2.8 mi./2450-ft. climb to Mt. Field via Avalon Trail, see Mt. Field chapter.

From summit of Field, Willey Range Trail descends S in three short, steep stages to Field-Willey col at 3.3 mi./3980 ft. Trail climbs out of col and meanders along ridgecrest, traversing several small knobs. Easy 0.2 mi. climb leads to two W outlooks on Willey and summit just beyond at 4.2 mi.

WINTER

The approach via Avalon Trail over Mt. Field is most often used; a large plowed area for parking is available at the Crawford's trailhead. After initial steep pitches, snowshoeing is pleasant along the ridge between Field and Willey. Many peakbaggers also include Mt. Tom on the itinerary. The SE approach is much more difficult, and possibly dangerous if icy in the vicinity of the ladders. Plowed parking is available beside US 302 at entrance to the side road to summer trailhead; the walk up this road adds 0.6 mi. round trip and 200 ft. of elevation gain. Deep snow improves the W outlooks over the Pemi Wilderness.

VIEW GUIDE

Taken together, the E and W outlooks provide a fine 270-degree view encompassing the Presidentials, Crawford Notch and the eastern half of the Pemigewasset Wilderness. Steep drop-offs on the E, S and W sides add a sense of drama and lofty isolation.

E Outlook: This small area of open ledge amidst the scrub is a fine lunch spot. You can sit and enjoy nearly all the view, though standing will expand the fringes. The views of the Presidentials and Webster Cliffs are excellent.

On the far L, looking N over the scrub, is the Dartmouth Range, with the Pliny Range above Mt. Deception and Mt. Cabot peering over in back. To the NE is the great mountain wall of the Presidentials. On the L the sharp Castellated Ridge leads up to Mt. Jefferson. Mt. Adams is behind and to the R of Jefferson, with Mt. Clay to the R. Mt. Washington looms to the R of Clay, with the foreshortened ridge of the Southern Peaks in front and below, including Clinton, Eisenhower, Franklin and jagged Monroe. To the R is the bare, level ridge of Boott Spur.

ENE across Crawford Notch are the great granite slabs on the face of Mt. Webster, with the small rock peak of Mt. Jackson behind and to the L. Carter Dome rises in the distance over Webster, with the Wildcats beneath. To the R of the Dome are the dark, wooded ridges of Mt. Isolation and Mt. Davis, with the Baldfaces, Sable and Chandler Mtns. beyond. Speckled Mtn. near Evans Notch is seen through the Isolation-Davis col. In the foreground the steep-faced ridge of Webster slants southward; over its R end, through a broad gap on Montalban Ridge, are the Doubleheads and Kearsarge North. Part of Maine's Pleasant Mtn. is visible behind and R of Kearsarge North.

To the SE is a magnificent view of the winding floor of Crawford Notch, striped by the Saco River, US 302 and the Notch railroad. The Notch bends R beneath Stairs Mtn., shaggy, flat-topped Mt. Resolution, Mt. Parker, and the rock-knob peak of Mt. Crawford. Beyond are the Green Hills in Conway. The ski slopes of Attitash are to the R of Mt. Crawford, and farther R is North Moat. Close by in this direction is the wooded backside of Frankenstein Cliff. Continuing to the R are West Moat, Table Mtn. and flat-topped Bear Mtn. To the R of Bear is distinctive Mt. Chocorua, with Bartlett Haystack below.

Closer in to the R, seen across a broad, forested plateau, is the notched summit of Mt. Bemis, with Mt. Tremont poking up behind. Mt. Paugus and Mt. Shaw (Ossipee Range) are seen over the R shoulder of Bemis. Due S are Mts. Nancy (L) and Anderson and Lowell (R), with Mts. Passaconaway and Whiteface between. The Sleepers and Tripyramids are spotted through the portal of Carrigain Notch. On the far R the view is closed in by the immense bulk of Mt. Carrigain.

W Outlook: This small, tiered ledge right on the Willey Range Trail provides an expansive view over the eastern Pemi Wilderness and surrounding mountains. It's best taken in while standing, though the central part can be seen while seated. On the L (S) the view begins with the Nancy and Sandwich Range peaks as described above. Massive, dominant Mt. Carrigain is seen beyond a rolling, forested upland, with Vose Spur below Signal Ridge on the L. To the R of Carrigain the view sweeps across the broad Shoal Pond Brook basin to the wide-spreading ridges of Mt. Hancock. There are good looks into the two remote ravines of Carrigain Branch and that of Crystal Brook. Scar Ridge and Mt. Hitchcock are seen to the R of Hancock's pointed NW peak. The stripings of old logging roads can be seen on the flanks on Nancy, Carrigain and Hancock.

In this SW direction you look almost straight down at Ethan Pond, with a broad spruce-covered plateau leading out to the low, rolling ridge of Shoal Pond Peak. A slice of Shoal Pond can be seen at the base of this ridge. In this direction the East Branch valley opens out to the ski trails on Loon Mtn., with Carr Mtn. in the distance on the L and Mts. Kineo and Cushman to the R. Bulky Smarts Mtn. is still farther away, behind and R of Cushman. To the R of this broad gap in the mountains is Whaleback Mtn., with a level ridge leading across to Mt. Flume; Mt. Moosilauke rises behind this ridge, and Bondcliff is in front of Flume, obscuring much of its summit.

To the R of Bondcliff the great bulk of Mt. Bond rears from the valley of the North Fork. Mt. Guyot is to the R of Bond. Mt. Lincoln peers over to the L of Guyot, and the serrated crest of Lafayette is on the R, just S of W. Looking due W, in the foreground is the wooded backside of Whitewall Mtn. with the ledgy Zeacliffs and Zealand Ridge beyond, and South Twin to the R. Farther R is slide-marked North Twin. The ledgy spur of Nubble Peak is to the R of North Twin, with Vermont's Mt. Mansfield on the horizon and the wooded knob of West Field close by and below. On the far R is Mt. Hale, its flanks scarred by talus slopes and clearcuts.

NO. OF 4000-FOOTERS VISIBLE: 33

Zealand Mountain

ELEVATION: 4260 ft./1298 m ORDER OF HEIGHT: 31
LOCATION: N edge of Pemigewasset Wilderness, Town of Lincoln
USGS MAP: 7½′ South Twin Mtn.

GEOGRAPHY

The flat, wooded, viewless summit of Zealand Mtn.—the highest swell on the elongated Zealand Ridge—is not an inspiring objective in itself. But there are sweet rewards on the long trek in, including brook and pond scenery in the Zealand valley, a spectacular wilderness vista from Zeacliff, and a ridge walk through boreal forest. Zealand is an interior ridge, far removed from major roads, and were it not for the USFS seasonal Zealand Rd. it would be very remote indeed.

The wooded crest extends for nearly two miles, from a high col with neighboring Mt. Guyot on the SW to the lofty Zeacliffs (ca. 3700 ft.), overlooking glacier-carved Zealand Notch on the E. The true summit of Zealand Mtn. is 0.1 mi. N of the Twinway at the W end of the ridge. From here a spur ridge runs N, with a large talus slope on the W side above the isolated upper basin of Little River. These rock slides are prominent when viewed from the Twins across the valley. This ridgeline is continued N as the "Little River Mountains," passing over an intermediate trailless peak known as

North Zealand, South Hale or Zeale (3700 ft.) and culminating in Mt. Hale. On the W side of this ridge the Little River flows N through a long valley.

Between Zealand's main summit and the Zeacliffs is a 4030-ft. knob known as "Zeacliff Pond Peak," with cliffs overlooking tiny Zeacliff Pond (3700 ft.), which is tucked into a tiny bowl on the S side of the ridge. On the NE side of Zealand Ridge are the headwaters of Whitewall Brook, which tumbles E past Zealand Falls Hut, then flows S through Zealand Notch. At the NE base of the ridge is beaver-dammed Zealand Pond, with outlets flowing both S into Whitewall Brook and N into Zealand River. On the SE side of the ridge is a large basin drained into the North Fork by Jumping Brook, and a smaller valley drained by the outlet brook from Zeacliff Pond.

The Zealand region was ravaged by fires in 1886 and 1903, but has recovered from that devastation and is now a beautiful, peaceful country well worth exploring.

NOMENCLATURE

Zealand Mtn. was originally included under the general title of "Little River Mtns.," referring to the ridge between Little River on the W and Zealand River on the E. This name was used in Charles H. Hitchcock's geological survey in the 1870s. "Mt. Thompson" was another early name, bestowed during an 1879 exploration led by veteran guide Allen "Old Man" Thompson.

Sometime in the late 1800s the name "New Zealand" was applied to the general region W of the Willey-Rosebrook Range. It appeared in Sweetser's 1876 guidebook and on Walling's 1877 map. The origin is uncertain, but may have been a humorous reference to the area's remoteness. The "New" was apparently removed by the Zealand railroad and post office in the 1880s for convenience. Features bearing the Zealand name include a ridge, a mountain, a notch, a waterfall, a river, a pond, a valley, and a set of cliffs.

HISTORICAL HIGHLIGHTS

First Ascent: Unknown

1871: Members of Hitchcock's geological survey explore Zealand region, including Little River Mtns. and Zealand Notch; may have visited summit of Zealand.

1879: Benjamin A. MacDonald and guide Allen Thompson traverse Zealand Notch; account of trip appears in Bethlehem, N.H. tourist paper, *The White Mountain Echo*.

1884–1885: Timber baron J. E. Henry begins construction of logging railroad up Zealand valley. Line eventually extends through Zealand Notch to Shoal Pond. Logging operations continue until 1897.

1886: First Zealand fire sparked on July 8 in logging slash; 12,000 acres burned.

1888: AMC explorers Eugene B. Cook and William H. Peek, guide Charles

E. Lowe and hired hand climb to high point of Zealand, coming across Little River valley from Twin Range. They measure summit at 4348 ft. and find initials "A.M.F." carved in tree in 1872.

1893–1900: Using J. E. Henry's equipment, George Van Dyke operates logging RR in Little River valley.

1903: After dry spring, second Zealand fire scorches 10,000 acres. Visitors call it "Death Valley" and "the climax of desolation."

1915: Zealand area added to WMNF, purchased for $6/acre from Henry company.

1923: WMNF Zealand Trail opened along old RR bed into Zealand Notch from N. Zealand Ridge Trail opened into notch from S, and extended up to Zeacliffs and along Zealand Ridge past summit of Zealand Mtn. to Mt. Guyot. (Today this route is part of Ethan Pond Trail, Zeacliff Trail, and part of Twinway.) Short spur paths constructed to Zeacliff outlook and Zeacliff Pond; shelter built by pond.

1931: AMC builds Zealand Falls Hut at NE base of ridge; opens in 1932. New section of trail links hut with Zeacliff outlook; this and rest of ridge trail is named Twinway.

mid-1930s: Civilian Conservation Corps starts construction of Zealand Rd.

1948: Zealand Rd. completed; not open all the way for auto traffic until 1960.

ca. 1960: Zeacliff Pond shelter removed. Short side path developed from Twinway to Zealand Mtn. summit.

1973: Zealand Falls Hut begins opening in winter on caretaker basis.

TRAIL APPROACHES

NORTHEAST APPROACH from Zealand Rd.

Zealand Trail, Twinway
11.4 mi. round trip, 2400-ft. elevation gain

TRAILHEAD (2000 ft.): From US 302, 2.2 mi. E of stoplight in Twin Mountain, follow USFS seasonal Zealand Rd. 3.5 mi. to parking area at end.

Zealand Trail starts up old logging RR grade, then splits R on bouldery bypass at 0.1 mi. After traversing spruce grove, trail briefly rejoins grade and makes R turn at 0.8 mi. where short spur L leads to ledges in Zealand River. Ascend gradually through conifers, then meander through brushy, swampy area with several stream crossings.

At ca. 1.8 mi. open swamp provides view of Zealand Ridge ahead. Cross boardwalk and skirt swamps and beaver meadows on L. At 2.1 mi. birch-lined aisle leads past pond on L with view across to Mt. Tom. Pass jct. with A-Z Trail on L at 2.2 mi./2450 ft., cross N outlet of Zealand Pond on bridge and skirt shore of pond on R. At 2.4 mi. short spur R leads to shore and view up to Zealand Ridge and Zealand Falls.

At 2.5 mi. turn R on Twinway (part of Appalachian Trail) for steep, rocky climb, past side path L to Zealand Falls, reaching AMC Zealand Falls Hut at

The view toward Whitewall Mtn. and Zealand Notch from atop the Zeacliffs, an eastern spur of Zealand Mtn.

2.7 mi./2637 ft. From here, enjoy good view from front of hut through Zealand Notch to Mt. Carrigain. Adjacent ledges on Whitewall Brook also have view down to Zealand Pond and out to Mt. Tom. Twinway bears R past hut, passing jct. R with Lend-A-Hand Trail to Mt. Hale at 2.8 mi. Cross two branches of Whitewall Brook, then begin long, steady climb, with rocky footing, through extensive white birch forest, mixing with conifers higher up. Reach crest of ridge at 3.9 mi./3700 ft. Here spur continues ahead to open ledges atop Zeacliff, with magnificent view over eastern Pemi Wilderness, and loops back to main trail at mucky spot. Between loop jcts., Twinway runs over ledgy hump with view W to peaks of Twin Range.

Continuing up scrubby ridge, pass jct. L with Zeacliff Trail at 4.0 mi. Gradual climb and descent leads to side trail L to Zeacliff Pond at 4.4 mi. (dropping 0.1 mi./100 ft. to tiny pond, with view of cliffs above and out to Mt. Carrigain). Twinway makes steep, rocky climb to ledge atop "Zeacliff Pond Peak" at 4.7 mi./4060 ft., with view SE. Trail then climbs easily up ridge through boreal forest. At 5.6 mi./4260 ft. reach cairn at high point of Twinway on Zealand Ridge; turn R on narrow, overgrown spur path and follow 0.1 mi. to small summit clearing and sign. No view here!

Zeacliff Trail Loop Option

Strong hikers can make a longer and steeper loop through Zealand Notch to the Twinway near Zeacliff using Ethan Pond Trail and Zeacliff Trail. From jct. below Zealand Falls Hut, follow Ethan Pond Trail S along old RR grade into Zealand Notch through birches, level with occasional washouts. At 1.3 mi. from jct. emerge on open rocks on side of Whitewall Mtn., with views up and down notch and across to Zeacliffs. Turn R here on Zeacliff Trail and descend steeply over talus to cross Whitewall Brook at 1.5 mi. Climb steeply up E side of Zealand Ridge, then more moderately up birch-wooded crest. Winding, steep route up through ledgy terrain leads to Twinway at 2.7 mi. Turn L for summit of Zealand Mtn. (1.7 mi. away) or R for Zeacliff outlook (0.1 mi.). Elevation gain on Zeacliff Trail is 1500 ft. from brook crossing. Loop is 1.2 mi. longer than direct route via hut, with extra 250-ft. elevation gain (due to descent to brook).

Southwest Approach from Mt. Guyot

Backpackers and hut-hoppers can also climb Zealand as part of a multi-day traverse of Twin Range. From jct. of Twinway and Bondcliff Trail, skirt open NE summit of Mt. Guyot (4580 ft.; stay on trail to preserve fragile vegetation) and make long, gradual to moderate descent down NE ridge with rocky footing. Look for view of Zealand talus part way down. Reach Zealand-Guyot col (4020 ft.) at 1.1 mi. from jct., then climb 0.2 mi./240 ft. to side path L to Zealand summit, 1.3 mi. from jct.

WINTER

Zealand Rd. is gated in winter and not open to public vehicle travel, effectively isolating Zealand Mtn. as much as Owl's Head or the Bonds. Winter parking is in the lot on the N side of US 302, 0.3 mi. E of the entrance to Zealand Rd. Road walking adds 3.8 mi. each way to the trip, for a marathon 19.0 mi. round trip with 2900-ft. elevation gain. Some winter peakbaggers ski or snowshoe in to Zealand Falls Hut (open on caretaker basis in winter) and use that as a base to day hike Zealand Mtn. (6.0 mi. round trip, 1700-ft. elevation gain from hut). Expect deep, drifted snow up on Zealand Ridge. Experienced bushwhackers sometimes approach the mountain via the USFS Haystack Rd., North Twin Trail and the trailless upper Little River valley and N ridge of Zealand, an arduous but interesting route with possible views from the top of the Zealand talus slope.

VIEW GUIDE

Zeacliff Outlook: The S-facing outlook ledges on the spur loop off the Twinway are one of the great view spots in the White Mountains, sweeping over the eastern Pemi Wilderness and several mountain ranges. On the far L, looking NNE, is Mt. Dartmouth in the Dartmouth Range. To the E the Presidentials rise majestically beyond Mt. Tom, with Mt. Jefferson to the L and Mt. Clay right above Tom. Mt. Washington is to the R of Tom, with Monroe, Eisenhower, Boott Spur and the top of Pierce farther R. Mts. Field and Willey are to the R of Washington. To the ESE is an impressive view across Zealand Notch to the scarred face of Whitewall Mtn., with its cliffs, talus slopes and ledgy S knob. The Ethan Pond Trail, which follows the bed of the old Zealand Valley logging railroad, cuts a line across the lower slopes. The Giant Stairs and Mt. Resolution are seen beyond Whitewall and the trailless ridge extending S from Mt. Willey. Kearsarge North pokes above the L end of Resolution. Farther R are Mt. Crawford, a sharp rock peak, and Mt. Parker, with Black Cap Mtn. between them. North Moat and Mts. Bemis and Nancy are visible beyond the broad spruce-wooded plateau in the foreground. Shoal Pond is in line with North Moat and Norcross Pond gleams at the R base of Mt. Nancy. The ledgy gash of Thoreau Falls can be seen below, in line with the Bemis-Nancy col.

To the SE is a classic vista of the spires of Mts. Anderson and Lowell, U-shaped Carrigain Notch, and massive, triple-humped Mt. Carrigain, seen across extensive rolling wildlands. Bear Mtn. is over Anderson's L shoulder, and sharp-peaked Mt. Tremont and Mt. Chocorua's Three Sisters Ridge are sighted through the gap between Anderson and Lowell. Part of Mt. Paugus is seen through Carrigain Notch. To the R of Carrigain is the low, flat-topped knob of The Captain, with Mt. Whiteface and East Sleeper in the distance. Farther R, almost due S, the sprawling ridges of Mt. Hancock fill a large section of the horizon, with the gaping valley of Crystal Brook revealed beyond the long valley of the North Fork. The Osceolas, the West Peak of Mt. Tecumseh, Mt. Hitchcock and Scar Ridge are to the R of the Hancocks. To the SW and close by is the great mass of Mt. Bond, showing a bare spur ridge on the L.

NO. OF 4000-FOOTERS VISIBLE: from Zeacliff Outlook, 15; from Zealand Mtn. summit, 20 (theoretical, through the trees).

The Bonds

MOUNT BOND

ELEVATION: 4698 ft./1432 m ORDER OF HEIGHT: 14
LOCATION: Twin Range, Town of Lincoln
USGS MAP: 7½′ South Twin Mtn.

WEST BOND

ELEVATION: 4540 ft./1384 m ORDER OF HEIGHT: 16
LOCATION: Twin Range, Towns of Lincoln and Franconia
USGS MAP: 7½′ South Twin Mtn.

BONDCLIFF

ELEVATION: 4265 ft./1300 m ORDER OF HEIGHT: 30
LOCATION: Twin Range, Town of Lincoln
USGS MAP: 7½′ South Twin Mtn.

GEOGRAPHY

The three peaks of the Bonds, situated at the S end of the Twin Range, are among the most remote, yet dramatic summits in all the White Mountains. Lying deep within the federally-designated Pemigewasset Wilderness, the open summits of the Bonds offer unrivaled views of mountains, valleys and unbroken forests in every direction. Nowhere else in the Whites can the hiker find such a sense of removal from civilization. From many angles, the Bonds—West Bond and Bondcliff in particular—are impressive mountains to look *at* as well as *from*, with cliffs, slides and scree fields marking their steep slopes.

The Bonds rise sharply out of the Franconia Brook valley to the W and the valley of the North Fork of the East Branch to the E. Mt. Bond is the anchor peak of the range, lying three miles S of the summit of South Twin. A bald area at the very summit permits panoramic views. To the N the ridge runs over a wooded sub-peak, then dips to a 4380-ft. col with Mt. Guyot, whose rounded double summits are one mile N. Just S of this col a spur ridge extends SW to West Bond (see below). Two major ridges extend S from Mt. Bond, enclosing the valley of Black Brook. The SW ridge is dominated by Bondcliff (see below); the SE ridge runs for three miles out to the East Branch.

On the E, Mt. Bond's huge mass slopes endlessly down toward the North Fork between Thoreau Falls and the main stem of the East Branch. Its NE slopes drain into Jumping Brook, a major tributary of the North Fork. High up on one of its several E ridges, but not accessible by trail, is a unique alpine zone seen best from the area around Thoreau Falls. On its W side the summit of Bond drops steeply, with large scree slopes, into the upper valley of Hellgate Brook, a wild, twisting basin that is enclosed by all three Bond peaks.

The tiny rock peak of West Bond is perched atop a narrow, steep-sided ridgecrest running SW from the main ridgeline near the N end of Mt. Bond. The narrow crest is about 0.3 mi. long and bears three small knobs; the easternmost is the true summit. The deep, winding valley of Hellgate Brook separates West Bond from Bondcliff to the S. The steep S and SE slopes of West Bond are striped with five great slides that are seen to advantage from the nearby crags of Bondcliff and serve as landmarks from more distant southern viewpoints. The N side of the ridge is somewhat less steep, with several ridges and ravines extending into the hidden valley of Redrock Brook. These northern slopes are splotched with extensive talus fields. The horseshoe of ridges formed by West Bond on the S, Mt. Guyot on the E, and the SW ridge of South Twin on the N enclose a remote, trailless area at the head of Redrock Brook featuring two glacial cirques, numerous rock slides, and a tiny tarn in the northern cirque, known as Bear Pond or Redrock Pond. To the W the ridge of West Bond broadens as it descends 2500 ft. to the Franconia Brook valley.

The summit of West Bond offers unparalleled views into the Redrock and Hellgate valleys and across the latter to Bondcliff, the fine series of crags and ledges SW of Mt. Bond. Bondcliff is probably best known for its ragged cliff face dropping off several hundred feet into Hellgate Brook valley on its NW flank. "Surely the best photo opportunity in the mountains is looking towards slide-scarred West Bond with the fractured cliffs in the foreground," wrote one White Mountain guidebook author of Bondcliff's summit vista. N of the summit a bare ridge extends nearly a mile across to the SW shoulder of Mt. Bond. To the E is the valley of Black Brook. To the W a broad ridge runs over two wooded spurs (3314 ft. and 2889 ft.) before descending to the Franconia Brook valley; this ridge forms the S side of the Hellgate Brook basin. Another ridge leads S from Bondcliff, soon passing over a sharp, wooded 3900-ft. spur, then fanning out into three sub-ridges that drop away to the East Branch valley.

The Bonds are about as far away from civilization as one can get in the Whites. The closest trailhead to either Bond or West Bond (at the end of Zealand Road) is 8.2 mi. away. For Bondcliff, the closest trailhead is 9.1 mi. away at the Lincoln Woods lot off the Kancamagus Highway.

NOMENCLATURE

The three peaks of the Bond Range are named for Professor George P. Bond, an early mapmaker and geographer affiliated with Harvard University. Bond was responsible for producing the first highly respected map of the White Mountains area back in 1853. The name "Mt. Bond" was assigned to the "southernmost summit of the Twin Range" by the Appalachian Mountain Club in 1876. (At the same time, they named the next peak to the N after another noted geographer, Arnold Guyot.) For many years, Bondcliff was referred to as The Cliffs or The Cliffs of Bond. One group of early explorers of the peaks identified Mt. Bond as "Craggy Mtn.," and the AMC group that made the first ascent of the Bonds in 1871 originally proposed the name, "Mt. Percival," after a poet and geologist from Connecticut. West Bond was just known as a western spur of the range for many years; only after the 4000-Footer Club was formed in 1957 did it actually receive a name.

HISTORICAL HIGHLIGHTS

First Ascent: The first known ascent of at least one, and possibly all three Bonds, was made in 1871 by two members of Charles Hitchcock's geological survey team—Warren Upham and an unidentified Dartmouth College student. Working from a camp a mile up Franconia Brook in what was then true wilderness, four of the group climbed up the ridge of Owl's Head, then Upham and his companion dropped E into the valley and ascended the Bond ridge via "the western spur," noting "the almost perpendicular face of rock, like some castle wall . . . at the top of the south peak on its northwest side." In relating his findings in *Appalachia* in 1876, Upham said, "The view [from Mt. Bond] is wholly of forest-covered mountains on every side, and I think no evidence is seen of the works of man, except for the small settlement on the summit of Mt. Washington."

1882: A. E. Scott leads party of six on week-long bushwhack epic over Twin Range. Trip includes ascent of North Twin, South Twin, Mt. Bond, and Mt. Field (in Willey Range). Account of adventure appears in April 1883 *Appalachia*.

1883: Trail from South Twin to Bonds is cut by Scott, others. Also, trail is spotted, cleared from Bondcliff to East Branch by way of Bear Brook (Black Brook). No attempt is made to cut path from Bond to Bondcliff, however.

1902: Overgrown and little-used path over Twins and Bonds refurbished by AMC.

1903–1910: Working from Camps 9, 10 and 14 off Franconia Brook spur of logging railroad, J. E. Henry's crews strip timber from W slopes of Bonds.

1907: Great fire starts on Owl's Head and consumes much of remaining timber on W slopes of Bonds. Present birch forest in much of area is legacy of fire.

1907: First AMC Guide lists trail from Mt. Bond to North Fork.

1913: New log shelter, to be known as Guyot Shelter, is built near spring between Mts. Guyot and Bond.

1916: Charles Blood (AMC) proposes new path from Bond to Bondcliff.

1916–1931: Timber crews from Henry Co. and Parker-Young Co. advance up North Fork of East Branch along another RR spur. Working from Camps 22, 22A, 23 and 23A, they ravage E slopes of Bonds.

1920: Lower portion of North Fork Trail from Mt. Bond is rerouted S to railroad nearer to North Fork Jct.

1920–21: Side trail is cut from Bond to Bondcliff.

1924: Tireless trail-builder Karl Harrington extends Twin Range Trail from summit of Mt. Bond down to Bondcliff, and then out to logging railroad line on East Branch of Pemi. Former trail from Bond to North Fork Jct. is abandoned.

1926: Original Guyot Shelter replaced by new log structure.

1929: Path over Twins-Bonds dubbed "Most Troublesome Trail in White Mountains" by Paul Jenks (AMC).

1934: Section of former Twin Range Trail between new Twinway trail near Mt. Guyot and logging rail line now called Bondcliff Trail.

1939: AMC crews construct third Guyot Shelter.

1960: For first time, AMC Guide describes bushwhack route to summit of West Bond; hikers are cautioned to allow at least three hours for the short but arduous round trip. That year first known winter ascent of Bonds is made by party led by Bob Collin, via Zealand Ridge and Mt. Guyot. Feat is repeated next day by Robert and Miriam Underhill and Merle Whitcomb, from Galehead Hut.

1963: Group led by Collin makes spectacular winter traverse of West Bond, up from cirque in Redrock Brook valley and down W ridge to Franconia Brook.

1966: AMC guide notes that side trail to West Bond is "well-worn" and takes just 25 min. each way. Path is soon officially adopted as "West Bond Spur."

1971: Tent platforms added at Guyot Shelter campsite.

1980: Bondcliff is added to 4000-Footer list when it's determined that elevation gain from Bond-Bondcliff col to summit exceeds prerequisite 200 feet.

1984: Bonds are included in 45,000-acre Pemigewasset Wilderness created by Congress.

TRAIL APPROACHES

South Approach from Kancamagus Highway (NH 112)

Bondcliff only

Lincoln Woods Trail, Wilderness Trail, Bondcliff Trail
18.2 mi. round trip, 3100-ft. elevation gain

Bondcliff and Mt. Bond

Lincoln Woods Trail, Wilderness Trail, Bondcliff Trail
20.6 mi. round trip, 3950-ft. elevation gain

Bondcliff, Mt. Bond and West Bond

Lincoln Woods Trail, Wilderness Trail, Bondcliff Trail, West Bond Spur
22.6 mi. round trip, 4600-ft. elevation gain

Trailhead (1160 ft.): Lincoln Woods parking area on N side of Kancamagus Highway (NH 112), 5.6 mi. E of Exit 32 off I-93 in Lincoln.

Though exceptionally long, the approach to the Bonds from the S is never difficult as the trail (at least to Bondcliff) mostly follows either an old logging RR grade or old logging roads. Only the last quarter-mile to Bondcliff's summit and the half-mile ascent of Bond from Bondcliff can be considered difficult.

From Lincoln Woods parking area, cross suspension footbridge over

East Branch of Pemigewasset River and turn R onto Lincoln Woods Trail along wide, level bed of J. E. Henry's East Branch & Lincoln RR (1893–1948), with many ties still astride trail. Easy walking leads to jct. L with Osseo Trail at 1.4 mi./1300 ft. and Camp 8 clearing just beyond. Trail approaches wide, rocky river at 1.6 mi. with view of Bondcliff upstream. At 2.6 mi. Black Pond Trail splits L. At 2.9 mi./1440 ft. is side trail L to Franconia Falls (0.4 mi.).

Continue ahead across footbridge over Franconia Brook and bear R onto Wilderness Trail near boundary sign for Pemigewasset Wilderness. After bypass of mucky area continue along RR grade, mostly away from river, crossing "One-Mile Brook" at 3.9 mi. Reach former Camp 16 tenting area (now closed) and jct. L with Bondcliff Trail at 4.7 mi./1600 ft.

Bear L here onto Bondcliff Trail and ascend moderately, then gradually N along relocated section of trail to W of Black Brook. At 5.8 mi. trail swings R and joins old logging road. Grade is easy, footing a bit rocky, through young conifers to first crossing of Black Brook at 6.1 mi./2100 ft. Second crossing is at 6.6 mi/2360 ft. Swing R and dip to third crossing, sometimes dry, at 7.2 mi./2780 ft. Trail horseshoes around minor ridge and climbs long rock staircases, leveling on scrubby slope at 3000 ft. and crossing small gravel slide with view across to steep E side of Bondcliff, crowned by rock peak. Just beyond is fourth crossing of brook, in steep ravine. Trail loops around to R, bears L up tiny ridge, then at 7.9 mi./3360 ft. swings L again to pick up old logging road for slabbing ascent across steep slope. Spindly birches and young conifers crowd edges of footway.

At 8.4 mi./3650 ft. trail swings to R, with rocky footing. Reach crest of Bondcliff's S ridge at 8.8 mi./3960 ft. and bear R for steady climb, passing view R to Mt. Carrigain. At 9.0 mi. you must negotiate short but difficult ledge scramble, emerging at top to wide views S and W. Climb easily through scrub, then completely in open to flat, ledgy summit of Bondcliff at 9.1 mi./4265 ft. Here there are incomparable wilderness views in every direction.

To continue to Mt. Bond, follow Bondcliff Trail to N along barren ridge. Trail is exposed for next mile and this section should not be traversed in bad weather. Follow markings carefully and keep back from W edge, which drops off in steep cliffs. In fair weather, this is one of most spectacular ridge walks in Whites. Trail descends along barren ridge at easy grade to long, level 4060-ft. col, with impressive views across to slides on West Bond. Trail continues in open as it begins ascent of SW slope of Mt. Bond, soon becoming steeper and rougher. At ca. 10.0 mi., halfway up side of Bond, trail enters scrub and continues rugged climb, attaining open summit of Bond at 10.3 mi./4698 ft. High point is just to R of trail, with superb 360-degree view.

To proceed to West Bond, continue N on Bondcliff Trail, entering conifer woods and descending to minor col. Climb slightly over N hump of Mt. Bond and drop easily, then more steeply to jct. L with West Bond Spur at 10.8 mi./4500 ft. (Side trail to Guyot Shelter, 0.2 mi. long, is 0.2 mi. farther N on Bondcliff Trail.) Turn L here and descend steadily on narrow trail

The late afternoon sun reflects brilliantly off the ledges of remote Bondcliff.

through dense firs to col at 11.1 mi./4340 ft. Ascend at moderate grade, then quite steeply up E end of summit, scrambling over rocks to top of small, sharp peak of West Bond at 11.3 mi./4540 ft. Views are matchless, especially across Hellgate valley to Bondcliff and over Redrock cirques to South Twin.

Northeast Approach from Zealand Road (FR 16)

For options below, add 0.2 mi. for easy round trip to Zealand Mtn. summit.

West Bond only

Zealand Trail, Twinway, Bondcliff Trail, West Bond Spur
16.4 mi. round trip, 3950-ft. elevation gain

Mt. Bond only

Zealand Trail, Twinway, Bondcliff Trail
16.4 mi. round trip, 3800-ft. elevation gain

Mt. Bond and West Bond

Zealand Trail, Twinway, Bondcliff Trail, West Bond Spur
17.4 mi. round trip, 4150-ft. elevation gain

Mt. Bond, West Bond and Bondcliff

Zealand Trail, Twinway, Bondcliff Trail, West Bond Spur
19.8 mi. round trip, 5000-ft. elevation gain

TRAILHEAD (2000 ft.): From US 302, 2.2 mi. E of stoplight in Twin Mountain, follow USFS seasonal Zealand Rd. (FR 16) 3.5 mi. to parking area at end.

A somewhat shorter alternative (especially for reaching Bond and West Bond) is the approach from the Zealand valley by way of AMC's Zealand Falls Hut and Zealand Mtn. (another 4000-footer). Though shorter by a couple of miles, there's significantly more elevation gain with an out-and-back trip to the Bonds since you'll be climbing the summit cones of Mt. Bond and Zealand Mtn. twice.

For description of route via Zealand Trail and Twinway as far as side trail to summit of Zealand Mtn. (5.6 mi.), see chapter on that mountain. From Zealand summit side trail, Twinway makes fairly steep descent to Zealand-Guyot col (4020 ft.) at 5.8 mi. Trail now begins moderate climb up long, heavily wooded NE ridge of Mt. Guyot. Grade eases on shoulder at 4200 ft., but footing is very rocky in places. Trail makes sharp L at 6.6 mi./4380 ft. and ascends steadily again to broad NE summit of Mt. Guyot at 6.8 mi./4580 ft. Here trail emerges into open; please stay on defined treadway to protect alpine vegetation. Descend to jct. L with Bondcliff Trail at 6.9 mi./4508 ft. Here there are fine views W over Redrock Brook valley to Owl's Head and Franconia Range.

Turn L here on Bondcliff Trail and traverse barren ridge to SW summit of Mt. Guyot at 7.1 mi./4580 ft. From this rounded alpine summit there are excellent views in all directions to the peaks in and around the Pemi Wilderness. Continue S along Bondcliff Trail in open, then descend into woods to small col and over minor hump to main Guyot-Bond col at 7.5 mi./4380 ft. Here side trail leads L 0.2 mi., with 250-ft. elevation loss, to Guyot Shelter (accommodates 12) and Campsite (with 6 tent platforms). There is also a fine, reliable spring here that makes the down-and-up side trip well worthwhile for thirsty Bonds trekkers. As many hikers are not into torturing themselves with 20-mile-plus day hikes, the Bonds are a popular destination with backpackers; though remote, this overnight destination is usually filled to capacity on summer/fall weekends.

From this jct., Bondcliff Trail ascends steadily to jct. R with West Bond Spur at 7.7 mi./4500 ft. West Bond is 0.5 mi. along spur; Mt. Bond is 0.5 mi. ahead on Bondcliff Trail, with Bondcliff 1.2 mi. beyond.

North Approach

Another, lesser used approach to the Bonds, primarily for backpackers, is from the N, either from Galehead Hut or from the Little River valley. Either approach entails ascents of North and/or South Twin. For detailed descriptions of routes to these summits, see North and South Twin chapter. From South Twin, follow Twinway S steeply down off summit cone. Trail continues on easy grades along high, broad ridge wooded with high scrub. At 0.9 mi. from South Twin pass over hump with limited views ahead to Guyot and Bond and back towards South Twin. After reaching South Twin-Guyot col (4380 ft.), trail climbs gently through scrub along W slope of Guyot and meets jct. with Bondcliff Trail (4508 ft.) 2.0 mi. S of South Twin summit. Follow Bondcliff Trail S over SW summit of Mt. Guyot and on to Bonds as described above.

WINTER

Due to their remoteness, the Bonds are among the hardest peaks to "bag" during the winter months. Although it makes for a grueling 20-mile day, most hikers choose to ascend all three summits in a single day, rather than have to make one or two return trips. The usual route taken is from the S (Kancamagus Highway) along the Lincoln Woods, Wilderness and Bondcliff Trails. The first 4.7 mi. on Lincoln Woods and Wilderness Trails are usually well-tracked out and provide a quick approach. With unbroken snow, the remaining 4.4 mi. to Bondcliff can take many hours. It's easy to lose the trail as you climb into the scrub on the S side of Mt. Bond. The Twinway N of Mt. Bond has some of the deepest snow in the Whites.

The approach from Zealand is impractical as a day-hike as Zealand Road is closed to motor vehicle traffic. One possibility is to stay at Zealand Falls Hut (open on caretaker basis; winter-rated sleeping bag needed) and day-hike the Bonds from there, nabbing Zealand along the way. This would cut the trip to all three Bonds down to 14.6 mi. round trip with 4300-ft. elevation gain.

The best time of winter to tackle the Bonds is in early to mid-March, owing to the extra hours of daylight available. It's best done on a clear, relatively calm day. As all three peaks are open (particularly Bondcliff), exposure to the winter wind and cold is always a concern on the Bonds; full winter clothing and gear are needed, and crampons may be required for the open ridge between Bondcliff and Bond.

VIEW GUIDE

All three Bonds are rated among the top viewing spots in the White Mountains for their expansive wilderness vistas. Warren Upham, along with a companion the first to climb the Bonds back in 1871, was captivated by what he saw: "From these summits, especially from Mt. Bond, which best overlooks the East Branch valley, the prospect is extensive and grand. As far as the view extends, we see only mountains and valleys and forest. . . . All is silent untrodden forest, and all around are the lofty foreheads of our highest mountains." After a recovery from the rapacious logging of the early 1900s, these Pemi views are once again perhaps the finest in the mountains.

Mt. Bond View: The highest of the Bonds has the most comprehensive view, because Bond itself blocks out parts of the vistas from Bondcliff and West Bond. To the E Bond offers a great sweep over the eastern Pemi Wilderness. To the NE, beyond the basin of Jumping Brook, the mighty

Standing atop the ragged cliff face of Bondcliff, with the scarred walls of West Bond in the background.

Presidentials tower above the Willey Range, with the prominent ledges of Whitewall Mtn. on the E side of Zealand Notch in front. Mt. Jefferson rises to the L of Mt. Tom, and Mt. Washington is to the L of Mt. Field. Carter Dome pokes up to the L of Mt. Willey. To the ENE the broad upper valley of the North Fork extends out to Ethan Pond at the base of Mt. Willey; the ledges of Thoreau Falls can be seen in line with the summit of Willey, as can the bare shoulder on the E ridge of Bond right below. To the R of Willey are the Webster Cliffs with the Baldfaces beyond.

To the E the lower North Fork valley and the ridge informally known as "Shoal Pond Peak" are in the foreground; beyond, a spruce-clad plateau extends out to the trailless ridge between Mt. Willey and the Nancy Range. Beyond this ridge are the Doubleheads, the Giant Stairs, Mt. Resolution and Mt. Crawford, and Kearsarge North. The Nancy Range is ESE, with North Moat behind. To the SE is the huge, shapely bulk of Mt. Carrigain. To its R is the sprawling mass of Hancock, with the great ravine of Crystal Brook carved into the S side of its rounded summit. Passaconaway and Whiteface peer over the L shoulder of Hancock, and Tripyramid, Huntington and Kancamagus are to the R.

To the S Sandwich Dome is seen through Mad River Notch, with the

Osceolas and Hitchcock on the R. To the WSW you look down on the rearing crags of Bondcliff, with Loon and distant Cardigan beyond. Scar Ridge is to the L of Bondcliff, with Mt. Kearsarge above on the horizon. To the R of Bondcliff are Carr, Kineo and Cushman in the mid-distance, with Whaleback closer in and farther R. To the R of Whaleback are Flume and Liberty with Moosilauke hovering beyond. The rocky S peak of Owl's Head is in front of Liberty. The main mass of Owl's Head is in front of the central part of the Franconia Range.

Due W and close by is the slide-scarred spine of West Bond, with Lincoln and Lafayette soaring behind. The sharp peak of Garfield is to the R of West Bond, and in this direction vast horizons extend out to Vermont's Green Mountains, including Mt. Mansfield to the L of Garfield. To the N the bulky Twin Range winds over bald Mt. Guyot and out to South and North Twin on the L. Farther R is the broad, wooded Zealand Ridge, with Hale, Cherry and the Nash Stream mountains out to the L. Mt. Waumbek is over Zealand, with Cabot nosing over on the L. To the NNE is Zeacliff, with the Dartmouth Range, Crescent Range and distant Maine mountains beyond.

West Bond View: The tiny rock peak of West Bond is perhaps the ultimate wilderness viewpoint in the White Mountains, providing a splendid sense of lofty isolation amidst a maze of high ridges and deep valleys.

The most striking view is S across the wild valley of Hellgate Brook to the arching crest of Bondcliff, with its ragged line of crags in full frontal view. Rising beyond Bondcliff and the scree-splotched ridge that extends L to Mt. Bond is a tumult of rumpled mountains. Between Bond and Bondcliff you see (L to R) the distant Moats, the scarred face of Mt. Lowell, the great bulk of Carrigain and its satellite, Vose Spur, Chocorua and Paugus to the R of Carrigain, and the massive sprawl of Hancock, with Passaconaway on its L and Whiteface, Tripyramid, Huntington and Kancamagus on its R. Directly over Bondcliff are Mad River Notch, Sandwich Dome, Hitchcock and the Osceolas, with Tecumseh to the R. Farther R sections of the wide, rocky East Branch can be seen leading out to Scar Ridge and Loon Mtn. Mt. Kearsarge is on the distant horizon above Scar Ridge. To the SW, past the S end of the Owl's Head ridge, are Whaleback and the graceful peaks of Flume and Liberty, with Moosilauke beyond.

To the W the lofty Franconia Ridge soars above the N end of the long, low wooded ridge of Owl's Head. The slash of Lincoln Slide is prominent to the R of Mt. Lincoln. From Mt. Lafayette the bumpy Garfield Ridge stretches across to the rocky pyramid of Mt. Garfield. Below these peaks is the remote forested basin at the headwaters of Franconia Brook. Mt. Mansfield can be spotted on the horizon between Lafayette and Garfield.

The view N across the wild cirques of Redrock Brook is unique to West Bond. The rocky crown of South Twin rises above the L, or northern of the bowls. Tiny Bear Pond can be glimpsed at the base of a talus slope on the floor of the ravine. The southern and closer of the glacial basins bears two large slides facing towards West Bond. The L slide is long and narrow; the R is a huge, wide gash. Both fell in 1994. To the R is the bald double dome of Mt. Guyot. Mts. Waumbek and Cabot are seen through the col to the L of Guyot, and Mts. Jefferson and Clay are visible through the col on Guyot's R. To the R of Clay the tip of Mt. Washington just pokes over the N shoulder of Mt. Bond. The main mass of Bond shuts out any distant views to the E.

Bondcliff View: The open flat ledges atop Bondcliff are one of the great hangout spots in the Whites. Some devotees maintain that this is the richest viewpoint of all among the Bonds. Most dramatic is the broadside view of West Bond's steep, slide-scored ridge, seen NNW across the deep valley of Hellgate Brook. Many a hiker has posed on a cliff-edge crag for a photo with this impressive backdrop. Northward the barren ridge stretches away towards the scrubby dome of Mt. Bond. To the R of Bond, Mt. Clay, Mt. Washington and Boott Spur rise behind Mt. Field. To the ENE the broad valley of the upper North Fork leads out to Mt. Willey; Carter Dome pops out above Willey. Farther R is the nearby ridge known as Shoal Pond Peak; in succession behind it are the ridge between Willey and the Nancy Range, Montalban Ridge, and the Baldface Range and Doubleheads. Just S of E, beyond the two S knobs of Shoal Pond Peak, are Mts. Bemis and Nancy, with Kearsarge North behind to the L. Of special note is the vista SE across the broad, spruce-cloaked upper valley of the East Branch—known as the Desolation region—to Mts. Anderson and Lowell and mighty Mt. Carrigain, showing its distinctive three-humped profile. North Moat is seen over Lowell. To the R of Carrigain is the great bulk of Hancock and its wild N ridges leading down to the East Branch. Chocorua is nicely framed between the two big peaks. To the R of Hancock are waves of peaks and ridges, including Whiteface, Tripyramid, Huntington, Kancamagus, and Sandwich Dome through Mad River Notch. Looking due S are the Osceolas above Hitchcock. Tecumseh is behind and to the R of the Osceolas. Farther R are the several summits of Scar Ridge, with Loon lower on its R. Cardigan is seen on the horizon over Loon, and Carr, Kineo and Cushman are to the SW. Farther R and closer is the ridge of Whaleback, truncated on its L end and on the R leading across to Mt. Flume. Moosilauke is behind Flume on the L and the notched peak of Liberty is to the R. The Franconia Range continues across to Little Haystack; South Kinsman pokes over its low point. To the W, you gaze down into the deep, winding valley of Hellgate Brook, which leads out to Franconia Brook valley and a broadside view of the long, massive, wooded ridge of Owl's Head just beyond. Above the R (N) end of Owl's Head are Mt. Lincoln, with the Y-shaped Lincoln Slide to the R, and the high, serrated crest of Lafayette. To the NW are the upper Franconia Brook basin, Garfield Ridge and the sharp peak of Mt. Garfield, then the view swings back around to the nearby ridge of West Bond.

NO. OF 4000-FOOTERS VISIBLE: from Mt. Bond, 38; from West Bond, 23; from Bondcliff, 28.

Mount Carrigain

ELEVATION: 4700 ft./1433 m   ORDER OF HEIGHT: 13
LOCATION: SE Edge of Pemigewasset Wilderness, Town of Lincoln, Township of Livermore
USGS MAP: 7½′ Mount Carrigain

GEOGRAPHY

Few peaks in the White Mountains can match the grandeur, spectacle and beauty of this towering mass, which for more than a century has been revered by climbers. Viewed from any angle, it is a dominant and easily idenified landmark. Being the most centrally situated major peak in the region, Mt. Carrigain offers a sweeping, unmatched view of the Whites, and in particular of the remote Pemigewasset Wilderness. It was once accurately described as the "great watch tower of the wilderness."

Mt. Carrigain lies in the SE corner of the federally-designated Pemigewasset Wilderness, with its main ridgeline serving as both the Wilderness boundary and the Lincoln-Livermore town line. Its summit rises 2650 ft. from the valley of the East Branch of the Pemi River at Stillwater Junction (to its N), and approximately 2060 ft. from the height-of-land in Carrigain Notch, just to its E.

As viewed from the N, Carrigain's main ridgeline descends sharply to the NE toward its namesake notch in a characteristic triple-humped profile. The ridge features two round subsidiary peaks, a nameless 4260-ft. knob and Vose Spur (3862 ft.), one of New England's 100 highest summits and a frequent destination of bushwhacking peakbaggers. Carrigain Notch is a wild, remote pass separating Carrigain's sprawling mass from the rugged, inaccessible peaks of Mts. Lowell and Anderson to the E. From its height of land (2638 ft.) flow Carrigain Brook to the S, into the Sawyer River, and Notch Brook to the N, towards the headwaters of the East Branch.

To the SW, the main summit ridge drops 1500 ft. to a connecting ridge linking Carrigain with Mt. Hancock. The most prominent peak on this rough ridge, which is scarred on its S side by inviting cliffs and ledges, is 3520-ft. Carrigain Pond Peak (also known as The Captain), trailless and rarely visited by backcountry explorers. The Captain overlooks a long, remote valley drained by a northern tributary of the Sawyer River. To the NE of this peak is seldom-visited Carrigain Pond (3180 ft.), a four-acre tarn which forms the headwaters of the Carrigain Branch, flowing N into the Pemi..

To the NW, a long wooded ridge drops steeply down into the area known as Desolation. In the early part of the 20th century this area was heavily logged by crews working for railroad lumber baron James E. Henry. For several years, a logging camp (Camp 20) was sited here. A short distance north of Desolation is the confluence of the East Branch of the Pemigewasset

River and Carrigain Branch, called Stillwater. On the E side of the NW ridge is a deep, wild ravine facing N.

Just SE of the main summit, and only a few hundred feet lower, is the lofty crest of Signal Ridge, Carrigain's open, knife-edged southeastern ridgeline that boasts as wild a view as any one spot in the mountains. Its perspective on Vose Spur, Carrigain Notch, and the slide-scarred wall of Mt. Lowell is exceptional. Beyond the crest, Signal Ridge gradually extends to the S and SE into the upper Sawyer River valley.

NOMENCLATURE

The mountain is named for former New Hampshire Secretary of State Philip Carrigain (1772–1842), who served in that post from 1805 to 1810. Carrigain is best known for producing one of the state's earliest maps, published in 1816, which showed many of the northern mountains for the first time. The name of the mountain first appeared in an 1857 atlas.

Signal Ridge was originally called "Burnt Hat Ridge," from an 1873 incident in which a storm overtook an exploring party atop the ridge and blew the hat of one of the climbers into their campfire. Its present name derives from surveying days in the late 1800s.

Vose Spur was named in 1876 for George L. Vose, an assistant in Charles H. Hitchcock's geolgical survey and an active member of the White Mountain Club of Portland, Maine, which specialized in exploring the Carrigain region.

HISTORICAL HIGHLIGHTS

First Ascent: Mt. Carrigain was first climbed by Arnold Henri Guyot (1807–1884) and his party of explorers in August 1857. It is thought that Guyot and his companions ascended the mountain from what is now known as Carrigain Notch, climbing over Vose Spur and another intermediary peak before reaching the summit. Despite "scratched face and hands, bruised feet and well-worn clothes," wrote S. Hasting Grant, one of the dozen adventurers accompanying Guyot, "I don't begrudge the pains taken in the least. Quite the contrary . . . the outlook was quite beyond anything yet seen."

Guyot was a Swiss scientist well-known for his study of glaciers, and was affiliated with Princeton University at the time of his Carrigain ascent. He roamed widely across the White Mountains and probably climbed more 4000-footers than anyone else before the 1870s. Guyot was also an early mapmaker and is credited with proving that New Hampshire's Mt. Washington was not the highest peak east of the Mississippi, as was previously believed. A 4580-ft. peak on the Twin-Bond Range is named in his honor.

1869: George Vose, local guide John C. Cobb, and artist George Morse, on geological survey expedition, attempt summit climb from Sawyer River valley by route known as "Cobb's Stairs." Group reaches Signal Ridge (later dubbed "Burnt Hat Ridge"), thinking it is summit; clouds obscure true summit, however, unbeknownst to group until descent is well underway.

1871: Geology survey party including Warren Upham reaches summit in what is likely second ascent of peak, ascending from East Branch up NW slope of mountain through open spruce woods. They measure elevation as 4678 ft.

1873: During expedition to mountain, group of climbers decide to form White Mountain Club of Portland, Maine, which devotes much of its time to visiting less-explored reaches of White Mountains. Over next couple of years, members climb Carrigain three more times, with August 1875 trip featuring a descent from summit N into virgin forest of Pemi Wilderness. Member George F. Morse completes profile of view from Carrigain which is reproduced in atlas published by Hitchcock's geological survey.

1876: Town of Livermore, in which major portion of mountain lies, is chartered by state. Party led by guidebook editor Moses Sweetser climbs Carrigain from SW.

1877: Saunders family establishes logging rail operation in Sawyer River valley, Livermore. Operation is noted for relatively conservative cutting tactics.

1879: AMC cuts first trail up mountain, following for most part "Cobb's Stairs" route up the steep E side of Signal Ridge. Path is called Mt. Carrigain Trail.

1880: Webster Wells, writing in *Appalachia,* describes August 1879 bushwhack excursion from Mt. Hancock to Mt. Carrigain. Along tortuous ridge walk, group stumbles upon remote Carrigain Pond; are probably first humans to ever visit pond.

1896: AMC Snow-Shoe Section members make probable first winter ascent of peak. Group includes Miss M. A. Furbish.

1898: Section of trail up mountain is relocated due to lumbering operations. New route follows more closely today's Signal Ridge Trail.

1906: AMC opens new path through Carrigain Notch. Trail runs from village of Livermore to North Fork Jct. on East Branch, a distance of 11.25 mi.

1910: N.H. Timberland Owners Association funds construction of fire lookout on summit, one of first in state. Ownership is taken over by state in 1911, U.S. Forest Service in 1933–34.

1910–1914: Logging crews of J. E. Henry occupy Camp 20 in Desolation area. Twenty-five million board feet of timber are removed from Vose Spur, Mt. Carrigain and Mt. Hancock.

1912: Heavily logged-over area around Carrigain Pond is described thusly by Maurice Osborne: "Scarcely a green thing showed around its desolated shore. . . . Here was Carrigain Pond, now desecrated, profaned, and laid bare to the vulgar gaze."

1927: November flood washes out bridges, road bed of Sawyer River logging railroad. One year later, sawmill at Livermore village shuts down for good.

1932: New route up Carrigain from N is established by AMC to provide access from new Zealand Falls Hut. Desolation Trail begins from Stillwater area and climbs to summit first via old logging road, then through virgin forest at higher elevation. At about same time, Mt. Carrigain Trail is renamed Signal Ridge Trail.

1936: Due to fire danger created by softwood slash left over from lumber operations, Forest Service temporarily closes off major portion of East Branch drainage to public entry. Affected trails include Carrigain Notch and Desolation Trails.

1940: New 20-ft. steel fire lookout's tower erected on summit by USFS.

ca. 1940: Carrigain Notch Trail rerouted through Desolation area and former logging camp (Camp 20) site. Original portion of trail running to Shoal Pond Trail is listed in AMC Guide as Stillwater By-Pass.

1948: Summit fire lookout post placed on inactive status by USFS.

ca. 1948: First 2.2 mi. of Carrigain Notch Trail from Livermore now designated as part of Signal Ridge Trail.

1949: New log shelter (Desolation) accommodating 12 campers is built near jct. of Carrigain Notch and Desolation Trails.

1955: Carrigain Notch Trail terminus now at Stillwater. Section of trail from there to North Fork Jct. designated part of Wilderness Trail from Lincoln.

1966: AMC Guide lists recently built extension of Nancy Pond Trail from outlet of Norcross Pond to Carrigain Notch Trail, one mile E of Desolation Shelter.

1982: Old summit fire tower taken down; replacement observation tower erected by USFS, Young Adult Conservation Corps.

1984: 45,000-acre Pemigewasset Wilderness is added to National Wilderness Preservation System. North slope of Mt. Carrigain lies within wilderness boundary.

Early 1990s: Bold 450-lb. black bear nicknamed "Brutus" terrorizes campers in Desolation region.

1995: Sawyer River Rd. washed out by major October storm, is not repaired for three years.

1997: Desolation Shelter is dismantled.

TRAIL APPROACHES

South Approach from Sawyer River Road (FR 34)

Signal Ridge Trail

10.0 mi. round trip, 3250-ft. elevation gain

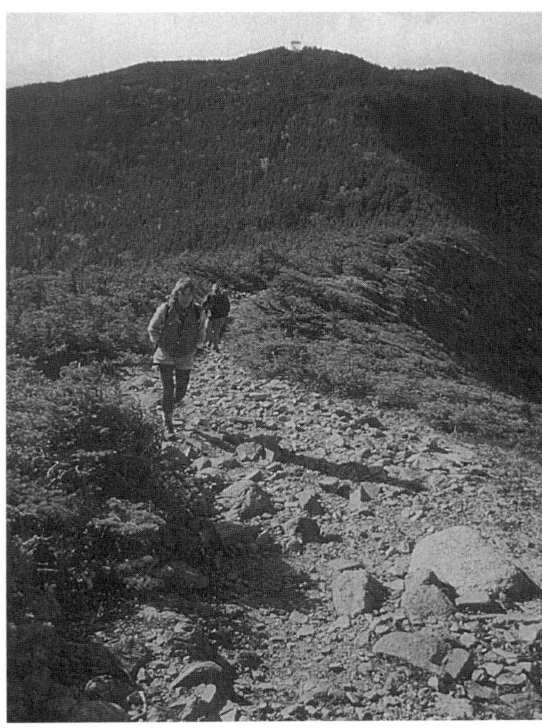

Hikers push on across Signal Ridge as the main summit of Mt. Carrigain rears up behind them.

TRAILHEAD (1480 ft.): The Signal Ridge Trail begins off Sawyer River Road 2.0 mi. from its jct. with US 302, which is approximately 3.7 mi. from Bartlett and just N of the bridge over Sawyer River. The trailhead parking lot is on the L just past bridge over Whiteface Brook.

This is the usual approach to Carrigain. After an easy two-mile start, there is a long, steady climb to the spectacular crest of Signal Ridge, where excellent views are enjoyed before the final short push to the summit.

From parking area, walk back across road bridge to start of trail on L, which quickly joins old logging road. At 0.2 mi., Whiteface Brook is crossed. In times of high water, stream crossing can be difficult. It can be avoided by bushwhacking from Sawyer River Road along S bank of river to point where trail is met. Following along S bank of brook, trail climbs at easy grade past series of nice pools and cascades, then climbs away from stream at 0.8 mi. before leveling out as grade of another logging road is met. At 1.4 mi., unmaintained Carrigain Brook Road (FR 86) to end of Sawyer River Road is passed on L. Then jct. with Carrigain Notch Trail (1.7 mi. / 1900 ft.) to Desolation / Stillwater area is reached on R.

Signal Ridge Trail continues straight ahead, crossing Carrigain Brook almost immediately (may be difficult in high water). After passing through boggy area and crossing another stream, level grade ends and long ascent of ridge begins with sharp L turn off logging road (2.4 mi.). After several switchbacks, trail takes sharp R at 2.8 mi./2800 ft. and begins mile-long traverse of old road angling its way up E side of ridge through small birch and conifer growth. Footing is rocky. Look for occasional views (on R) through trees toward Carrigain Notch and cliffs of Mt. Lowell. At 3.8 mi./3700 ft. trail turns sharp L off logging road and via series of twists and turns begins steep ascent to S end of Signal Ridge, reached at 4.5 mi./4420 ft. Trail passes over bare, level ridgecrest with steep dropoff on R. Here there are excellent views E and W and toward wooded mass of tower-topped summit just ahead to NW. Especially notable is view E across Carrigain Notch to gravelly slides, cliffs and talus on W face of Mt. Lowell, with Vose Spur close by on L and Webster Cliffs, Willey Range and Presidentials beyond. To SW is wild view to lumpy ridges of Mt. Hancock, with profile of The Captain's cliffs below.

From N end of open ridge, trail drops into sag, angles toward S slope of summit, and eventually reaches site of old firewarden's cabin. From clearing, trail continues on L, bears R and climbs more steeply to summit ridge, then steers R again to main summit and observation tower at 5.0 mi./4700 ft.

North Approach from Stillwater/Desolation

Desolation Trail

3.8 mi. round trip, 2500-ft elevation gain (from Carrigain Notch Trail)

Trailhead (2180 ft.): One of the most remote and wild trails in the mountains, Desolation Trail begins at the jct. with Carrigain Notch Trail near the site of the former Desolation Shelter.

Mostly following old logging roads, the trail approaches the summit from the NW via a long wooded ridge E of Carrigain Branch valley. This approach is much steeper and rougher than the Signal Ridge approach, but is the most direct approach up the mountain from the East Branch and Zealand areas.

Trail leaves Carrigain Notch Trail at sharp R turn near tributary of Carrigain Branch. It initially follows old logging railroad grade, then veers L onto ancient logging road which climbs at moderate grades. As nice stand of birches is met, trail merges onto long, straight road dug into W side of ridge. At ca. 3150 ft. trail follows this amazing road across to E side of ridge, where it is cut into side of steep slope. There are occasional glimpses into deep ravine on L. At 1.3 mi/3650 ft., trail leaves road and grade quickly becomes very steep, climbing over wet rocks and numerous stone steps while passing through shady stand of virgin spruce. Look back for occasional views N into Pemi Wilderness. Watch footing carefully through this steep, rugged section, where even J. E. Henry's bold loggers decided not to cut. Eventually, as trail climbs to crest of steep NW ridge, grade lessens and footway improves. At 1.8 mi. swing L for brief traverse before final sharp pitch leads to summit and tower, 1.9 mi. from Carrigain Notch Trail.

Loop Option

A nice, but ambitious alternative to the traditional out-and-back ascent via Signal Ridge Trail is the loop hike through Carrigain Notch with the summit ascent via Desolation Trail. From Signal Ridge Trail, steer R onto Carrigain Notch Trail 1.7 mi. from Sawyer River Road and cross Carrigain Brook 60 yd. from jct. Trail approaches notch on easy grades, passing beaver pond on L with view up to lower Signal Ridge and crossing several stony brookbeds. At 3.3 mi./2200 ft., small gravelly opening in brook to R opens view up to Vose Spur. Trail soon steepens and works up W side of wild Carrigain Notch, reaching height-of-land and Pemigewasset Wilderness boundary at 4.0 mi./2637 ft. Trail now begins moderate descent on N side of notch, utilizing mostly old logging roads with occasional bypasses to L. In this area trail passes through deep conifer forest with wild, almost primeval feel. At 5.8 mi./2140 ft., trail turns L onto old logging railroad grade at jct. with Nancy Pond Trail and follows easy grade for 0.8 mi., passing through old logging camp site (Camp 20) just before meeting Desolation Trail to Mt. Carrigain at 6.7 mi./2180 ft. Turn L here to continue loop hike, following Desolation Trail to summit, then descending via Signal Ridge Trail. Total for loop, 13.6 mi., elevation gain 3650 ft.

(Carrigain Notch Trail continues R at jct., passing by former Desolation Shelter site in 0.1 mi. and terminating in 0.7 mi. at 2050-ft. Stillwater Jct., where Wilderness Trail to Kancamagus Highway in Lincoln bears L and Shoal Pond Trail to Zealand area bears R and crosses East Branch of Pemigewasset River. Please note that no camping is allowed within ¼ mi. of old shelter site.)

WINTER

Mt. Carrigain is a challenging peak to reach in winter, mainly because the access road to the Signal Ridge trailhead (Sawyer River Road) is gated at US 302. This adds four miles to a round-trip hike, making it 14.0 mi. total from start to finish, with 3800-ft. elevation gain. Frequently winter trampers will don cross country skis for the two-mile trek from the highway to the trailhead. The ski out is particularly nice as it's all downhill from the trailhead to US 302. If breaking trail, the mile-long slab up the E side of Signal Ridge is very tiresome. While most of the hike up Carrigain is in the sheltered woods along the road and trail, the traverse of treeless Signal Ridge may pose some problems for hikers, especially in times of stormy weather. Fortunately, the summit mass of Carrigain frequently shelters Signal Ridge from the winter's often brutally cold NW winds. On a calm, sunny winter day, the crest of Signal Ridge is one of the finest spots in the hills.

VIEW GUIDE

Carrigain's isolated central position in the Whites gives it a commanding perspective on the region, and indeed the summits of 43 of its 4000-footer brethren can be seen from the top, tying it with Mt. Washington for top honors in that regard. The all-encompassing view from Carrigain has extracted superlatives from hikers for more than a century. "From its central position a better idea of the arrangement of the White and Franconia Mts. is had than from any other point, perhaps, in the whole group," wrote George L. Vose, who visited the summit several times in the early 1870s. With unusual succinctness, guidebook editor Moses Sweetser noted that the view overlooks "many leagues of unbroken wilderness and stately mountains." Save this one for a clear day!

In addition to the nearly numberless summits visible from here, there is an unrivalled view over the vast (by New England standards) wild area of uplands in the eastern half of the Pemigewasset Wilderness. Ironically, these wilderness views would be limited by the dense fir growth atop the peak were it not for the observation tower that was renovated in 1982 for the benefit of Carrigain-climbers.

The N view over the Pemi Wilderness overlooks a basin of unbroken forest thousands of acres in area drained by the North Fork, Shoal Pond Brook and the East Branch of the Pemigewasset itself. To the NW this region of long valleys and low, rolling ridges is closed in by the high peaks of the Bond-Twin Range. The rounded, ledgy crest of Bondcliff is almost due NW, with the sharp rocky peak of Garfield and slide-marked ridge of West Bond to its R. Marching in quick succession along the Bond-Twin Range to the R are the summits of Mt. Bond, Mt. Guyot, South Twin and North Twin, with the top of its E slide visible. In front of North Twin, elongated Zealand Ridge extends R and out to the deep scoop of Zealand Notch—this is one of the best places for viewing that rocky pass. The sharply cut valley of Jumping Brook is seen below the summit of Zealand Mtn., at the L end of Zealand Ridge. Mt. Hale is sighted through Zealand Notch, and in the distance beyond Zealand and Hale are many distant ridges in northern Vermont. In the foreground, below Zealand Ridge and Zealand Notch, are the broad, spruce-clad valley of Shoal Pond Brook and its long, low neighboring ridge on the L (W), known as Shoal Pond Mtn.

Ledgy Whitewall Mtn. forms the R (E) wall of Zealand Notch, and from that summit a long ridge extends R to the Willey Range. Little, ledgy Mt. Oscar and shapely Cherry Mtn. are seen through a gap on the R side of Whitewall. Just E of N the broad upper plateau of the eastern Pemi stretches out to the base of the Willey Range peaks of Tom, Field and Willey. The glimmer of Shoal Pond can be spotted on the tableland, in line with the W spur of Mt. Field. There's an unusual view into a hidden basin enclosed by the W spur of Field, Field itself, and Willey. In the distance to the L of Tom are the peaks of the Nash Stream area, and the long ridge of Waumbek is seen over Field, with Mt. Cabot just peering over.

To the NNE, beyond the 4260-ft. spur of Carrigain, is a striking vista to the gravel-gashed Webster Cliffs, forming the E side of Crawford Notch, with the peaks of the Presidentials piled beyond. Jefferson and Washington are prominent, while the ridge of the Southern Presidentials is foreshortened. To the R of Mt. Washington and Boott Spur, looking NE, the high summits of the Carters rise above the Wildcats and upper Montalban Ridge, with Mts. Anderson, Nancy and Bemis in the foreground. Farther R, beyond nearby Mt. Lowell, are the Giant Stairs and gravel-splotched Mt. Resolution, with the Baldface Range in the distance. The Doubleheads and Iron Mtn. are farther to the R.

To the E is the prominent blue dome of Kearsarge North, with vast horizons in Maine beyond. A bit farther R the town of Bartlett is seen in the Saco valley, guarded by the ski slopes of Attitash Mtn. on the R. Cranmore Mtn. and Black Cap in the Green Hills, and Pleasant Mtn. in Maine, are behind Attitash. The graceful Moat Range is to the ESE. To the SE you look down on Signal Ridge, with the swath of the trail running across its crest. The jumbled peaks of Mt. Tremont and Owl Cliff are beyond, with Bear Mtn. behind and Bartlett Haystack to the L. Countless hills in western Maine and eastern N.H. are in the distance. To the R Chocorua is seen over the lower part of Signal Ridge.

Mt. Paugus is seen over the flat crest of nearby Green's Cliff. Just E of S is a beautiful spread of the Sandwich Range high peaks, seen beyond the broad Albany Intervale: Passaconaway, Whiteface, Sleepers and Tripyramid. Bulky Sandwich Dome is set back to the R, beyond the eastern ridges of Mts. Huntington and Kancamagus. To the SSW, past the western part of Kancamagus, Mt. Kearsarge is seen on the horizon, with Mt. Monadnock peeping over on the L. To the R of Kancamagus are the Osceolas, with Tecumseh popping up between them and the two main rounded summits of Huntington in front.

To the SW is the wild, sharp South Peak of Hancock with Scar Ridge and more distant mountains such as Carr (L) and Smarts (R) beyond. Vermont's Mt. Ascutney is on the horizon to the L of Carr, over the twin E summits of Scar Ridge. To the R of Scar Ridge's main summit is ski-trailed Loon Mtn. with Mt. Cube and Vermont's Killington and Pico in the distance. Close by to the WSW is the rounded hump of North Hancock, with massive Moosilauke rising beyond.

To the W, Mt. Wolf and Whaleback Mtn. are seen over the craggy NW Peak of Hancock. Mts. Abraham and Ellen are far beyond, in the Green Mtns. Just to the R are Mts. Flume (L) and Liberty (R), with South Kinsman between them and North Kinsman to the R. Camel's Hump in Vermont raises its distinctive profile to the R of North Kinsman, over the ridge connecting Liberty with the higher Franconias. To the WNW Mts. Lincoln and Lafayette dwarf the ridge of Owl's Head beneath them. The V-shaped Lincoln Slide is especially prominent. From here the view swings back around to the Bonds.

NO. OF 4000-FOOTERS VISIBLE: 43

Galehead Mountain

ELEVATION: 4024 ft. / 1227 m ORDER OF HEIGHT: 44
LOCATION: Garfield Ridge, Town of Franconia
USGS MAP: 7½′ South Twin Mtn.

GEOGRAPHY

This wooded mountain is situated on the E end of Garfield Ridge and appears as a rather inconspicuous hump from most perspectives. It sits at the head of the Gale River to the N and the Pemi Wilderness to the S, but is dwarfed by its higher, more spectacular neighbors to the E and W. To the E, 4902-ft. South Twin Mountain towers nearly 900 ft. above Galehead's summit, while to the W lies Mt. Garfield (4500 ft.) and several of its subordinate peaks (including Mts. Pam and East Garfield).

The North Branch of the Gale River flows off the mountain's lower slopes to the N, draining out through a long, deep mountain valley followed by the Gale River Trail. On the mountain's SE slope drains Twin Brook, which runs for nearly two miles SW before converging with Franconia Brook near 13 Falls Campsite. This scenic mountain valley is traversed by the Twin Brook Trail, which passes through a stunning stand of white birches found on Galehead's lower south-facing slopes. Galehead forms the western wall of this valley, while South Twin and its 4357-ft. SW spur rise sharply on the opposite side of the stream. A long spur ridge runs SSW from Galehead's summit down to the 13 Falls area; a little more than halfway down this ridge is a flat-topped 2962-ft. knob fronted by small cliffs. To the W of Galehead's summit and this spur ridge is a secluded valley drained by the E fork of Franconia Brook.

NOMENCLATURE

Galehead Mtn.'s name is tied directly to the river (Gale River) which originates on its N slopes and flows NW, eventually into the Ammonoosuc River. The headwaters of the North Branch of the Gale River flow off the slopes of Galehead and North and South Twin Mtns. According to *The History of Franconia* by Sarah N. Welch, Gale River is named for Susannah Gale, daughter of an early town resident on whose farm "the Gale Spring is located and across which the river flows."

HISTORICAL HIGHLIGHTS

First Ascent: Unknown
1904–1909: J. E. Henry's crews conduct intensive logging operations on S

slopes of Galehead, working from Camp 13 at end of Franconia Brook spur line of East Branch & Lincoln RR. 1907 fire sears lower S slopes.

1914: Charles Blood leads week-long expedition over Garfield Ridge, scouting out proposed trail linking Twin Range with Mt. Lafayette.

1915: Trail is established between South Twin and Haystack Lake (Garfield Pond).

1916: Garfield Ridge Trail is completed.

1926: Galehead Shelter, accommodating 8–10 campers, is built by AMC in area known as Surveyor's Clearing.

1929–30: Galehead Trail, branch path from Gale River Trail (previously established route to Garfield Ridge Trail E of Mt. Garfield via Garfield Stream and Hawthorne Falls) opens. Path leaves trail 3 mi. from state highway, ascends steep ravine at head of North Branch of Gale River, and meets ridgeline near shelter site.

1932: AMC completes construction of new Galehead Hut at cost of $10,527.98. Structure stands about 100 yards W of former shelter.

1938: In aftermath of September hurricane, hut is inaccessible as windthrown trees block every approach trail onto Garfield Ridge.

ca. 1940: E end of Garfield Ridge Trail now coincides with upper portion of Galehead Trail.

1951: Hut visitors Jack and Ruth Frost begin effort to establish trail from hut to Galehead summit. Work is completed following July.

1952: AMC maps list Galehead Mt. for first time.

1953: Trail to summit receives permanent name, Frost Trail.

1954: Heavy rains from two hurricanes cause landslide, flooding along Gale River Trail.

1960: Former Galehead Trail renamed Gale River Trail; old route up valley of Garfield Stream that once bore this name has been abandoned.

1962: AMC takes over maintenance of Frost Trail.

1968: AMC opens Twin Brook Trail from S, providing access to Galehead area from 13 Falls.

1975: Revised USGS maps elevate summit to 4000-ft. status. Previously, summit elevation was listed as 3948 ft.

1982: Fiftieth anniversary of Galehead and Zealand Huts opening is celebrated.

1999: Crews begin dismantling of original AMC hut and start construction of replacement facility.

2000: New Galehead Hut opens in June. State-of-the-art facility, including handicap accessible ramp, costs upwards of $450,000. Later in summer group of disabled hikers makes landmark ascent up Gale River Trail to hut. Supported by family, friends, volunteers, wheelchair-bound Craig Gray, Nicole Haley and Geoff Krill successfully make way to hut. Making same trek on crutches are Souley Marzouk and Dr. Susan Murray.

TRAIL APPROACHES

NORTH APPROACH from Gale River Loop Road (FR 92)

Gale River Trail, Garfield Ridge Trail, Frost Trail
10.2 mi. round trip, 2450-ft. elevation gain.

TRAILHEAD (1600 ft.): From jct. of US 3 and Trudeau Rd., between Franconia Notch and Twin Mountain, drive SE on USFS gravel Gale River Rd. (FR 25). Bear L at 0.6 mi. and turn sharp R at 1.3 mi. onto Gale River Loop Rd. (FR 92). Parking area for Gale River Trail is on L at 1.6 mi. This approach via the scenic Gale River valley is quickest, most direct approach to Galehead. It is also used by hikers headed up to South Twin or to hut.

From parking area, Gale River Trail crosses small brook and then leads S at easy grades on W side of Gale River's North Branch, keeping well back from stream. Approach river at 1.4 mi. and cross to E side on footbridge at 1.7 mi. Trail becomes rougher along bank, crosses tributary, then recrosses North Branch of Gale River on step stones at 2.5 mi./2250 ft., usually a fairly easy crossing. Grades continue easy through slide outwash areas to open gravel bank at 3.1 mi./2580 ft, with interesting view up to high ridges of Twins. Beyond, trail begins to steepen, and at 3.5 mi. commences stiff climb up rock staircases, reaching jct. with Garfield Ridge Trail at 4.0 mi./3390 ft.

Turn L here for moderate, rocky climb on Garfield Ridge Trail through deep, mossy coniferous forest. Reach AMC Galehead Hut at 4.6 mi./3780 ft. From hut, Frost Trail drops into sag, passes through blowdown patch, then at 0.1 mi. passes jct. L with Twin Brook Trail to Pemi Wilderness. Trail soon jogs R and begins 250-ft. climb to summit. At 0.3 mi. from hut, at top of steep pitch, side trail L leads to nice viewpoint S into Twin Brook valley and up to massive wall of South Twin. Easy climbing leads to summit cairn at clearing in woods, 0.5 mi. from hut.

Other Approaches
There are three additional ways to reach Galehead Hut and the Frost Trail, but all involve significantly more climbing and mileage.

The Twin Brook Trail provides the best access to Galehead from the S. It leaves from 13 Falls Campsite (2196 ft.) near Franconia Brook and climbs 2.6 mi. to its terminus at Frost Trail, 0.1 mi. from hut. The lower end of trail at 13 Falls begins 8.1 mi. from Kancamagus Highway in Lincoln. It is reached via Lincoln Woods and Franconia Brook Trails, a long easy walk along old railroad grades. Twin Brook Trail bears E and NE as it climbs out of Franconia Brook valley and enters splendid birch forest. Middle mile of trail traverses four minor ridges of Galehead Mtn. before bearing N to jct. with Frost Trail. Distance from 13 Falls to Galehead summit is 3.0 mi. (one-way) with 1850-ft. elevation gain.

From the W, Garfield Ridge Trail from Franconia Ridge and Mt. Garfield terminates at hut, 6.6 mi. from its start atop Mt. Lafayette. Garfield Ridge

Trail, a link in the Appalachian Trail, is accessed by Mt. Garfield and Gale River Trails to N and Franconia Brook Trail from S. The distance between Galehead Hut and Mt. Garfield is 3.1 mi. This trail is noted for its rough terrain and many ups and downs.

The Twinway, linking Galehead Hut with AMC's Zealand Falls Hut, is primary E approach to mountain. Twinway runs 7.0 mi. from hut to hut and along way passes near or over Mts. Zealand, Guyot and South Twin. The 0.8 mi. stretch from South Twin to Galehead Hut is exceedingly steep, dropping 1150 ft. in elevation.

WINTER

The Gale River Loop Rd. is closed to auto travel in winter, adding 3.2 mi. round trip on snowmobile-packed road to approach via Gale River Trail (total 13.4 mi.). Parking is available on N side of US 3 by jct. with Trudeau Rd. Toughest snowshoeing is approach to Garfield Ridge Trail and isolated short, steep pitches on Frost Trail to summit. Few winter hikers will strike out only for Galehead; they'll usually add one or both of the nearby Twins, making for either a tiring out-and-back trip or a strenuous loop over No. Twin and down to Haystack Road. (See Twin Mountain chapter for mileage / distance.)

Note also that Galehead Hut is closed in winter.

VIEW GUIDE

Back in the mid-1950s, when the trail to Galehead's summit was still quite new, visitors marveled at "a panorama that extends from Osceola and Tecumseh on the south through to Jay Peak on the Canadian border in Vermont—not to mention the unsurpassed view of nearby Franconia Ridge." Unfortunately, tree growth at the summit has all but eliminated any views of note; in fact, only the peaks of Franconia Ridge (to the W) and the crown of neighboring Mt. Garfield are seen over the trees that now envelop most of the actual summit. If you stand on the cairn you may be able to spot the Osceolas and Tecumseh to the S.

Though there's not much to look at from the summit, there are two decent viewpoints at or near the mountaintop. From the vicinity of Galehead Hut, South Twin Mtn. looms high above to the SE, while more to the S are seen the Twin Brook and Franconia Brook valleys, with Owl's Head Mtn. rising up out of the latter. Above and beyond Owl's Head is wooded Scar Ridge near the Kancamagus Highway and the upper slopes of Loon Mtn. in Lincoln. More to the W are seen Galehead's rounded, wooded summit mass and behind it to R is sharp peak of Mt. Garfield.

Views to the S are also gained from a ledge L off the Frost Trail 0.3 mi. from the hut. The view is similar to that found at hut, but from a vantage point 200 feet higher. To the L of Scar Ridge are now seen Mts. Tecumseh and Osceola near Waterville Valley, while far in the distance to the SW are several peaks in south-central New Hampshire. Nearby to the E, South Twin looms massively across the upper valley of Twin Brook.

NO. OF 4000-FOOTERS VISIBLE: 11

Mount Garfield

ELEVATION: 4500 ft./1372 m ORDER OF HEIGHT: 17
LOCATION: Garfield Ridge, Town of Franconia
USGS MAPS: 7½′ South Twin Mtn., 7½′ Franconia

GEOGRAPHY

The conical 4500-ft. peak of Mt. Garfield is one of the most dramatic and recognizable in the White Mountains. Lying midway between Mt. Lafayette and South Twin Mtn., the mountain is the culminating point of rugged Garfield Ridge, notorious among hikers for the many ups and downs along its six-mile length. Garfield's bare, pointed peak, standing at the head of the great mountain amphitheater that encircles the lush western Pemigewasset Wilderness, is its most striking attribute.

Garfield's long forested northern slopes sweep gracefully upward from the Gale River valley. On the NW side the slopes are drained by Burnt, Spruce, and Thompson Brooks, all draining into the South Branch of Gale River. To the NNE is cliff-faced Flat Top Mtn. (3248 ft.), a trailless spur overlooking Garfield Stream, a fork of the North Branch of Gale River. This stream tumbles down over Hawthorne Falls and several unnamed cascades.

The mountain's steep, rocky S face presents a much more rugged aspect, overlooking the remote upper drainage of Franconia Brook. When the continental glaciers ground their way S during the Ice Age, they gave Garfield a smooth N slope where the ice flowed uphill, and a rugged S face where the downward pull of the ice plucked chunks of rock away.

Near the western base of the summit cone, about a half-mile distant, lies Garfield Pond, a small tarn nestled amidst the conifers at an elevation of 3800 ft. From the pond Garfield Ridge runs SW over a 3885-ft. hump, then rises to the North Peak of Mt. Lafayette. On the E the cone of Garfield drops precipitously to a 3420-ft. col, beyond which Garfield Ridge twists eastward over two unnamed knobs (3667 ft. and 3590 ft.) and continues on to Galehead Mtn.

Another prominent feature of Garfield is its southern spur that abruptly ends in an impressive wall of cliffs overlooking the NW corner of the Pemi Wilderness. These inaccessible precipices are especially prominent when seen from the summit of Mt. Lafayette.

NOMENCLATURE

Originally known as the Haystack (for its symmetrical profile), the Franconia Haystack, and also Hooket, the mountain was renamed in August 1881 in honor of U.S. President James Garfield, who earlier in the year had been struck down by an assassin's bullet. The new name, proposed by Frances A. Willard, was officially bestowed upon the mountain by the selectmen of Franconia, in which a major portion of the mountain rests.

HISTORICAL HIGHLIGHTS

First Ascent: It is likely, though not absolutely certain, that a group of Dartmouth College students, all members of Prof. Charles H. Hitchcock's geological survey team, were the first to reach the summit of Garfield (then known as Mt. Haystack) early in the summer of 1871. C. H. Conant, Jonathan Smith, and (possibly) C. W. Hoitt are also credited with first discovering Garfield (Haystack) Pond during this same geological expedition.

1878: E. B. Cook of AMC leads five climbers on bushwhack trek across Garfield Ridge, starting atop Mt. Lafayette and proceeding E. At Haystack Lake, group meets three fishermen bound for trout streams in trackless wilds of Pemi Wilderness. On climb to summit, Cook reports "we soon came upon traces of previous visitors."

1881: Moses Sweetser's guidebook describes trailless trek to mountain as "surpassingly difficult, leading through long unbroken thickets of dwarf spruce."

1881: Franconia selectmen officially change name of mountain to Garfield, in honor of President James Garfield.

1883: W. L. Hooper of AMC bushwhacks from Twins across Garfield Ridge to Mt. Garfield and on to Mt. Lafayette.

1897: AMC cuts path starting at Profile and Franconia Notch RR bridge over Gale River and running up NE ridge to summit of Garfield.

1902: Forest fire ravages N slopes of mountain.

1904–1909: J. E. Henry's men are logging S slopes of Mt. Garfield from Camp 13 and railroad line to SE. 1907 fire burns S slopes of mountain.

1914: Charles Blood leads week-long expedition on ridge, scouting out proposed route for new trail that will connect Twin Range with Mt. Lafayette.

1915: First trail is established between South Twin and Haystack Lake.

1916: AMC guide lists two routes to summit. One leaves from state highway (today's Route 3), follows North Branch of Gale River and Garfield Stream, passes by picturesque Hawthorne Falls on NE slope of mountain, then climbs to new Garfield Ridge Trail in low col E of Mt. Garfield. This is later named Gale River Trail. Second route (Garfield Trail) follows South Branch of Gale River, then steers SE through forested area burned over in 1902.

1917: Garfield Ridge Trail is finally completed. First Garfield Pond shelter constructed; rebuilt in 1925.

1918: AMC votes to officially change name of Haystack Lake to Garfield Pond.

1940: 14-foot square forest fire lookout cabin is constructed on summit by CCC crews. Materials are hauled up by tractor road. It remains in operation through 1948. Cement foundation is all that remains of cabin today. Franconia Brook Trail opened to Garfield Ridge from 13 Falls in valley to S.

Late 1950s: Trail past Hawthorne Falls disappears from hiking guides.

1971: Garfield Ridge Campsite is established 0.4 mi. E of summit. It serves as replacement for Garfield Pond Shelter, closed that same year due to overuse and lack of reliable water source. Garfield Pond Cut-Off is abandoned.

TRAIL APPROACHES

North Approach from Gale River Loop Road (FR 92) in Bethlehem

Garfield Trail
10.0 mi. round trip, 3000-ft. elevation gain

Trailhead (1500 ft.): Garfield Trail starts from Gale River Loop Road (FR 92), 1.2 mi. from US 3. To reach trailhead, leave highway 0.3 mi. W of intersection with Trudeau Road. Avoid R fork, and continue until road turns sharp L and crosses bridge. Parking lot is on R.

Although a lengthy walk with 3000-ft. elevation gain, this hike is mellow as the trail mostly follows old logging and tractor roads that once serviced the summit fire lookout cabin.

First 0.7 mi., relocated by Forest Service in 1991, leads over narrow, bumpy hemlock-clad embankment before rejoining old trail near E side of Gale River's South Branch. After two stream crossings and long, gentle ascent through hardwood forest, trail begins to pass through fine white birch forest at 2.8 mi. in area once called Burnt Knoll after early 1900s fire. Trail then turns sharp L, enters conifer forest, and begins first of seven long switchbacks. At L turn marking start of last switchback (3800 ft.), look for nice view towards Mt. Lafayette through stand of dead trees. Note: Former Garfield Pond Cut-Off departed here on R before its abandonment in early 1970s.

Trail slabs around cone of mountain at moderate grade, meeting with Garfield Ridge Trail at 4.8 mi./4180 ft. Turn R for steep, rocky 0.2 mi. scramble to open, ledgy summit, located a few yards S (left) of trail at 5.0 mi./4500 ft. Highest point bears old foundation of lookout cabin; best viewing spots are on S side. (Note: From Garfield Ridge Trail jct., 0.2 mi. descent to E leads to Garfield Ridge Campsite, elevation 3900 ft., which features 12-person log lean-to and seven four-person tent platforms. Campsite is staffed and maintained by AMC; fee is charged in summer and fall.)

Other Approaches
While there are approaches to the summit from all four points of the compass, only the N approach from Route 3 is popular with day-hikers. The others, such as the E and W approaches via the rocky Garfield Ridge Trail, are used primarily by backpackers.

From Mt. Lafayette and Franconia Ridge, it's a rugged 3.5-mi. walk to Garfield's summit, with many ups and downs totaling 1200 ft. of elevation gain. From summit of Mt. Lafayette, Garfield Ridge Trail runs across bare N ridge, over beautiful North Peak, and descends in open to jct. L with Skookumchuck Trail at 0.8 mi./4680 ft. Trail descends steeply to treeline and drops through mossy fir woods to col at 1.7 mi./3740 ft. Climb over 3885-ft. hump, passing obscure side path R leading to wild outlook towards Owl's Head Mtn. Trail meanders along ridge, then climbs easily to tiny Garfield Pond at 3.0 mi./3860 ft. (Side path L leads to shore of lily-dotted pond.) From here climb is steep and rocky to summit of Garfield, 3.5 mi. from Mt. Lafayette.

From AMC's Galehead Hut to E, it's a 3.1 mi. trek to Garfield summit, with 1400 ft. elevation gain. From hut (3780 ft.), Garfield Ridge Trail descends to jct. R with Gale River Trail at 0.6 mi./3390 ft. Ridge trail then traverses series of humps with several short, steep ups and downs, passing partial outlook S to Owl's Head Mtn. near top of first major hump. Catching glimpses of daunting steep side of Garfield ahead, drop to deep col and jct. L with Franconia Brook Trail at 2.2 mi./3420 ft. Climb from here is very steep and rocky, wet in places, rising nearly 1100 ft. in 0.9 mi. Pass jct. R with spur to Garfield Ridge Campsite (view) at 2.7 mi./3900 ft., and jct. R with Garfield Trail at 2.9 mi./4180 ft. Last pitch is very steep to summit at 3.1 mi./4500 ft.

From the S, hikers can join Garfield Ridge from deep recesses of Pemi Wilderness via Franconia Brook Trail. But it's 10.3 mi. from closest highway (Kancamagus Highway in Lincoln) to ridge trail, and another 0.9 mi. of very steep climbing from this trail intersection to summit. From 13 Falls Campsite, climb to Garfield's summit is 3.1 mi. (one-way) with 2300-ft. elevation gain.

WINTER

Winter on Garfield tends to be long and brutal. As the summit area is treeless and exposed, it can be quite inhospitable, especially during a snowstorm, or when bone-rattling winds are ripping across the mountaintop from the NW.

The access road to the Garfield Trail is not open in winter, so any ascent of the mountain from US 3 will require a 1.2-mi. road walk each way, for a total trek of 12.4 mi. Although the grade is never steep along the Garfield Trail, the snow accumulates to a great depth on the mountain's north-facing slope and snowshoes are generally required from the end of November until early May. The comfortable grade makes it a good snowshoeing trail. The final quarter-mile pitch to the summit along the Garfield Ridge Trail can be very icy, and caution is required on both the ascent and descent of this steep, ledgy section of trail.

VIEW GUIDE

Garfield's sharp, ledgy summit is one of the premier viewing perches in the Whites, especially on the S side looking down into the remote, mountain-ringed valleys of the western Pemigewasset Wilderness. This summit deserves a long visit on a clear day.

Looking L, to the E, the high, massive summits of North and South Twin loom just three miles away. A high shoulder, striped with fir waves, extends to the L from North Twin, with Mts. Adams and Jefferson poking above and distant Goose Eye and Old Speck in the Mahoosucs to the L. The top of Mt. Washington peers over just to the R of North Twin's summit. The low hump of Galehead is seen in front of the great, scree-streaked bulk of South Twin. Galehead Hut can be spotted on the level col between these peaks. To the SE, beyond the broad, birch-wooded upper basin of Franconia Brook, are the other peaks of the Twin-Bond Range: bald Guyot, scarred with many rock slides, peering over the great SW ridge of South Twin; Bond rising behind and to the L of the sharp peak of West Bond; and the craggy face of Bondcliff. Mt. Carrigain's dome rises in the back between West Bond and Bondcliff, and Mt. Hancock is to the R of Bondcliff. Looking SSE down the Franconia Brook valley, Mts. Passaconaway, Whiteface and Tripyramid are in the distance to the R of Hancock, above Mts. Huntington and Hitchcock.

Close by to the S the rounded, wooded mass of Owl's Head dominates the interior of the western Pemi Wilderness. Beyond Owl's Head on the horizon are the Osceolas and Scar Ridge, with Mt. Tecumseh behind and between them. To the R of Owl's Head, looking SSW, the graceful pyramids of Mts. Flume and Liberty rise beyond the valley of Lincoln Brook. Mt. Kearsarge is in the distance between them. Down below, in line with Liberty, is the long, spruce-clad ridge that extends S from Garfield. Nearby to the SW looms the great wall of Franconia Ridge, with Mt. Lafayette impressively revealed from base to serrated crest. The tip of Cannon can be seen over the R shoulder of Lafayette.

To the N and NW there are sweeping views across extensive lowlands into northern N.H. and Vermont, though these are hard-pressed to compete with the compelling wilderness vistas to the S. The villages of Franconia and Littleton can be seen to the NW, with Vermont high points such as Mt. Mansfield and Jay Peak on the horizon. A bit E of N are the mountains of the Nash Stream Forest. To the NNE the long ridge of Mts. Starr King and Waumbek in the Pliny Range is seen beyond Cherry Mtn., with Mt. Cabot and the Pilot Ridge extending to the L. The village of Twin Mountain is at the base of Cherry Mtn., and part of Jefferson village is visible below Mt. Starr King. Farther R the Crescent Range is seen over the 3813-ft. spur of North Twin known as Nubble Peak.

NO. OF 4000-FOOTERS VISIBLE: 30

North and South Hancock

NORTH HANCOCK

ELEVATION: 4420 ft./1347 m ORDER OF HEIGHT: 21
LOCATION: S edge of Pemigewasset Wilderness, Town of Lincoln
USGS MAPS: 7½′ Mount Carrigain, 7½′ Mt. Osceola

SOUTH HANCOCK

ELEVATION: 4319 ft./1316 m ORDER OF HEIGHT: 26
LOCATION: S edge of Pemigewasset Wilderness, Town of Lincoln, Township of Livermore
USGS MAPS: 7½′ Mount Carrigain, 7½′ Mt. Osceola

GEOGRAPHY

The sprawling mass of Mt. Hancock dominates the south-central region of the Pemigewasset Wilderness. Though its ridges are densely wooded and its summit views are partly restricted, upon closer inspection this turns out to be a very interesting mountain. It has long held an aura of mystery and inaccessibility and offers a wilderness flavor not found on the more popular White Mountain ridges.

Hikers on the Hancock Loop Trail—the only path on the mountain—traverse only a small central section of an entire range of Hancock peaks and ridges. The main ridge stretches over 4 miles from N to S. At its N end it rises from the East Branch of the Pemigewasset River over several minor summits to the trailless NW Peak (4020 ft.), a sharp knob with cliffs on its NE face. This peak bore a fire tower for a few years after the 1938 hurricane. A long, narrow ridge connects the NW Peak with the flattened dome of North Hancock; to the W of this ridge is the isolated valley of Cedar Brook. On the W flank of the ridge is a prominent gravelly slide that fell in 1927. On the S face of North Hancock is the Arrow Slide, a great Y-shaped gash that identifies the peak from afar and once served as the climbing route to the summit. On the W a 3100-ft. saddle joins North Hancock with the E spurs of trailless Mt. Hitchcock (3620 ft.).

A high, curving ridge joins North Hancock with South Hancock, which has a precipitous E face and appears as a sharp wooded pyramid from some angles. Part way along this ridge is a subsidiary summit sometimes referred to as "Middle Hancock." On the W this central ridge encloses a wooded bowl that forms the headwaters of the Hancock Branch, North Fork. The ridge continues S from South Hancock to a bold, trailless spur (3940 ft.) that overlooks Hancock Notch (2820 ft.) and the headwaters of Sawyer River. Across Hancock Notch to the S rises trailless Mt. Huntington (3700 ft.)

From Middle Peak a rough, tangled ridge runs E towards Mt. Carrigain, dropping steeply at the E end to its col with the rock-faced nubble known as "The Captain" (3520 ft.), hidden between Hancock and Carrigain. On the S side of Hancock's E ridge are two small glacial cirques that drain into the Sawyer River. In addition to its main N-S ridge, Hancock throws out two more prominent ridges to the N. Between the main ridge, which bears the NW Peak, and the middle northerly ridge is the supremely wild valley of Crystal Brook, with a steep headwall on the N side of North Hancock. This slide-scarred basin is well seen from Zeacliff to the N. The middle and eastern of Hancock's three N ridges enclose the valley of the W fork of Carrigain Branch. The main stem of Carrigain Branch flows down from Carrigain Pond at the NE base of The Captain. This valley is enclosed by Mt. Carrigain and the easternmost of Hancock's N ridges.

NOMENCLATURE

The original name for the mountain was "Pemigewasset Peak," as coined by geographer Arnold Guyot on his 1860 map of the White Mountains, for its proximity to the East Branch of the Pemigewasset River. The current name was applied in the 1870s by state geologist Charles H. Hitchcock in honor of John Hancock, the first patriot to sign the Declaration of Independence, though Dr. Edward Tuckerman contended that the name in fact honored a 19th-century lumberman.

HISTORICAL HIGHLIGHTS

First Ascent: Unknown.

1876: Moses Sweetser's guidebook notes of Hancock that "its extent and shape are vaguely represented on the maps because much of the adjacent country is still unexplored."

1878: AMC trampers are exploring the region; cylinder placed on summit for hikers to register in.

1879: Party led by AMC explorer Webster Wells climbs Hancock from North Fork, traverses ridge from Hancock to Carrigain, discovers Carrigain Pond. Three-day expedition also includes ascents of Mts. Anderson and Lowell. Trip described in July 1880 *Appalachia*.

1894–1904: Lumber baron J. E. Henry builds logging railroad up Hancock Branch and on into North Fork drainage to SW of Hancocks. Slopes are heavily cut over.

1907: First edition of AMC guidebook recommends that pathless Hancock be ascended from East Branch via long N ridge.

1908: Party of 30, "many of them ladies," is recorded in summit cylinder. Crude, short-lived trail cut from S using logging roads and Arrow Slide.

1927: AMC *Bulletin* lists club trip from town of Lincoln via train to Parker-Young lumber camp. Itinerary includes climb of Hancock and dinner at lumber camp.

1932–1945: Parker-Young Co. logs Cedar Brook valley on NW side of Hancock, mainly from Camp 24 on spur logging RR from East Branch. Slash from logging and blowdown from 1938 hurricane creates fire hazard. Firetower is erected on NW Peak and for several years around 1940 area is off limits to hikers, patrolled by WMNF rangers.

1936: Parker-Young Co. sells 69,969 acres in East Branch watershed, including Hancocks, to U.S. Forest Service for $2.50 per acre, retaining cutting rights for 20 years.

1955: AMC guidebook cautions that ascent of Hancock is "a stunt to be undertaken only by strong trampers with knowledge of woodcraft who should be prepared to camp overnight." Various approach routes are used for bushwhack climbs, with Arrow Slide a favorite. About this time Kancamagus Highway is extended to hairpin turn (present-day trailhead), eliminating long walk from Lincoln and making Hancock more accessible. Highway is linked with Conway in 1959.

1957: Interest in Hancock surges with creation of 4000-Footer Club. AMC trip in May places 46 trampers on North Hancock, and 41 ascend South Hancock on September jaunt.

1960: AMC group including Robert and Miriam Underhill make first winter circuit of Hancock peaks.

1965–1966: AMC's Worcester Chapter cuts Hancock Loop Trail. As reported in *Appalachia,* first hiker to traverse the trail upon completion in 1966 is "a Mr. Waterman of the New York Chapter." For many years thereafter Hancock is one of Guy Waterman's favorite peaks.

TRAIL APPROACHES

South Approach from Kancamagus Highway (NH 112):

North and South Hancock

Hancock Notch Trail, Cedar Brook Trail, Hancock Loop Trail
9.6 mi. round trip, 2650-ft. elevation gain

North Hancock only

Hancock Notch Trail, Cedar Brook Trail, Hancock Loop Trail
8.4 mi. round trip, 2400-ft. elevation gain

South Hancock only

Hancock Notch Trail, Cedar Brook Trail, Hancock Loop Trail
8.0 mi. round trip, 2200-ft. elevation gain

TRAILHEAD (2129 ft.): Parking is at the Hancock Overlook on the Kancamagus Highway, just E of the hairpin turn and 4.7 mi. E of the Lincoln Woods parking area. Parking at trail's start at hairpin turn is strictly prohibited.

The hike to the Hancocks features a gentle approach with many stream crossings followed by a steep climb to the top of either peak. The two summits are linked by a wooded ridge trail; most hikers do the loop over both Hancocks.

From overlook parking, descend path past kiosk and carefully cross highway at hairpin turn to sign for Hancock Notch Trail. Trail follows old railroad grade built by J. E. Henry's logging crews in 1890s. Walking is easy through mixed woods, with occasional dips at washouts. Cross small brook at 0.6 mi. and continue up grade through spruces, passing spot with view over North Fork of Hancock Branch at 1.2 mi. Turn R up bank at 1.4 mi., heading NE along S side of North Fork. Look L for glimpse of high, sharp wooded peak of South Hancock rising over trees. Trail weaves across three small brooks and swings R to jct. with Cedar Brook Trail at 1.7 mi. / 2520 ft.

Turn L on Cedar Brook Trail and climb moderately, then make five crossings of North Fork interspersed with easy stretches through spruce woods and along boggy openings. Some crossings may be difficult at high water, but can be avoided with unofficial bypass paths. After fifth crossing reach jct. with Hancock Loop Trail at 2.4 mi. / 2720 ft. Turn R on Loop Trail and quickly make final crossing of North Fork, then climb moderately through conifers and birch; higher up there are glimpses L through trees to North Hancock and Arrow Slide. Reach Loop Jct. at 3.5 mi. / 3320 ft. Loop will be described from North Peak to South Peak.

Turn L on North Link and descend to dry brookbed; by walking 200 ft. L you can access outwash of Arrow Slide and look up to upper slabs. Trail ascends moderately at first but soon shoots up very steeply, parallel to but away from slide. Grade is relentless and footing rough for most of climb to North Peak, with loose rock underfoot in places. Nearing top trail angles left and moderates, reaching broad wooded summit at 4.2 mi. / 4420 ft. Here Ridge Link to South Peak goes R and side path descends 150 ft. L to outlook ledge with good view S to Osceolas and Sandwich Range.

From jct., wild, winding Ridge Link meanders across summit plateau, then descends at easy / moderate grades through ridgetop fir woods to 4180-ft. col. Trail rises easily to "Middle Peak" at 5.1 mi. / 4300 ft. Dip to another 4180-ft. col, then climb easily up narrow ridge, passing partial views through trees back to N and R (NW) to Arrow Slide on North Hancock and beyond to Owl's Head and Franconia Range. Pass small viewpoint on L looking E and attain wooded summit of South Hancock at 5.6 mi. / 4319 ft. Short side path drops L to small ledge with view SE over Sawyer River valley.

From summit, South Link begins steep descent NW back to Loop Jct. A short distance down, trail offers narrow view across Pemi Wilderness to Owl's Head and Franconias. Grade is steep most of way down to Loop Jct., reached at 6.1 mi./3320 ft. From here it is 3.5 generally easy mi. back to trailhead.

There are no other day-hike trail approaches to the Hancocks. Backpackers can make longer approaches via Hancock Notch Trail from the E or Cedar Brook Trail from Pemigewasset Wilderness to N.

WINTER

A challenging but fun winter trip, relatively easy up to Loop Jct. if North Fork crossings have good snow bridges. The climb up either peak is steep and difficult snowshoeing, requiring vigorous step-kicking or crampon-clawing. Snow piles deep on the ridge, and the Ridge Link may be very hard to follow. Along the way it offers neat winter-only views into various nooks and crannies of the Pemi Wilderness. In late winter, with a deep platform of snow, South Hancock can become a wonderful wilderness watchtower with views over the trees in several directions. Parking area at Hancock Overlook is plowed.

VIEW GUIDE

North Hancock Outlook: This sunny granite outcrop has a 180-degree panorama to the S, though you must stand to see over the scrub for the full effect. To the far L is dark, tower-topped dome of Mt. Carrigain, just 2½ mi. away, with Kearsarge North seen over its R shoulder. Maine's Pleasant Mtn. and Black Cap Mtn. are visible beyond the ski slopes of Attitash. Farther R are Mt. Tremont and Bear Mtn., with the Moat Range beyond. Close by to SE is the wooded ridge leading over to South Hancock; rising beyond are the high peaks of the Sandwich Range. Mt. Chocorua is seen above Middle Hancock, Mts. Paugus and Pasaconaway are between Middle and South Hancock, and Mts. Whiteface and Tripyramid are over the R side of South Hancock.

Farther R, looking nearby to the S, is the long, dark ridge of Mt. Huntington, scarred with scree slopes, and the more distant Mt. Kancamagus, the tops of the two Flat Mtns. and Sandwich Dome rising beyond. The most striking view is S down the North Fork basin to the rippled, slide-marked ridge of Osceola, with the East Peak on the L and the main summit in the middle. The many summits of Scar Ridge extend to the R of Osceola, with low spurs of Mt. Hitchcock in front. Mt. Cardigan can be spotted over the notch between Osceola and Scar Ridge with Mt. Sunapee to its L. Stinson Mtn. is to the R of the double-summit eastern Scar Ridge peak, while Vermont's Mt. Ascutney is to the R of the sharp middle peak of Scar Ridge. Carr Mtn. and Mt. Kineo are seen over the main Scar Ridge summit, with distant Smarts Mtn. to the R. The ski trails of Loon Mtn. are farther R, with Mt. Cushman to the L. Mt. Cube is beyond Loon and Vermont's Killington and Pico are on the horizon to the R. Mt. Moosilauke anchors the view on the far R, with the sharp nearby peak of Mt. Hitchcock in front and below.

South Hancock Outlook: This small ledge, with a steep drop-off in front, offers an unusual view to the E and SE. Mt. Carrigain is close by to the L, with Signal Ridge trailing to the R. The town of Bartlett is seen in the Saco valley with the high dome of Kearsarge North beyond and the Attitash ski slopes to the R. The broad Sawyer River valley leads out to lumpy Mt. Tremont and Owl's Cliff, with Sawyer Pond at their base. North Moat is beyond Tremont, with Black Cap Mtn. and Pleasant Mtn. in Maine to the L and farther away. Bear Mtn. rises over Owl's Cliff, with Middle and South Moat behind to the L. On the R of the Sawyer River valley is the wooded backside of Green's Cliff, with Mt. Chocorua on the horizon. To the R of Chocorua are its Sandwich Range neighbors, Mt. Paugus and dark, cone-shaped Mt. Passaconaway.

NO. OF 4000-FOOTERS VISIBLE: from North Hancock summit, 41 (theoretically, through the trees); from North Hancock outlook, 9; from South Hancock summit (best in winter): 37.

Owl's Head Mountain

ELEVATION: 4025 ft./1227 m ORDER OF HEIGHT: 43
LOCATION: Western Pemigewasset Wilderness, Town of Franconia
USGS MAP: 7½′ South Twin Mtn.

GEOGRAPHY

Rising aloof and remote deep in the Pemigewasset Wilderness, Owl's Head Mtn. suffers from a terrible reputation among peakbaggers. Nine miles by trail from the Kancamagus Highway, its flat, wooded summit offers a quintessential non-view. "Owl's Head is everything a mountain should not be," lamented one weary hiker after completing the trek. "It is a mountain that has much to be modest about," wrote another.

But Owl's Head does have its rewards. The approach up the Lincoln Brook Trail brings you through a deep valley with a wonderful sense of isolation. The views of that valley and the "back side" of the Franconia Range from the mountain's western slide are one-of-a-kind. The committing length, potentially difficult stream crossings, and steep scrambling at the end make this one of the most memorable of all the 4000-footer hikes.

The wooded ridge of Owl's Head sprawls several miles N and S in the center of the western Pemigewasset Wilderness. On the W, N, and E it is surrounded by a great horseshoe of higher mountains: the Franconia Range,

Garfield Ridge, and the Twin-Bond Range. Deep valleys separate Owl's Head from its taller neighbors. On the W and S is the sharply cut valley of Lincoln Brook, while on the N and E the mountain is bounded by the broad trough of Franconia Brook. The two brooks join near the SE base of the mountain.

At the NW end of Owl's Head a broad saddle (3180 ft.) divides the headwaters of Lincoln and Franconia Brooks and links the mountain with the E side of Mt. Lafayette. From here the Owl's Head ridge rises SE to the narrow N-S crest, which is nearly level at the 3800–4000 ft. level for a mile. The 4025-ft. summit is about in the middle of the long ridgecrest. Finding this highest point proved mettlesome for early Owl's Head peakbaggers.

A half-mile S of the summit the ridge dips to a col before rising to the sharp 3660-ft. cone at the S end—the true "Owl's Head." Seen from the S, this peak is a wooded spire. On its SE side the "Owl's Head" thrusts out a flat-topped 3060-ft. spur that ends in a prominent cliff. On the W side of the mountain, between the summit and the "Owl's Head," is a steep slide of broken rock that plunges into Lincoln Brook valley and provides part of the climbing route to the peak.

The E side of the mountain is broken by several truncated ridges and three brook ravines. A series of talus fields is strung along the lower E slopes towards the N end. Although its ridgecrest is thickly wooded with conifers, the sides of Owl's Head are largely cloaked in a paper birch forest that grew up after a forest fire devastated the region in 1907.

NOMENCLATURE

Owl's Head Mtn. takes its name from the sharp peak at the S end of the ridge. This local name was used in Moses Sweetser's guidebook as early as 1881, and it appeared on the Appalachian Mountain Club's 1887 map of the White Mountains. This moniker has also been applied to two other summits in the White Mountains, one a cliff-faced knob at the south end of the Benton Range, the other a spur of Cherry Mtn. In all three cases the summit was thought to resemble the shape of the wise bird's head. The Owl's Head in the Pemigewasset Wilderness has also been called the "Franconia Owl" for its location in the SE corner of the town of Franconia. The name "Wilderness Mountain" was proposed by a climber in the 1930s, but never caught on.

HISTORICAL HIGHLIGHTS

First Ascent: Probably 1871, by small party of Dartmouth College students working for Charles H. Hitchcock's geological survey. Four members climbed to top of ridge; two continued N along crest, possibly crossing actual summit. Trip described by Warren Upham appeared in first issue of *Appalachia*, 1876.

1903–1910: J. E. Henry's crews push logging RRs up valleys of Franconia and Lincoln Brooks and cut virgin forest off much of Owl's Head. Logging camps are established along both brooks.

1907: Huge fire kindled by lightning in dry slash rages for two weeks and burns over Owl's Head and surrounding ridges. In 1908 hikers on Lafayette observe "a country of charred stumps and dry stream beds."

1931: AMC trailman Nathaniel Goodrich publishes list of 4000-footers in *Appalachia* and climbs Owl's Head from Greenleaf Hut.

1936: AMC Guide describes route to Owl's Head, descending from Franconia Ridge via Lincoln Slide, then bushwhacking up to summit from Lincoln Brook; est. 9 hrs. round trip from Greenleaf Hut. Hiker Murray H. Stevens writes up bushwhack route from Galehead Hut, down valley of Twin Brook and up N ridge of Owl's Head.

Late 1930s: Franconia Brook Trail and Lincoln Brook Trail opened along old logging RR beds.

1949: Blazed trail laid out from Lincoln Brook up N end of ridge, but is short-lived.

Late 1950s: With formation of 4000-Footer Club in 1957, route up W slide becomes standard approach, first described in 1960 *AMC Guide*.

1959: First recorded winter ascents made by two parties on March 8, one led by Robert Collin, other consisting of Robert and Miriam Underhill and Merle Whitcomb. Only Underhill group reaches "true" summit.

1960: AMC group led by Al Robertson scouts entire ridge and marks new summit location.

1963: Bob Collin returns with group and traverses entire ridge in winter—final ascent of nine-day Pemi winter epic in era of unbroken trails.

1984: Owl's Head and surrounding valleys included in new Pemigewasset Wilderness.

TRAIL APPROACHES

South Approach from Kancamagus Highway (NH 112)

Lincoln Woods Trail, Franconia Brook Trail, Lincoln Brook Trail, Owl's Head Path

18.0 mi. round trip, 2900-ft. elevation gain

Trailhead (1160 ft.): The grueling walk to this remote summit starts from the Lincoln Woods parking area on the N side of the Kancamagus Highway (NH 112), 5.6 mi. E of Exit 32 off I-93 in Lincoln.

The long walk to Owl's Head features 8 miles of pleasant valley trekking, largely on old logging RR grades, and 1 mile of steep climbing. The crossings of Franconia and Lincoln Brooks are very difficult in high water.

From parking lot, cross suspension footbridge over East Branch of Pemigewasset River and turn R on Lincoln Woods Trail along wide, level bed of J. E. Henry's East Branch & Lincoln RR (1893–1948), with many ties

The wooded mass of Owl's Head Mtn. as seen from Franconia Ridge.

still astride trail. Easy walking leads to jct. L with Osseo Trail at 1.4 mi./1300 ft. and Camp 8 clearing just beyond. Trail approaches wide, rocky river at 1.6 mi. with view of Bondcliff upstream. At 2.6 mi. Black Pond Trail splits L. At 2.9 mi./1440 ft. is side trail L to Franconia Falls (0.4 mi.).

Continue ahead across footbridge over Franconia Brook and bear L and up on Franconia Brook Trail. Follow another RR grade N, crossing Camp 9 Brook twice. At 3.9 mi. follow detour R around beaver swamp with glimpses L to cliffs and sharp S peak of Owl's Head. Cross Camp 9 Brook again and bear L back to RR grade at 4.2 mi. and turn R to follow it (note this turn for return trip). At 4.6 mi./1760 ft. bear L on Lincoln Brook Trail and traverse SW through blowdown area. Turn R on RR grade and cross large Franconia Brook at 5.1 mi.—easiest route is to L. Cross Lincoln Brook at 5.5 mi. and follow trail on N curve up deep valley through yellow birches, with glimpses of cliffs up to R. Trail is occasionally rough along bank. Cross tributary at 6.8 mi. and Liberty Brook at 7.4 mi. Pass through Camp 12 clearing and cross to E side of Lincoln Brook at 7.6 mi. Reach large cairn at base of Owl's Head slide at 8.0 mi./2560 ft.

Turn R on unsigned path and ascend steeply, reaching lower ledges of slide at 8.1 mi. Cairns mark routes up steep slide, easiest on R, with mix of ledge, loose rock, gravel—use caution. Enjoy views back across Lincoln Brook valley to Franconia Ridge. Reach top of slide at 8.3 mi./3200 ft., where tiny spring bubbles out of crack in ledge. Follow well-trodden but rough path steeply up through fir woods, angling to L. Grade moderates at 8.8 mi. Meander along ridgecrest to small clearing, cairn and possibly sign at small knob that is true summit at 9.0 mi.

High Water Route
To avoid difficult crossings of Franconia and Lincoln Brooks, experienced hikers can follow unmaintained path starting at end of Franconia Falls side path and leading 1.5 mi. along W bank of Franconia Brook and S bank of Lincoln Brook, meeting Lincoln Brook Trail 0.9 mi. from its S jct. with Franconia Brook Trail.

North Approach from 13 Falls Campsite

Backpackers can also approach Owl's Head via the little-used N end of Lincoln Brook Trail from 13 Falls Campsite (2180 ft.), located at the N jct. of Franconia Brook and Lincoln Brook Trails (8.1 easy mi. from Kancamagus Highway via Lincoln Woods Trail and Franconia Brook Trail). This is a highly scenic area with multiple cascades at the site of logging Camp 13. From jct. by campsite, follow Lincoln Brook Trail across ledgy brookbed with view up to N ridge of Owl's Head. Trail passes series of cascades on W fork of Franconia Brook, then crosses stream and climbs steadily to boggy height-of-land between Owl's Head and Mt. Lafayette at 1.5 mi./3180 ft. Trail descends along W side of upper Lincoln Brook, crossing to E side at 2.6 mi. Descend to jct. L with Owl's Head Path at 3.5 mi./2560 ft. Turn L for 1.0 mi./1500-ft. climb to summit.

The circuit around Owl's Head from Kancamagus Highway via Lincoln Woods Trail, Franconia Brook Trail and Lincoln Brook Trail, including side trip to summit, is 21.6 mi. with 3500-ft. elevation gain.

N approach can also be made from AMC's Galehead Hut by descending 0.1 mi. on Frost Trail and 2.6 mi. on Twin Brook Trail to 13 Falls Campsite, with beautiful white birch forest in lower half. Round trip to Owl's Head summit from Galehead Hut is 14.4 mi. with 4800-ft. elevation gain.

WINTER

Owl's Head is one of the most challenging winter peaks in the Whites. The W slide is often icy and dangerous, requiring crampons, ice axe and great caution. Many winter climbers opt for a bushwhack ascent up the E side of the mountain from Franconia Brook Trail near Hellgate Brook, starting with a potentially dicey crossing of Franconia Brook. The 2200-ft. climb to the ridge is steep and arduous. Lucky climbers may find a ledge with a fine view E to the Twin-Bond Range. Either ascent route is for fully-equipped snowshoers with solid winter experience.

VIEW GUIDE

Summit views are nonexistent on the ground, though Eugene Daniell III (who has climbed Owl's Head ca. 20 times) notes in the *AMC White Mountain Guide* that "excellent views are sometimes obtained from the summit area by ambitious tree-climbers." It was not always thus, for up through the early 1970s the guide mentioned vistas of the Franconias and Bonds near the summit. Miriam Underhill took spectacular photos of the Twin-Bond Range from Owl's Head on the March 1959 ascent mentioned above; one was printed in her autobiography, *Give Me the Hills*.

The W slide does offer a unique view across the remote Lincoln Brook valley to the "back" (E) side of Franconia Ridge. Mt. Liberty is seen to the L (SW) above the basin of Liberty Brook. W across the valley are the craggy peaks of upper Franconia Ridge—Little Haystack, Lincoln, Lafayette—and the V-shaped gravel gash of Lincoln Slide. Up the valley to the R (N) are the headwaters of Lincoln Brook and the W end of Garfield Ridge beyond, and a slice of Mt. Garfield itself.

NO. OF 4000-FOOTERS VISIBLE: 22 (entirely theoretical, through the trees).

North and South Twin Mountain

NORTH TWIN

ELEVATION: 4761 ft./1451 m ORDER OF HEIGHT: 11
LOCATION: Twin Range, Towns of Bethlehem and Franconia
USGS MAP: 7½′ South Twin Mtn.

SOUTH TWIN

ELEVATION: 4902 ft./1494 m ORDER OF HEIGHT: 8
LOCATION: Twin Range, Town of Franconia
USGS MAP: 7½′ South Twin Mtn.

GEOGRAPHY

North Twin and South Twin are the two highest and northernmost peaks of the Twin Range, the loftiest ridge between the Presidentials and the Franconias. Both offer superb views of the Pemigewasset Wilderness and surrounding mountains and out to distant horizons.

North Twin is massive, rounded and thickly wooded to the top, but ledgy outlooks near the summit provide wide views E and W. Several ridges run out on its NE side to the long, deep valley of Little River. To the W several wooded buttresses drop into the basin drained by the North Branch of Gale River. Between these valleys a high ridge with many gray "fir waves" extends NW from the summit, swinging down over an intermediate peak, then NE to the wooded eminence known as Nubble Peak (3813 ft.). This trailless peak is one of New England's "Hundred Highest" and is guarded by steep ledges on its E flank. Its N side bears the distinctive "check-mark" slide, prominently seen from US 3 in the village of Twin Mountain, which lies in the Ammonoosuc River valley N of North Twin. On the NW slope of Nubble Peak is a striking little rock cone known as Haystack Mtn. or The Nubble (2712 ft.), thought by geologists to be the core of an ancient volcano. On the E side of North Twin, at the head of a deep valley draining into Little River, is a great slide with its top starting just below the summit. Another long, prominent slide fell on the N side of North Twin in an October 1995 rainstorm, at the head of a hidden valley between the main summit and Nubble Peak. Southward the summit ridge runs over a small rock knob before dropping to the 4460-ft. col between the Twins.

The summit of South Twin is a small rocky peak rising from a long, massive, heavily wooded ridge. The top is quite open and is marked by two rock knobs just a few yards apart. A broad, semi-open shoulder extends N to the col with North Twin. To the SE the high ridge extends 2 miles to the rounded double summit of Mt. Guyot. A broad buttress spreads NE to the Little River valley; E and SE of the summit is a two-pronged ravine scored with several slides and draining into Little River.

On the W the slopes of South Twin drop steeply to a col with Galehead Mtn. and down into the deep valleys of Twin Brook and Gale River's North Branch. Just S of the summit is a 4723-ft. spur; from this a prominent ridge runs SW for several miles between Twin Brook and Redrock Brook, ending at the deep trough of Franconia Brook. Two trailless knobs crown the upper end of this ridge; the first (4580 ft.) is bare and rocky on top; the second (4357 ft.) is wooded and sometimes referred to as SW Twin. On the S side of this ridge is the northern of two slide-scarred glacial cirques at the head of Redrock Brook, bearing a tiny tarn, Bear Pond, on its floor. The wild Redrock valley is enclosed by the SW ridge of South Twin, the ridge between South Twin and Mt. Guyot, Guyot itself, and West Bond.

NOMENCLATURE

The name "Twin Mts" was originally applied to these neighboring peaks by geographer George P. Bond on his 1853 map. The nearby town to the north shares the name of Twin Mountain. North Twin looms large in the view from the town, but the summit of South Twin is hidden.

HISTORICAL HIGHLIGHTS

First Ascent: Probably 1871, by New Hampshire state geologist Charles H. Hitchcock and a Dartmouth student, who ascend both North Twin and South Twin as part of the state geological survey. "Scarcely any mountains are more difficult to reach than these, on account of the stunted growth near their tops," lamented the intrepid geologist. Hitchcock's report on the survey includes a profile of the view from North Twin.

1876: Moses Sweetser's guidebook describes an eight-mile route to South Twin via Little River and a W branch near its head, based on information provided by Assistant State Geologist Joshua H. Huntington. Dwarf conifers atop ridge are again noted as impediment: "Frequently the most rapid mode of advance is found by lying flat on the ground and crawling under the bristling boughs."

1882: In August, A. E. Scott leads AMC party of six—three men, three women—on week-long bushwhack epic over Twin Range. They spend first night high on N slope of North Twin and battle to summit on second day, bivouacing in rain beside slide, then proceed over South Twin on third day, marveling at the view. Trip continues over Mt. Bond and Mt. Field before ending in Crawford Notch. Scott writes up adventure in April 1883 *Appalachia*.

1883: AMC cuts Twin Range Trail, leading from Twin Mtn. House into Little River valley, up North Twin, then over South Twin and Bond. Path is dedicated during outing of 30–40 trampers led by A. E. Scott; group spends night at camp on slope of North Twin built by Charles E. Lowe.

1893–1900: Timber mogul George Van Dyke logs Little River valley, hauling wood out via railroad.

1903–1909: Logging crews employed by J. E. Henry cut slopes of SW ridge of South Twin from Camps 12 and 13 along Franconia Brook and Camp 14 by Redrock Brook, all on spurs of East Branch & Lincoln logging RR.

1915: AMC trailmasters Paul Jenks, Charles Blood, Nathaniel Goodrich and others cut Garfield Ridge Trail from South Twin summit to Garfield Pond. Trail is completed in 1916, connecting Twin and Franconia Ranges.

1925: AMC builds Galehead Shelter in col at W base of South Twin summit cone.

ca. 1930: Portion of Twin Range Trail from Little River valley abandoned. AMC cuts new 2½-mile North Twin Loop, ascending from Gale River valley on W.

1932: AMC builds Galehead Hut on small hump near site of shelter. Trail from hut to South Twin and across ridge to Guyot and Zealand is renamed "Twinway" and connects Galehead and Zealand Falls Huts. New Galehead Trail provides approach to hut and South Twin from N via Gale River valley.

ca. 1935: Trail from Little River valley up North Twin re-opened by WMNF as North Twin Trail. New Little River Trail opened by WMNF leading 6½ miles up Little River valley, connecting with Twinway at South Twin-Guyot col. This trail is abandoned in late 1950s.

1938: W side of North Twin Loop from Gale River valley obliterated by hurricane. Portion of trail between Twins retains this name until ca. 1950, then re-named North Twin Spur.

1968: Twin Brook Trail from S opened by AMC, providing access to Galehead Hut and South Twin from Pemi Wilderness.

1975: WMNF opens gravel Haystack Rd. from US 3, shortening approach hike to North Twin.

TRAIL APPROACHES

NORTHEAST APPROACH from USFS Haystack Rd. (FR 304)

North Twin only

North Twin Trail
8.6 mi. round trip, 2950-ft. elevation gain

North and South Twin

North Twin Trail, North Twin Spur
11.2 mi. round trip, 3700-ft. elevation gain

TRAILHEAD (1800 ft.): From US 3, 2.3 mi. W of stoplight in Twin Mountain, drive 2.5 m. S on gravel Haystack Rd. (FR 304) to parking area and sign for North Twin Trail at end.

The hike up North Twin is two trips in one—an easy ramble along Little River, followed by a grinding climb up a NE ridge. The trail starts at easy grade through hardwoods mostly on bed of old logging RR, following boulder-filled river. There are three crossings of river that are very difficult in high water. The third crossing is at 1.9 mi./2350 ft. Trail bears away from river and ascends moderately into fir forest, then more steeply over eroded footway. Ascent is quite steep for 0.5 mi. starting at 3.5 mi./3600 ft. At ca. 4.0 mi./4400 ft. is first view N and E from outcrop. Grade eases through high scrub to magnificent outlook ledge on L at 4.2 mi., with wide view E. Continue gently up ridge to jct. with North Twin Spur at 4.3 mi./4761 ft. Here short side path leads R over actual summit of North Twin (wooded) to open ledge with fine view W.

North Twin Spur descends moderately down S ridge of North Twin, reaching 4460-ft. col between Twins at 4.8 mi. Climb up to shoulder of South Twin to open level stretch with views, then continue up through high scrub to open rocky summit of South Twin and jct. with Twinway at 5.6 mi.

NORTHWEST APPROACH from Gale River Loop Road (FR 92)

(For all options, add 1.0 mi./250 ft. for round trip to Galehead Mtn. summit)

Gale River Trail, Garfield Ridge Trail, Twinway, North Twin Spur
South Twin only: 10.8 mi. round trip, 3350-ft. elevation gain
South and North Twin: 13.4 mi. round trip, 4100-ft. elevation gain
Loop over South and North Twin (with carspot at North Twin Trail): 11.0 mi., 3650-ft. elevation gain

TRAILHEAD (1600 ft.): From jct. of US 3 and Trudeau Rd., between Franconia Notch and Twin Mountain, drive SE on USFS gravel Gale River Rd. (FR 25). Bear L at 0.6 mi. and turn sharp R at 1.3 mi. onto Gale River Loop Rd. (FR 92). Parking area for Gale River Trail is on L at 1.6 mi.

This approach via Gale River valley is often used to climb South Twin alone, or in combination with Galehead. If two cars are available, a loop hike over both Twins is an excellent option.

From parking area, Gale River Trail crosses small brook and leads S at easy grades on W side of Gale River's North Branch, keeping well back from stream. Approach river at 1.4 mi. and cross to E side on footbridge at 1.7 mi. Trail becomes rougher along bank, crosses tributary, then recrosses North Branch of Gale on step stones at 2.5 mi. / 2250 ft., usually a fairly easy crossing. Grades continue easy through slide outwash areas to open gravel bank at 3.1 mi. / 2580 ft., with interesting view up to high ridges of Twins. Beyond, trail begins to steepen, and at 3.5 mi. commences steep climb up rock staircases, reaching jct. with Garfield Ridge Trail at 4.0 mi. / 3390 ft.

Turn L here for moderate, rocky climb on Garfield Ridge Trail through deep, mossy coniferous forest. Reach AMC Galehead Hut at 4.6 mi. / 3780 ft. Water available here in-season; partial views S into Pemi Wilderness and up to Galehead Mtn. and Mt. Garfield. (From hut, Frost Trail leads 0.5 mi R to summit of Galehead Mtn.) Continue ahead on Twinway. After short, steep drop into col, begin grueling climb up well-constructed rocky footway, rising 1100 ft. in 0.8 mi. Trees shrink to scrub and views open back to W as you approach top of climb. Reach open rocky summit of South Twin and jct. with North Twin Spur at 5.4 mi. / 4902 ft. Turn L on North Twin Spur to continue to summit of North Twin in 1.3 mi.

South Approach via Twinway

Backpackers and hut-hoppers can approach South Twin via Twinway from Mt. Guyot to S. From open area at jct. of Twinway and Bondcliff Trail near summit of Guyot (good views W here towards Owl's Head and Mt. Lafayette), Twinway rambles easily along broad, thickly wooded ridge leading towards South Twin. Cross knob with limited views 1.1 mi. from jct. Grades continue easy / moderate until fairly steep 0.3 mi. climb to summit of South Twin at 2.0 mi.

WINTER

Haystack Rd. is closed in winter, adding 5.0 mi. round trip to approach via North Twin Trail (total 13.6 mi. / 3400 ft. for North Twin, 16.2 mi. / 4150 ft. for both Twins). Parking is tight off US 3 at entrance to Haystack Rd.; you may need to shovel out a space. Hope for good snow bridges at Little River crossings. The upper part of North Twin Trail is a grind-it-out snowshoe climb. The high wooded col between the Twins has some of the deepest snowpack in the mountains. Gale River Rd. is also closed to auto travel in winter, adding 3.2 mi. round trip on snowmobile-packed road to approach via Gale River Trail (total 14.0 mi. / 3650 ft. for South Twin, 16.6 mi. / 4400 ft. for both Twins out-and-back, 15.1 mi. / 3950 ft. for loop over both Twins with car-spot at entrance to Haystack Rd.) Parking is available on N side of US 3 by jct. with Trudeau Rd. Toughest snowshoeing is approach to Gar-

The view from the summit of South Twin takes in Mts. Galehead and Garfield, plus the peaks of Franconia Ridge.

field Ridge Trail and steep climb from Galehead Hut (closed in winter) to South Twin; crampons may be needed on exposed upper cone in crusty or icy conditions.

VIEW GUIDE

North Twin, E Outlook: This is a premier ledge perch jutting above the scrub, offering a 180-degree panorama which features a fine view of the Presidentials.

To the R (S) the massive rock-crowned summit of South Twin looms close at hand, with Loon Mtn. and distant Mt. Kearsarge to the R. The tops of Bond, Guyot, North Hancock and Passaconaway poke above nearer ridges on the L. To the SE the view opens out to Zealand Mtn., scarred by an extensive talus slope, and the long NE ridge of Guyot with triple-humped Carrigain and the four peaks of the Nancy Range beyond. Mt. Chocorua is seen over Carrigain's Vose Spur, pointed Mt. Tremont is sighted through Carrigain Notch, and Bear Mtn. is between Mts. Anderson and Lowell, over the Zealand talus. North Moat peeks over Mt. Bemis, with the Attitash ski slopes to the L. More to the L are Mts. Parker and Resolution and the Giant Stairs, with Kearsarge North behind the Stairs.

Looking E the three peaks of the Willey Range are seen beyond the deep Little River valley and the long ridge that connects Zealand Ridge with Mt. Hale. Doublehead Mtn. in Jackson pops up over the col between Willey and Field. Mt. Isolation is seen to the R of and behind Mt. Tom, with Sable Mtn. to its R.

To the NE the chain of Southern Presidential peaks and the rocky shoulder of Boott Spur lead up to Mt. Washington. To the L of Washington the sharp peaks of Adams and Jefferson rise beyond nearby Mt. Hale. Farther L is the darkly wooded Dartmouth Range with Old Speck Mtn. in the Mahoosucs in the distance and the Crescent Range to the L. To the NNE is Cherry Mtn., with the long crest of Mt. Waumbek and the Pliny Range to the R and Mt. Cabot and the Pilot Ridge to the L. On the far L, looking N, are the mountains of the Nash Stream region seen beyond the plains of Whitefield and Jefferson.

North Twin, W Outlook: This open, sun-struck ledge is just a few yards W of the true summit and affords a superb vista of the Franconia Range and the Pemigewasset Wilderness. On the far L (S) is the nearby rocky crown of South Twin, with Mt. Tecumseh and Scar Ridge on the R, rising above a SW spur of South Twin. Loon Mtn. is just R of Scar Ridge, with Mt. Kearsarge on the horizon in central N.H.. To the SSW is a dramatic view, down past Galehead Mtn. and its namesake hut, into the deep, remote valley of Franconia Brook, guarded on the R by the rib-like ridges of Owl's Head. Mt. Flume's pyramid is seen over the crest of Owl's Head, with Mt. Cardigan to the L on the horizon. A long, graceful ridge connects Flume with Mt. Liberty to its R, with the rounded hump of Galehead in the foreground.

To the R of Galehead you look SW across the broad uplands at the head of Franconia and Lincoln Brooks to the high, sharp-edged crests of Mts. Lincoln and Lafayette—perhaps the finest single vista from North Twin. Shapely Mt. Garfield rises to the R of Lafayette and closer, beyond the wooded humps of Garfield Ridge. Looking W and WNW there are long views into Vermont beyond the low northern spurs of Lafayette and Garfield, with the tilted profile of Camel's Hump standing out on the horizon. Continuing around through the NW to the N, the views sweep across extensive lowlands out to Mt. Mansfield, Jay Peak, Burke Mtn. and other Vermont landmarks on the horizon.

South Twin Summit: This open rock peak affords an impressive panorama of peaks and ridges. Fine perches can be found around either of the adjacent rocky knobs at the summit. The rounded mass of North Twin is close by on the N, with long vistas on either side. The Nash Stream mountains are seen to the R of North Twin, and farther R, to the NNE, are Cherry Mtn. with Mt. Cabot and the Pilots beyond on the L and Mt. Waumbek and the Pliny Range behind on the R. To the NE and close by is Mt. Hale, with the Dartmouth and Crescent Ranges beyond. Old Speck is in the distance over Mt. Dartmouth. Swinging to the R, the view takes in an excellent panorama of the Presidentials beyond the long ridge running R (S) from Mt. Hale to Zealand Mtn., and the Rosebrook Range. Adams, Jefferson and Clay are on the L, Washington rises in the center, and Boott Spur presides above the ridge of the Southern Presidentials on the R. Mt. Tom is seen below Mt. Pierce, and to the R the Willey Range extends across to Mts. Field and Willey, due E. Mt. Isolation and the Baldfaces are in back and L of Field, with Sable and Chandler to the R. The Doubleheads are prominent off the R slope of Willey.

Just S of E is the scree-splotched ridge of Zealand Mtn., seen close by across the Little River valley. In the distance are the Giant Stairs and Mt. Resolution, with Kearsarge North beyond over Resolution and Pleasant Mtn. in Maine behind to the R: Mt. Parker and Black Cap Mtn. are farther to the R. To the SSE are Mts. Bemis and Nancy with North Moat over Nancy. Farther R are Mts. Anderson and Lowell, with Bear Mtn. and Mt. Tremont sighted through Carrigain Notch. To the SE Mt. Carrigian's triple hunps rise over the broad N summit of nearby Mt. Guyot, with Mt. Paugus behind to the R. To the SSE the high crest of the Twin Range twists over the bald S summit of Guyot, scarred by rock slides, to the pyramid of Mt. Bond. Cone-shaped Passaconaway is behind Bond on the L, and North Hancock is in back on the R, with Whiteface behind it and Tripyramid to the R. The ridge of West Bond sweeps out to the R from Bond; over the saddle between them are Mts. Huntington and Kancamagus. Sandwich Dome is over the R end of West Bond's crest, and farther R are the Osceolas rising above Mt. Hitchcock. Mt. Tecumseh's sharp peak is over Osceola's R shoulder, due S.

Farther to the R you look out over two SW spurs of South Twin to the East Branch valley and Scar Ridge looming at the end. Loon is to the R of Scar Ridge, with Mt. Kearsarge far away on the skyline. Farther R, to the SSW, Mt. Cardigan is visible well beyond Whaleback Mtn.'s sharp knob. To the R the pyramids of Mts. Flume and Liberty rise above lowly Owl's Head, with Carr Mtn. above Flume and Smarts Mtn. to the R of Liberty. From Liberty a long ridge runs R to Little Haystack, with Moosilauke rising beyond, to the SW.

To the WSW is a fine broadside look at the upper Franconia Range, viewed across the rolling wildlands of the western Pemigewasset Wilderness, with Lafayette presenting its characteristic long, serrated profile. Due W is Mt. Garfield's pointed peak, with Mts. Abraham and Ellen to the L on the horizon in Vermont. From the W edge of the summit, where the Twinway begins its steep descent, you can look down on the hump of Galehead Mtn. Over Garfield's R shoulder are Big Bickford and Scarface Mtns., northern spurs of Lafayette, and Camel's Hump on the skyline. Farther R and closer in is Flat Top Mtn., scarred by a curving slide. Above Flat Top are expansive lowlands, including the village of Franconia, and Mt. Mansfield on the horizon. Farther R, to the NW, are the low, twin humps of Mts. Cleveland and Agassiz near Bethlehem. To their R and far away is northern Vermont's Jay Peak. Looking NNW, beyond a spur ridge of North Twin marked by twin slides, the view sweeps over more lowlands out to Burke and Umpire Mtns. and other peaks in Vermont's Northeast Kingdom.

NO. OF 4000-FOOTERS VISIBLE: from North Twin, 27 from summit, 3 additional from E outlook; from South Twin, 35.

Mount Flume

ELEVATION: 4328 ft./1319 m ORDER OF HEIGHT: 25
LOCATION: Franconia Range, Town of Lincoln
USGS MAPS: 7½′ Lincoln, 7½′ Mt. Osceola

GEOGRAPHY

Mt. Flume is the southernmost 4000-footer in the Franconia Range, and is distinguished by its slide-scarred western face and its ledgy, knife-edged summit. Travelers on I-93 and US 3 in the Lincoln area can't help but notice the great slides which scar the mountain from summit to base. These slides came down in 1883, as did the smaller, more grown-up slides seen on Mt. Liberty's south-facing slope. When viewed from Mt. Liberty's 4459-ft. summit, Flume's impressive slides angle down and away from the summit at a grade seemingly impossible to negotiate.

The mountain's narrow summit ridgecrest, no more than 8–10 feet wide, drops off steeply on both its E and W flanks and the view directly down the length of the W-facing slides can be dizzying. Looking E from the summit, over and through the trees which line that side of the peak, one sees the Pemigewasset Wilderness and its jumble of remote peaks and twisting valleys.

Mt. Liberty, Flume's closest 4000-ft. neighbor, is to the NW, separated by a deep col some 450 ft. lower than Flume's summit. To the S a long, level heavily wooded ridge connects Flume with flat-topped Whaleback Mtn. (3586 ft., also known as Osseo Peak). From Whaleback several lower knobby spurs extend S and E.

Two spur ridges run to the E off the main summit ridge of Flume. The Osseo Trail from the East Branch valley follows the upper portion of the southernmost of these ridges, which is steeply truncated and scored by slides. The more northerly ridge drops off into the Lincoln Brook valley and toward tranquil Black Pond, a tiny four-acre lakelet bordering the southern reaches of the Pemi Wilderness. Between Flume's two E ridges is the valley of Birch Island Brook.

On the opposite side of Mt. Flume, the broad, deep valley of Flume Brook runs WSW from the base of the slides to the famous Flume Gorge, the Pemigewasset River, and US 3. Extending W from an unnamed 3834-ft. summit less than a mile SSW of Mt. Flume is Hardwood Ridge, a long, wooded spur bordering Flume Brook valley on the S. Another ridge runs SW off the 3834-ft. knob, dipping to a col and then rising to steep-sided, trailless Big Coolidge Mtn. (3294 ft.), the southernmost peak of the Franconia Range.

NOMENCLATURE

The mountain borrows its name from the famous 700-ft. natural granite gorge near the mouth of Flume Brook. According to legend, The Flume was discovered in 1808 by "Aunt Jessie" Guernsey while the 93-year-old woman was fishing in the remote wilds of the Pemigewasset watershed. Flume Brook, which passes through the gorge, originates on the lower slopes of Mt. Flume and provides the link between the mountain and the much-visited gorge, which is owned by the State of New Hampshire.

HISTORICAL HIGHLIGHTS

First Ascent: Unknown

1808: While on a fishing trip into the unexplored wilds just S of Franconia Notch, 93-year-old "Aunt Jess" Guernsey discovers Flume Gorge.

1835: English writer Harriet Martineau visits Franconia Notch, Flume. A description of region and narrative of her journey appears three years later in Vol. II of book, *Retrospect of Western Travel.*

1847–48: First Flume House, near entrance to Flume Reservation and Gorge, is built, probably by William Kenney and Ira Coffin. Building is then sold to Richard Taft, who opens hotel for business in 1849.

1871: Flume House burns to ground.

1872: Second Flume House, built on foundation of original hotel, opens.

1883: Landslides come crashing down off Mts. Flume, Liberty, dislodging suspended, egg-shaped boulder in Flume Gorge.

1891: Moses F. Sweetser's guidebook describes trailless route to summit by way of Flume Brook. "The journey is arduous, the choice being given of the rolling stones of the brook or the thickets at its side."

1902–1907: Lower E slopes of Mt. Flume are logged by J. E. Henry's crews, working from Camp 7 on East Branch & Lincoln RR. Operation includes short-lived incline railway on N side of Osseo Brook.

1906: With assistance from AMC, North Woodstock Improvement Association completes Franconia Ridge Trail, extending it from logging railroad by East Branch up Osseo Peak and across to Mts. Flume and Liberty.

1917: AMC establishes new trail to summit by way of old slide. Path is initially known as Mt. Flume Trail, but by 1928 is listed in guidebooks as Flume Slide Trail.

1918: Fire claims Second Flume House.

1928: Franconia Notch becomes Forest Reservation and State Park.

1949: Section of Franconia Ridge Trail from upper terminus of Flume Slide Trail to Kancamagus Highway in Lincoln is renamed Osseo Trail.

1983: Due to condominum construction at S terminus near Lincoln, Osseo Trail is relocated. Path now begins off Wilderness Trail (1.4 mi. from Kanc Highway) and ascends ridge from SE.

TRAIL APPROACHES

SOUTHWEST APPROACH from Lincoln Woods (Wilderness) Trail

Lincoln Woods Trail, Osseo Trail, Franconia Ridge Trail
11.2 mi. round trip, 3150-ft. elevation gain

Trailhead (1160 ft.): Lincoln Woods parking area on N side of Kancamagus Highway (NH 112), 5.6 mi. E of Exit 32 off I-93 in Lincoln.

This is the lone approach to Mt. Flume from the valley of the East Branch of the Pemigewasset River. It starts off on an old logging railroad, then follows a relatively new and well-engineered path (1983) that ascends the mountain via a SE spur ridge. Upper sections of the trail are steep and are negotiated by several wooden staircases—it has been reported that there are 396 rock and wooden steps on Osseo Trail.

From parking area, cross suspension footbridge over East Branch and turn R on Lincoln Woods Trail along wide, level bed of J. E. Henry's East Branch & Lincoln RR (1893–1948), with many ties still astride trail. Easy walking leads to jct. L with Osseo Trail at 1.4 mi. / 1300 ft. Osseo Trail starts out in W direction at level grade in hardwood glade beside Osseo Brook, then starts to climb easily and soon joins former incline logging RR grade. Heading now more NW, trail advances on easy to moderate grade up brook valley, first on RR grade, then on old logging roads for long, pleasant stretch of walking. At 3.5 mi. / 2300 ft., trail begins steeper ascent of ridge to R via switchbacks through birch forest. Once atop ridge, trail meanders up through conifers and birch, then begins steep, winding climb up nose of ridge, leading to several sets of wood ladders and staircases. At 4.6 mi. / 3475 ft., at top of long ladder, look for signed viewpoint ("Down-Look") up on R. Here there is memorable view NE and E into Pemi Wilderness, including Owl's Head, the five 4000-footers of Twin-Bond Range, and Nancy Range and Carrigain up long valley of East Branch. Especially fine is view into slide-marked cirques at head of Redrock Brook, between South Twin and Guyot. Flume's summit looms close by on L.

After more staircases, main ridge is attained and trail levels out, meandering through firs. At 5.1 mi. / 3800 ft., in large flat area, trail heads R toward Flume's narrow ridgecrest. Flume Slide Trail comes in on L at 5.5 mi. / 4220 ft., just past side path L to viewpoint looking W. For summit, go straight on Franconia Ridge Trail for final 0.1 mi. climb, ending with scramble up jagged rock outcrops along W edge of narrow summit ridge. Use caution as there are steep drops to L. High point is open ledge at N end of crest.

West Approach from US 3

Mt. Flume only

Whitehouse Trail, Liberty Spring Trail, Flume Slide Trail, Franconia Ridge Trail

9.6 mi. round trip, 3100-ft. elevation gain

Mts. Flume and Liberty loop option

Whitehouse Trail, Liberty Spring Trail, Flume Slide Trail, Franconia Ridge Trail, descent via Liberty Spring Trail

10.9 mi. round trip, 3650-ft. elevation gain

Mts. Liberty and Flume, out-and-back

via Liberty Spring Trail ascent
10.2 mi. round trip, 4250-ft. elevation gain

TRAILHEAD (1400 ft.): These routes begin in a hiker's parking area on the E side of US 3, 0.1 mi. N of the parking area for Flume Visitor Center. If driving N on I-93, take Exit 1 off Franconia Notch Parkway and proceed 0.5 mi. N on US 3 to exit on R for hiker's parking. Coming S on I-93, parking area is on L, 0.2 mi. S of Exit 1.

The ascent via Flume Slide Trail is the most direct approach to the summit from the W, and is extremely steep and difficult in its upper section as it follows the route of one of the mountain's old slides. Because many of the rock slabs which the route passes over are extremely dangerous when wet, this route is not recommended in times of wet weather. Hikers will also encounter difficulties while descending via this trail, therefore it is not generally used as a descent route. Hikers not comfortable with such steep terrain are advised to use the Osseo Trail route to Mt. Flume, or ascend Mt. Liberty via Liberty Spring Trail, go out-and-back to Mt. Flume on Franconia Ridge Trail, and descend from Mt. Liberty. See Mt. Liberty chapter for details.

From parking area, follow Whitehouse Trail up onto hardwood plateau and N along rolling course parallel to parkway. Descend to paved Franconia Notch Recreation Trail (the bike path) at 0.6 mi. Turn L on bike path and follow it over bridges across minor brook and Pemigewasset River, passing jct. L with Cascade Brook Trail at W side of second bridge. From here to jct. with Flume Slide Trail, the route is part of Appalachian Trail. On far side of bridge, at 0.8 mi., turn R off bike path onto white-blazed Liberty Spring Trail.

Trail traverses northward across hardwood slope, then swings back to R and climbs to jct. R with Flume Slide Trail at 1.4 mi./1800 ft. Flume Slide Trail initially follows old logging road, then veers more to the E while traversing lower slopes of Mt. Liberty. Ascending via mostly easy grades, trail makes several minor stream crossings in first 1.5 mi., and eventually meets and crosses Flume Brook 1.9 mi. from jct. with Liberty Spring Trail. After crossing and recrossing main brook several times in next half-mile, path climbs away from brook and gradually emerges onto gravel outwash of slide. At 4.0 mi./2850 ft. ascent of slide begins over wet ledges and loose rocks, with occasional views available. If hiking with or near someone else, be aware of rocks dislodged by hiker above you or by your footwork. Much of climb is over steep, smooth ledges that are slick when wet. Some hikers may be driven to woods along edges of trail. After half-mile of unrelieved climbing, trail steers L for final steep ascent of ridgecrest. Atop ridge, Franconia Ridge Trail to summit leaves L and Osseo Trail to East Branch valley leaves R. Follow Franconia Ridge Trail 0.1 mi. N to summit ledges.

Loop Option

From the W, a loop over Mts. Flume and Liberty can be made via the Flume Slide, Franconia Ridge and Liberty Spring Trails. Since it is inadvisable to descend the Flume Slide Trail, most hikers will instead take that trail *up* Mt. Flume, follow Franconia Ridge Trail 1.1 mi. N to Mt. Liberty, then continue N on ridge to terminus of Liberty Spring Trail 0.3 mi. from summit. From there, Liberty Spring Trail is taken 2.9 mi. back to Whitehouse Trail.

From Mt. Flume, Franconia Ridge Trail descends to knob N of summit, then drops down to Liberty-Flume col (3900 ft.). From col, trail begins stiff 550-ft. climb up Liberty, heading mostly in westerly direction. From open summit of Mt. Liberty, head N down and over ledges and into woods until Liberty Spring Trail is reached. (For detailed description of Liberty Spring Trail see Mt. Liberty chapter.)

By spotting vehicles, one at Lincoln Woods and one at the lot above Flume Visitors Center, it's also possible to do a point-to-point traverse over Mt. Flume or Mt. Liberty and Mt. Flume, using Liberty Spring Trail or Flume Slide Trail for ascent and Osseo Trail for descent. Total mileage for Mt. Flume-only traverse is 10.4 mi. For Flume/Liberty traverse mileage is 10.7 mi.

WINTER

The most popular (and therefore most likely to be beaten out) route to Flume is via Mt. Liberty, which is usually climbed in conjunction with the former. Be aware that the trail between the two summits may be hard to follow in places, especially in the open, windswept woods in the col between Liberty and Flume. Use caution on the summit ledges, especially if icy. Due to its steepness, the Flume Slide Trail is not recommended for winter travel. The Osseo Trail from the East Branch valley is another option, but it does not see anywhere near the winter use of the Mt. Liberty approach and features some steep, difficult snowshoeing in the vicinity of the staircases. Summit views to the E are better in winter with a deep snow platform.

VIEW GUIDE

Unlike the other Franconia Ridge peaks, the summit of Mt. Flume is partially wooded, thus there is not a full 360-degree view from any one spot. But Flume's ledges have excellent open views W, S and N, and by standing atop the highest ledges one can also gain a good view E into the Pemigewasset Wilderness.

Because the mountain is set off to the SE from the taller peaks of Franconia Ridge, Flume offers a unique perspective looking N up the range. Close by to the NW is the shapely peak of Mt. Liberty, displaying a prominent talus patch on its side. The tip of Cannon is seen on the R side of Liberty's summit. To the R of Liberty is a fine view of the bare peaks of Lincoln and Lafayette, the latter looking especially sharp from this angle. Just E of N is a beautiful look up the remote valley of Lincoln Brook to the sentinel of Mt. Garfield standing guard at its head. (From here around to the SE you must stand to get the full view over the scrub.) The Lincoln Brook valley is closed in on the R by the long, level-topped ridge of Owl's Head, with a sharp wooded peak prominent at its S end. To the NNE, over Owl's Head, Galehead Mtn. can be spotted, with North Twin looming behind and Mt. Cabot in the distance to the L. Swinging around through the ENE you gain a sweeping view of the other peaks of the Twin-Bond Range with their many slides and cliffs. Bondcliff is especially impressive. Mt. Jefferson is seen over Mt. Guyot, and Mt. Washington is to the L of Mt. Bond.

Mt. Willey is just R of Bondcliff's summit, with Carter Dome to the R and beyond; Wildcat is beneath the Dome and hard to spot. A bit farther R and closer in, Mt. Isolation can be picked out along the upper Montalban Ridge. The Baldface Range, Giant Stairs and Mt. Resolution are seen to the ENE. Peering over the scrub to the E, you can gain a beautiful perspective of the East Branch valley leading for miles out to the Nancy Range. On the R the valley is closed in by the great bulks of Carrigain and Hancock, with a prominent slide marking the side of the ridge to the L of North Hancock. Kearsarge North pops out over the Nancy Range in the distance. The wooded Mts. Hitchcock and Huntington occupy a large area to the ESE, with Chocorua beyond. To the SE are the Sandwich Range peaks of Passaconaway and Tripyramid. To the SSE, seen beyond nearby spur ridges, are the Osceolas, Sandwich Dome, Tecumseh and Scar Ridge. The ski trails on Loon can be seen almost due S.

To the SSW, beyond the lowly hump of Big Coolidge Mtn., portions of the Pemigewasset valley can be seen, including part of the town of North Woodstock and many distant hills. To the SW and close by is the high wooded shoulder of Hardwood Ridge, forming the S wall of the Flume Brook basin; Mt. Liberty closes the valley in on the R. The view in this westerly direction is especially dramatic, as these ridges form a wide portal through which you gaze out at Moosilauke, Mt. Wolf and the Kinsmans. Parts of I-93 can be seen in the valley. Most exciting of all is the dizzying look down the steep slides into the great wooded bowl of Flume Brook. On very clear days many of the Green Mountains line the horizon, including Camel's Hump through the col between the Kinsmans, and on occasion even some Adirondack peaks can be espied, such as Dix Mtn. through the gap to the L of Mt. Abraham.

NO. OF 4000-FOOTERS VISIBLE: 33

Mount Lafayette

ELEVATION: 5260 ft./1603 m ORDER OF HEIGHT: 6
LOCATION: Franconia Range, Town of Franconia
USGS MAP: 7½′ Franconia

GEOGRAPHY

With an elevation of 5260 ft., Mt. Lafayette stands as the highest mountain in the Franconia Range and the tallest peak in the White Mountains outside of the Presidential Range. Besides its lofty ranking, it also possesses a summit view rivaled by few mountains anywhere in the East. The entire upper portion of the mountain lies above timberline and is home to rare and fragile alpine plants. Visitors to this unique mountain environment are urged to remain on the marked trails at all times to protect the alpine vegetation.

Mt. Lafayette is the northernmost 4000-footer along the Franconia Range, which rises out of the Pemigewasset Valley to the W and the Ammonoosuc River drainage to the N. A mile to Lafayette's S along the bare, narrow, rocky ridgecrest, beyond an intermediate 5020-ft. hump sometimes called Truman Peak, lies its craggy neighbor, 5089-ft. Mt. Lincoln.

From Lafayette's high point the open summit ridge extends one half-mile N over several rocky knobs to the rounded North Peak (5060 ft.), giving the mountain a characteristic serrated, sloping profile when seen from E or W. From here the main ridge swings NE, descends below treeline, and runs three miles over several rough, wooded humps to Mt. Garfield. From the North Peak another ridge descends NW, then splits into two spurs, one extending N and then W for several miles over Big Bickford Mtn. (3261 ft.), Scarface Mtn. (2802 ft.) and Bickford Mtn. (2380 ft.), the other dropping NW towards I-93.

Spur ridges running W from the main summit form the eastern wall of Franconia Notch. The broad upper ridge descends a mile W to a 4200-ft. shoulder. Here, just below treeline, are the two boggy Eagle Lakes, tiny alpine tarns at the base of Lafayette's exposed summit cone. On a nearby shelf is the Appalachian Mountain Club's Greenleaf Hut, named for Col. C. H. Greenleaf, former proprietor of the Profile House in Franconia Notch. From this shoulder the high, sweeping Agony Ridge descends SW between Franconia Notch and Walker Brook, forming the route of Old Bridle Path. The broad, steep W face of this ridge walls in the Notch across from the great Cannon Cliffs. This slope is littered with landslides, some of which fell as recently as 1959.

From the W shoulder of Lafayette another shorter ridge descends NW to the wild, rocky cleft of Eagle Pass (2980 ft.); on the far side of this gap is craggy Eagle Cliff (3420 ft.), a ragged line of precipices directly across I-93 from the NE slopes of Cannon Mtn.

Several deep ravines guard the main summit mass to the NW and SW. Lafayette Brook drains out of the seldom-visited ravine to the NW. This deep basin is flanked by Eagle Cliff ridge on one side and an unnamed ridge running NW from the North Peak on the other. Much of this drainage, best seen from a bridge on the Franconia Notch Bike Path, is a part of the Lafayette Brook Scenic Area; several slides scar its upper slopes. In the latter part of the 19th century, doctored photographs and postcards frequently depicted an exaggerated "snow cross" which would appear in Lafayette Brook ravine in the spring. The cross was apparently inspired by William Henry Johnson's famous 1873 photograph, "Mountain of the Holy Cross," which also depicted a snow cross, but not the one on Mt. Lafayette. To the N of the above-mentioned unnamed ridge, in the valley between it and Big Bickford Mtn., flows Skookumchuck Brook, which drains in a westerly direction, eventually merging with Lafayette Brook. E of the Big Bickford ridge is the valley drained by the South Branch of Gale River.

SW of the summit is the deep, sharply carved Walker Ravine, out of which flows the northern branch of Walker Brook. Hikers ascending the mountain via the Old Bridle Path gain an excellent perspective on this ravine while traversing the heights of Agony Ridge. The southern branch of Walker Brook flows out of a second ravine cut into Franconia Ridge halfway between Mts. Lafayette and Lincoln. The two ravines of Walker Brook are separated by a short spur ridge running up to the main ridge and culminating in the 5020-ft sub-peak between Mts. Lafayette and Lincoln.

The E slopes of Lafayette drop 2000 ft. along a broad front into the NW corner of the Pemigewasset Wilderness, drained by the deep, broad Lincoln Brook valley and the upper Franconia Brook valley. This remote area is guarded to its N by sphinx-like Mt. Garfield and to the E and SE by the forested mass of Owl's Head Mtn. A broad, boggy height-of-land (3180 ft.) links Owl's Head to Lafayette and divides the Lincoln Brook and Franconia Brook headwaters.

NOMENCLATURE

The peak is named after the French soldier, statesman and American Revolutionary War hero, Marquis de Lafayette (1757–1834), who was hailed as a hero during a stay in the United States in 1824–25. The mountain, previously identified on maps as "Great Haystack," was renamed Mt. Lafayette on October 19, 1825, the 44th anniversary of the famous Battle of Yorktown, which ended the Revolutionary War. According to White Mountain historian Frederick Kilbourne, Yale University president Timothy Dwight, who twice visited the White Mountains (in 1797 and 1803), at one time proposed the mountain be called Wentworth Mountain, presumably for Governor Benning Wentworth.

HISTORICAL HIGHLIGHTS

First Ascent: While it is not known for certain who was first to reach the summit, the first "recorded" ascents took place in 1826, the same year the first trail up the mountain was built. One early account of a climb to the summit appeared in the *Concord Register* and the *New Hampshire Statesman*, both in September 1826. The following year, the *American Journal of Science and Arts* published "Notice of an Ascent up Mt. Lafayette and of Irised Shadows" by Forrest Shepard. This article chronicled an August 7, 1826, ascent by the author, a Mr. Sparhawk of Dartmouth College, and a local guide.

1826: First trail up mountain (forerunner of today's Greenleaf Trail) is constructed. Path ascends by way of Eagle Pass.

1835: Lafayette House tavern is built in Franconia Notch by Stephen and Joseph Gibbs.

1837: Norwich University founder Capt. Alden Partridge leads excursion of student cadets to summit.

1850: Landslide crashes down mountain at head of Walker Brook ravine.

1852: New bridle path up mountain from Lafayette Place to Eagle Lake is opened. Path was probably used as footpath previously.

1853: 110-room Profile House opens in Notch. Lafayette House is moved and incorporated into Profile House complex. Also, Greenleaf Trail is widened for use as bridle path to summit.

ca. 1855: Mt. Lafayette Summit House, crude structure at top of mountain, is built. Building falls into disrepair sometime around 1865, though exact date remains unknown.

Late 1850s: Mt. Lafayette House, a small hotel, is built near site of present-day Lafayette Campground. It is destroyed by fire in spring of 1861.

1858: Henry David Thoreau, on second visit to White Mountains, camps out at base of Lafayette, climbs summit the following day. Also, Sylvester Marsh (who later builds Cog Railway up Mt. Washington) receives charter from state legislature to build steam railway up Lafayette, but financial difficulties and Civil War scuttle plans.

1882: Proposal is advanced to build tourist railroad from Profile House to summit, but project is abandoned.

Mid-1880s: Trail route is opened across ridge from Lafayette to Lincoln and Little Haystack.

1897: Old path up mountain from Lafayette Place (Old Bridle Path) is reopened, but because of logging in area, quickly falls into disrepair. Second attempt to reopen trail takes place in 1901, but again, trail is quickly obliterated.

1905: Original Profile House is torn down to make way for new structure.

1914: Charles Blood leads week-long expedition along Garfield Ridge, scouting out proposed route for new trail that will connect Twin Range with Mt. Lafayette. Trail is ultimately completed in 1917.

1923: Second Profile House leveled by major fire. Soon afterwards, hotel baron Karl Abbott sells Franconia Notch holdings (including Old Man of Mountain) to state of New Hampshire.

1929: Old Bridle Path reopened by AMC.

1930: Greenleaf Hut, built on W spur ridge near Eagle Lake, opens.

ca. 1937: Skookumchuk Trail from US 3 to Garfield Ridge Trail, just N of Lafayette's North Peak, is built.

1938: September hurricane strikes New England. Greenleaf Trail "obliterated by fallen trees and more than half a dozen slides," reports *Appalachia* in June 1939 issue. Upper section of Old Bridle Path "is a blind mess of churned-up vegetation."

1948: Heavy rain on June 24 touches off landslide which blocks Franconia Notch highway.

1954: Account of early overnight stay on summit in 1827 appears in December issue of *Appalachia*. Includes description of crude stone shelter atop mountain.

1956: Plane crash-lands on mountain 150 yards off Old Bridle Path. Pilot, one passenger walk away with minor injuries.

1959: Longtime state worker Clyde Smith lays out Falling Waters Trail from Lafayette Campground to ridge near summit of Little Haystack Mtn. Also, October 24 landslide buries Notch highway in 27 feet of debris.

Late 1970s: In effort to protect trampled alpine vegetation, AMC and WMNF crews build scree wall defining trail across Franconia Ridge.

1980: Laura and Guy Waterman adopt Franconia Ridge Trail; during nearly two decades of their stewardship trail is carefully improved and vegetation recovers.

TRAIL APPROACHES

West Approach from Franconia Notch Parkway (I-93) at Lafayette Place

Mt. Lafayette only

Old Bridle Path, Greenleaf Trail
8.0 mi. round trip, 3600-ft. elevation gain

Loop over Mt. Lafayette and Lincoln

Old Bridle Path, Greenleaf Trail, Franconia Ridge Trail, Falling Waters Trail
8.8 mi. loop, 3850-ft. elevation gain

Trailhead (1780 ft.): Old Bridle Path starts at large hiker's parking area on E side of Franconia Notch Parkway, across from Lafayette Place Campground. Parking is also available on W side of road, with 0.1 mi. paved path leading under road to E side.

The scenic Old Bridle Path, combined with the Greenleaf Trail from Greenleaf Hut to the summit, is the most popular ascent route for hikers bound solely for Mt. Lafayette. The last 0.6 mi. of route is completely in open and should be avoided in bad weather. Because ridge is exposed and narrow, it's a dangerous place in a thunderstorm. While above treeline, hikers should walk only on marked footpath to protect the delicate alpine vegetation on ridge.

From parking area, Old Bridle Path and Falling Waters Trail coincide for

0.2 mi., at which point Falling Waters Trail diverges R, crossing Walker Brook on footbridge. Old Bridle Path continues along brook for 50 yds., then turns L and begins easy traverse to N through beautiful hardwood forest, then swings to E and SE into extensive stand of birch. At 1.1 mi./2400 ft. yellow-blazed trail crosses WMNF boundary, makes slight dip, then veers sharply L on bank above Walker Brook. Trail soon swings away from stream and climbs steadily through open conifer and birch forest. Returning to edge of ravine, at 1.6 mi./3020 ft. trail makes another sharp L turn and begins steeper climb up to S end of Agony Ridge. Where trail turns L, look for viewpoint on R across Walker Brook valley and up to Mt. Lincoln.

After steady climb of 0.3 mi., first extensive viewpoints looking across Walker Brook ravine and up to Franconia Ridge are reached at 1.9 mi./3400 ft. Views widen even more as path continues up spine of ridge. First (and steepest) of three humps along Agony Ridge is soon reached, followed by easier ascents of remaining humps. Look for occasional viewing spots on both sides of path (including views W to Cannon, Kinsmans and Moosilauke) as trail gains elevation and eventually levels, reaching Greenleaf Hut at 2.9 mi./4220 ft.

From hut, pick up Greenleaf Trail and drop down into scrub, passing S of Eagle Lakes. Path passes over several knobs and soon begins ascending ridge to summit, with fine views back toward hut, Cannon Mtn. At 3.4 mi., trail breaks above treeline and climbs more steeply, following stone steps and cairns on winding route. At 3.8 mi./5000 ft. swing around large ledge on R of trail, then angle to R up to summit at 4.0 mi./5260 ft., where Garfield Ridge Trail enters on L and Franconia Ridge Trail on R.

SOUTH APPROACH from Mt. Lincoln

If traversing open ridge from Mt. Lincoln (see that chapter for its approaches), follow Franconia Ridge Trail N off summit, descending to 4900-ft. saddle before climbing to top of rocky 5020-ft. hump at 0.5 mi. From atop this knob, look for Lincoln Slide on slope to E, with Pemi Wilderness beyond. Trail then drops to second saddle, where patch of scrub is found in 4900-ft. col. Trail then climbs steeply to summit of Lafayette, 1.0 mi. from Mt. Lincoln.

WEST APPROACH from Franconia Notch Parkway (1–93) at Cannon Mtn.

Greenleaf Trail
7.6 mi. round trip, 3300-ft. elevation gain

TRAILHEAD (1980 ft.): The Greenleaf Trail is the shortest and oldest route to the summit, but because it lacks the fine views of some of the other approaches, it is the least used of those originating in Franconia Notch.

The trail starts from the Cannon Mtn. Aerial Tramway parking lot and climbs to Greenleaf Hut by way of Eagle Pass, the narrow cleft on the ridge

Mt. Lafayette and Eagle Cliff Ridge as seen from Artist's Bluff in Franconia Notch.

running NW from the summit. The way is almost completely in the woods. From the hut, however, much of the way to the summit is above treeline and thus exposed to the weather.

From parking lot, follow paved sidewalk (bike path) to Parkway underpass, turn L for very short distance, then right into the woods where sign marks start of footpath. At first, path climbs at easy grade and parallels highway (below and on R). It soon begins climbing more steadily, and after passing outwash of slide below Eagle Cliff, ascends via series of switchbacks to Eagle Pass (1.5 mi./2980 ft.), where a boulder on R provides view back to Cannon Cliffs. Trail is nearly level through boulder-strewn pass, with sheer cliff looming up to L. Beyond, you swing around to R and head more S, beginning zigzag ascent of NW shoulder on trail frequently littered with loose rocks. Use care ascending or descending rocks during wet weather. As height of shoulder is reached, grade moderates for final approach to hut, where Old Bridle Path from Lafayette Place comes in on R. See above for description of trail from hut to summit.

Northwest Approach from US 3

Skookumchuck Trail, Garfield Ridge Trail
10.2 mi. round trip, 3550 ft. elevation gain

Trailhead (1700 ft.): Skookumchuck Trail begins at parking lot off US 3 just N of its split with I-93, 2 mi. past Cannon Mtn. Ski Area and 0.3 mi. S of the US 3/NH 141 jct. The lot doubles as parking area for N end of Franconia Notch bike path, which leaves from S end of lot.

Probably the least used of the various approaches to Mt. Lafayette, the Skookumchuck Trail route is a pleasant, albeit longer alternative, with attractive woods and nearly a mile of above treeline walking over the N ridge of Lafayette along Garfield Ridge Trail.

Initially trail heads S, staying well above highway and crossing and recrossing grassy logging road several times. At 1.1 mi., former section of trail from old Rt. 3 comes in on R just as Skookumchuck Brook is reached. Path follows course of stream E, climbing on mostly easy grades until small tributary is crossed at 1.8 mi./2400 ft. Trail then steers L and climbs steeply away from brook on long set of stone steps and continues walk up valley through attractive birch forest, spectacular at fall foliage time. Moderate climb continues up slope until crest of ridge connecting Lafayette with Big Bickford Mtn. is attained at ca. 2.9 mi./3500 ft. Here trail swings R (S) and meanders up ridge through deep fir forest.

At 3.6 mi./4200 ft., after attaining flat NW shoulder, summit of North Lafayette is seen ahead. Trail drops slightly, heads more easterly, and begins final climb to ridgeline over rocky, rougher treadway, emerging above treeline a short distance before meeting with Garfield Ridge Trail at 4.3 mi./4680 ft. Ledges on E side of jct. offer striking view down into remote NW corner of Pemi Wilderness, with Owl's Head and Bond Range beyond to SE.

Turn R (S) at jct. and begin short, steep climb in open up to rounded peak of North Lafayette 4.6 mi./5080 ft. This is superb viewpoint in its own right, with far fewer visitors than main summit. After slight descent into sag, trail follows open ridgecrest S over several little knobs to main summit at 5.1 mi./5260 ft., where Franconia Ridge Trail continues straight ahead along ridge and Greenleaf Trail diverges R to Greenleaf Hut.

WINTER

A winter ascent of Mt. Lafayette, no matter which approach you choose, is a serious undertaking with extensive exposure to wind, storms, whiteouts, and a possible mix of snow, ice and rock on the exposed summit cone and ridge. One steep pitch on Greenleaf Trail just below the summit is particularly tricky if coated in ice or hard snow. Full winter clothing and gear, including crampons, is required. Old Bridle Path is the most popular winter ascent route and is usually packed out shortly after any snowfall. Still, it's always wise to carry snowshoes on any ascent of summit as it is easy to get turned around while traveling above treeline during stormy weather and it's quite possible that you'll end up in one of the mountain's trailless ravines, where great amounts of snow can collect, even in the mildest of winters.

VIEW GUIDE

Few visitors to Mt. Lafayette will dispute the notion that its summit is among the finest in the White Mountain range. And even though some observers rate its view inferior to that of several of its sister peaks along Franconia Ridge, the mountain's overall perspective of the surrounding country is unsurpassed. Of special note are the views S down the rocky spine of the ridge, E over the vast Pemigewasset Wilderness, and W across Franconia Notch.

Looking S down the barren crest of Franconia Ridge is the slightly lower summit of Mt. Lincoln, while just over Lincoln's E slope can be seen the tip of Mt. Liberty. The unmistakable pyramid-shaped peak of Mt. Flume is seen further to the L. The ski trails of Loon Mtn. can be seen between Liberty and Flume, while Scar Ridge rises to the L of Flume. In back of and L of Scar Ridge are Waterville Valley's Mt. Tecumseh and Sandwich Dome, while the peaks of Mt. Osceola are farther L, extending E from Scar Ridge. Mt. Shaw in the Ossipee Range is in the distance to the L of East Osceola.

To the SE, beyond the lower valley of Lincoln Brook, the sprawling, wooded mass of Mt. Hitchcock rears up out of the southern Pemigewasset Wilderness, a little E of the Osceolas. Above Hitchcock are slide-scarred Mt. Tripyramid (R) and the dark pyramid of Mt. Passaconaway (L). Mt. Kancamagus is in front of Tripyramid and Mt. Huntington is below Passaconaway, with Mt. Paugus behind to the L.

The long, flat mass of Owl's Head Mtn. dominates the nearby Lincoln Brook valley landscape to the E and SE, with its notable slide towards its S end. Above Owl's Head ridge, looking L-R, are the crags of Bondcliff, majestic Mt. Carrigain, and the Hancocks. The peaks of the Nancy Range are seen over Bondcliff, and North Moat rises to the L of Carrigain, over Vose Spur. The top of Mt. Chocorua is seen peering up over South Hancock's main summit.

To the E and NE is a dramatic view across the broad, remote valleys of the upper Franconia and Lincoln Brook drainages to the Twin-Bond Range and the Presidentials beyond. In late September this rolling birch-clad upland is carpeted in gold. Mt. Bond is just S of E over the lower N end of the Owl's Head ridge, with West Bond in front and Kearsarge North beyond to the R. To the L are Mt. Guyot's two rounded alpine summits, with many rock slides in front, while Stairs Mtn. and the Doubleheads in Jackson are seen above the connecting ridge between Guyot and Mt. Bond. Mt. Willey, near Crawford Notch, peers up just to the L of Guyot, with Mt. Field to the L and the Baldfaces beyond. Farther to the L, Mt. Washington and the Presidentials rise up behind the Twins. Mt. Washington's summit is just to the L of South Twin, with Boott Spur Ridge running to the R from Washington and Carter Dome visible over the S end of Boott Spur. Mts. Jefferson and Adams are seen over North Twin, and the round hump of Galehead Mtn. huddles below and between the Twins.

Swinging around more to the L, Mt. Garfield and its long connecting ridge with Lafayette are seen to the NE. The cliffs at the end of Garfield's long, wooded S arm are in full view. Old Speck (L) and Goose Eye (R) in the

Mahoosuc Range are seen on the horizon in the direction of these cliffs. Beyond the village of Twin Mountain, Cherry Mtn. runs diagonally above Garfield Ridge, with Mt. Waumbek seen over its summit and Mt. Cabot and the Pilot Range seen more to the L. Well in the distance above the town of Whitefield are the many peaks of New Hampshire's North Country, including the bald summits of the Percy Peaks near Stark. To the N and close at hand is Lafayette's rocky, rounded North Peak and a nearer knob, with a vast sweep of lowlands beyond. The Nash Stream mountains are on the horizon to the R of North Peak. Just to the L of North Peak are the low twin summits of Mts. Agassiz and Cleveland in Bethlehem. Agassiz's 2370-ft. summit is notable for its mountaintop structure.

To the NW, I-93 snakes its way along the Gale River valley and through Franconia village. Way in the distance, above the waters of the Connecticut River and Moore Reservoir, is northern Vermont's Jay Peak. Echo Lake and Bald Mtn. in Franconia Notch State Park are visible low and close by, more to the L. On the horizon above them, beyond many miles of lower country, spreads Mt. Mansfield, Vermont's highest peak.

Directly W is Cannon Mtn., with its precipitous cliffs dropping off sharply into the Notch and ski trails on the slopes to the R. The Cannon Balls and the Kinsmans, extending S from Cannon along Kinsman Ridge, form the backdrop for Lonesome Lake, which is seen below South Kinsman's summit. Black and Sugarloaf Mtns. in the Benton Range are seen between the Kinsmans. Several more Green Mountain peaks, some 70 miles away, are visible well off to the W. These include Camel's Hump (over the R slope of Cannon) and Mts. Abraham and Ellen (between Cannon's main summit and its NW spur). On the very clearest days, several peaks in the Adirondacks can be seen over and to the R of Cannon's summit and L of Mt. Abraham. Further SW is Mt. Killington, to the L of South Kinsman.

Mt. Moosilauke is to the SW over the lower end of Kinsman Ridge, with Mt. Wolf in front and Mt. Ascutney in SE Vermont seen to the L. Looking down the Pemigewasset Valley to the SSW one can see Mts. Kineo and Carr near Rumney, with the more distant southern and central N.H. summits of (L to R) Mts. Kearsarge, Monadnock, Sunapee and Cardigan seen far off on the horizon over North Woodstock village and the long ridge of Kineo.

NO. OF 4000-FOOTERS VISIBLE: 38

Mount Liberty

ELEVATION: 4459 ft./1359 m ORDER OF HEIGHT: 18
LOCATION: Franconia Range, Town of Lincoln
USGS MAP: 7½′ Lincoln

GEOGRAPHY

The sharp rock peak of Mt. Liberty is a distinctive landmark towering above lower Franconia Notch near the S end of the Franconia Range. Seen from the vicinity of the Flume Visitor Center, Liberty is a massive pyramid of a mountain, wooded except for its craggy crown, the shape of which has been likened to "Washington lying in state." From the summit ledges the hiker is rewarded with a magnificent 360-degree view over Franconia Notch, the Pemigewasset Wilderness and dozens of peaks.

Liberty's near neighbor to the SE is slide-scarred Mt. Flume, which is set back from the Notch and separated by a deep, broad col. Flume Brook drains the broad basin S of Mt. Liberty and W of Mt. Flume and flows down through the famous Flume Gorge at the SW base of Liberty. A short, sharp ridge descends S from the summit into this valley. To the N a long, gentle, wooded ridge joins Liberty with Little Haystack Mtn. two miles up the range.

On the W, the broad slopes of Liberty sweep gracefully upward from the Pemigewasset River valley at the S end of Franconia Notch. The Pool, a deep rock-walled pothole in the river, is a notable landmark at the foot of the mountain. A long slide scars the SW face of Liberty. To the E is the remote valley of Lincoln Brook, deep in the Pemigewasset Wilderness; on the other side of this drainage is the S end of Owl's Head Mtn. A broad spur ridge extends NE from Liberty into the Pemi; on the N side of this ridge is the basin of Liberty Brook, a tributary of Lincoln Brook. On the E side of the Liberty-Flume col is a cirque-like valley that also drains into Lincoln Brook.

NOMENCLATURE

In the early 1800s Liberty was known as one of the Franconia Haystacks, for when seen from the S the peaks of Flume, Liberty, Little Haystack, Lincoln and Lafayette appear as a chain of sharp, pyramidal peaks. No one is sure who bestowed the name of Liberty on this particular mountain, but it appeared as early as 1852 in a *Harper's Magazine* article, "Scenery of the Franconia Mountains," by William Macleod.

HISTORICAL HIGHLIGHTS

First Ascent: Unknown.

1813: Improved road through Franconia Notch completed.

Late 1800s: Sawmill in operation at Whitehouse Bridge on Pemigewasset River, at W base of Mt. Liberty. Settlement of 20 families develops here, with all buildings painted drab red.

1876: E. C. Pickering of AMC and B. P. Moore of Baltimore ascend Liberty from Flume House (hotel near The Flume) and spend 3 hours making observations at summit; they leave AMC register bottle at top. Account appears in March 1877 *Appalachia*.

1880s: Moses Sweetser's guidebook says of Mt. Liberty: "A long day is needed for the exploration of this summit; and a skillful guide should be taken."

1883: Major landslides occur on W slopes of Mts. Liberty and Flume.

1889: Under direction of Frank O. Carpenter and Franklin Clark, steep trail, dubbed "The Air Line," is built from Flume House to summit of Liberty. Path is extended along ridge to Little Haystack. Route up to Liberty is soon devastated by logging.

1903–1907: J. E. Henry's crews are logging in Lincoln Brook valley on E side of Liberty, operating from Camp 11 along spur line of East Branch & Lincoln Railroad.

1906: In cooperation with AMC, Karl P. Harrington and R. J. Jackman of North Woodstock Improvement Association open S section of Franconia Ridge Trail, extending from Henry's logging railway on East Branch across Osseo Peak and Mt. Flume to Mt. Liberty. Liberty Camp, open shelter accommodating six, is built at site of spring high up on new AMC trail ascending Mt. Liberty from W.

1916: 2nd edition of AMC guidebook describes the AMC path up Mt. Liberty, leaving from upper end of The Flume. Trail crosses burned area partway up, threading among "huge rocks and luxuriant raspberry bushes." Upper part of Carpenter's old path is "nearly impassable" due to logging and fire.

1921: Whitehouse Bridge Trail completed, extending from Kinsman Pond near North Kinsman Mtn. down to Whitehouse Bridge over Pemigewasset River, then following old logging road from former Whitehouse mill up W slope of Liberty to meet AMC path about 2 mi. above The Flume.

1922: New, larger shelter built at Liberty Spring, accommodates 12.

1928: After acquiring 6,000 acres with funds obtained through drive led by Society for Protection of NH Forests, State of New Hampshire creates Franconia Notch State Park.

1939: Another new shelter with space for 25 is constructed to replace former lean-to, which was destroyed by 1938 hurricane.

1970: AMC removes Liberty Spring Shelter and establishes tent platforms and caretaker at site.

1972: Section of trail between The Flume and Whitehouse Trail has been closed; Liberty Spring Trail now starts at Whitehouse Bridge.

1987: Whitehouse Bridge trailhead now closed due to construction of Franconia Notch Parkway; new Whitehouse Trail opened from parking area near Flume Visitor Center. This lengthens hike to Mt. Liberty by 0.8 mi. each way.

TRAIL APPROACHES

West Approach from US 3

Mt. Liberty only

Whitehouse Trail, Liberty Spring Trail, Franconia Ridge Trail
8.0 mi. round trip, 3250-ft. elevation gain

Mts. Liberty and Flume out-and-back

Whitehouse Trail, Liberty Spring Trail, Franconia Ridge Trail
10.2 mi. round trip, 4250-ft. elevation gain

Trailhead (1400 ft.): This route, the usual way to ascend Mt. Liberty, begins in a hiker's parking area on the E side of US 3, 0.1 mi. N of the parking area for Flume Visitor Center. If driving N on I-93, take Exit 1 off Franconia Notch Parkway and proceed 0.5 mi. N on US 3 to exit on R for hiker's parking. Coming S on I-93, parking area is on L, 0.2 mi. S of Exit 1.

After a warm-up approach, this climb to Liberty entails a long, steady slog up the W slope of the mountain followed by a short ridge walk to the summit. From parking area, follow Whitehouse Trail up onto hardwood plateau and N along rolling course parallel to parkway. Descend to paved Franconia Notch Recreation Trail (the bike path) at 0.6 mi. Turn L on bike path and follow it over bridges across minor brook and Pemigewasset River, passing jct. L with Cascade Brook Trail at W side of second bridge. From here to top of ridge route is part of Appalachian Trail. On far side of bridge, at 0.8 mi., turn R off bike path onto white-blazed Liberty Spring Trail.

Trail traverses northward across hardwood slope, then swings back to R and climbs to jct. R with Flume Slide Trail at 1.4 mi./1800 ft. Stay ahead on Liberty Spring Trail at easy grade, crossing brook at 1.9 mi. Climb moderately to sharp L turn at 2.3 mi./2350 ft. and traverse up slope to start of long, relentless climb through white birch and conifer forest. Footing is rocky in places. Steady grade continues, passing through open grove of firs just before reaching Liberty Spring Campsite at 3.4 mi./3870 ft. Ten tent platforms are to L; caretaker and fee in summer. Side path R leads to spring and partial view W. Liberty Spring Trail continues up at steep grade, reaching jct. with Franconia Ridge Trail at 3.7 mi./4260 ft. Turn R on ridge trail and wind up through conifers to small, level, ledgy ridge, with summit crags looming fortress-like just ahead. Traverse spine of open rock with views W and N and swing L, then R to scramble up open ledges to flat perches with panoramic views on summit at 4.0 mi./4459 ft.

To continue to Mt. Flume, follow southbound Franconia Ridge Trail off summit, which actually descends E off summit, dropping steeply over ledges and large rocks. Grade then moderates and trail swings SE to broad 3900-ft. col. Continue SE, then S on climb up N ridge of Mt. Flume and reach knife-edged summit at 5.1 mi./4328 ft. Retrace steps to return to Mt. Liberty and then trailhead; descent via Flume Slide Trail is not recommended. Climb back up Liberty entails 550-ft. elevation gain.

North Approach from upper Franconia Ridge

Strong day hikers or backpackers can fashion long loops over Franconia Ridge peaks with car spots at Lafayette Place and Liberty Spring trailheads. (These locations are 3.6 mi. apart.) Franconia Ridge Trail provides connection to Mt. Liberty from jct. with Falling Waters Trail (4760 ft.) near summit of Little Haystack Mtn. (See Mt. Lincoln and Mt. Lafayette chapters for descriptions of Falling Waters Trail and upper Franconia Ridge Trail.) From jct. with Falling Waters Trail, southbound Franconia Ridge Trail runs gradually out to S end of summit ridge of Little Haystack, then descends steeply over ledges into scrub; here there is fine view S down long, wooded ridge to Mts. Liberty and Flume. Grade soon eases and trail provides easy, pleasant ridge walk through fine fir forest. Reach 4060-ft. col between Little Haystack and Liberty about 1.1 mi. from Falling Waters Trail. Rise is gradual to jct. R with Liberty Spring Trail at 1.8 mi./4260 ft. Summit of Mt. Liberty is 0.3 mi. ahead on Franconia Ridge Trail.

Other Options
Really ambitious hikers can do a loop walk over Mts. Lafayette, Lincoln and Liberty. This loop entails an ascent from Lafayette Place via Old Bridle Path and Greenleaf Trail, a ridge walk on Franconia Ridge Trail, and a descent via Liberty Spring Trail and Whitehouse Trail to car spotted at Liberty Spring hiker's parking area. Total distance is 11.8 mi., with a 4350-ft. elevation gain. Hikers adding an out-and-back trip to Mt. Flume on this loop will increase the round-trip distance to 14.0 mi., and elevation gain to 5350-ft.

The option to walk back to Lafayette Place from jct. of Liberty Spring Trail/Whitehouse Trail (via Pemi Trail or bike path) will add 2.1 mi. to hike, so for Lafayette, Lincoln and Liberty it's 13.9 mi. round trip, 4720-ft. elevation gain; for Flume out-and-back it's 16.1 mi. round trip, 5720-ft. elevation gain.

WINTER

Mt. Liberty is a popular and moderately difficult winter 4000-footer. The Liberty Spring Trail is a long, uphill snowshoe slog but often has a good packed track. The last short climb over ledges at the summit may be crusty or icy; good snowshoe crampons or boot crampons may be required. Winter peakbaggers often include an out-and-back to Mt. Flume in the itinerary. The trail may be hard to follow in the open, windswept woods in the col between Liberty and Flume. Descent via the steep and difficult Flume Slide trail is definitely not recommended.

VIEW GUIDE

The open summit ledges provide one of the best 360-degree panoramas in the White Mountains. Perhaps the finest vista is eastward into the vast Pemigewasset Wilderness. Beyond a spur ridge of Mt. Flume there's a long look up the remote valley of the East Branch of the Pemigewasset, with Mts. Hancock and Carrigain looming to the R and the Nancy Range at the far end, to the L of Carrigain. Kearsarge North pops up over Mt. Anderson, and several Montalban Ridge summits and the Doubleheads are seen to the L of Mts. Nancy and Bemis. To the NE and close at hand the long wooded ridge of Owl's Head rises from the Lincoln Brook valley. Beyond is a broadside view of the Twin-Bond range: L to R, North Twin, South Twin, Mt. Guyot with its necklace of rock slides, West Bond in front of Bond (over the S peak of Owl's Head), and Bondcliff with its crags well displayed. The Presidentials rise beyond Guyot, including Mts. Adams, Jefferson, Clay, Washington (just to the R of Guyot), Monroe, Eisenhower and Boott Spur. The distant Baldfaces can be spotted just to the R of Bondcliff. At the other end of the range, to the L of North Twin, Mts. Starr King and Waumbek rise above Cherry Mtn., with Mt. Cabot behind to the L. To the NNE you gaze up the hidden valley of Lincoln Brook to the pyramid of Mt. Garfield at its head. Up the ridge to the N, beyond the rocky shoulder of Liberty, rises the bare peak of Mt. Lincoln, with the top of Lafayette just peering over.

Nearby to the SE is the great slide-scarred face of Mt. Flume, with Mts. Hitchcock and Huntington (nearer) and Chocorua and Paugus (in back) above. To the R of Flume is a jumble of peaks including Mt. Kancamagus (in front), Mt. Passaconaway, the Tripyramids, the Osceolas, Sandwich Dome, Tecumseh, and Scar Ridge, with Whaleback and Hardwood Ridge in the foreground. Farther R Loon rises beyond nearby Big Coolidge. Just W of S there's a long look down the Pemigewasset River valley, with parts of the towns of Lincoln and Woodstock nearby and many low hills and mountains in the distance. At your feet is the broad valley of Flume Brook. Distant Mt. Kearsarge and Mt. Cardigan can be picked out to the SSW, and more to the R are the ridges of Mts. Kineo, Carr and Cushman. Mt. Moosilauke rises impressively to the SW, with Mt. Wolf in front to the R. Down in the valley, to the L of Moosilauke, is the strip of North Lincoln along US 3, and in the distance Smarts Mtn. peeks over the long Blue Ridge, Moosilauke's SE spur. To the W across lower Franconia Notch are the rolling double summits of the Kinsmans with the humps of the Cannon Balls extending to the R. On clear days the Green Mountains span the western horizon. NW across the notch is the great bulk of Cannon Mtn., with its cliffs and talus slopes mostly revealed and the glimmer of Lonesome Lake glimpsed on a plateau to the L.

NO. OF 4000-FOOTERS VISIBLE: 32

Mount Lincoln

ELEVATION: 5089 ft./1551 m ORDER OF HEIGHT: 7
LOCATION: Franconia Range, Town of Franconia
USGS MAP: 7½′ Franconia

GEOGRAPHY

Mt. Lincoln and Mt. Lafayette, its slightly higher neighbor to the N, are the two major summits along the narrow, barren, steep-sided crest of the upper Franconia Range. Lincoln's craggy top presents views just as stunning as those from Lafayette, and with over two miles of continuous views the loop hike over the two summits is one of the most popular treks in the White Mountains. Because of the heavy use in this area, hikers should take extra care to remain on the trail to protect the fragile vegetation of the alpine zone.

From many angles Mt. Lincoln presents a sharp, rocky peak rising from the ridgeline. To the N the open ridge dips to a col, passes over a ledgy intermediate 5020-ft. peak, then rises to 5260-ft. Mt. Lafayette. To the S the ridge forms a knife edge with interesting rock formations as it descends from the summit of Lincoln, then it runs nearly level, still above treeline, to the small peak of Little Haystack Mtn. (4780 ft.) To the S of Little Haystack the ridgecrest descends into the woods and extends two miles to its next summit, Mt. Liberty.

To the W the slopes of Mt. Lincoln plunge steeply into Franconia Notch. The upper slopes are impressively craggy and are scarred with numerous slides and naked rock slabs. A sharp ridge, with a rocky arête near the top, drops westward right off the summit, then bends SW, dividing the ravine of Dry Brook on the S from that of the S branch of Walker Brook on the N. Another ridge descends W from the S end of the minor peak just N of Mt. Lincoln, splitting the two branches of Walker Brook. Two other westerly ridges come off Little Haystack Mtn., with the wet rock slab known as Shining Rock Cliff between them.

To the E the slopes of Lincoln drop sharply into the valley of Lincoln Brook in the Pemigewasset Wilderness, with Owl's Head Mtn. rising beyond. Between the base of Mt. Lincoln and Lincoln Brook is a remote 3000-ft. plateau holding two beaver ponds. On this side of the ridge, between Lincoln and the small peak to the N, is the Lincoln Slide, a huge Y-shaped gash of gravel that is a distinctive landmark from distant points.

NOMENCLATURE

In early days this sharp peak was included under the general term of the Franconia Haystacks, in reference to the array of pyramidal peaks pre-

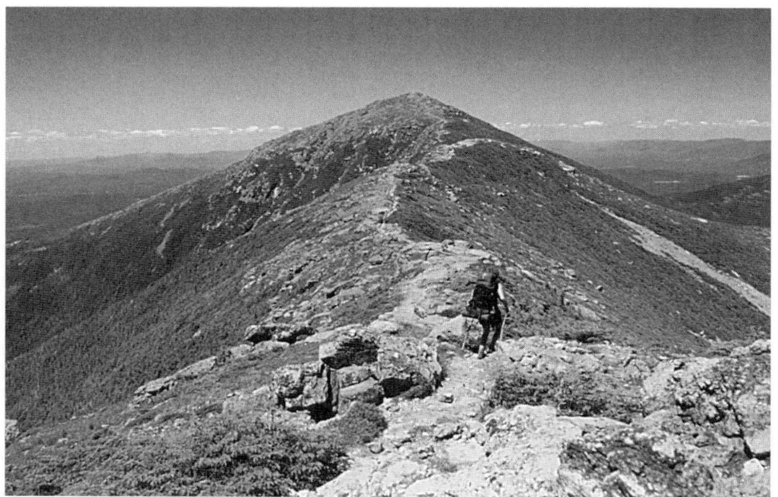

Looking north up the ridge toward Mt. Lafayette from a point near the summit of Mt. Lincoln.

sented by the Franconia Range when viewed from the S. The mountain was once called Mt. Pleasant, a name that appeared in Thomas Starr King's *The White Mountains: Their Legends, Landscape and Poetry.* (Not to be confused with Mt. Eisenhower, another former Mt. Pleasant.) Its current name honors President Abraham Lincoln. This name was apparently bestowed by a Mr. Fifield in the late 1800s.

HISTORICAL HIGHLIGHTS

First Ascent: Unknown. Geographer Arnold Guyot is presumed to have climbed it sometime during his extensive explorations in the White Mountains in the mid/late 1800s.

1876: Moses Sweetser's guidebook notes that from Mt. Lincoln "the views to the E., W. and S. are broad and beautiful." The walk from Lafayette over to Lincoln and the "South Peak" (Little Haystack) "takes about 2 hrs., and is comparatively easy" save for one belt of scrub. Much of the ridge is traversed by a "singular path-like trench, 1–2 ft. wide, which some people think has been made by countless generations of animals passing along the summit."

1880: Charles E. Fay and a companion climb Mt. Lafayette, then cross the ridge to Mt. Lincoln and descend partway along its W ridge before plunging down a "sunless gorge," negotiating a precipitous drop into the ravine of Walker Brook without benefit of ropes. They bushwhack out to road in Franconia Notch, emerging after dark. Trip is written up in May 1881 *Appalachia*.

Mid-1880s: Trail route is opened across ridge from Lafayette to Lincoln and Little Haystack.

1889: Trail built from Mt. Liberty N to Little Haystack.

1897: Frank O. Carpenter cuts trail up steep W ridge of Lincoln, but it is soon rendered impassable by logging.

1903–1907: Lower E slopes of Mt. Lincoln are cut over by J. E. Henry's loggers, working from Camps 12 and 13 on Lincoln Brook spur of East Branch & Lincoln RR.

1936: AMC guidebook describes route to Owl's Head Mtn. that includes descent from Franconia Ridge via Lincoln Slide.

1959: Working for N.H. Dept. of Parks, Clyde Smith builds cascade-rich Falling Waters Trail from Lafayette Place to Little Haystack Mtn.

Late 1970s: To help trampled alpine vegetation recover, AMC and WMNF crew builds scree wall defining trail across Franconia Ridge.

1980: Laura and Guy Waterman adopt Franconia Ridge Trail; during nearly two decades of their stewardship trail is carefully improved and vegetation recovers.

TRAIL APPROACHES

West Approach from Franconia Notch Parkway (I-93) at Lafayette Place

Mt. Lincoln only, out-and-back

Falling Waters Trail, Franconia Ridge Trail
7.8 mi. round trip, 3450-ft. elevation gain

Mt. Lincoln and Mt. Lafayette loop

Falling Waters Trail, Franconia Ridge Trail, Greenleaf Trail, Old Bridle Path
8.8 mi. loop, 3850-ft. elevation gain

Trailhead (1780 ft.): Falling Waters Trail starts at large hiker's parking area on E side of Franconia Notch Parkway, across from Lafayette Place Campground. Parking is also available on W side of road, with 0.1 mi. paved path leading under road to E side.

The steep but scenic Falling Waters Trail provides the shortest access to Mt. Lincoln. The last 0.8 mi. of this route is completely in the open and should be avoided in bad weather. Because the ridge is exposed and narrow, it's a dangerous place in a thunderstorm. Hikers should be sure to walk only on the marked footpath to protect the delicate alpine vegetation on the ridge.

From parking area, Falling Waters Trail and Old Bridle Path coincide for

0.2 mi., at which point Falling Waters Trail diverges sharp R to cross Walker Brook on footbridge. Trail climbs parallel to brook, then swings R at easy grade, traversing through hardwoods across base of Lincoln's W ridge. At 0.7 mi./2000 ft. Dry Brook is crossed (difficult in high water). Trail turns sharp L to follow rough course along brook past Stairs Falls (small but pretty) and Sawteeth Ledges. At 0.9 mi. recross brook at base of twisting Swiftwater Falls. Climb steep bank beyond, with view back to South Kinsman, then ascend moderately to lacy, 80-ft. Cloudland Falls at 1.3 mi/2600 ft. Steep climb to top of falls leads to view SW to Mt. Moosilauke, Mt. Wolf and SE spur of South Kinsman. Just above are two small waterfalls where two branches of Dry Brook converge.

Trail makes three crossings of N branch of brook (last at 1.6 mi./2860 ft.), then follows old logging road up to SE. After passing cleared view W, trail swings L and begins long, steep ascent through firs over rocky footway, with several short switchbacks. At 2.8 mi./4130 ft. side path descends 100 yards R to base of Shining Rock Cliff, large, wet rock slab that is dangerous to ascend. Here there is view W to Kinsmans and Moosilauke. Main trail continues direct ascent, emerging from scrub just below jct. with Franconia Ridge Trail at 3.2 mi./4760 ft., by summit of Little Haystack.

Turn L on Franconia Ridge Trail and traverse open, nearly level ridge on treadway well-defined by low rock walls. Views are spectacular to E and W; ahead Mt. Lincoln looms. Cross small rocky hump, then at 3.7 mi. traverse ledges on E side of wild knife edge section of ridge and climb up cone of Mt. Lincoln. Open rocky summit is reached at 3.9 mi./5089 ft.

North Approach from Mt. Lafayette

If traversing open ridge from Mt. Lafayette (see that chapter for its approaches), follow Franconia Ridge Trail S off summit, descending moderately in open on footway lined with scree walls. Patch of scrub is passed in 4900-ft. col. at 0.4 mi. Climb to top of rocky 5020-ft. hump at 0.5 mi.; in this area huge, gravelly Lincoln Slide can be seen down on slope to E, with Pemi Wilderness beyond. Dip to second 4900-ft. saddle and climb to summit of Mt. Lincoln, 1.0 mi. from Lafayette. Beyond, it is 0.7 mi. in open to jct. with Falling Waters Trail by summit of Little Haystack.

South Approach from Liberty Spring Trail

Franconia Ridge Trail can be followed from top of Liberty Spring Trail along wooded, mostly gentle ridge to jct. with Falling Waters Trail. This is most lightly used section of ridge trail. From Liberty Spring jct. (4260 ft.), Franconia Ridge Trail descends gradually for 0.7 mi. to 4060-ft. col between Liberty and Little Haystack. Ridge walk continues pleasant through nice fir forest until moderate, then steep climb leads to S end of Little Haystack ridge. Near top, ledge provides fine view S down ridge to Liberty and Flume. Trail levels through scrub, then emerges above treeline and reaches jct. L with Falling Waters Trail at 1.8 mi. from Liberty Spring jct.

WINTER

By White Mountain standards, Mt. Lincoln is a serious winter mountaineering destination with great exposure to wind and storms and a possible mix of snow, ice and rock on the ridge. Full winter clothing and gear, including crampons, are required. Falling Waters Trail is often packed out, but is a fairly difficult winter trail, especially if icy around the waterfalls. If descending Falling Waters after a ridge traverse, note that the trail may be hard to locate where it enters the scrub if it's not broken out.

VIEW GUIDE

Mt. Lincoln's sharp, open summit is a premier vantage for reconnoitering the Pemigewasset Wilderness to the E, Franconia Notch and mountains beyond to the W, and the Sandwich and Osceola groups to the S. Though smaller than the spacious summit of Lafayette, it is likely to be much less crowded.

To the N, up the ridge, is the nearby rocky pyramid of Mt. Lafayette. To the NE, beyond the Lincoln Slide and an eastern spur ridge dropping into the Pemigewasset Wilderness, is the distinctive cone of Mt. Garfield, with its S cliffs well-displayed. North Country mountains seen to the L of Garfield include Cherry, Waumbek and Cabot. To the R are the Twins with the high Presidentials beyond. Lurking close by to the E and SE, down in the Pemi, is the long, level, wooded ridge of Owl's Head, with the slide that provides the route up towards its summit seen towards the R (S) end of the ridge. Guyot, with its slide-scarred S cirque in full view, and the Bonds are seen over the N end of Owl's Head. Kearsarge North and Mts. Bemis and Nancy are seen over the crags of Bondcliff. To the R, over the middle of Owl's Head, are Anderson, Lowell and massive Carrigain. The Hancocks are beyond the S end of Owl's Head, with Chocorua in the distance. To the SE, over the mouth of Lincoln Brook valley, are the jumbled peaks of the Sandwich Range and the Osceolas.

To the S the barren Franconia Ridge stretches out to Little Haystack, with the pointed summits of Liberty and Flume offset to the L. Scar Ridge and Tecumseh are seen over Flume, with Sandwich Dome behind and L. Many distant hills can be seen in the S and SSW, beyond the Pemigewasset River valley. Moosilauke dominates to the SW beyond Mt. Wolf, with the ridges of the Carr-Kineo group off to the L. The Kinsmans are WSW across Franconia Notch, with Lonesome Lake nestling on a plateau in front of North Kinsman. On clear days a long chain of Green Mountain ridges can be seen across the western horizon. Just N of W, across the ravine of Walker Brook and the ledgy ridge followed by Old Bridle Path, is the great bulk of Cannon Mt. fronted by its huge cliffs and talus slopes.

NO. OF 4000-FOOTERS VISIBLE: 38

Cannon Mountain

ELEVATION: 4100 ft./1250 m ORDER OF HEIGHT: 36
LOCATION: Kinsman Ridge, Town of Franconia
USGS MAP: USGS 7½′ Franconia

GEOGRAPHY

A bulky, sprawling mountain at the N end of Kinsman Ridge, Cannon (or Profile) Mtn. is one of the most visited peaks in the region, and the reasons for that are multi-fold.

Besides being a mountain that tops the 4000-ft. mark in elevation, Cannon is home to the most recognizable face in the state—New Hampshire's granite symbol, the Old Man of the Mountain. It also boasts some of the state's most challenging downhill ski terrain, and lest we forget, its summit is serviced year-round by the Cannon Mountain Aerial Tramway, erected on the mountain in 1937 and put into service the following year.

Cannon Mtn.'s massive girth forms the S and W wall of scenic Franconia Notch. The peak rests solely in the town of Franconia, from which the notch below gained its name. Kinsman Ridge, of which Cannon is the northernmost peak, runs more than 10 miles S to N from Kinsman Notch to Franconia Notch. Mt. Wolf, the summits of North and South Kinsman Mtns., and the three intervening ridgeline humps known as the Cannon Balls (3769 ft., 3660 ft. and 3693 ft., E to W) are all southern ridgemates of Cannon. The Northeast Cannon Ball is one of New England's Hundred Highest peaks and is separated from the main mass of Cannon by the deep Coppermine Col.

The valley of the main stem of the Pemigewasset River separates Cannon Mtn. and the peaks of Kinsman Ridge from the craggy heights of Mt. Lafayette and the Franconia Range on the opposite side of the Notch. To the N, the minor mountain ridge connecting the summits of Bald Mtn. and Artist's Bluff serves as a natural barrier between the mountain's lower slopes and the deep valley in which lies Franconia village. W of the mountain lies the broad, flat Easton Valley, traversed by the Ham Branch of the Gale River. Into this valley flows Coppermine Brook, a scenic mountain stream draining a deep, secluded ravine enclosed by Cannon and the Cannon Balls. The beautiful Bridal Veil Falls is tucked into this basin.

Cannon itself is composed of three main masses, stretching out, more or less in an E-to-W pattern. The main summit, in the middle, houses the Aerial Tramway summit building, most of the ski lifts and trails, and a new (1995) observation tower and deck. A broad, level shoulder extends S from the summit, ending abruptly in cliffs overlooking Lonesome Lake, a 14-acre pond nestled on a high plateau to the S.

Cannon's flat-topped East Peak (3860 ft.) is home to the Old Man of the

Mountain and the sheared-off walls which form the spectacular Cannon Cliffs—at 1200 ft. the biggest rock face in the East and a renowned venue for rock and ice climbing. Below the cliffs is a vast, steep slope of large talus, also unrivalled in the eastern mountains. Slightly NW from the main summit is an open 3620-ft. foot sub-peak which formerly hosted the Mittersill ski resort. Cannon's main summit and the Mittersill summit are connected by the 1.75-mile long Taft Ski Trail, New Hampshire's first ski racing trail. Two ridges descend NW from the Mittersill peak, with Tucker Brook flowing between them, and another drops to the N.

Some 2000 ft. below Cannon's true summit, at the floor of the great mountain pass, lie two of the region's most scenic tarns—Echo and Profile Lakes. Between the two is the base terminal of the Aerial Tramway, which in just seven minutes can whisk as many as eighty passengers from the relative comfort of the notch floor to the oftimes cold and clammy mountaintop.

NOMENCLATURE

The mountain which we all know as Cannon Mtn. has been known alternately over the years by four different names. Its present name is derived from an oblong rock near the summit, which from a distance resembles the outline of a cannon. The mountain has also been called Profile Mtn. or Old Man's Mtn., in deference to the "Great Stone Face" which juts out from the mountain's easternmost shoulder. Philip Carrigain's 1816 map of New Hampshire, the most complete map of the state at that time, identified the mountain as Freak Mtn.. On one map from the mid-1800s, the NW peak of Cannon was named Mt. Jackson, presumably for President Andrew Jackson.

HISTORICAL HIGHLIGHTS

First Ascent: Unknown

1805: Luke Brooks and Francis Whitcomb, two workers on crew establishing early road through Franconia Notch, are first to "discover" Old Man of the Mountain while stopping for break at present-day Profile Lake.

1828: First printed account of Old Man appears, drawing more visitors to Franconia Notch.

1850: Nathaniel Hawthorne immortalizes Old Man in epic short story, *The Great Stone Face.*

1853: 110-room Profile House opens at base of mountain, approximately 500 ft. SE of present day tramway station. Hostelry is expanded over years and rebuilt in 1905, and gains renown as one of great grand hotels in White Mtns. In later years bridle path to Lonesome Lake is developed for use of guests.

1855: John Spaulding, in tourist guide *Historical Relics of the White Mountains* writes, "A footpath from the Lafayette House leads directly over the top of the old man's head and sometimes a mortal may be seen standing among the bristly hair (bushes) of the old man's foretop."

1859: Writer and fishing enthusiast William C. Prime discovers Lonesome Lake on plateau just S of Cannon. Seventeen years later (1876) he and William Bridges would build cabin on E side of pond.

1867: *Eastman's White Mountain Guide* makes reference to trail "which seems to lead almost directly from the front of the [Profile House] to the summit."

1874: State Geologist Charles H. Hitchcock notes that only the lower E summit of the mountain is generally visited, the apex being still covered by trees.

1879: Profile and Franconia Notch Railroad Co. constructs narrow-gauge RR from Bethlehem to Profile House.

1881: Trail built by AMC to Bridal Veil Falls.

1916: Rev. Guy Roberts of Whitefield and stone quarry superintendent Edward Geddes of Quincy, Mass. climb to top of Old Man and install turnbuckles in effort to prevent rocks which comprise profile from breaking off mountain. AMC guide notes that path from Profile House only goes to E summit; main summit "can be reached only by a hard scramble of about 1 hr. through dense scrub."

1917: AMC trail crews begin construction of Kinsman Ridge Trail, linking Kinsman Notch to the S with Cannon Mt. and Franconia Notch.

1918: Trail built from Lonesome Lake to Coppermine Col.

1923: Second Profile House (built after original hotel was torn down in 1905) is leveled by major fire. Soon afterwards, following extensive fund-raising drive led by Society for the Protection of NH Forests, hotel baron Karl Abbott sells Franconia Notch holdings (including Old Man) to state of New Hampshire. Franconia Notch becomes state park in 1928.

1928: Climbers Robert L. M. Underhill and Lincoln O'Brien make first ascent of Cannon Cliff.

1929: Hassler Whitney and Bradley Gilman climb exposed arête on Cannon Cliff, establishing famed Whitney-Gilman route.

1930: AMC leases, renovates former William C. Prime cabin on Lonesome Lake and opens it to use by campers.

1933: Civilian Conservation Corps cuts first ski racing trail (Taft Trail) on mountain, over NW summit. "A wide variety of turns lends excitement," notes a ski guidebook of the era. In subsequent years Coppermine Ski Trail is cut, leading from Taft Trail down to Bridal Veil Falls and NH 116.

ca. 1935: Shelter built near Bridal Veil Falls. Rough trail can be followed from there up to Kinsman Ridge between Middle and SW Cannon Balls.

1938: America's first Aerial Tramway, whisking visitors from floor of Notch to Cannon summit in minutes, opens for first summer season.

1939: Actress Bette Davis, staying in nearby Sugar Hill, becomes lost on hike along Coppermine Brook and is rescued by Arthur Farnsworth, whom she marries in 1940.

1945: Old Man of Mountain becomes official state symbol of New Hampshire.

1955: State park worker Clyde Smith locates and cuts new Hi-Cannon Trail, linking lower Lonesome Lake Trail to summit and Kinsman Ridge Trail.

1964: State builds, leases new structures at south end of Lonesome Lake. Is later purchased outright by AMC and operated as Lonesome Lake Hut.

1971: Ice climber John Bouchard makes legendary solo ascent of Black Dike on Cannon Cliff.

1988: Unique stretch of interstate highway, the Franconia Notch Parkway, is opened through Notch after years of controversy.

1991: Niels F. Nielsen retires after several decades of service as caretaker of Old Man; tradition is carried on by his son, David.

1995: New observation tower built on summit.

1997: Major rockfall in June occurs on Cannon Cliff; scars are easily visible from Franconia Notch Parkway. Among debris is mammoth boulder weighing an estimated 20–30 tons, which comes to rest a short distance above bike path through Notch.

TRAIL APPROACHES

NORTHEAST APPROACH from Franconia Notch Parkway (I-93) in Franconia.

Kinsman Ridge Trail
4.4 mi. round trip, 2100-ft. elevation gain

TRAILHEAD (1980 ft.): Cannon Mountain Aerial Tramway parking lot, off Exit 2 from Franconia Notch Parkway (I-93).

This trail provides the most direct ascent of the mountain, reaching the top of the Cannon Cliffs in just 1.5 mi. and the main summit in 2.2 mi. From Tramway parking lot, steer L of base station buildings to trailhead just up slope from picnic area. Trail enters woods L about 80 yards up slope. For first mile grade is moderately steep and steady, affording occasional views R through trees to Tramway towers. After turning E, away from Tramway, grade steepens and series of slick rock slabs are traversed in badly eroded section (use caution here). After entering coniferous forest the woods open up and trees begin to decrease in size. At 1.4 mi. grade levels out, and at 1.5 mi./3800 ft., side trail (signed) leads in short distance to top of exposed Cannon Cliffs, directly across Notch from Mt. Lafayette and peaks of Franconia Ridge. Views are spectacular here. From top of cliffs, regain Kinsman Ridge Trail and continue over wooded E summit. Following slight descent into wet, boggy area, climb through rough, bouldery stretch, scrubby and semi-open with views. Reach intersection with state-maintained Rim Trail at 2.0 mi./4050 ft. To reach summit and viewing tower, go L until signed trail on R is met at 2.2 mi. Proceed 100 yards up trail to observation tower deck. For summit Tramway station, follow loop

The bulky mass of Cannon Mtn (upper left), Franconia Ridge, and narrow Kinsman Pond as seen from North Kinsman.

trail from tower, or retrace steps back to Rim Trail and continue L (N), Rim Trail terminates at summit station.

SOUTHEAST APPROACHES from Franconia Notch Parkway and Lafayette Campground.

Lonesome Lake Trail, Dodge Cutoff, Hi-Cannon Trail, and Kinsman Ridge Trail
6.2 mi. round trip, 2350-ft. elevation gain

Lonesome Lake Trail, Hi-Cannon Trail and Kinsman Ridge Trail
5.6 mi. round trip, 2350-ft. elevation gain

Lonesome Lake Trail and Kinsman Ridge Trail
6.4 mi. round trip, 2350-ft. elevation gain

TRAILHEAD (1770 ft.): Lafayette Place Campground, on W side of Franconia Notch Parkway (I-93) between Exits 1 and 2.

Probably the nicest, most varied route to Cannon begins at Lafayette Campground, then heads up by way of Lonesome Lake, a scenic 14-acre pond nestled on a plateau high above Franconia Notch. Lonesome Lake Trail begins at footbridge over Pemigewasset River at S end of campground parking lot. Climbing largely on route of old bridle path, Lonesome Lake Trail first passes lower terminus of Hi-Cannon Trail at 0.4 mi./2040 ft., works up slope via two long switchbacks at easy to moderate grades, then veers L at 0.9 mi. for short, stiff climb to height-of-land. After brief descent,

E shore of Lonesome Lake is reached at 1.2 mi/2740 ft. Spur path ahead leads to shore and beautiful view across water to Kinsmans.

At signed intersection here, take Dodge Cutoff N for 0.3 mi., climbing easily to intersection with Hi-Cannon Trail (0.8 mi. from its lower terminus) at 1.5 mi./2960 ft. At 1.9 mi/3300 ft., nice outlook across floor of Franconia Notch to Mts. Lafayette and Lincoln is reached. A hundred yards further, Cliff House, natural rock shelter, is passed on R. Ascend steep ledgy area on wooden ladder, then pass by series of rock outcroppings on L with stunning bird's eye views of Lonesome Lake and S down Pemigewasset valley. View extends to Franconia Range on L and Kinsmans on R. Follow path on moderate climb to jct. with Kinsman Ridge Trail at 2.7 mi./3850 ft. Turn R and climb easily along S ridge, reaching summit area at 3.1 mi./4100 ft.

Other Approaches

Take Hi-Cannon Trail from its lower terminus, 0.4 mi. up Lonesome Lake Trail. Ascend 0.8 mi. via series of switchbacks to jct. with Dodge Cutoff at 1.2 mi./2960 ft. Follow route described above. Or, take Lonesome Lake Trail to pond (1.2 mi.), then continue ahead on same trail, first on 0.2 mi. segment of coinciding Around-the-Lake Trail. At 1.4 mi. bear R onto rougher, steeper upper section of Lonesome Lake Trail leading to Coppermine Col and jct. with Kinsman Ridge Trail at 2.3 mi./3400 ft. Bear R at intersection and climb very steeply up boulder-strewn W slope of Cannon (one pitch requires use of hands), meeting Hi-Cannon Trail on R at 2.7 mi./3850 ft. Bear L with Kinsman Ridge Trail to attain summit at 3.1 mi.

Various loop combinations are also possible using the approaches from Lafayette Campground.

Hikers or backpackers traversing the entire length, or just sections of the Kinsman Ridge Trail from the S will also find Cannon as their final major obstacle. Kinsman Ridge Trail runs 16.9 mi. from NH 112 in Kinsman Notch to I-93/Franconia Notch Parkway at N base of Cannon. The first 11.5 mi. from NH 112 are a link in the Appalachian Trail. Kinsman Ridge Trail passes over numerous summits, including Mt. Wolf, N. and S. Kinsman, the Cannon Balls, and Cannon Mtn. There are numerous approach trails from both the E and W. Consult *AMC White Mountain Guide* for complete descriptions.

WINTER

Windy conditions frequently prevail atop Cannon, especially in winter. Expect bitter cold winds, and plenty of snow (150 inches a year, on average). There are no easy winter ascent routes up Cannon. If ascending via Kinsman Ridge Trail, use caution for final half-mile from the top of Cannon Cliffs to summit ridge as drifted and blowing snow frequently obscure the trail. On Hi-Cannon route, beware of tricky ascent of ladder near Cliff House, a natural rock shelter about halfway up the mountain. The steep, rough section of the Kinsman Ridge Trail from Coppermine Col to jct. with Hi-Cannon Trail is not recommended as a winter ascent route.

VIEW GUIDE

The summit observation deck offers a 360-degree view, though the neighboring tower mars the vista to the N. In that direction the vast view extends out to the mountains of Vermont's Northeast Kingdom, including Burke and Umpire just W of N, and New Hampshire's Nash Stream region just E of N. The town of Littleton is seen below Burke, with the village of Franconia closer in to the L. To the NE the long-running Pilot and Pliny Ranges and Cherry Mtn. are seen beyond nearby Scarface and Big Bickford Mtns., northern spurs of Mt. Lafayette. Jefferson village spreads at the base of Mt. Starr King, and part of Twin Mountain village is seen below Cherry Mtn. Farther R distant Old Speck and Goose Eye in the Mahoosucs appear to the R of the Crescent Range.

The broadside view E across Franconia Notch to barren, slide-scarred Franconia Ridge is quite impressive, with Mt. Lafayette to the L and Mt. Lincoln to the R. The tops of Adams, Jefferson, Garfield and North Twin are visible over the L shoulder of Lafayette, with the sheer face of Eagle Cliff below. To the SE is the pointed peak of Mt. Liberty, with the Osceolas, Scar Ridge, Sandwich Dome, Mt. Tecumseh and Loon Mtn. to the R. Big Coolidge Mtn. is below Loon. To the S, the valley of the Pemigewasset River and I-93 stretches out to distant hills. To the R of the valley is Mt. Kearsarge in central New Hampshire, and farther R Mt. Cardigan peers over the long ridge of Mt. Kineo, with Carr Mtn. to the R.

To the SW the wooded humps of the Cannon Balls appear close at hand with the two Kinsmans looming impressively behind. The crest of Mt. Moosilauke peers over South Kinsman, and Moosilauke's SE spurs and the top of Mt. Wolf are seen above the L shoulder of South Kinsman. To the R of North Kinsman the sharp peaks of Killington and Pico cut the skyline in Vermont, with Sugarloaf and Black Mtn. in the Benton Range to the R. To the W many more of the Green Mtns. spread across the horizon beyond nearby Cooley and Cole Hills and the Connecticut River valley, including Camel's Hump just N of W and Mt. Mansfield to the WNW. To the NW are the twin summits of Jay Peak.

Cannon Cliffs: These flat, open ledges provide a superb view E across the floor of Franconia Notch to the high peaks of Franconia Ridge, including barren 5000-footers Mts. Lafayette and Lincoln. The pointed peak of Liberty is farther to the R. To the S, the winding Pemi River valley dominates the landscape, striped by I-93.

NO. OF 4000-FOOTERS VISIBLE: 16 (from summit observation deck)

North and South Kinsman

NORTH KINSMAN

ELEVATION: 4293 ft./1309 m ORDER OF HEIGHT: 28
LOCATION: Kinsman Ridge, Towns of Lincoln and Easton
USGS MAP: 7½′ Franconia

SOUTH KINSMAN

ELEVATION: 4358 ft./1328 m ORDER OF HEIGHT: 22
LOCATION: Kinsman Ridge, Towns of Lincoln and Easton
USGS MAPS: 7½′ Franconia, 7½′ Lincoln

GEOGRAPHY

The double peaks of Mt. Kinsman are the culminating points of the long ridge running S to N from Kinsman Notch (NH 112) to Franconia Notch (I-93), with South Kinsman's 4358-ft. elevation topping its sister peak by just 65 ft. They form an impressive wooded wall when viewed from the broad Easton valley to the W.

North Kinsman's ledgy E face drops off sharply to a flat narrow shelf in which rests remote Kinsman Pond (3740 ft.), a scenic five-acre tarn, long a favorite destination of backpackers. The peak, which is mostly wooded, is flanked to the NE by the rounded Cannon Balls, a series of three forested humps on the ridgeline between the Kinsmans and Cannon Mtn. A ledge on the E side of North Kinsman's summit opens a spectacular view out to the Franconia Range.

South Kinsman's summit, which is actually comprised of two readily apparent knobs, is flatter and less defined than the narrow North Peak. There is some dispute over which of the two summit knobs is higher. The U.S. Geological Survey map shows the northernmost knob as being the higher of the two. Trampers who have visited the mountaintop know, however, that the summit cairn has been built on the southernmost of the knobs. In any event, South Kinsman's summit is fairly open (due to a ridgetop forest fire sometime around 1870), and from different locations scattered around the summit fine views are obtained in all directions.

While Kinsman Pond lies at the base of North Kinsman's summit cone, the south summit has a watery neighbor of its own, scenic Harrington Pond, named after AMC trailbuilder Karl Harrington, who discovered the pond while laying out the proposed Kinsman Ridge Trail in 1917. This tiny acre-and-a-half pond, surrounded by wet, boggy terrain, rests on a 3300-ft. shoulder a mile S of the peak alongside the Kinsman Ridge Trail. For hikers headed N along the trail, the view of the mountain from the shore of Har-

The sheer east-facing slopes of North Kinsman drop off to hidden Kinsman Pond.

rington Pond is quite daunting as the peak's steep S slope forms a formidable wall ahead.

Several long, lower ridges extend off the main mountain mass of the Kinsmans. To the NW, 2470-ft. Bald Peak, accessible to hikers along the Mt. Kinsman Trail, provides a bird's eye view of the wide and flat Easton Valley, drained by the Ham Branch of Gale River. This sharp little peak, which is open on the top, is quite prominent as one travels along NH 116 through Franconia and Easton. Nearby also is steep-walled Kinsman Flume, a narrow, 400-ft. long gorge that writer John Jerome once mused "seems almost gaudy," lying as it does in the middle of an otherwise serene mountainside forest.

Though technically not a part of the mountain, Mt. Pemigewasset (2557 ft.), home to the famous Indian Head profile, rises several miles SE of South Kinsman. It is in direct line with Kinsman's extensive SE ridge, which tops out at 3655 ft. and rises abruptly from the flat forest floor just to the NW of the Indian Head. At the base of this ridge is tiny, secluded Mud Pond. A S spur of this massive SE ridge runs down to a broad, swampy plateau that holds 43-acre Bog Pond.

The main ridgeline from South Kinsman also extends a mile or so to the SW from Harrington Pond, where a ledgy crag at ca. 3000-ft. looks down upon the floor of the original Kinsman Notch (the mountain pass in which now runs the powerline from North Woodstock), with Mt. Wolf (3500 ft.) across to the S.

Cascade Brook, which runs E into the main stem of the Pemigewasset River, drains out of Kinsman Pond through a broad, wild basin E of the peaks. Eliza Brook drains the valley between the SW and SE ridges of South Kinsman and flows into Bog Pond, Bog Eddy, Harvard Brook and the Pemigewasset River. Whitehouse Brook drains the lower E slopes of South Kinsman. Kendall Brook, Judd Brook, Slide Brook and Reel Brook are among the streams which flow off the mountain to the W. A W spur ridge of North Kinsman, bordering the N side of the Slide Brook basin, bears an extensive set of bare ledges that are prominent from the Easton valley.

NOMENCLATURE

The mountain, its namesake pond, and the narrow mountain passageway (Kinsman Notch) dividing Mt. Wolf and Kinsman Ridge from Mt. Moosilauke are named for early Easton settler and farmer Nathan Kinsman. He, his wife, and four children arrived in the unpopulated valley W of the mountain in 1782 after relocating N from the Ipswich, Massachusetts area. Their journey through the mountain wilderness, with an ox-drawn cart hauling all their worldly possessions, is one of legendary status in the White Mountains.

HISTORICAL HIGHLIGHTS

First Ascent: Probably Dartmouth College graduates A. A. Abbott and A. M. Bacheler, members of Prof. Charles H. Hitchcock's 1871 geological survey team which explored many heretofore unreached areas of the White Mountains. Hitchcock himself acknowledges that Abbott and Bacheler were the first to discover Kinsman Pond, which at an elevation of 3740 ft. rests just 553 ft. below North Kinsman's summit. One can only surmise that these two mid-19th century explorers eventually made their way to the mountaintop as well.

1782: Nathan Kinsman and family arrive in Easton Valley and become first permanent settlers in area that is now Town of Easton.

1816: Name of Kinsman Mtn. first appears on map produced by N.H. secretary of state Philip Carrigain.

1876: Town of Easton is officially established per state legislative action. Previously, land was part of Town of Landaff.

1880: Benjamin MacDonald, in piece appearing in tourist paper, *The White Mountain Echo and Tourists' Register*, describes visit to recently discovered Kinsman Flume and Bald Peak on mountain's W slopes.

1881: Guidebook editor Moses Sweetser writes: "The ascent of this formidable peak is rarely undertaken, so great is the labor in comparison with the reward." Says best ascent route from west is via Slide Brook.

1910: First official trail to North Kinsman is established by Frederick Tuckerman and A. B. Hubbard. "Trail commences at Cecil Bowles farm in Easton . . . and is about three and a half miles in length," reports *Appalachia*.

1911: Tuckerman and Hubbard extend trail to South Kinsman.

1917–1919: AMC crews cut Kinsman Ridge Trail, linking Kinsman Notch with Franconia Notch. Future N.H. governor Sherman Adams is among workers on trail crew.

1920: Karl Harrington oversees work on trail from Whitehouse Bridge to Kinsman Pond. Route (called Kinsman Pond Trail) was cut several years earlier by Forest Service, but was not maintained. Same trail is also extended E to shelter on Mt. Liberty.

1921: Open log shelter accommodating 12 backpackers is constructed at Kinsman Pond.

1924: AMC builds small log shelter near Eliza Brook, several miles S of Kinsmans along ridge trail.

1926: Harrington writes of Kinsman traverse in book, *Walks & Climbs in the White Mountains*.

1930: Fishin' Jimmy Trail from Lonesome Lake to Kinsman Pond is cut by AMC. Eliminates tedious climb over Cannon Balls to terminus of Lonesome Lake Trail in Coppermine Col.

Mid-1930s: Kinsman Cabin is built along Mt. Kinsman Trail to accommodate growing number of skiers frequenting White Mountains.

1934: AMC guidebook provides brief description of Kinsman Ski Trail which runs 3 mi. from Mt. Kinsman Trail to col between S and Middle Cannon Balls.

1939: Ski guide to Eastern U.S. describes Kinsman Ski Trail as "sporty with many sudden pitches which keep the skier on the alert."

1950s: Powerline is built from North Woodstock to Easton, crossing over Bog Pond and through notch between South Kinsman and Mt. Wolf. In 1970s this corridor is considered but rejected as alternative route for I-93 instead of Franconia Notch.

Late 1950s: Basin-Cascades Trail built by state park workers.

1965: Veteran AMC trail-builder Charles Blood recalls construction of Kinsman Ridge Trail in *Appalachia* article titled, "Evolution of a Trailman."

1982: Forest Service decides to remove Kinsman Cabin and rehabilitate site.

TRAIL APPROACHES

West Approach from NH 116, Easton Valley and Franconia

North Kinsman only

Mt. Kinsman Trail, Kinsman Ridge Trail
8.2 mi. round trip, 3263-ft. elevation gain

North and South Kinsman out and back

Mt. Kinsman Trail, Kinsman Ridge Trail
10.0 mi. round trip, 3913-ft. elevation gain

Trailhead (1030 ft.): Mt. Kinsman Trail begins at Franconia-Easton town line and runs 3.7 mi. to Kinsman Ridge, intersecting the latter 0.4 mi. from

North Kinsman's summit. Parking is sparse at trailhead and is limited to immediate roadside. The trailhead is 4 mi. S of Franconia village and I-93 and is marked by prominent stone gate just past Easton/Franconia town-line marker.

The ascent via the Mt. Kinsman Trail from Easton Valley is the primary western approach to the Kinsmans. As South Kinsman is much tougher to reach from points S (on either the E or W side of the range), most peakbaggers opt to hit both peaks on a single hike. Backpackers traversing the Kinsman Ridge Trail are the exception, as are hikers who might have spotted vehicles at the Reel Brook and Mt. Kinsman trailheads, both off NH 116.

From gate, trail heads SE and follows old logging roads. Blazes are few and far between, so watch for directional arrow at 0.5 mi. indicating where trail bears R. At 1.1 mi., trail crosses WMNF boundary near wet section. After short bypass loop to L, trail turns R, then quickly L and climbs to former site of Kinsman Cabin at 1.5 mi. Turn R to cross stream, and another in 0.3 mi., and at 2.1 mi./2300 ft. reach Flume Brook. Just after brook is crossed, look for side path R leading 150 yards to Kinsman Flume, a deep eroded dike several hundred feet long.

Less than 100 yards past side trail to flume, another path branches R, this one leading 0.2 mi. to bare, flat summit of Bald Peak (2470 ft.), the prominent spur of Mt. Kinsman with good views W over Easton valley, SW to Mt. Moosilauke and mountains in Vermont, and E to looming wall of North Kinsman.

Once past Bald Peak spur, trail ascends another 1.6 mi. to its terminus along Kinsman Ridge. First mile is on moderate grades, with only an occasional steep pitch marring climb. Last half-mile to the ridgeline is more difficult, requiring in one spot short ladder to ascend ledge.

From jct. with Kinsman Ridge Trail at 3.7 mi./3900 ft., bear R and climb steeply 0.4 mi. to North Kinsman summit, with some ledge scrambling. As you attain summit, note pointed boulder on L, about 30 yards N of sign indicating short path L to summit outlook. This rock is true summit of mountain. Summit outlook path leads in 25 yards L to ledge from which stunning panorama of Franconia Ridge is obtained. Proceed 70 yards further along beaten path through scrubby trees, a muddy area, and down a six-foot ledge to open rock face with dizzying view down to Kinsman Pond.

To reach South Kinsman, continue S on Kinsman Ridge Trail, descending 270 ft. to col between summits, with peek towards Vermont and Mt. Moosilauke en route. From col, begin steady 350-ft. climb to South Kinsman summit. Trail first reaches scrubby N knob, where cairn 15 yds. to E marks high point. After slight drop into sag, trail continues 0.1 mi. to bare S knob, from which excellent views in all directions are obtained. Take care not to trample fragile alpine vegetation in mini-alpine zone here.

To return to trailhead, reverse direction and climb back up North Kinsman. After passing over summit, descend steeply and bear L at point where Mt. Kinsman Trail to NH 116 enters.

EAST APPROACHES from Franconia Notch Parkway/I-93

North Kinsman only

Lonesome Lake Trail, Cascade Brook Trail, Fishin' Jimmy Trail, Kinsman Ridge Trail
8.2 mi. round trip, 2900-ft. elevation gain

North and South Kinsman out and back

Lonesome Lake Trail, Cascade Brook Trail, Fishin' Jimmy Trail, Kinsman Ridge Trail
10.0 mi. round trip, 3550-ft. elevation gain

There are numerous eastern approaches to the Kinsmans from Franconia Notch State Park. A majority of hikers will initiate their assaults on either the Lonesome Lake Trail from Lafayette Campground (1770 ft.) or the Basin-Cascades Trail from The Basin (1520 ft.). There is no parking at the lower end of the Cascade Brook Trail, eliminating that as a viable approach for most hikers.

Probably the most heavily used approach utilizes portions of the Lonesome Lake, Cascade Brook, Fishin' Jimmy and Kinsman Ridge Trails. This route begins at Lafayette Campground in Franconia Notch State Park and reaches summit of North Kinsman in 4.1 mi. and summit of South Kinsman in 5.0 mi.

Yellow-blazed Lonesome Lake Trail begins at wooden bridge over Pemigewasset River and immediately passes through section of state park campground. Ascending on moderate to easy grades via two long, sweeping switchbacks, trail climbs 1000 ft. in 1.2 mi. to NE corner of Lonesome Lake (see Cannon Mtn. chapter for more detailed description).

At three-way junction at NE corner of lake, turn L along shoreline and follow Cascade Brook Trail 0.3 mi. to jct. with Fishin' Jimmy Trail. Continue ahead on Fishin' Jimmy and cross Lonesome Lake's outlet, proceed past dock and AMC's Lonesome Lake Hut, and follow trail along mostly level, heavily-forested terrain, but with several significant ups-and-downs. For next 1.5 mi., as trail swings along southern slopes of middle and south Cannon Balls, treadway is rough with alternating steep and moderate stretches. Steepest pitches have wooden steps pinned to ledges. As trail nears Kinsman Pond, it levels out and passes through wet area of sphagnum moss, reaching Kinsman Jct.(3750 ft.), four-way trail intersection near N end of pond, 2.0 mi. from Lonesome Lake and 3.5 mi. from trailhead.

Take Kinsman Ridge Trail S for steady 0.6 mi. climb to North Kinsman summit, with occasional views to N. Along steep, rocky way, Mt. Kinsman Trail from Easton comes in on R, 0.2 mi. from Kinsman Jct. Follow Kinsman Ridge Trail S additional 0.9 mi. for South Kinsman (See Mt. Kinsman Trail description above).

From Basin Parking Area (1520 ft.)

North Kinsman only

Basin-Cascades Trail, Cascade Brook Trail, Kinsman Pond Trail, Kinsman Ridge Trail
9.2 mi. round trip, 2800-ft. elevation gain

North and South Kinsman out and back

Basin-Cascades Trail, Cascade Brook Trail, Kinsman Pond Trail, Kinsman Ridge Trail
11.0 mi. round trip, 3450-ft. elevation gain

North Kinsman only

Basin-Cascades Trail, Cascade Brook Trail, Fishin' Jimmy Trail, Kinsman Ridge Trail
9.8 mi. round trip, 2800-ft. elevation gain

North and South Kinsman out and back

Basin-Cascades Trail, Cascade Brook Trail, Fishin' Jimmy Trail, Kinsman Ridge Trail
11.6 mi. round trip, 3450-ft. elevation gain

If starting out at The Basin area, navigate the maze of paths around The Basin and find the start of the scenic (but rough) Basin-Cascades Trail. Follow up alongside ledgy Cascade Brook, passing Kinsman Falls at 0.4 mi., crossing brook at 0.5 mi., and skirting Rocky Glen Falls at 0.9 mi.. Meet Cascade Brook Trail at 1.0 mi./2084 ft. Turn R here on Cascade Brook Trail and cross stream on rocks, climb along NE bank of brook, then meet Kinsman Pond Trail at 1.5 mi./2294 ft. For Lonesome Lake and Fishin' Jimmy Trail route (along Appalachian Trail), follow Cascade Brook Trail up rocky old logging road another 0.8 mi. Look for Fishin' Jimmy Trail on L. For shorter, more direct route to Kinsman Pond, steer L onto Kinsman Pond Trail, which immediately crosses stream and ascends moderately on old logging road. Trail is rough and eroded in spots as it passes through beautiful boreal forest. After crossing stream at 2.8 mi., trail runs for short distance in brook bed, then grade eases. Outlet brook from pond is crossed at 3.4 mi. and S end of pond is reached at 3.6 mi. Trail then traverses rocky E shore of pond, with impressive views up to ledgy wall of North Kinsman, and passes by Kinsman Pond Shelter (and tentsites) at NE end of pond. Kinsman Jct. is reached at 4.0 mi./3750 ft. Turn L here on Kinsman Ridge Trail to reach North Kinsman at 4.6 mi. and South Kinsman at 5.5 mi.

Other Approaches
From the N and S, the Kinsmans are accessible via the Kinsman Ridge Trail, which runs 16.9 mi. between NH 112 at Kinsman Notch and Franconia

Notch Parkway (I-93) at the base of Cannon Mtn. Kinsman Ridge Trail is intersected by numerous side trails N of the Kinsmans, allowing backpackers a variety of entry points. See Cannon Mtn. chapter for details. Several footpaths also join Kinsman Ridge Trail several miles S of Harrington Pond. The closest is the Reel Brook Trail, a moderate, muddy 2.9 mi. climb with 1200-ft. elevation gain and several brook crossings. The trailhead (1400 ft.) is on a side road 0.6 mi. off NH 116 in Easton.

These approaches are utilized primarily by backpackers, including Appalachian Trail thru-hikers, who usually ascend the Kinsmans from the S. The section leading N from Reel Brook Trail jct. (2600 ft.) crosses a powerline with views E over Bog Pond and descends to Eliza Brook Shelter (2400 ft.) at 1.0 mi. from jct. It then ascends alongside beautiful Eliza Brook, with many cascades, to tiny, secluded Harrington Pond at 2.4 mi./3400 ft., where South Kinsman's ledgy ridge looms ahead. The precipitous 1.1 mi. climb up South Kinsman from the pond is one of the most grueling stretches of the AT in the White Mountains, with ledgy scrambles and good views S. Summit of South Kinsman is reached 3.5 mi. from Reel Brook Trail, with elevation gain of 2000 ft. From trailhead of Reel Brook Trail, one-way climb to South Kinsman is 6.4 mi. with 3200-ft. elevation gain. With car spot at start of Mt. Kinsman Trail on NH 116, a rugged traverse of both Kinsmans is possible. Total distance 11.4 mi., with 3500-ft. elevation gain.

WINTER

As is usually the case with summer hikers headed to the Kinsmans, winter trampers tend to "bag" both summits in the same trip rather than make a second separate trip for the one they didn't get the first time around. As space for cars is limited alongside NH 116, it may be difficult in winter to find adequate parking near the Mt. Kinsman Trail at the Easton-Franconia town line—bring a shovel! This trail has good, mostly moderate grades for snowshoeing. Parking, however, is not a problem for hikers bound for the Kinsmans from the E as the parking lots in Franconia Notch at both Lafayette Campground and The Basin are regularly plowed.

The Fishin' Jimmy Trail from Lonesome Lake can be decidedly treacherous in winter, particularly along its steeper sections, which tend to ice up quickly. The hike up to Kinsman Pond via the Kinsman Pond Trail tends to be a more pleasant experience than in summer as the rocky stream bed over which upper portions of the trail run is usually blanketed under several feet of snow.

The unpaved road into the Reel Brook trailhead off NH 116 is not plowed and the trail itself receives little, if any, use in winter, thus plans including this trail are not recommended.

VIEW GUIDE

North Kinsman: The E outlook is a table-flat ledge with a spectacular view across Franconia Notch to the barren, slide-scarred Franconia Range, with Lonesome Lake nestled on a plateau in the foreground. This is one of the finest of all views to Lafayette and Lincoln. The ridge followed by Old Bridle Path sweeps down below the peaks. The tips of Garfield, Adams and Jefferson can be seen over the L shoulder of Lafayette. Cannon and the Cannon Balls are nearby to the L, with distant Old Speck to the R of Cannon. Cherry Mtn. and Mts. Starr King and Waumbek are to Cannon's L, and Mt. Cabot is over Cannon's NW Peak, with the Pilot Ridge trailing off on the L. Farther L much of New Hampshire's North Country can be seen in the distance. To the R, Franconia Ridge extends to Mts. Liberty and Flume, with Mts. Carrigain (to the L of Liberty) and Hancock (North Peak between Liberty and Flume, South Peak to the R of Flume) peering over. A jumble of mountains is seen to the SE, including Mts. Huntington, Chocorua, Paugus, Kancamagus, Passaconaway and Tripyramid, the Osceolas, Scar Ridge, Tecumseh, Sandwich Dome and Loon Mtn. Ski Area. Big Coolidge is seen closer in below Osceola. Nearby South Kinsman is seen to the far R. From the lower ledge there's a dramatic view right down at Kinsman Pond, 600 ft. below.

South Kinsman: The best views are from the more open S knob, where from various ledges around the plateau you can cobble together a 360-degree panorama. To the E Franconia Ridge rises above the nearby scrub (though not as dramatically as from North Kinsman). Bond and Bondcliff peek over to the R of Little Haystack. Carrigain is seen between Liberty and Flume, with the Hancocks to the R of Flume. Farther R Mts. Hitchcock and Huntington peer over the level ridge of Whaleback. To the SSE Mts. Passaconaway, Tripyramid, the tip of Whiteface, and Osceola rise above nearby Big Coolidge Mtn. Farther R are Scar Ridge and Loon Mtn., with Mt. Tecumseh and Sandwich Dome beyond. Mt. Shaw in the Ossipee Range is to the L of Tecumseh.

To the S, Bog Pond sprawls across a high plateau guarded by Mt. Wolf on the R, with a long look down the Pemigewasset valley to the L. Mts. Kineo, Cushman and Carr are beyond Mt. Wolf, and on clear days Cardigan and Mondanock are visible. The great bulk of Moosilauke rises to the SW; in the foreground, in a pocket on a shoulder of Kinsman Ridge, is the glimmer of Harrington Pond. Mt. Clough is to the R of Moosilauke, and farther R, looking WSW, are the Benton Range peaks of Jeffers, Sugarloaf and Black.

To the W there's a wide sweep of Vermont's Green Mountains beyond the Connecticut River valley, including Breadloaf Mtn., Mts. Abraham and Ellen, and Camel's Hump. Mt. Mansfield and Jay Peak are seen more to the NW. Looking N, the sharp wooded cone of North Kinsman thrusts up above Kinsman Pond, with many North Country ridges beyond. The Nash Stream mountains are seen in line with Kinsman Pond and the bald Percy

Peaks are to the R, over the Cannon Balls. Farther R are the NW Peak and main summit of Cannon Mtn. Over the ridge between these two Cannon summits are Mt. Cabot and the Pilot Ridge (L) and Mts. Starr King and Waumbek (R). Cherry Mtn. is seen over the main summit of Cannon.

NO. OF 4000-FOOTERS VISIBLE: from North Kinsman, 22; from South Kinsman: 21.

Mount Moosilauke

ELEVATION: 4802 ft./1464 m ORDER OF HEIGHT: 10
LOCATION: Towns of Benton, Woodstock and Warren
USGS MAPS: 7½′ Mt. Moosilauke, 7½′ Mount Kineo

GEOGRAPHY

Since the mid-1800s Mt. Moosilauke has had a large and devoted following among White Mountain hikers. This massive, bald-topped giant has it all: horizon-stretching views, a grassy alpine zone, beautiful forests, wild ravines, waterfalls, and a network of varied and interesting trails. It also has as fascinating a history as any 4000-footer save Mt. Washington. In the 20th century it has become known as "Dartmouth's mountain," for the Hanover college has had a long association with Moosilauke, and in fact owns the E side of the mountain.

Located SW of Franconia Notch, Moosilauke dominates the countryside for miles around. It is a large mountain mass with several subsidiary summits and ridges. The main summit is a broad, gently sloping dome crowned with an alpine zone of about 100 acres. A narrow, scrubby ridge leads a mile southward to the prominent South Peak (4523 ft.), which is bare on top and offer excellent views, especially to the W. From South Peak a long ridge runs S over the minor summits of Hurricane Mtn. (3015 ft.), Chokecherry Hill (2971 ft.) and Bald Hill (2397 ft.). The E slopes of this ridge are drained into the Baker River by Big Brook, Little Brook and Merrill Brook.

To the W the deep Tunnel Brook Notch, drained northward by Tunnel Brook, divides the main summit of Moosilauke from its trailless neighbor, Mt. Clough (3561 ft.). Many slides have scarred the E face of Clough, and a chain of beaver ponds is strung along the floor of the notch. On the W slope of Moosilauke between the main summit and South Peak is a deep, slide-scarred ravine carved out by SW-flowing Slide Brook, which drains into Oliverian Brook.

NW of the main summit is a cirque-like valley known as Benton Ravine or Tunnel Ravine, marked by a long slide on its E wall. A Dartmouth Outing Club (DOC) trail and cabin were once located in this basin. A major ridge runs N from the main summit to the wooded dome of Mt. Blue (4529 ft.), with a spur ridge splitting off to the NW; the latter ridge carries the Benton Trail and forms the E side of Benton Ravine. From Mt. Blue another spur ridge, this one trailless, continues N over several nameless wooded humps before descending to the Wild Ammonoosuc River. Between this and the Benton Trail ridge is the deep, wild, ravine of Little Tunnel Brook, which flows NW and is laced with hidden waterfalls, once known as the Nine Cascades.

From Mt. Blue the main ridge curves SE to Mt. Jim (4172 ft.) and Mt. Waternomee (3940 ft.), enclosing the magnificent cirque known as Jobildunk Ravine, where the Baker River takes its rise. This now-trailless glacial basin has a cliffy headwall and a flat floor dotted with beaver ponds and meadows. On the shelf above the headwall is a small bog that was once a tiny pond known as Deer Lake.

To the NE the steep slopes of Mts. Blue and Jim form one wall of glacier-carved Kinsman Notch, site of the famed Lost River caverns and picturesque Beaver Pond along NH 112. Kinsman Ridge rises on the far side of the pass. The precipitous drop of Beaver Brook has created a long series of scenic cascades on this slope, accessible along the Beaver Brook Trail. There are more cascades on trailless Stark Falls Brook to the N. To the N the Notch is drained by the Wild Ammonoosuc River; to the E the Notch and the NE slopes of Waternomee are drained by Lost River.

The high Blue Ridge continues several miles S from Mt. Waternomee, enclosing the upper valley of Baker River; the E slopes of Moosilauke itself form the other wall of this valley. The DOC has named several of the minor knobs on Blue Ridge after prominent club members: Mt. Braley (3770 ft.), Mt. Kirkham (3341 ft.) and Sayre Peak (3157 ft.). The E slopes of the Blue Ridge are drained by Walker Brook and tributaries of Jackman Brook. From Kirkham a spur ridge runs S to a 2531-ft. saddle that divides the Moosilauke massif from Mt. Cushman (3221 ft.) to the S; NH 118 crosses this height-of-land.

On the SE side of Moosilauke's main summit a flat spur ridge runs across the barely discernible East Peak (4660 ft.). Between the South and East Peaks is the ravine of Gorge Brook, a partially formed cirque striped with slides on its SW side. On the headwall are waterfalls once known as The Pleaides or Seven Cascades. Gorge Brook is the first major tributary of the Baker River as it flows S and E to Plymouth; the two streams meet close by the DOC's Ravine Lodge, location of the major trailhead on the SE side of the mountain.

NOMENCLATURE

It's believed that the name "Moosilauke" derives from the Abenaki Indian words "moosi" and "auke," which mean "bald place." A version of this name,

"Mooselauk," appeared in print as early as 1755, and various other spellings were used over the next hundred years. Philip Carrigain's 1816 map of New Hampshire used the term, "Moosehillock," and this variant gained wide acceptance for many years. The present spelling of "Moosilauke" first appeared in an 1852 article on "The Mountains of New Hampshire" by C. E. Potter. Within a few years this became the standard name for the mountain. Sentiment appears evenly divided as to whether the name should be pronounced "moos-i-lawk" or "moos-i-lawk-ee."

Mt. Waternomee was named for a chief of the Abenaki tribe (see below). This spur was originally named Blue Mtn., and today's Mt. Blue was once called Waternomee. The name switch took place in 1876. Jobildunk Ravine was supposedly named for three early explorers of the area—Joe, Bill and Duncan.

HISTORICAL HIGHLIGHTS

First Ascent: Although local legend avers that earlier climbs were made by the Indian chief Waternomee in 1685 and two of Rogers' Rangers in 1759, a more widely accepted (though still not certain) first ascent was by local moose hunter Chase Whitcher ca. 1773.

1685: According to legend, Waternomee, an Abenaki sachem, crosses the mountain with a group of his men en route from the Pemigewasset River valley to the Connecticut River valley. They are driven off summit by fierce storm brewed by Gitche Manitou, the Great Spirit dwelling atop peak.

1712: Lt. Thomas Baker leads thirty troops along river that would later bear his name, then called Asquamchumauke ("water of the mountain place"). They ambush Indian encampment by river near present-day Plymouth and kill Waternomee.

1759: Two of the famed Rogers' Rangers are said to wander onto Moosilauke during retreat from raid on St. Francis in Quebec. Robert Pomeroy dies at summit, other Ranger is found by old trapper in Gorge Brook ravine and is nursed back to health.

1767: First settlers arrive in nearby town of Warren.

ca. 1773: Moose hunter Chase Whitcher reportedly makes ascent of mountain, calls it "a cold place."

ca. 1800: Scientific expedition including Dr. Ezra Bartlett and Samuel Knight explores mountain.

1817: Champion walker Alden Partridge climbs South Peak, writes article for *American Monthly Magazine*.

1840: First trail on mountain, from Glencliff on SW, is cut by local residents; this later becomes bridle path. Today's Glencliff Trail follows part of route.

ca. 1840: Mrs. Daniel Patch becomes first woman to climb Moosilauke; she fixes cup of tea at summit.

1851: Boston, Concord & Montreal Railroad is extended into Warren, launching era of logging in Moosilauke area. Small logging operations and sawmills spring up in surrounding towns.

1858: Bridle path is built to summit from Breezy Point to S.

1859: Bridle path built up Moosilauke from NW—precursor to present Benton Trail.

1860: Six-room hotel, 30 ft. × 15 ft. and made of stone, is built on S side of summit by local entrepreneurs. Opens for business on July 4 with brass band entertaining throng of 1,000 visitors. Building, variously known as Prospect House, Summit House and Tip-Top House, is expanded in 1872, 1881, 1901.

1869–1870: Geologist Joshua H. Huntington and photographer Amos F. Clough occupy Summit House for January and February, establishing precedent for winter occupation of Mt. Washington following year. Their pioneering observations on Moosilauke include measurements of fierce storms and then-record wind of 100 mph. Experience is written up in Charles H. Hitchcock's book, *Mount Washington in Winter*.

1870: Moosilauke Mountain Road Co. incorporated, upgrades bridle path from Breezy Point to Carriage Road, charges tolls. Road is operated into early 1900s; last toll is collected in 1919.

1870: William Little publishes lengthy, colorful *History of Warren*, including many tales of Moosilauke.

ca. 1876: Jim and Daniel Clement, builders of Carriage Road, spend full year living in Summit House.

1880: Thomas Wentworth Higginson writes article for *Atlantic Monthly* magazine describing bushwhack exploration of Gorge Brook ravine in search of Pleaides Cascades.

1882–83: Warren historian William Little helps scout and build trail from North Woodstock to Moosilauke, later named Little's Path. It is obliterated by logging after turn of century.

1884: Current edition of Moses Sweetser's guidebook devotes five pages to description of view from Moosilauke. Mentions great slide on W slope, with recently constructed path leading to it from Summit House.

1889: Charter is secured for "Moosilauke Railroad Company" to build railway to summit, but plans never come to fruition.

1899–1914: Fall Mountain Paper Co. strips softwood timber off slopes of Moosilauke in Kinsman Notch area and in drainages of Tunnel Brook and Little Tunnel Brook; logs are driven down Wild Ammonoosuc River. In same period G. L. Johnson operation logs extensively on S side of Kinsman Notch and on side of Mt. Waternomee, and in inaccessible basin of Stark Falls Brook.

1901: Logger William R. Park, Jr. builds gravity railroad to serve logging operation in upper Baker River valley, starting at junction with Gorge Brook.

1909: Dartmouth Outing Club (DOC) is formed.

1912: DOC members Carl E. Shumway and G. S. Foster make first ski ascent of Moosilauke, skiing all the way from Hanover and back in five-day epic.

1914–1917: U.S. Forest Service purchases substantial acreage in Moosilauke area.

1915: Tunnel Brook Trail established through valley at W base of Moosilauke. Glencliff Trail taken over by DOC.

1916–1924: Champlain Realty Co. logs in upper Baker River valley.

1916: Beaver Brook Trail built from Kinsman Notch to summit; upper part follows old route of Little's Path. Benton Trail adopted by DOC.

1920: Dartmouth alumni purchase 100 acres on summit, including Summit House, and donate to college.

1924: Model T Ford makes first automobile ascent of mountain—takes 3 hours to top. Another Model T repeats feat in 1926 or 1927, and third auto climb is made with jeep in 1949.

1927: First downhill skiing race in U.S. is held on Carriage Road in April; Charles Proctor wins with time of 21 minutes. Winter cabin built at summit.

1927: Major storm causes slides in Gorge Brook ravine.

1930: Shelter built in lower Tunnel (Benton) Ravine; abandoned ca. 1980.

1931: Cabin built in Jobildunk Ravine by DOC; abandoned after 1938 hurricane.

1932: Shelter built by Beaver Pond in Kinsman Notch. Short-lived trail built up over East Peak to summit.

1933: DOC cuts legendary Hell's Highway Ski Trail down W side of Gorge Brook ravine, described as "the steepest and most difficult trail in New England, requiring expert technique." That year first National Downhill Championship Race is held on Carriage Road. DOC skier Henry Woods wins with time of 8 minutes; Harry Hillman, for whom Hillman's Highway in Tuckerman Ravine is named, comes in second.

1933: Dartmouth purchases 933 acres from Parker-Young Co. and converts old logging camp into Ravine Camp; this burns in 1935.

Mid-1930s: CCC opens old road between Warren and Woodstock—today's NH 118.

1935: Hurricane Trail built over S slope of Moosilauke. Short-lived Pleiades Trail built up Gorge Brook headwall. Tunnel Ravine Trail cut through Tunnel (Benton) Ravine up to Benton Trail; abandoned in 1940s.

1937–38: New Ravine Lodge is built at base of Gorge Brook from virgin spruce cut nearby.

1938: Hurricane devastates old growth in Jobildunk Ravine and wipes out Hell's Highway with slides. Parker-Young Co. salvages fallen timber in mid-1940s.

1939: DOC cuts Dipper and Snapper ski trails.

1942: Summit House burns, presumably struck by lightning. Foundation is still in place today.

1942: On night of January 14, B-18 bomber on anti-submarine patrol along coast wanders off course in snow squalls and crashes into side of Mt. Waternomee. Two crewmen are killed; despite darkness, cold, wind and deep snow, five are miraculously rescued by teams quickly assembled in nearby town of Lincoln.

ca. 1946: Gorge Brook Trail cut.

1949: Ridge Trail built over Mts. Waternomee and Jim, and Asquamchumauke Trail cut up through Jobildunk Ravine; latter is abandoned ca. 1973.

1957: 2nd winter cabin built below summit; removed in 1979. New shelter constructed at base of Beaver Brook Trail.

1965: Dartmouth acquires another 1,179 acres on E side of mountain thanks to generosity of alumnus H. Pennington Haile.

1966: Very steep Slide Trail opened up old landslide in Gorge Brook ravine; abandoned ca. 1980.

1979: Dartmouth acquires remainder of land in Jobildunk Ravine and Ravine Lodge area; total ownership is 4,500 acres.

1983: Al Merrill Ski Trail opened on slopes of Blue Ridge. John Rand Cabin built.

1989–90: Upper Gorge Brook Trail relocated to NE.

1991: Snapper Trail relocated.

1993–1994: Carriage Road widened and improved by DOC. New Beaver Brook Shelter built high up on Beaver Brook Trail. Upper part of Beaver Brook Trail relocated over Mt. Blue, away from former route along rim of Jobildunk Ravine.

TRAIL APPROACHES

Moosilauke is blessed with a variety of scenic trail approaches from various directions. From any direction the final stretch to the summit is exposed to wind and weather and should not be attempted if conditions are unfavorable. It is not as exposed or potentially dangerous as the Presidentials or upper Franconia Ridge, but this is still a big mountain that deserves respect. Please stay on marked trails to protect fragile vegetation in Moosilauke's alpine zone. When leaving summit, follow signs carefully to make sure you descend correct trail.

Southwest Approach from Glencliff

Glencliff Trail, Carriage Road
7.8 mi. round trip, 3300-ft. elevation gain

Trailhead (1480 ft.): Take NH 25 to the tiny village of Glencliff, between Warren and Haverhill. Turn N onto High St. and drive 1.2 mi. to parking area for Glencliff Trail on R. The trail starts at a sign a few yards back down the road.

This route provides a long, steady ascent to the ridge near South Peak and a final easy approach along the partly open crest. It is part of the Appalachian Trail. From trailhead, climb up to old farm road and follow it up through open pastures, bearing L into woods to jct. R with Hurricane Trail at 0.4 mi./1680 ft. Glencliff Trail ascends steadily through mixed woods, then open hardwoods. At ca. 1.5 mi. enter conifer zone and slab along slope, crossing several small brooks. At 2.5 mi./3600 ft. trail swings R for steeper climb through fir forest. Good views W are available from talus slope on R at 2.8 mi./4300 ft. Grade is more moderate to jct. R with side trail to South Peak at 3.0 mi./4460 ft. Glencliff Trail ends at Carriage Road a few yards beyond. (Side trip to 4523-ft. South Peak adds 0.4 mi round trip with 100-ft. elevation gain. Beyond shallow col this path rises through scrub and over rocks to open summit, with excellent views in all directions, especially down to slides and beaver ponds in Tunnel Brook Notch to NW.)

At end of Glencliff Trail, turn L on Carriage Road. This wide trail rises gradually through high scrub, passing side trail R to viewpoint overlooking Gorge Brook ravine and main summit at 3.3 mi. Dip slightly and leave scrub at 3.7 mi.; from here to summit trail is completely exposed to weather. Climb easily up well-defined footway through open, grassy terrain, reaching broad summit and foundation of old Summit House at 3.9 mi./4802 ft.

NORTHWEST APPROACH from Tunnel Brook Rd.

Benton Trail
7.2 mi. round trip, 3100-ft. elevation gain

TRAILHEAD (1700 ft.): Take NH 112 to a point 0.5 mi. E of its eastern jct. with NH 116 and turn S onto Tunnel Brook Rd. (FR 147), which is paved at first, then gravel. Bear L at jct. at 1.4 mi. and continue to sign and parking area for Benton Trail on L at 3.0 mi.

Benton Trail provides a moderately graded climb along an old bridle path with especially attractive forests, a view partway up, and a final approach along open N ridge. This is one of the most lightly used approaches to Moosilauke. From trailhead, descend short distance to cross Tunnel Brook at 0.2 mi. (difficult at high water) and climb across logging road and up through recently logged area of hardwoods. Continue steadily up through open uncut hardwoods, then mixed forest to ledge on L at 1.3 mi./2800 ft. with excellent view into steep Little Tunnel Ravine and N to Kinsmans. Grades are easy to moderate through woods along edge of ravine, then up broad slope. Pass spring on R at 2.2 mi./3700 ft. and continue steadily up through beautiful boreal fir forest. At 4400 ft. is side path R to view SW. Shortly after passing short path R to wider W view, reach jct. L with Beaver Brook Trail at 3.2 mi./4550 ft. Benton Trail, now on Appalachian Trail, continues ahead, reaching treeline at 3.3 mi. and angling R up to top of open N ridge with sweeping views around northern horizon. Enjoy exhilarating stroll along nearly level crest following line of tall cairns, reaching summit at 3.6 mi./4802 ft.

Cairns mark the way along the open and exposed summit ridge of Mt. Moosilauke.

NORTHEAST APPROACH from NH 112 in Kinsman Notch

Beaver Brook Trail, Benton Trail
7.6 mi. round trip, 3100-ft. elevation gain

TRAILHEAD (1870 ft.): Beaver Brook Trail, part of the Appalachian Trail, starts from large parking area on S/W side of NH 112 in Kinsman Notch, 0.5 mi. W of entrance to Lost River.

Beaver Brook Trail is the steepest approach to Moosilauke and is very rugged in its first 1.5 mi., both on ascent and descent, climbing alongside a cascading brook. The upper portion provides some views along the ridge of Mt. Blue and concludes with an open walk along Moosilauke's N ridge on the Benton Trail. From parking area, trail runs nearly level to pair of crossings of Beaver Brook on footbridges. At 0.2 mi. swing R and begin to climb alongside brook, soon reaching first cascade. Trail is now very steep, with rock and wood steps and hand rungs helping at toughest spots. Cascades are nearly continuous along brook. Use caution in wet weather as rocks can be slippery.

At 1.1 mi./3400 ft. trail veers L away from main brook and becomes somewhat less steep, though hardly easy. At 1.5 mi./3750 ft. side trail R leads to DOC Beaver Brook Shelter, with view NE. Trail continues moderate climb, then eases to high plateau between Mt. Blue and Mt. Jim. Here, at 1.9 mi./4050 ft., is jct. L with Asquam-Ridge Trail. Bear R on Beaver Brook Trail and climb gradually across face of Mt. Blue, with some rough footing. At 2.5 mi. sharp R takes you on relocated stretch of trail, away from former route along rim of Jobildunk Ravine. Climb fairly steep and rough section to point just below summit of Mt. Blue. Pass two partial views to L. After short descent into col, trail rises to jct. with Benton Trail at 3.4 mi./4550 ft. Turn L on Benton Trail for final approach along open N ridge to summit of Moosilauke at 3.8 mi./4802 ft.

SOUTHEAST APPROACH from Ravine Lodge Rd.

Gorge Brook Trail
7.4 mi. round trip, 2550-ft. elevation gain

TRAILHEAD (2460 ft.): Gorge Brook Trail begins at end of Ravine Lodge Rd., which leaves NH 118 7.2 mi. from NH 112 near North Woodstock and 5.8 mi. from NH 25 near Warren. Drive 1.6 mi. up this gravel road and turn around in cul-de-sac at end (no parking here), then parallel park on R (W) side of road near stairway to DOC Ravine Lodge.

Gorge Brook Trail is perhaps the easiest and most popular ascent route to Moosilauke. A 1989–90 relocation eased the grades on the upper climb and opened several fine views partway up. Two possible loop options using this trail are described in addition to the out-and-back climb.

From your car, walk back to cul-de-sac at end of road and past kiosk with view up to mountain. In short distance Gorge Brook Trail descends L at sign, then swings L to drop to footbridge over Baker River at 0.2 mi./2360 ft. Turn L on far side of bridge as Asquam-Ridge Trail goes R. At 0.3 mi. turn R as Hurricane Trail continues ahead. Gorge Brook Trail rises moderately over rocky footway, then grade eases. Cross brook on bridge at 0.6 mi./2620 ft.; on far side is jct. L with Snapper Trail. Continue up alongside brook, recrossing on bridge at 1.3 mi. At 1.6 mi./3200 ft. turn sharp R by plaque and traverse E, then swing L and climb moderately to NE. Join old logging road at 2.1 mi. and pass fine cleared outlook S to Mt. Kineo and Carr Mtn. at 2.3 mi./3850 ft.

Trail now winds up slope through deep fir forest to two outlooks at 2.9 mi./4300 ft. Second vantage has good view NE to Franconia Range and Presidentials beyond Mts. Jim and Waternomee. Steady climb continues, bending L at 3.1 mi. to traverse scrubby, semi-open section called "The Balcony." At 3.3 mi. turn R on shoulder known as East Peak along corridor through high scrub. Emerge from scrub at 3.5 mi. and ascend in open to summit at 3.7 mi./4802 ft.

Loop Option for Descent
An attractive option to returning down Gorge Brook Trail is loop over S ridge via Carriage Rd. and Snapper Trail. From summit, head S in open down Carriage Road with S ridge and South Peak in sight ahead. Descend into high scrub at 3.9 mi. and enjoy easy walking along ridge, passing side path L to outlook over Gorge Brook ravine at 4.3 mi. Reach jct. R with Glen-

cliff Trail at 4.6 mi./4460 ft. (For visit to South Peak and more good views, add 0.4 mi. round trip and 100-ft.elevation gain; side path leaves a few yards down Glencliff Trail on L.)

For descent, continue down reconstructed Carriage Road; downgrade is steady and trail is wide enough to open views S and E in several places. At 5.8 mi./3360 ft. turn L on Snapper Trail. Grades are mostly easy as this path traverses slope through birch groves, dropping to Gorge Brook Trail at 6.9 mi. Turn R to return to trailhead in 0.6 mi., with 100-ft. climb at end. Loop total is 7.5 mi. with 2550-ft. elevation gain.

Asquam-Ridge Trail Loop Option
Asquam-Ridge Trail offers longer, lightly-used ascent route to Moosilauke, with descent via Gorge Brook Trail. From Ravine Lodge Rd., take Gorge Brook Trail down to bridge over Baker River at 0.2 mi. On far side turn R on Asquam-Ridge Trail and follow upstream at easy grades with nice brook scenery. Logging road comes in from R over bridge at 0.7 mi. At 1.7 mi./2900 ft. trail turns R, crosses footbridge over river and ascends gradually to jct. R with Al Merrill Loop at 2.1 mi./3000 ft. Bear sharp L here and climb at easy grade, then more steeply to ridgecrest between Mt. Waternomee and Mt. Jim, passing through open, moss-draped fir forest. Climb rocky stretch to wooded 4172-ft. summit of Mt. Jim (high point is just to R) at 3.8 mi., then dip to blowdown-strewn flat area and jct. with Beaver Brook Trail at 4.1 mi./4050 ft. From here follow Beaver Brook Trail and Benton Trail to summit of Moosilauke at 6.0 mi. Descend via Gorge Brook Trail. Total for loop is 9.7 mi. with 2700-ft. elevation gain.

WINTER

Moosilauke is an alluring objective in winter, but should be attempted only with favorable weather conditions. Fierce W winds often batter the upper ridge. Crampons may be required for the final open approach. The Gorge Brook Trail has excellent grades for snowshoeing and lots of views on the way up, and is largely protected from prevailing winds almost to the top. Ravine Lodge Rd. is not plowed, adding 1.6 mi. each way to the trip, plus an extra 400-ft. elevation gain (total 10.6 mi. round trip, 2900-ft. elevation gain). Plowed parking is available off NH 118 at the road entrance. Glencliff Trail is also good for snowshoeing, though the upper section of this route is more exposed to wind; the trailhead parking area is plowed. Beaver Brook Trail is sometimes used as a winter approach, but its steep grades along the cascades are quite difficult for snowshoeing and possibly dangerous in icy conditions. The road into the Benton Trail is not plowed. Skiers have long used the 5-mile long Carriage Road from Breezy Point to the S for winter ascents (and descents!) This route is shared with snowmobilers, who are supposed to turn back below Glencliff Trail jct. but sometimes ride on up the ridge.

VIEW GUIDE

Main Summit: Moosilauke has long been renowned for the breadth and variety of its views, taking in large portions of the White Mountains, central New Hampshire, the Connecticut River valley and Vermont. Wrote one 19th-century visitor, Rev. Washington Gladden, "The view from the summit of Moosilauke is, on the whole, the most thoroughly satisfactory and inspiring view I have ever seen."

To the NE the blue-green jumble of the White Mountains is piled ridge upon ridge out to the Presidentials. The sharp peaks of Mts. Lafayette and Lincoln are prominent over nearby Mt. Wolf. The cliff face of Indian Head is seen low down to the R of Wolf. South Twin is seen behind and R of Lincoln/Little Haystack, with Mts. Adams and Jefferson in the distance and farther R. The crest of the Franconia Range sweeps gracefully over to Mt. Liberty, with slide-scarred Guyot peering over and Mt. Washington towering on the horizon, flanked by Clay on the L and Boott Spur on the R. The striped face of Flume is to the R of Liberty, with Mt. Bond behind on the L, Bondcliff on the R. Willey is to the R of Bondcliff and Carter Dome and Wildcat hover on the horizon farther R. From Flume a ridge extends R to Whaleback Mtn., marked by large gravel slides, and Big Coolidge in front. The distant Baldfaces are seen to the R of Whaleback, with Mt. Nancy to the R. Down to the ENE are the towns of North Woodstock and Lincoln in the basin where the Pemigewasset River and its East Branch join.

Lumpy Mt. Hancock looms above Mt. Hitchcock up the East Branch valley, with Carrigain peering over its L shoulder. Kearsarge North pops out to the R of Hancock, through Hancock Notch, with Mt. Huntington on the R. Loon Mtn. is in the foreground under Huntington.

To the E distant North Moat and Bear Mtn. rise over nearer Scar Ridge, with the Osceolas looming to the R. Farther R the three peaks of Tripyramid are sighted through Thornton Gap, with Whiteface over Tecumseh on the R. Part of Chocorua is seen to the L of North Tripyramid, and the tip of Passaconaway is just visible on the R of Middle Tripyramid. More to the R is the bulk of Sandwich Dome above ledgy Fisher and Dickey Mtns., with the Ossipee Range farther afield to the R. Looking SE, beyond nearby ridges, are Red Hill, the Squam Range, Lake Winnipesaukee, the Belknap Range and many distant hills.

To the S, just a few miles away, are the long, wooded ridges of Mt. Kineo (L) and Carr Mtn. (R). Stinson Mtn. is behind and R of Kineo. Mt. Kearsarge is to the L of Carr on the horizon, and bald Cardigan is to the R of Carr. On very clear days Mt. Monadnock and Sunapee Mtn. can be espied to the R of Cardigan. Looking SW the spine of Moosilauke's S ridge stretches out to South Peak on the L; the sharp Croydon Peak is right above South Peak. Tower-topped Smarts Mtn. is to the R of South Peak, and Vermont's Mt. Ascutney is beyond and farther R. The bright ledges of Mt. Cube are prominent due SW over Moosilauke's S ridge. Farther R, beyond the chopped-off

Webster Slide Mtn., are Lake Tarleton, Piermont Mtn. and the distinctive sharp peaks of Killington and Pico on the horizon, joined by a long ridge. In the middle distance is the broad valley of the Connecticut, a patchwork of fields, woods and small towns.

This wide-sweeping view continues around to the W, with low Blueberry Mtn., dark with spruce and spotted with ledges, nearby in front; Vermont's Breadloaf Mtn. is in the distance over Blueberry. To the R the ridge of the Benton Range rises from Blueberry to the long ridge of Jeffers Mtn. with the broad, wooded Mt. Clough in front and more of the Green Mountains arrayed across the horizon. Mts. Abraham and Ellen are right over Jeffers, and on exceptionally clear days a few peaks of the Adirondacks—Dix, Marcy, Gothics, Algonquin, Rocky Peak Ridge and Giant (L to R)—can be picked out to the L of Abraham, and New York's Whiteface pops up through a gap to the R of Ellen. To the WNW is the N end of the Benton Range, with The Hogsback and the cone of Sugarloaf on the L and ledgy Black Mtn. on the R, and a bit of Long Pond visible in front. Camel's Hump is beyond The Hogsback and the mid-distance Signal Mtn. Range, and Mt. Mansfield sprawls far beyond Black. Farther R are the twin Jay Peaks in northern Vermont.

Seen to the N are the mountains near Willoughby Lake in Vermont, including Hor, Pisgah and Burke. To the NNE are the peaks of the Nash Stream region, just N of the White Mountains. Swinging more to the NE, the Kinsmans are dominant, with Cabot over North Kinsman (L) and Cannon poking above South Kinsman (R). Waumbek's long ridge is seen to the R of South Kinsman, with Cherry Mtn. in front and Mt. Lafayette to the R.

South Peak View: This bare spur has a fine view also, sweeping the horizon to E, S and W. To the N is a fine close-up view of the main summit of Moosilauke, looking like a peak from the Scottish Highlands. Also unique to South Peak is the striking view NW down into the deep Tunnel Brook Notch between Moosilauke and Mt. Clough, with good looks at the beaver ponds on the floor of the gap and the huge slides on the E face of Clough.

NO. OF 4000-FOOTERS VISIBLE: 34 (from main summit)

Mount Osceola and East Osceola

MOUNT OSCEOLA

ELEVATION: 4340 ft./1323 m   ORDER OF HEIGHT: 23 (tie)

LOCATION: Towns of Lincoln and Waterville Valley, Township of Livermore

USGS MAPS: 7½′ Mt. Osecola, 7½′ Waterville Valley

EAST OSCEOLA

ELEVATION: 4156 ft./1267 m ORDER OF HEIGHT: 34
LOCATION: Towns of Lincoln and Waterville Valley, Township of Livermore
USGS MAP: 7½′ Mt. Osceola

GEOGRAPHY

Mt. Osecola and its rugged East Peak form the NW wall of the high, mountain-ringed basin of Waterville Valley. The mountain's ridgeline serves as the boundary line between the bustling tourist community of Lincoln and the unpopulated township of Livermore. It also serves as a separating line between the forested East Branch country to the N and the heavily developed Waterville Valley area to the S.

The 4340-ft. main summit, with its ledgy top and suberb vista, has been the most popular hiking destination in the Waterville Valley region for well over a century. Flat-topped East Osceola, on the other hand, stands on the opposite spectrum as one of the White Mountains' least distinguishable high peaks. Unlike its sister peak, the summit is completely wooded, prompting one New Hampshire peakbagger to quip, "the summit view is definitely—and exclusively—coniferous."

The Osecola range runs E to W, with its cluster of four summits separated by less than two miles. Just W of the main summit are the Middle Peak (4220 ft.) and the sharp, knobby West Peak (4114 ft.), both trailless. To the N, the ridge is drained into the valley of the Hancock Branch through steep ravines by several branches of Pine Brook. To the S, several ridges descend towards Waterville Valley, while flat-topped Breadtray Ridge ends abruptly in a bluff overlooking Thornton Gap. This 2300-ft. pass separates Osceola from Mt. Tecumseh to the S, and from here the West Branch of Mad River flows eastward while Eastman Brook flows to the W. Osceola Brook has carved a deep S-facing ravine between the main summit and East Peak.

The broad E face of East Osceola drops off precipitously into the deep, glacier-carved hollow of Mad River Notch. Seldom-visited Mt. Kancamagus (3728 ft.) rises out of the notch on the opposite side. Draining N from the notch is the South Fork of Hancock Branch. Just S of the 2300-ft. height-of-land in the notch rest the remote Upper and Lower Greeley Ponds, headwaters of the S-flowing Mad River. A lower spur, faced with a line of cliffs, extends NE from East Osceola at the N end of the Notch. At the S end of the pass a SE spur of East Osceola ends abruptly in the sheer Painted Cliff. Greeley Brook flows out of a broad ravine S of this precipice.

To the W of the Osceolas, beyond a 3100-ft. pass, Scar Ridge extends NW across several subsidiary summits to its main summit (3774 ft.) and then descends to Loon Mtn. above the town of Lincoln. Scenic East Pond is located on a shelf just S of the Osceola-Scar Ridge col.

Over the years numerous slides have scarred the mountain on both its E and N slopes. Two prominent slides litter the slopes of East Osceola as it rises out of Mad River Notch. Several other slides, the most prominent of which came down as recently as November 1995, mark the N slopes and are best seen from various points along the Kancamagus Highway. Viewed from this angle, the Osceola Ridge has an especially wild and rugged look. Another slide in a SE ravine below the main summit is well-seen from the floor of Waterville Valley.

Split Cliff, a spectacular rock outcropping a quarter-mile N of the main summit, for many years was reached via a side trail off the main path between Osceola and East Osceola. Bushwhackers who have successfully battled their way through the scrubby ridgetop vegetation to reach this spot say its view N into the wilds of the Pemi Wilderness is unmatched. This ragged rock face can be seen from outlooks along the Kancamagus Highway.

NOMENCLATURE

The mountain is named for the famous Seminole Indian chief who hailed from Florida's Everglades. Chief Osceola was one of the Indian leaders in the Second Seminole War against the United States, which lasted from 1835 to 1842. He employed early "guerilla warfare" tactics against government troops who were carrying out a U.S. plan to transport Seminole Indians from Florida to Oklahoma. He was taken prisoner in 1837 and died in captivity a year later.

No one knows for sure who gave the mountain its name, but Nathaniel L. Goodrich, author of a 1952 history of the Waterville Valley region, surmised that it might have been 19th-century Valley resident, E. J. Connable, formerly of Jackson, Michigan. His reasoning was that some early guidebooks mentioned a "Wisconsin tourist" as being the person to name at least one other peak (Mt. Tecumseh) in the Valley. "It is tempting to surmise that Wisconsin is an error for Michigan . . . but that is just guessing," wrote Goodrich. The author also points out that on Arnold Guyot's 1860 map of the region, Mt. Osceola was listed as Mad River Peak.

HISTORICAL HIGHLIGHTS

First Ascent: Possibly by Capt. Samuel Willard, a colonist heading up an expeditionary force that was sent into the White Mountains in 1725 to look for Indian activity in the region. An expedition journal recounts a climb of a high mountain in the East Branch region, presumably Mt. Osceola.

1830: Nathaniel Greeley settles in Waterville Valley.

1850s: Greeley establishes first trail up mountain. Greeley's route (later a bridle path) ascended the "second ridge west of Osceola Brook" and climbed four and a half miles through "virgin forest never touched by the axe."

1881: Guidebook editor Moses Sweetser compares summit view with that of Mts. Carrigain and Willey "for its wide sweep over the Pemigewasset Forest and the surrounding peaks."

1884: A "comfortable bark-camp" is built on crest of Osceola.

1885: Privately published account of overnight stay on mountain—"One Night in a Mountain Camp: Story of the Ascent of Osceola in 1885"—appears in print.

1888: Waterville Atheletic and Improvement Association (WAIA) is formed.

Early 1890s: International Paper Company (IPC), owner of much of the forest land in and around Waterville Valley, begins timber harvesting operations on Noon and Jennings Peaks.

1890 or 1891: Southernmost slide on East Osceola comes crashing down on E-facing slopes.

1891: AMC group, meeting in Waterville Valley, summits main peak on snowshoes.

1896: Rev. Julius Ward adds new chapter, "Snow-Shoeing on Osceola," to his 1890 book, *The White Mountains: A Guide to Their Interpretation*.

1897: Second slide occurs on East Osceola, creating N slide overlooking Mad River Notch.

1900: A. L. Goodrich lays out trail through steep ravine separating main and east peaks. Path strikes ridgeline in col, then climbs via ridgecrest to main summit.

1910: New Hampshire Timberland Owners Association and state forestry department fund construction of wooden fire tower atop Osceola.

1915: State fire warden C. B. Shiffer marks out new trail from Thornton Gore to summit. Includes stretch of trail through virgin forest. Over time, path goes by name of Breadtray Ravine Trail, Breadtray Trail and Osceola West.

1923: Wooden fire lookout tower is replaced with new steel tower.

1926: IPC sells Valley timber holdings to Parker-Young Company, which threatens to run logging railroad line into Mad River Notch.

1928: U.S. Forest Service pays $1.05 million for 23,000 acres in and around Waterville Valley, saving Mad River Notch from logging.

1933–34: Construction of Tripoli Road, connecting Waterville Valley with Pemigewasset River valley to W, is undertaken by Forest Service, CCC. Road follows old logging railroad grade, former Waterville Path.

1934: AMC guide includes first mention of new trail up and over summit of East Osceola. East Peak Trail begins in col between two peaks, runs up to summit, and then down into Mad River Notch to the Upper Greeley Pond.

1938: Hurricane of 1938 demolishes acres of virgin spruce on Breadtray Ridge, forcing closure of new Breadtray Ridge Trail. Fire break along ridge from East Pond region to Upper Greeley Pond is cut by Forest Service.

1942: Forest Service replaces lookout tower with new structure.

1946: AMC guide says old Breadtray Ridge, Osceola Trails have been combined into Mt. Osceola Trail.
1954: Heavy rains from pair of summer hurricanes touch off three new landslides on mountain.
1955: Fire tower atop main summit is manned for final season.
1969: Greeley Ponds Scenic Area designated by Forest Service.
1985: Summit fire tower is removed by Forest Service.
Mid-1980s: North end of Mt. Osceola Trail at Mad River Notch is relocated away from base of north slide.
1995: Huge slide falls on N slope between main summit and Middle Peak.

TRAIL APPROACHES

The Mt. Osceola Trail (WMNF) is the lone trail up the mountain. Its southern terminus is along Tripoli Road (FR 30), while its northern terminus is in Mad River Notch, where it meets the Greeley Ponds Trail 1.3 mi. from the Kancamagus Highway and 3.8 mi. from the Livermore Trail from Waterville Valley. The trail runs a total distance of 5.7 mi.

Unless your hiking party has spotted vehicles at both the Tripoli Road and Kancamagus Highway trailheads, the only practical way to "bag" the two summits in a single trip is an over-and-back trek from either trailhead. Ascending the peaks from Tripoli Road is the easier of the two approaches as the total elevation gain is less and the climbing is significantly less steep than via Mad River Notch.

Southwest Approach from Tripoli Road

Mt. Osceola only

Mt. Osceola Trail
6.4 mi. round trip, 2050-ft. elevation gain

Mt. Osceola and East Osceola out and back

Mt. Osceola Trail
8.4 mi. round trip, 2950-ft. elevation gain

Trailhead (2280 ft.): Mt. Osceola Trail leaves from a parking lot on the N side of Tripoli Road near its height-of-land, 7.0 mi. from I-93 at Exit 31.

The climb out of Thornton Gap is on moderate grades and the main summit is reached in a relatively easy 3.2 mi. Trail initially runs NE on old road with one section of very rocky footing, then turns sharp L through a nice glade of white birches. At 1.3 mi., start series of switchbacks leading to top of connecting Breadtray Ridge. Huge bowl separates this ridge from main summit mass, and through trees to NE Osceola's summit is seen on opposite side of the cirque.

Attaining main ridge, trail swings R through wide, flat area, then after

A hiker gazes off toward Osceola's wooded East Peak from the ledges atop the main summit.

passing through open stand of spruce and fir, begins moderate, winding ascent over rougher terrain. Wet ledges may be icy in late fall. As ascent of main ridge begins, look for views S across Thornton Gap to Mt. Tecumseh and W to Breadtray Ridge. At 3.0 mi., trail makes abrupt R turn for final climb to summit. Upon reaching summit area, concrete abutments to former fire tower are passed while side path on L (signed) leads in short distance to fine N outlook. Several hundred feet past first tower abutments are second set of concrete supports. Just past these, at 3.2 mi./4340 ft., are Osceola's main summit ledges.

To reach East Osceola, trail departs L (N) from second concrete abutments. For first half-mile, as trail descends to col, grade of trail alternates between level terraces and steep, rough pitches. Especially challenging is short, steep chimney just above low point on connecting ridge. Most descending hikers will detour L around chimney.

From col, reached at 3.8 mi./3820 ft., trail climbs steeply up East Osceola cone. About halfway up, look for rock ledge on L offering nice view N and W. From ledge it is 0.2 mi. to trailside cairn marking viewless summit, attained at 4.2 mi./4156 ft.

Northeast Approach from Kancamagus Highway

East Osceola only

Greeley Ponds Trail, Mt. Osceola Trail
5.6 mi. round trip, 2216-ft. elevation gain

East Osceola and Mt. Osceola out and back

Greeley Ponds Trail, Mt. Osceola Trail
7.6 mi. round trip, 3116-ft. elevation gain

TRAILHEAD (1940 ft.): Hikers bound for the summits from the Kancamagus Highway should park at Greeley Ponds trailhead, 4.5 mi. E of Lincoln Woods hiking trailhead and USFS information center. (This is 0.2 mi. E of trailhead for Greeley Ponds X-C ski trail.)

Follow Greeley Ponds Trail on gradual ascent through mixed woods, with two stream crossings at 0.3 mi. and some muddy, rocky footing. At 0.9 mi. trail turns L on old logging road and rises at easy grades to height-of-land in Mad River Notch at 1.3 mi./2300 ft., where Mt. Osceola Trail intersects on R. Turn R and ascend on moderate grade for first 0.8 mi., approaching and then passing under cliffs of NE spur of East Osceola. At sharp R turn, trail begins very steep half-mile climb alongside century-old slide. Trail angles up across broken ledges on upper portion of slide at ca. 3700 ft., with fine view straight down at green-tinted Upper Greeley Pond, E to Mt. Kancamagus and NE to many distant peaks. Trail remains steep, ending with scramble up eroded gully to shoulder of East Osceola; look here for side path R leading to outlook W to main ridge of Osceola and Scar Ridge. Trail turns L and continues fairly steep climb to knob at N end of ridge, then moderates as summit is approached, reaching high point at 2.8 mi./4156 ft.

To reach main peak, follow trail as it drops past past fine outlook N and W, reaching col at 3.2 mi./3820 ft. After negotiating chimney at start of ascent, continue on alternating steep and easy grades 0.5 mi. to summit ledges at 3.8 mi./4340 ft.

WINTER

Motor vehicle access to the Tripoli Road end of the Mt. Osceola Trail is non-existent in winter as the road is gated at both its E and W ends. For that reason, most winter climbers choose to ascend the peaks from the NE by way of the Greeley Ponds Trail and Mad River Notch. The steep climb up East Osceola can be very difficult when there is poor snow cover, or if the track is too hard-packed. Crampons should be carried for this section and also for the very steep pitch just above the col. With deep snow, additional views open up on the ridgecrest approach to main summit.

VIEW GUIDE

Mt. Osceola: The main summit has perhaps the finest view of any major peak in the southern White Mountains. The summit ledges, facing E atop a cliff, afford a grand view of the surrounding mountain landscape. A short side path through the woods several hundred feet W of these ledges leads to another fine outlook, with a memorable view of the jumble of forest-covered mountains around the Pemigewasset Wilderness.

The main ledge looks out across the deep ravine of Osceola Brook, with its headwall meeting the crest of the ridge at the col with East Peak. Mt. Kancamagus is behind and to the R of East Peak. Across this valley runs a long, low ridge extending from East Osceola S to Waterville Valley. To the ESE and well above this ridge are the towering peaks of Mt. Tripyramid, including the slide-scarred North Peak, with The Sleepers and Mt. Whiteface to the R and ledgy Mt. Chocorua, the Moats, and Bear Mtn. to the L. Mt. Passaconaway peeks out just to the L of North Tripyramid

Osceola's East Peak is the dominant feature to the NE, with Mt. Tremont rising above. The sharp summit of Bartlett Haystack is to the R of East Peak over Owl's Cliff, with Kearsarge North above. A short section of the Kancamagus Highway is visible just above the col with East Peak. Rugged Mt. Huntington rises above the highway to the N, with remote Mt. Hancock seen just to the L. Mt. Willey appears between the summits of Mt. Hancock, while Mt. Tom is to the L of North Hancock.

The curving dome of Mt. Carrigain rises high above Huntington's ridgeline. To its R are the lower peaks of Montalban Ridge (including prominent Stairs Mtn.), and the more distant Baldfaces and Doubleheads. To Carrigain's L rises dominant Mt. Washington, with the Southern Presidentials in front and Jefferson and Adams to the L.

Further N, the distant peaks of the Bond-Zealand area are seen above the lower, jumbled peaks of Mt. Hitchcock (to the L of Mt. Huntington), including South Twin, West Bond, Bondcliff, Bond, and Zealand. Mts. Waumbek and Cabot can be seen in the distance to the R of Zealand Ridge. Galehead Mtn. peeks out at the L base of South Twin. To the L of the Bond Range, Mt. Garfield rises out of the western Pemi Wilderness, high over indistinct Owl's Head Mtn.. The Franconia Brook valley forms a trough on the R of Owl's Head. To the L of Garfield are the Franconia Ridge peaks, with Mt. Liberty appearing the sharpest from this vantage.

The S view from Osceola's ledges takes in the developed Waterville Valley area. Massive Sandwich Dome, and its subsidiary summits, Jennings and Noon Peaks, provide a dramatic backdrop for the many condos and hotels in the Valley. The Ossipee Range is seen over the long, low ridge of the northern Flat Mtn. Osceola's nearest neighbor to the S, Mt. Tecumseh, appears just across Thornton Gap, while a series of smaller peaks lining the Mad River valley are seen to the L of Tecumseh. On clear days the distant peaks of Monadnock and Kearsarge may be spotted to the L of Tecumseh's summit.

Osceola's NW outlook provides a clear view into the western Pemi Wilderness and peaks farther W, with Garfield, Owl's Head, the Franconias, Cannon, the Cannon Balls, the Kinsmans, Wolf and Moosilauke all on display. Mt. Mansfield can be seen in the distance to the R of Wolf. The lower, southern extremities of Franconia Ridge are seen below the middle peaks of Kinsman Ridge.

Also from this vantage point, the trackless West Peak of Osceola appears enticingly close, while a bit further to the W are seen Scar Ridge and Black Mtn. Vermont's Mt. Mansfield is on the horizon above West Peak. The East Branch valley, meanwhile, is seen snaking its way between Mts. Hitchcock and Flume. The hairpin curve on the Kancamagus Highway is below the NW summit of Mt. Hancock and to the L of a minor summit along the ridge between East Osceola and the main peak.

East Osceola: East Osceola's summit vista is about as lacking as they come. If not for an obstructed view to the N and W (found at the end of a short, beaten path leading W from the summit cairn), there'd be no view at all worthy of mention.

Elsewhere on the mountain there are at least two notable vistas. The best of the pair is found a quarter-mile W of and below the summit on a trailside ledge. From here, an unobstructed sweep of the mountains to the N—from the Kinsmans E to Mt. Carrigain—is obtained, similar to the NW outlook on the main summit. A good view to the E and N is found along the approach route via Mad River Notch, from the top of the slide that is crossed high up on East Osceola's N ridge. The look down at green-tinted Upper Greeley Pond is striking. Mt. Kancamagus rises above the pond across Mad River Notch, with Mt. Tremont, Kearsarge North and North Moat beyond. The Tripyramids are seen to the R of Kancamagus, along with Mts. Passaconaway and Chocorua. Peaks visible to the L, looking NE, include the Doubleheads, Baldfaces, Carters, Carrigain, Jefferson, part of Washington, Huntington, and Hancock.

NO. OF 4000-FOOTERS VISIBLE: Mt. Osceola, 41; East Osceola, 41 (by working hard for views through the trees).

Mount Passaconaway

ELEVATION: 4043 ft./1232 m ORDER OF HEIGHT: 42
LOCATION: Sandwich Range, Towns of Waterville Valley and Albany
USGS MAPS: 7½′ Mount Tripyramid, 7½′ Mount Chocorua

GEOGRAPHY

Passaconaway is a great wooded dome in the heart of the Sandwich Range, rising majestically above the broad Albany, or Swift River Intervale to the N and the Wonalancet lowlands and Lakes Region to the S. Though cloaked in forest, Passaconaway's symmetrical crown offers good views S, E and N.

Trail approaches can be made from several directions to this handsome and interesting mountain.

Beyond a broad, flat col (3260 ft.), a long, high ridge connects Passaconaway with Mt. Whiteface to the SW, enclosing The Bowl, a beautiful glacial cirque harboring old-growth forest and drained by the Wonalancet River. The steep headwall of The Bowl, marked by a rock slab, plunges from the Passaconaway-Whiteface col. A short ridge runs S from the summit of Passaconaway, dividing The Bowl from a smaller cirque-like basin to the E. The W flank of the mountain falls sharply into the long valley of Downes Brook.

A major ridge runs SE over the sub-peaks of "Nanamocomuck" (3340 ft.) and "Wonalancet Hedgehog" (3140 ft.) to the low gap of Paugus Pass (2220 ft.), which separates Passaconaway from Mt. Paugus to the E. These spurs give Passaconaway a trademark stair-step profile when seen from the S. Extending NE from Nanamocomuck is Square Ledge (2670 ft.), with a great E-facing cliff overlooking the broad upper valley of Oliverian Brook. A western tributary of this brook drains the valley between Square Ledge and Passaconaway itself, the route traversed by Passaconaway Cutoff.

From Wonalancet Hedgehog another ridge runs S over Hibbard Mtn. (2940 ft.) and Mt. Wonalancet (2780 ft., once known as Toadback); these peaks along with Wonalancet Hedgehog are known as the Wonalancet Range. Hedgehog Mtn., sometimes called the "Albany Hedgehog" (2532 ft.), is a detached, ledgy spur to the NNE of Passaconaway. Most of these lower peaks offer good views.

The mountain is also marked by prominent slides on its NW (the Downes Brook Slide) and E slopes.

NOMENCLATURE

The mountain was originally dubbed "North Whiteface" on Arnold Guyot's 1860 map. Its present name was bestowed in the 1870s by state geologist Charles H. Hitchcock in honor of Passaconaway, "Son of the Bear," the legendary sachem, or chief, of the Penacook tribe, which lived in the lower Merrimack valley. He ruled a powerful confederation of tribes through much of the 1600s and was peaceably inclined to the white settlers who had established a toehold along the New England coast. He was reputed to be a great warrior, hunter and sorcerer. Legend holds that upon his death ca. 1682 he was borne to the summit of Agiochook (Mt. Washington) in a sleigh drawn by giant wolves, there to join the Council of the Gods. Among his children were the chieftains Wonalancet and Nanamocomuck, for whom spurs of the mountain are named. Kancamagus, "the fearless one," was his grandson.

HISTORICAL HIGHLIGHTS

First Ascent: Unknown. Possibly climbed by Arnold Guyot in mid-1800s.
1869: George L. Vose climbs Passaconaway for N.H. Geological Survey.

1876: Charles E. Fay (first President of the AMC, which is formed that year) and worker from U.S. Coastal Survey traverse trailless ridge from Mt. Whiteface and ascend Passaconaway. Sweetser's guidebook describes ascent route from Albany Intervale via Downes Brook; other routes suggested from Wonalancet and summit of Mt. Whiteface.

1880: Trail cut up Oliverian Brook valley to summit by James M. Shackford, a farmer from Albany Intervale—commissioned by AMC.

1891: Dicey's Mill Trail from S cut by local residents led by the AMC's Charles E. Fay. AMC contributes $25 to effort. They build Passaconaway Lodge by base of summit cone. (This shelter is rebuilt in 1899, 1925 and 1953. In 1948 it is renamed Camp Rich, after Edgar J. Rich, a prominent Wonalancet Out Door Club member.)

1892: Innkeeper Kate Sleeper and others organize Wonalancet Out Door Club. AMC snowshoers make winter ascent of Passaconaway.

Early 1890s: Huge landslide falls off side of mountain into Downes Brook valley; later becomes route of Downes Brook Slide Trail.

1890s/Early 1900s: Square Ledge, Wonalancet Range and Walden Trails are opened, the latter named for Arthur Walden, famed breeder of sled dogs and husband of Kate Sleeper.

1906: AMC cuts trail from summit to top of Downes Brook Slide.

1914: Thanks to work of Kate Sleeper and WODC, The Bowl's virgin forest is preserved from logging and added to WMNF.

1914–15: Lumber camps active in Downes Brook valley.

1916: Charles Edward Beals, Jr. chronicles history of Albany Intervale in *Passaconaway in the White Mountains*, describes Passaconaway as "the loftiest, wildest, yet most symmetrical, most awe-inspiring mountain of the Sandwich Range." Short-lived trail, "Walden Cut-Off," is built from Dicey's Mill up to col between Passaconaway and Wonalancet Hedgehog.

1925: Oliverian Brook Trail constructed by WMNF. Passaconaway Mountain Club opens Passaconaway Cutoff. This trail discontinued ca. 1940 after flood and slides, reopened 1965. PMC also builds trails to Potash Mtn. and Albany Hedgehog, then disappears from history. Buildings at Dicey's Mill have disappeared. J. Brooks Atkinson (later to become Pulitzer Prize winner) writes about sojourn at Camp Rich and descent of Downes Brook Slide in *Skyline Promenades*.

1938: Hurricane destroys virgin spruce along Dicey's Mill Trail; two landslides scar side of mountain.

ca. 1960: Downes Brook Slide Trail abandoned.

1984: Sandwich Range Wilderness (25,000 acres) created by Congress, includes most of Mt. Passaconaway.

1998: January ice storm decimates second-growth hardwoods on southern slopes.

1998: WODC begins major restoration of Walden Trail.

2000: Camp Rich collapses and is removed.

TRAIL APPROACHES

NORTH APPROACH from Kancamagus Highway (NH 112)

Oliverian Brook Trail, Passaconaway Cutoff, Square Ledge Trail, Walden Trail
10.2 mi. round trip, 2800-ft. elevation gain.

TRAILHEAD (1238 ft.): Parking area is at end of side road off Kancamagus Highway 1.0 mi. W of Bear Notch Rd.

This is a long wooded approach with steep climbing at the end. From parking area, follow Oliverian Brook Trail through turns to L and R, pass view up to Passaconaway from old clearcut, then stroll at easy grades on logging roads and section of old logging RR bed; several stretches of nice brookside scenery. At 1.9 mi./1500 ft. bear R on Passaconaway Cutoff. Gentle upgrade continues past brook crossing at 2.4 mi. Steadier climb leads into spruces, then through white birches, with Passaconaway looming up to R. Turn R on Square Ledge Trail at 3.6 mi./2550 ft. Pass through dip and ascend to bottom of slide at 3.9 mi.; careful scramble up to L provides good view N. Ascent is steep from this point. Bear R on Walden Trail at 4.3 mi./3300 ft. and pass jct. L with East Loop (which traverses 0.2 mi. to Dicey's Mill Trail) at 4.4 mi. Continue on Walden Trail for steep, winding ascent up cone through wild fir woods. Pass S outlook on L at 4.9 mi. and make short, steep climb to E outlook on R at 5.0 mi. Just beyond, side path R leads 0.3 mi./300 ft. down to N outlook. A few yards farther is jct. with Dicey's Mill Trail; summit, with limited view S, is reached by short side path L.

Loop Option from North via Square Ledge
11.4 mi. loop, 2950-ft. elevation gain.

An interesting descent variation can be made over the great E-facing cliff of Square Ledge. At jct. of Square Ledge Trail and Passaconaway Cutoff, continue ahead on Square Ledge Trail, climbing over knolls to summit of Square Ledge in 0.4 mi. Here obscure side path R leads to outcrop with view up to Mt. Passaconaway and out to Paugus Pass; use caution as ledge drops off abruptly. Traverse ridge to top of main cliff at 0.6 mi. from jct., with view across Oliverian Brook valley to Mt. Paugus; this spot may be posted during peregrine falcon nesting season, April 1–August 1—please heed restrictions on signage. Here trail turns R for very steep descent below cliffs to jct. L with Square Ledge Branch Trail at 1.0 mi./2000 ft. Turn L on Branch Trail and descend moderately to crossing of Oliverian Brook and Oliverian Brook Trail at 1.5 mi. Turn L here for easy descent, with two brook crossings before jct. with lower end of Passaconaway Cutoff at 2.9 mi. Continue ahead another 1.9 mi. to trailhead.

SOUTH APPROACH from Wonalancet

Dicey's Mill Trail
9.2 mi. round trip, 2950-ft. elevation gain

Trailhead (1140 ft.) Parking area off Ferncroft Rd., 0.5 mi. from NH 113A in Wonalancet.

This is a steady, moderate route, wooded to the top. From parking area, trail follows Ferncroft Road NW, crosses field by house, and enters WMNF and Sandwich Range Wilderness at 0.8 mi. Climb easily through hardwoods on long S-curve and cross brook by Dicey's Mill, site of former sawmill, at 2.3 mi./2020 ft. Trail makes long, steady ascent up E side of a ridge through ice-damaged hardwoods, with glimpses of Passaconaway ahead and Wonalancet Range to R. At 3.7 mi./3300 ft. reach jct. with Rollins Trail on L at crest of ridge. Soon pass site of Camp Rich and jct. with East Loop on R. Dicey's Mill Trail zigzags up summit cone through wild conifer forest. At top of climb trail passes restricted view L (W), from Mt. Tecumseh around to Willey Range, and meets Walden Trail by side path R to summit at 4.6 mi./4043 ft. Continue ahead on Walden Trail for side path L to N view and beyond to E view.

Loop Options

Loop options over less-used trails with good views can be fashioned from Ferncroft Rd. parking area in combination with descent via Dicey's Mill Trail.

Old Mast Road and Walden Trail

9.4 mi. round trip, 3300-ft. elevation gain

This loop features a pleasant approach, followed by steep, rough climbing with views. From Ferncroft, follow Old Mast Road on well-graded, easy to moderate climb through hardwoods to four-way jct. at 2.0 mi./2350 ft. Turn L on Walden Trail and ascend steep, rough section on E side of Wonalancet Hedgehog, recently improved by WODC. Short spur R at 2.6 mi./3000 ft. leads to ledge with fine view E including impressive look at Mt. Paugus. Easier climbing leads to 3140-ft. summit of Hedgehog at 2.7 mi.; side trail L leads 100 yards to ledge with wide view S. At 2.8 mi. another spur leads L to a S viewpoint. Walden Trail dips to jct. L with Wonalancet Range Trail at 2.9 mi. Continue ahead on Walden Trail, dropping steeply past view N towards Mt. Washington and down to col at 3.2 mi./2900 ft. Ascend steep, rough pitch to summit of Nanamocomuck at 3.6 mi./3340 ft. Dip to saddle, then rise to jct. R with Square Ledge Trail at 4.1 mi./3300 ft. Walden Trail passes East Loop at 4.2 mi. and climbs steeply up cone of Passaconaway, passing S outlook at 4.7 mi. and E outlook at 4.8 mi. Continue short distance farther to jct. with Dicey's Mill Trail and side path to summit. Descend via Dicey's Mill Trail.

Wonalancet Range Trail and Walden Trail

9.8 mi. round trip, 3450-ft. elevation gain

This loop offers mostly moderate climbing with good views. From Ferncroft, follow Old Mast Road for 0.1 mi. and turn L on Wonalancet Range Trail. Grades are easy through hemlocks and hardwoods, then steeper with

Mt. Passaconaway as viewed from the open ledges of nearby Hedgehog Mtn.

a very steep pitch through spruces to jct. R with "Short-Cut" at 1.5 mi./2350 ft. (This trail slabs up and across side of Mt. Wonalancet, rejoining Range Trail in 0.4 mi.) Range Trail climbs steeply L to rock slab (use caution) with view SE at 1.7 mi./2550 ft. Ascent continues to Mt. Wonalancet summit (no view) at 1.9 mi./2780 ft. Descend easily N to col and jct. R with "Short-Cut" at 2.3 mi./2600 ft., then climb moderately to Hibbard Mtn. at 2.7 mi./2940 ft. Side path leads R to view S over Mt. Wonalancet to Lakes Region; in 100 yds. Range Trail crosses ledge with impressive view W to Mt. Whiteface rising from depths of The Bowl. Trail continues easily along ridge to meet Walden Trail at 3.3 mi./3100 ft. Turn L to reach Mt. Passaconaway in 1.9 mi., as described above. Descend via Dicey's Mill Trail.

Loops with Mt. Whiteface can be fashioned using Rollins Trail along connecting ridge. Combine N route to Passaconaway with Dicey's Mill, Rollins, Kate Sleeper and Downes Brook Trails and 1.0 mi. road walk on Kancamagus Highway (15.6 mi., 3700-ft. elevation gain). With S route to Passaconaway via Dicey's Mill Trail, use Rollins and Blueberry Ledge Trails (11.9 mi., 3850-ft. elevation gain).

WINTER

Parking areas are plowed at both the Oliverian Brook Trail and Ferncroft trailheads. The most popular winter route is the Dicey's Mill Trail, a good, moderately graded snowshoe route with a few steep pitches on the cone. Passaconaway and Whiteface are often combined via the Rollins Trail and rugged Blueberry Ledge Trail. The Rollins Trail is a long, tiring section and may be very hard to follow. Views S at the actual summit are better in winter with the lift of deep snows.

VIEW GUIDE

Passaconaway's summit is thickly wooded, but there are three good outlooks and two restricted ones at various points around the top. The true summit has a very limited view SW towards Mt. Whiteface. Just to the W along Dicey's Mill Trail is a ledge with a limited view NW through the trees. The best views are found at the S, E and N outlooks.

S Outlook: This small, sunny ledge located beside the Walden Trail at 3900 ft. provides a wide view over the Lakes Region. On the L is the nearby wooded hump of Nanamocomuck, with distant hills to the SE. The Wonalancet Range—Mts. Hibbard and Wonalancet—runs out to the S, and in the distance, beyond the mouth of the Wonalancet River valley, is Lake Winnipesaukee. The big water is flanked by the Ossipee Range on the L and Red Hill on the R, with the double-peaked Belknap Range on the horizon. Farther R Squam Lake shimmers between Red Hill (L) and Mt. Israel (R); the latter is seen over the SE ridge of Mt. Whiteface. On the horizon are the twin Uncanoonucs near Manchester, Mt. Kearsarge (directly over Israel), and, on a clear day, Mt. Monadnock over Squam Lake.

The most striking vista here is SW to the long, steep-sided ridge of Mt. Whiteface, just two miles away, rising above The Bowl and a S spur ridge of Passaconaway. Over the R shoulder of Whiteface are Sandwich Dome and its sharp spur, Jennings Peak. In clear weather Killington and Pico Peaks can be seen far off in Vermont. On the far R is the forested dome of East Sleeper.

E Outlook: A ledge beside the Walden Trail at the E end of the summit plateau opens a fine 180-degree vista, with a dramatic dropoff in front. This may be the nicest lunch spot on the mountain. On the far L Mt. Washington and the Presidentials rise above the nearer Mt. Tremont and Owl's Cliff. To the R the Wildcats and Carters are seen in the distance through Bear Notch, the gap between Bartlett Haystack, a sharp cone on the L, and the long ridge of Bear Mtn. on the R. Ledgy Iron Mtn. is to the L of Bear, and the Baldfaces rise above Bear, with Doublehead below and to the R. Close at hand under Bear are the white ledges of Hedgehog Mtn. To the R of Bear is fire-scarred Table Mtn., below the wooded humps of West Moat Mtn. Farther R Kearsarge North lifts its pyramid behind the high ridge of North Moat Mtn. Beyond the broad Albany Intervale the Moat Range runs to the R over Middle and South Moat, with ledgy spurs thrust out into the lower Swift River valley.

Eastward the rocky crest of Chocorua dominates the view, with the rounded Three Sisters on the L and the sharp summit on the R. Over the L shoulder of Chocorua is Maine's long, level Pleasant Mtn. Lumpy Mt. Paugus sprawls nearer and below Chocorua, spotted with ledges and crumbling granite cliffs. Below Paugus is the wooded backside of Square Ledge. In this direction the city of Portland on the Maine coast, 60 mi. away, may be spotted on crystal days. On the R (SE), the view continues around to the Wonalancet Hedgehog, and out to the Ossipee Range, Lake Winnipesaukee and the Belknaps.

N Outlook: Perhaps Passaconaway's finest viewpoint is a small opening perched on the steep N slope, atop what Beals (1916) called a "lofty eagle-nest of a cliff." You have to descend 0.3 mi. and 300 ft. from the summit to this point, but in clear weather it's worth the trouble. The view is a northward sweep of mountain country, with a tremendous dropoff below to the lower slopes of Passaconaway.

On the far L is the pointed peak of North Tripyramid, with the Osceolas to the R and the flat ridge of The Fool Killer beneath. South and North Kinsman rise in the distance above Mt. Kancamagus. Mts. Flume and Liberty are almost in line to the R of Kancamagus, followed by Mts. Lincoln and Lafayette and the sharp pyramid of Mt. Garfield. Mt. Huntington sprawls beneath the Franconias, presenting impressive cliffs on its W spur. Mt. Hitchcock can be seen behind Huntington. To the R of Garfield is the long wooded mass of Mt. Hancock, with Mt. Bond and South Twin over its R shoulder. The cliffy nubble of The Captain pokes up from the low point between Hancock and its impressive neighbor to the R, Mt. Carrigain, with Zealand Mtn. beyond The Captain. To the R of Carrigain and its spurs is a beautiful look through Carrigain Notch, with Vose Spur on the L and Mt. Lowell on the R. Below the Notch and closer is granite-faced Green's Cliff, and nearer still is ledgy Potash Mtn., seen across the lower Downes Brook valley.

Mts. Tom, Field and Willey are arrayed behind the Nancy Range, just R of Carrigain Notch. Over the R shoulder of Potash is the glimmer of Church Pond on the floor of Albany Intervale. Mt. Webster rises far above and beyond the pond, and the Southern Presidentials march upward to the dramatic peak of Mt. Washington, about 22 mi. to the N. Mt. Tremont is below Washington, and from here the view continues around to Chocorua on the eastern horizon, as described under the E Outlook.

NO. OF 4000-FOOTERS VISIBLE: 40.

Mount Tecumseh

ELEVATION: 4003 ft./1220 m ORDER OF HEIGHT: 47 (tie)
LOCATION: Town of Waterville Valley, Township of Livermore
USGS MAP: 7½′ Waterville Valley

GEOGRAPHY

Among the higher peaks of the White Mountains, Mt. Tecumseh (along with Mt. Isolation) holds the dubious distinction of being the shortest of the tallest. These two peaks are overtopped by each of the other 46 White

Mountain 4000-footers. Tecumseh is also among the most visited mountains in New Hampshire as it is home to Waterville Valley Ski Area, one of the state's busiest winter resorts. The ski area dominates the mountain's east-facing slopes and operates with a special use permit issued by the U.S. Forest Service. For hikers Tecumseh presents a fairly short and moderate hike with some interesting views along the ridgetop.

Tecumseh is the culminating point of the string of mountains which stretch 5–6 mi. NNE from Thornton to the broad Waterville Valley. Tecumseh, Mt. Osceola, Mt. Kancamagus, the Tripyramids, and Sandwich Dome form a ring of peaks that almost completely surrounds the scenic resort community at Waterville. The mountain is flanked on the E and W by two great valleys. The Waterville Valley, through which the Mad River flows, sits to the E. The broader Pemigewasset River valley, with its headwaters well to the N, lies further to the W along the I-93 corridor. Mt. Osceola rises just to the N of Tecumseh, separated only by narrow Thornton Gap (or Waterville Gap, 2300 ft.), through which runs the seasonal Tripoli Road (connecting I-93 with Waterville Valley).

The jumble of peaks that rise from the S and extend all the way to Tecumseh's sharp, pointed summit, begins with 2132-ft. Cone Mtn. in Thornton. The ridgeline thrusts higher and higher as it rises toward Tecumseh, with prominent, ledgy Welch Mtn. (2605 ft.) and Dickey Mtn. (2734 ft.) passed first. From Dickey a long ridge extends N to trailless Green Mtn. (3536 ft.), Tecumseh's closest neighbor to the S along the scrubby ridge. A ridge runs SW from Green over Hogback Mtn. (2770 ft.) and Fisher Mtn. (2609 ft.). Shattuck Brook drains the valley between Dickey and Hogback/Fisher.

The main summit of Tecumseh, which appears rather inconspicuous from some vantage points, is actually quite sharp, prompting one early White Mountain guidebook writer to say it is "one of the most interesting sections of natural architecture in the mountain region." The pyramid-shaped summit, with its "lofty pile of white rocks" features a narrow ridge-crest which drops off sharply on all sides. The best profile of the summit is seen from a vantage point along the ridgetop Sosman Trail connecting the main summit with the top of the ski area.

The mountain has two subsidiary summits which are also accessible by trail. Tecumseh's wooded 3766-ft. West Peak, over which passes the Mt. Tecumseh Trail from Tripoli Road, was formerly considered one of New England's 100 Highest peaks, and for a time was regularly an objective of peakbaggers. The West Peak was removed from the list in 1985 after the U.S. Geological Survey determined that the mountain was 24 ft. lower than previously believed. West Tecumseh's long gentle ridge to the SW extends out to Bald Mtn., a prominent, bare knob occasionally reached by bushwhacking hikers. Between this and the main Green-Tecumseh ridge is a large trailless valley drained by Haselton Brook. Three short, ledgy ridges, prominent when seen from the W, especially in winter, extend into this valley from the W side of the Green-Tecumseh ridge.

Waterville Valley Ski Area's highest chairlifts extend to the top of White Peak (3860 ft.), Tecumseh's other long and flat subsidiary summit. This area is reached from the main summit by the Sosman Trail, or from the eastern base of the mountain by a network of ski trails.

In addition to Haselton Brook on the SW, major streams which flow off the mountain are Tecumseh Brook to the E, Hardy Brook to the SE, and Johnson Brook to the W.

NOMENCLATURE

Like a number of other southern White Mountain peaks, this mountain bears the name of a legendary Indian chief described by one historian as "the most extraordinary Indian in American history." Mt. Tecumseh is named for the great Shawnee chief who unsuccessfully tried to unite the tribes of the Ohio region in an effort to ward off encroachment of their homeland by westward bound settlers. Tecumseh's unsuccessful campaign was crushed on Nov. 7, 1811, when warriors led by his twin brother, Tenkswatawa (who was also known as the Shawnee Prophet), were routed by U.S. soldiers in the infamous Battle of Tippecanoe. Following the failed Indian campaign, Tecumseh (1768–1813) allied himself with the British during the War of 1812 and was eventually killed in the Battle of the Thames in Ontario, Canada. Coincidentally, Tecumseh's birthplace in Ohio was in a village on the Mad River. That is the same name as the river which flows S through New Hampshire's Waterville Valley.

To this day there remains a cloud of mystery over who gave the mountain its name. Early maps of the region simply referred to the peak as Waterville Mountain. But the name Tecumseh was certainly bestowed upon the mountain by 1874, when state geologist Charles H. Hitchcock issued his comprehensive report on the *Geology of New Hampshire*. He said the name was given to the mountain by Campton photographer E. J. Young, who produced several early stereographs of the Waterville Valley area.

It has also been speculated that E. J. Connable of Jackson, Michigan, who first came to Waterville Valley in 1859, may have come up with the permanent names for both Tecumseh and neighboring Mt. Osceola. Guidebook author Moses Sweeter added to the name-calling in early editions of his popular *Osgood's White Mountains* by relating that the mountain was also known locally as Kingsley's Peak, "a title recently conferred in honor of himself by a gentleman who imagined he was its discoverer."

HISTORICAL HIGHLIGHTS

First Ascent: Unknown

1830: Nathaniel Greeley arrives in Waterville Valley and establishes permanent residency.

1850s: Greeley orchestrates construction of network of walking paths in and around Valley. His trail system, the first in the Whites, includes paths to Tecumseh, Osceola, and Sandwich Dome.

1879: AMC cuts new trail to summit via "steep ridge north of Tecumseh Brook."

1880: Sweetser describes several possible routes to summit, noting approach from Waterville is shortest and best. Other possibilities include three routes of ascent from SW, including one over Fisher and Green Mtns., and ascent from S over Welch Mtn. Of ridge walk between Green Mtn. and main summit, Sweetser writes, "In some places the easiest way to advance is on hands and knees, so dense and spiky is the upper growth."

1888: Waterville Valley Athletic and Improvement Association is formed, becomes active trail-building group.

1891: Twenty-one AMC members take part in February excursion to Waterville Valley. Snowshoe treks include ascents of Tecumseh, Osceola, Tripyramids.

1892: A. L. Goodrich espouses virtues of Waterville Valley area in *Appalachia* (January 1892). Article includes sketch map of Valley and existing trail system.

1909: Woodstock and Thornton Gore Railroad (1909–1914), operated by Woodstock Lumber Company, begins operation along Eastman Brook valley NW of Tecumseh, following for most part grade of modern day Tripoli Road.

1920s: Hiking trail is relocated to S side of Tecumseh Brook due to logging.

1928: Forest Service pays $1.05 million for 23,000 acres in and around Waterville Valley.

1933–34: Construction of Tripoli Road, connecting Waterville Valley with Pemigewasset River valley to W, is undertaken by Forest Service, CCC.

1934: First ski trail on mountain is cut.

1937: Forest Service approves construction of new ski trail (Tecumseh Trail) on mountain. Work is done by CCC. Trail runs two miles with vertical descent of 1900 ft.

1939: In aftermath of destructive Hurricane of 1938, Forest Service establishes Tecumseh Fire Trail from height-of-land on Tripoli Road to summit. Trail mainly follows fire barrier strip on ridge leading to summit.

1940: Forest Service considers, rejects proposal for installation of ski lift on Tecumseh Trail.

1940: AMC guide includes descriptions of Haselton Brook and Johnson Brook Trails. Haselton Brook Trail (formerly the Bald Mt. Trail) approaches mountain from SW and joins Mt. Tecumseh Trail 0.4 mi. N of summit. Johnson Brook Trail enters from W, 1.6 mi. N of summit.

1952: AMC trailman Nathaniel Goodrich chronicles region in book, *The Waterville Valley*, and notes that "when our itch for bushwhacking became unbearable, a favorite cure was to climb Tecumseh, then fight our way all down the ridge to Welch and the six-mile bridge."

1966: Former Olympic skier Tom Corcoran and his Waterville Company open new Mt. Tecumseh Ski Area. Shortly thereafter Waterville Valley Athletic and Improvement Association opens Sosman Trail along ridgecrest.

1985: West Peak of Tecumseh is removed from New England 100 Highest list as new geological survey reveals peak is 24 ft. shorter than previously thought.

1991: Lower section of Mt. Tecumseh Trail from E is rerouted away from ski slopes.

TRAIL APPROACHES

East Approach from Waterville Valley Ski Area

Mt. Tecumseh Trail
5.0 mi. round trip, 2200-ft. elevation gain

Trailhead (1840 ft.): From Waterville Valley, Mt. Tecumseh Trail begins on W side of ski area access road, just across from northernmost parking lot (Lot 1).

The Mt. Tecumseh Trail, which runs 5.6 mi. from the base of Waterville Valley Ski Area, over the summit, and on down to Tripoli Road (FR 30) just W of its height-of-land, is the lone base-to-summit hiking trail on the mountain. Because the two trailhead lots are miles apart, few trampers traverse the entire length of the trail, opting instead to climb and return from the summit via the same route. For the purposes of this guide, each approach is considered separately.

The trail from the ski area immediately strikes off into woods, crosses small stream, then continues 0.3 mi. along S side of Tecumseh Brook. Trail then bears sharp R across brook (arrow and double-blazed) and continues along new section of trail opened in 1991. From here, trail climbs steeply over rough and rocky footway onto small ridge, which it follows for a quarter-mile through hardwoods. At 1.1 mi., trail drops back down to brook, recrosses, and climbs via switchbacks steeply out of ravine to old logging road, where original path is regained. Look here for sign directing hikers 20 yards to L, where beaten path leads to edge of ski slope and fine views E and NE. A second side path to ski slopes and lift is passed a short distance later.

Continuing along logging road, trail begins long, moderate ascent through grove of birches. As elevation is gained, width of road narrows significantly. Upon reaching head of Tecumseh Brook ravine (on R), trail veers NW and steepens, then levels out before reaching intersection with Sosman Trail to the top of ski area at 2.2 mi. For several hundred feet the two trails coincide, before Sosman Trail forks L and in 0.2 mi. reaches summit via switchbacks from the W. At fork, Mt. Tecumseh Trail swings R, drops into sag, circles around summit to NE, passes viewpoint looking SE, and climbs steeply to summit at 2.5 mi./4003 ft.

Northwest Approach from Tripoli Road

Mt. Tecumseh Trail
6.2 mi. round trip, 2600-ft. elevation gain

Trailhead (1820 ft.): From N, Mt. Tecumseh Trail begins at parking lot on S side of Tripoli Road, 1.3 miles W of Mt. Osceola Trail and 5.7 mi. E of I-93 (Exit 31) in Woodstock.

This approach offers a more interesting and secluded approach to Tecumseh. From parking, trail quickly drops down to cross Eastman Brook (may be difficult at times of high water), then climbs up onto old logging road which is followed on easy to moderate grades for 1.3 mi. After reaching 2980-ft. saddle, trail turns L and steepens as it climbs to crest of Tecumseh's W ridge. A short side trail R provides partial view NW toward Mt. Moosilauke and Kinsman Notch.

Trail continues over series of three knobs; true summit of West Peak is last, or easternmost knob, reached at 2.4 mi./3766 ft. Beyond, drop into 3620-ft. col between West Peak and main summit. At first, trail ascends from col at moderate grade, then more steeply, finally reaching excellent outlook N at 3.0 mi. Continue on easy grade several hundred feet more to summit.

South Approach

The Sosman Trail, established a few years after Waterville Valley Ski Area opened in 1966, provides an alternative approach to the summit. It runs 0.8 mi. from the top of the ski slopes N to the main summit. Sosman Trail attacks summit cone from W, over rock-strewn footway. From ski area, trail strikes off across the ridge (N) from flat, rocky area marked with cairns. About halfway along, two viewpoints are passed. The first, which looks E, is marked by log bench. The second, offering vistas NW, is a bit further along on L. From here trail descends rock ledge (good views of sharp summit cone), passes through level stretch of forest, then meets Mt. Tecumseh Trail 0.2 mi. from main summit. Continue straight ahead several hundred feet to fork. Bear L for approach via Sosman Trail, R for Mt. Tecumseh Trail approach.

WINTER

As Tripoli Road is not maintained for winter motor vehicle traffic, and is in fact gated at both the I-93 and Waterville Valley ends, it is impractical to consider the NW approach, or an end-to-end hike of Mt. Tecumseh Trail. Nearly all winter trampers will start and end their hikes up the mountain at the base of the ski area, taking the Mt. Tecumseh Trail to the summit. Since the ski area parking lot generally fills up quickly in the morning, especially on weekends, don't expect to find a space anywhere near the trailhead near unless you're an early riser.

For those hikers who wish to either ascend or descend via the ski trails, be on the lookout for fast moving skiers and snowboarders. Be forewarned, also, that you're likely to receive many a curious glance from those schussing down the mountain's steep slopes.

VIEW GUIDE

Summit Area: The actual summit offers limited views, and as vegetation atop the mountain continues to thrive, there's less and less to look at as time progresses. While the summit once afforded better-than-average views, especially E, one has to stand nearly tiptoe now to gain a decent perspective on the Osceola Range to the N and Mt. Tripyramid and other Sandwich Range peaks to the E.

The best views NE are obtained from a ledge a few yards down from the actual summit. A well-worn path leads to this spot. To the N and E are seen Tecumseh's closest neighbor, Mts. Osceola and its East Peak. Just to the L of East Osceola are South Hancock and Mt. Carrigain. Behind and higher is Mt. Washington, with Mt. Clay, Mt. Adams, and Mt. Jefferson to the L. Mts. Monroe, Eisenhower and Pierce can be seen under Clay. To the R of East Osceola, on the other side of the Mad River valley, is the long wooded mass of Mt. Kancamagus, with the Carters, Wildcats, the Giant Stairs and Mt. Resolution, the Baldface Range, Kearsarge North, and the Moats beyond.

Partial easterly views are available from the Mt. Tecumseh Trail as it ascends the steep summit cone, or by poking around the summit itself. Most impressive are the three peaks and two slides of Mt. Tripyramid across the valley, with Mt. Passaconaway peeking over on the R and the Sleepers and Mt. Whiteface farther R. To the SE is the dark bulk of Sandwich Dome.

Splendid views N and W to the peaks of the Franconia Notch region and the western Pemi Wilderness are found from an outlook along the Mt. Tecumseh Trail 0.1 mi. N of the summit. Cannon Mtn., the Cannon Balls and North and South Kinsman are to the NW. To the R of Cannon-Kinsman, poking up well above the peaks of nearby Scar Ridge, are Mts. Flume, Liberty, Lincoln and Lafayette. To their R is the sharp summit of Mt. Garfield, towering well above the round dome of Owl's Head Mtn. Farther R are the peaks of the Twin-Bond Range, including Galehead, South Twin, West Bond, Bondcliff, and Mt. Bond. Also seen is Tecumseh's West Peak, less than a mile away.

Sosman Trail Outlooks: Arguably, the mountain's most stunning vistas are those obtained from the viewpoints established several years ago along the ridgeline Sosman Trail. The first outlook, attained after a short scramble up a steep slope 0.4 mi. S of the summit, offers a sweeping view NW of Mt. Moosilauke, Kinsman Ridge, Scar Ridge, the peaks of Franconia Ridge, Owl's Head, and Garfield. Mt. Mansfield and other Vermont peaks can be seen on the horizon. Closer at hand to the NNE is the spruce-clad, arrow-like peak of Tecumseh.

A bit further along the trail, this time on the L, is a long wooden log bench where one can sit and enjoy a sweeping vista to the E and NE of Waterville Valley, taking in everything from East Osceola to the Tripyramids.

Wide views E are also available from the ski slopes, which run approximately 1.8 mi. from top to bottom. Treading down the skiways tends to be tedious and very hard on the knees and is not recommended as a method of descent.

NO. OF 4000-FOOTERS VISIBLE: 36 (from summit)

North and Middle Tripyramid

NORTH TRIPYRAMID

ELEVATION: 4180 ft./1274 m ORDER OF HEIGHT: 32
LOCATION: Sandwich Range, Town of Waterville Valley
USGS MAP: 7½′ Mount Tripyramid

MIDDLE TRIPYRAMID

ELEVATION: 4140 ft./1262 m ORDER OF HEIGHT: 35
LOCATION: Sandwich Range, Town of Waterville Valley
USGS MAP: 7½′ Mount Tripyramid

GEOGRAPHY

A triad of sharp peaks along its ridgecrest and two huge slides on its flanks mark Tripyramid as one of the most distinctive and rugged mountains in the Whites. It rises in the Sandwich Range Wilderness between Waterville Valley on the SW and the Albany Intervale on the NE. North and Middle Peaks are official 4000-footers, while the South Peak (4100 ft./1250 m) lacks the requisite 200-ft. rise from its col. The North Peak is somewhat detached from the other two. There are partial views E and W from Middle Peak and a restricted vista NE from North Peak. The best views are found atop the North Slide (mostly bare granite ledge on the NW flank of North Peak) and the South Slide (a slide of gravel and broken rock on the SW flank of South Peak). A variety of trails provide scenic and rugged approaches to Tripyramid.

Scaur Peak (3605 ft.) is a prominent, sharp-peaked spur connected to North Peak by a level ridge on the NW. Livermore Pass (2900 ft.) separates Scaur Peak from Mt. Kancamagus on the NW. The wonderfully-named, flat-topped Fool Killer (3548 ft.) juts to the E from North Peak, overlooking the valley of Sabbaday Brook. From The Fool Killer a spur ridge extends NE to the Swift River valley.

The high, rounded domes of West Sleeper (3881 ft.) and East Sleeper (3840 ft.) connect South Tripyramid with Mt. Whiteface on the SE.

The N slopes of the mountain are drained by the broad basin of Pine Bend Brook. On the E Sabbaday Brook flows down to the Swift River through a long, curving valley between the Tripyramids, The Fool Killer, The Sleepers, and a long N spur ridge of East Sleeper. On the W side of Tripyramids, Avalanche Brook flows down from a ravine between North Peak and Scaur Peak, while Slide Brook tumbles down from the base of the South Slide. These brooks unite at the W base of the mountain.

NOMENCLATURE

Early names for this three-headed mountain included "Saddle Mtn." and "Waterville Haystacks." One 1860 map called the mountain "Passaconaway," but that same year the geographer Arnold Guyot published his map and applied the name "Tripyramid." In 1876 state geologist Charles H. Hitchcock adopted Guyot's "Tripyramid" name in his *Geology of New Hampshire* and moved "Passaconaway" to another 4000-footer in the Sandwich Range.

The Fool Killer received its name because of its deceptive appearance when viewed from Albany Intervale, where it blends in with the main bulk of Tripyramid. On at least one occasion an exploring group reached the top of this spur ridge, only to discover that the real objective loomed much higher beyond a thickly wooded connecting ridge.

HISTORICAL HIGHLIGHTS

First Ascent: Unknown, possibly by Arnold Guyot in mid-1800s.

1830: Nathaniel Greeley settles in Waterville Valley.

1840s: Settlers clear two patches of land near western base of Tripyramid, named "Swazeytown" and "Beckytown."

1869: First South Slide falls in October rainstorm.

1874: Charles E. Fay and three others ascend South Slide and traverse the three peaks to "unveil the mysteries" of this little-known mountain.

1875: Guidebook editor Moses Sweetser and surveying party climb Tripyramid from Waterville and cross over Mt. Whiteface to town of Sandwich. Route up South Slide to South Peak is written up in his 1876 guidebook. Trip is said to "occupy a long and workful day."

1879: AMC opens Livermore Trail (then called "American Institute of Instruction Path") from Beckytown through Livermore Pass and on to Sawyer River valley to N.

1880: AMC members scout Sabbaday Brook valley as route for trail to Tripyramid, but decide expense of this long route is too great to justify completion.

1885: North Slide and second South Slide fall in August downpour. One visitor writes that the South Slides have "made the fair mountain a desert of rock." Rev. Dr. J. M. Buckley makes exciting ascent up newly bared ledges of North Slide, barely escapes fall in crumbling stone near apex.

1890s: Active logging at western base of mountain; several camps established, including Depot Camp, Flume Brook Camp, and Avalanche Camp.

1892: AMC snowshoers scale North Peak—perhaps the first winter ascent.

ca. 1904: Trail is cut above North Slide and is soon extended across ridge. Sleeper Trail built to connect South Slide and Mt. Whiteface.

ca. 1915: Logging in Sabbaday Brook valley to E.

1916: Tripyramid makes first appearance in AMC guidebook. In addition to North and South Slides and Sleeper Trail, book describes route up Sabbaday Brook valley using logging roads and slide on E side of mountain.

1924: New slide falls on E slope. Sabbaday Brook Trail soon established, using older slide in upper portion.

mid-1930s: Pine Bend Brook Trail built from Albany Intervale to North Peak.

1938: Hurricane obliterates part of Sleeper Trail; remains obscure until ca. 1960 due to logging.

mid-1950s: Scaur Ridge Trail opened.

1984: Tripyramids included in newly created Sandwich Range Wilderness.

TRAIL APPROACHES

West Approach from Waterville Valley

Livermore Trail, Mt. Tripyramid Trail via North and South Slides
11.0 mi. loop, 3000-ft. elevation gain

Trailhead (1580 ft.): Livermore Rd. (Depot Camp) parking area just off Tripoli Rd., 1.8 mi. from NH 49 in Waterville Valley.

The loop over the Tripyramid slides is one of the most exciting and challenging hikes in the Whites. It's best to ascend the steep granite slabs of the North Slide and descend the gravelly South Slide. Some hikers will be uncomfortable on the North Slide, and it should be avoided if wet or icy. The Scaur Ridge Trail (see below) is a safer alternative for the ascent.

From parking area, walk up Livermore Trail, here a wide gravel road, at easy grades. Cross Depot Camp clearing at 0.3 mi. with glimpse of Tripyramid ahead and continue up road past Greeley Ponds Trail and many other trail junctions. Sloping meadow on R provides limited views at ca. 1.0 mi. Pass cascades in Avalanche Brook on R just after jct. with Cascades Path/logging road at 2.1 mi.

Trail from S Slide comes in on R at 2.6 mi./2000 ft. Continue at moderate grade up Livermore Rd., passing Avalanche Camp clearing on L at 3.1 mi. Turn R on narrow trail to N. Slide at 3.6 mi./2400 ft. Cross Avalanche Brook and ascend moderately to base of slide at 4.1 mi./2900 ft. Scramble up exposed granite slabs—steepest and smoothest at bottom; follow blazes carefully. Higher up footing improves and views open dramatically to W and N. Follow R fork of slide and exit top L corner at 4.6 mi./3900 ft. Climb steeply through woods to Pine Bend Brook Trail at 4.8 mi.; turn R and quickly reach 4180-ft. summit of North Peak with limited view NE.

After offering glimpse of triangular Middle Peak close ahead, combined Mt. Tripyramid/Pine Bend Brook Trails descend easily to col and jct. L with Sabbaday Brook Trail at 5.3 mi./3850 ft. Cross col and climb steeply to Middle Peak at 5.6 mi./4140 ft. with outlooks W and E. Descend to col, then make short climb to South Peak with partial view back to N, reaching narrow summit at 6.0 mi./4100 ft. Drop steeply to top of S Slide at 6.2 mi./3900 ft. Descend carefully over steep gravel, ledge and broken rock with wide views W and S, passing jct. L with Kate Sleeper Trail. Views continue to bottom of slide at 6.6 mi./3100 ft. Grade eases along old logging road beside Slide Brook, passing Black Cascade at 7.7 mi., just before crossing Cold Brook. Cross Avalanche Brook and meet Livermore Road at 8.4 mi; turn L for easy 2.6 mi. walk back to car.

Scaur Ridge Trail alternate route to North Peak

Continue on Livermore Rd. 0.2 mi. beyond trail to N Slide and turn R on Scaur Ridge Trail for moderate 1.2 mi. ascent to Pine Bend Brook Trail. Turn R here for easy traverse followed by rugged climb to North Peak, reaching summit 2.0 mi. from Livermore Rd. This adds 1.0 mi. to loop distance.

NORTH APPROACH from Kancamagus Highway

North Peak only

Pine Bend Brook Trail
8.0 mi. round trip, 2800-ft. elevation gain

North and Middle Peaks

Pine Bend Brook Trail, Mt. Tripyramid Trail
9.6 mi. round trip, 3300-ft. elevation gain

TRAILHEAD (1370 ft.): Pine Bend Brook Trail starts at sign (limited roadside parking) on S side of Kancamagus Highway (NH 112) 1.0 mi. W of Sabbaday Falls parking area.

This is a varied trail with a mix of easy and steep grades and limited views. First two miles are at easy grades, with several brook crossings, first leading SSW, then more to the W around N end of Fool Killer. Forest is hemlock and spruce, then hardwoods. At 2.2 mi./2100 ft. enter Sandwich Range Wilderness, cross brook bed, and climb more steeply up W side of ravine. At 2.6 mi./2550 ft. turn L for steep climb out of ravine, then bear R to ascend brushy ridge with limited views N. At 3.1 mi. reach crest of ridge between Scaur Peak and North Peak. Bear L to jct. with Scaur Ridge Trail at 3.2 mi./3440 ft. Pine Bend Brook Trail traverses crest of this wild ridge, with view R up to North Peak and its slide and glimpses L out to N, then swings

North (L) and Middle Tripyramid from South Peak.

R for steep, winding, ledgy climb to summit of North Peak, reached at 4.0 mi./4180 ft., just beyond jct. with trail from N Slide. Limited view NE; for excellent views W and N, descend 0.2 mi./300 ft. on N Slide trail to top of slide. To reach Middle Peak, continue 0.8 mi. along Mt. Tripyramid Trail from North Peak as described above, then retrace steps over North Peak and descend to trailhead via Pine Bend Brook Trail.

NORTHEAST APPROACH from Kancamagus Highway

North and Middle Peaks

Sabbaday Brook Trail, Mt. Tripyramid Trail
11.4 mi. round trip, 3140-ft. elevation gain

TRAILHEAD (1320 ft.): Sabbaday Brook Trail starts at Sabbaday Falls picnic area on S side of Kancamagus Highway (NH 112) 3.3 mi. W of Bear Notch Road.

This trail provides a beautiful walk up a secluded valley, ending with a steep climb to the ridge. Sabbaday Brook Trail starts as graded path, passing side loop L to Sabbaday Falls at 0.3 mi. Cross Sabbaday Brook three times from 0.7 to 0.9 mi.—difficult at high water. Trail soon picks up old logging road on E bank above brook, commencing lovely wilderness walk up hardwood valley; glimpses R to Fool Killer, West Sleeper and South Tripyramid. Recross brook at 2.8 mi./2100 ft., wind up floor of valley and cross mossy brook twice more. Trail swings L at final crossing at 4.1 mi./2900 ft. and cuts across E slope of Tripyramid, passing view down valley to Mt. Passaconaway. Turn R near top of old slide at 4.5 mi./3300 ft; view E to Fool Killer, Passaconaway and Chocorua. From here climb is very steep and rough, reaching crest of ridge and Mt. Tripyramid Trail at 4.9 mi./3860 ft. Turn L (S) for Middle Peak (0.3 mi., 280 ft. elevation gain), or R (N) for North Peak (0.5 mi., 320 ft. elevation gain).

Other Options

A nice loop hike over the Middle and North Peaks can be done by combining the Pine Bend Brook Trail, Mt. Tripyramid Trail, and Sabbaday Brook Trail, then adding a 1.0 mi. road on the Kancamagus Highway walk back to your starting point. The total distance of the loop is 11.0 mi., with 3100-ft. elevation gain.

The Tripyramids can also be approached from the SE via the Kate Sleeper Trail. This remote ridgecrest path runs from the jct. between the two summits of Mt. Whiteface 0.8 mi. down to a 3400-ft. col and jct. with Downes Brook Trail. From here it traverses Sleeper Ridge and its two rounded, wooded summits, East Sleeper and West Sleeper, then climbs to cross slide (good views SW) and meet Mt. Tripyramid Trail near top of South Slide, 2.5 mi. from Downes Brook Trail, with 900 ft. elevation gain. Strong hikers can use Kate Sleeper Trail with Downes Brook Trail and Sabbaday Brook Trail to make long, tough loop that includes Whiteface and all Tripyramid summits: 18.0 mi. (including 1.3 mi. road walk) with 4500-ft. elevation gain.

WINTER

Pine Bend Brook Trail is the most popular approach, though it has several challenging steep sections. The L turn out of the ravine at 2.6 mi. is easy to miss. Sabbaday Brook Trail is a scenic winter approach if brook crossings are frozen, but the upper part is very steep. The Slide loop is hazardous in winter and not recommended. Scaur Ridge Trail provides a long but safer approach in winter (13.2 mi. round trip to both peaks). Views from North Peak are much improved with deep snowpack.

VIEW GUIDE

By far the best views from Tripyramid are from atop the North and South Slides. Even if you opt not to do the slides loop on the Mt. Tripyramid Trail, in clear weather the side jaunt down to the North Slide from North Peak is well worth the effort of the 0.4 mi. round trip from the summit of North Peak, with a steep 300-ft. climb on the way back.

North Slide View: The widest section of the North Slide, a short distance below its apex, overlooks a grand sweep of mountain country to W and N. There are some rock seats to be found here.

On the far L, looking W, is the distinctive cone of Mt. Tecumseh, with part of Waterville Valley Ski Area on the L and its West Peak on the R. Mt. Moosilauke fills the horizon through Thornton Gap, the pass between Tecumseh and Osceola. Flat-topped Breadtray Ridge forms the R (N) side of the gap. The rugged, slide-scarred Osceolas are WNW across the upper basin of Mad River, with nearby Flume Peak closer and far below East Osceola. The distant Kinsmans are seen over the cliffy NE arm of Osceola, with Big Coolidge beneath. Whaleback, Liberty and Flume are to the R.

To the NW is the long, darkly wooded bulk of Mt. Kancamagus, with Mts. Lafayette and Lincoln over its middle, and Mt. Hitchcock and Owl's Head over the highest Kanc summit on the R. Mt. Garfield's pyramid is over the R shoulder of Kancamagus. The double summit of Mt. Huntington is next to the R, with Bondcliff and West Bond above and beyond. Mt. Bond is to the R of West Bond, with South Twin between them. Just R of the Bonds and closer are the Hancocks, with Scaur Peak close at hand and below. Looking due N, massive Carrigain rises to the R of Hancock's long E ridge and the nubble of The Captain. Whitewall Mtn. and Cherry Mtn. are sighted through the gap between Hancock and Carrigain. On Carrigain's R, over Signal Ridge, is Mt. Willey, and farther R, on the E side of Carrigain Notch, is slide-streaked Mt. Lowell. Between Willey and Lowell are Mt. Weeks (L) and Mt. Deception (R).

To the R of Lowell are Mt. Nancy and the Webster Cliffs. Next to the R are the Presidentials, including Jackson, Pierce, Eisenhower, Jefferson, Monroe, and Mt. Washington soaring above Oakes Gulf. A bit farther down the slide the view opens out more to the R to Boott Spur, Montalban Ridge, the Wildcats and the Carters.

North Peak View: Standing only, there is a limited vista NE over the trees to the Presidentials, Carters, Baldfaces, Moats and nearer peaks such as Bear, and Church Pond down on the Albany Intervale.

Middle Peak, W View: A small outlook ledge a few yards W of the trail, just N of the summit, overlooks the Waterville Valley region. On the far L (S) is nearby South Tripyramid. Massive Sandwich Dome is to its R, with sharp Jennings Peak at its R end and Flat Mtn. beneath. Mts. Monadnock and Kearsarge can be seen in the distance over the L shoulder of Sandwich, and of many distant hills to the R (SW), Mt. Cardigan and Vermont's Mt. Ascutney stand out. The long, low ridge of Snows Mtn. is close by in this direction, beyond which are the Mad River valley and the ledgy peaks of Welch and Dickey. Stinson Mtn. is to the L of and beyond Welch. The long flat ridge of Green Mtn. joins Dickey with Tecumseh to the R. Carr Mtn.'s spread is over the L end of Green, with Smarts Mtn. and Vermont's Killington and Pico in the distance a bit farther L. Over the R shoulder of Green is the long crest of Mt. Kineo. Between Carr and Kineo is Mt. Cube.

W across the valley are Mt. Tecumseh and the Waterville Valley ski trails, with Tecumseh's West Peak to the R. Massive Moosilauke is perfectly framed by Thornton Gap. To the R, over Osceola's Breadtray Ridge, are lower Kinsman Ridge, and Signal Mtn. and Camel's Hump in Vermont. The view NW to the Osceolas is especially fine from this angle. The crumbling Painted Cliff is prominent on a spur of East Peak, with the Kinsmans and two Cannon Balls to the R. On the far R are Whaleback, the four Franconia Ridge peaks, Mt. Hitchcock, Owl's Head, and Garfield, all seen over the nearer ridge of Mt. Kancamagus.

Middle Peak, E View: From the summit ledge of Middle Peak is an interesting view E over the trees along the Sandwich Range. On the far L (NE) is Kearsarge North rising over Bear Mtn. and West Moat. Close at hand and far below is the ledgy knob of Potash Mtn. Beyond the Swift River valley the long ridge of the Moats fills the horizon. Close in to the R of the Moats is dark, bristling Hedgehog Mtn.

Eastward is a fine view of Mt. Chocorua, with Maine's Pleasant Mtn. in the distance to the L and the N ridges of Paugus beneath. Farther R and most striking is the great wooded dome of Passaconaway, rising above a N spur ridge of East Sleeper. To the R of Passaconaway a long ridge runs up to Mt. Whiteface. Between these peaks are glimpses of Silver Lake, Green Mtn. in Effingham and Ossipee Lake. Through gaps in the trees to the R (SE) are the Ossipee Range, Lake Winnipesaukee and the Belknap Range over the nearby humps of the Sleepers.

South Slide View: The top of the South Slide offers an unusual vista over the wild, mostly trailless region between Tripyramid and Sandwich Dome. There's an excellent rock seat just below the top of the slide. On the L (SE) is a long SW arm of Sleeper Ridge, over which are seen the Ossipee Range, Lake Winnipesaukee, and the Belknaps. Sprawling, tower-topped Red Hill rises beyond the rounded, southern Flat Mtn. Farther R, due S, is the S end of Flat Mountain Pond. At your feet is a broad spruce-wooded plateau holding two beaver ponds. Above is the wild cut of Lost Pass, the gap between the Sleepers and the northern Flat Mtn., with Mt. Israel seen beyond. The Flat Mtn. ridge extends R to massive, double-summited Sandwich Dome. Monadnock and Kearsarge are visible to the L of Sandwich's summit, and Mt. Cardigan can be seen to the R.

Nearby to the SW is long, low Snows Mtn., with Stinson Mtn. beyond and Welch and Dickey to the R. Farther R is Green Mtn. leading up to Mt. Tecumseh. Between Dickey and Green are seen distant Killington in Vermont, Smarts Mtn., and Carr Mtn., while Mt. Cube and Mt. Kineo are seen above Green.

NO. OF 4000-FOOTERS VISIBLE: from North Tripyramid, 36 (somewhat theoretical, perhaps in winter only); from Middle Tripyramid: 36.

Mount Whiteface

ELEVATION: 4020 ft./1225 m ORDER OF HEIGHT: 45
LOCATION: Sandwich Range, Town of Waterville Valley
USGS MAP: 7½′ Mount Tripyramid

GEOGRAPHY

With its great S cliff and long, steep-sided ridgecrest to the N, Whiteface strikes a bold and commanding pose in the center of the Sandwich Range Wilderness. The precipitous face of the mountain thrusts southward from the main line of the range and looms, sphinx-like, 3000 ft. above the lowlands of Wonalancet (once known as Birch Intervale) and Whiteface Intervale to the S. It is the southernmost of the White Mountain 4000-footers. Though the true summit is viewless, from the ledgy S summit (3994 ft.), just 0.3 mi. away, there are wide views over the lake country, and other vantages just below on the Blueberry Ledge Trail provide vistas in other directions. A good trail system offers several varied and interesting approaches.

From the true summit a narrow, humpy ridge, traversed by the Rollins Trail, extends nearly two miles N to a broad col with Mt. Passaconaway, enclosing the beautiful glacial cirque known as The Bowl. In this secluded valley, drained by Wonalancet River, are woods that have never been logged —a rarity in the White Mountains. To the E, across The Bowl, is the lower Wonalancet Range. On the W side of the N ridge is the remote upper valley of Downes Brook, a major tributary of the Swift River. Two large slides have fallen off the steep side of this ridge.

Bold ridges run S from either side of the S summit; the basin between them, below the S cliff, is drained by White Brook. The Blueberry Ledge Trail tackles the rocky SE ridge, while the McCrillis Trail climbs the SW ridge. The Blueberry Ledges are an extensive area of gently sloping open rock slabs, fringed with scrub spruce, low down on the mountain's SE ridge.

To the SW are the ravines of Whiteface River and its East Branch, and beyond that the remote region around picturesque Flat Mountain Pond and the two Flat Mtns. Just to the W of the main summits is the broad, flat-topped West Spur (3580 ft.), with a cliff-faced ridge running S. Beyond West Spur to the NW the Whiteface massif is connected to Mt. Tripyramid by the high, rolling Sleeper Ridge, named for Kate Sleeper, a community leader, innkeeper and trails activist from Wonalancet.

NOMENCLATURE

"Whiteface" is an obvious reference to the prominent cliff on the S slope of the mountain. Guidebook editor Moses Sweetser averred that the rock face was bared by a great landslide in October 1820. However, the name predates that slide, appearing in Jeremy Belknap's 1784 journal and on Philip Carrigain's 1816 map. Timothy Dwight referred to it as "White-Faced Mtn." in his 1831 *Northern Traveller*, while geographer Arnold Guyot labeled the peak "South Whiteface" on his 1860 map, distinguishing it from "North Whiteface"—today's Passaconaway.

HISTORICAL HIGHLIGHTS

First ascent: Unknown. The mountain was mentioned as early as 1784 in Dr. Jeremy Belknap's journal. The geographer Arnold Guyot probably climbed it in the mid-1800s.

1820: Landslide strips soil and vegetation off steep south face.

1869: George L. Vose ascends Whiteface and makes detailed observations for NH Geological Survey. Work of survey moves mountain from town of Albany to Waterville.

1871: U.S. Coast Survey erects signal station on summit.

1876: Sweetser's guidebook describes path to summit from McCrillis Farm in Whiteface Intervale, later becomes McCrillis Trail. Describes summit view as "one of the most beautiful in the state."

1891: Kate Sleeper opens inn at Wonalancet Farm.

1892: Community leader Katherine Sleeper and other trails enthusiasts found Wonalancet Out Door Club (WODC).

1895: Thomas S. Wiggin cuts Wiggin Trail up SE ridge to summit.

1899: Gordon H. Taylor blazes Blueberry Ledge Trail, joining Wiggin Trail below upper ridge; route is specifically marked for snowshoeing. Dr. William H. Rollins cuts Rollins Trail along N ridge towards Mt. Passconaway. Camp Shehadi built between north and south summits using proceeds from lecture by Shehadi Abdullah Shehadi, a native of Syria then living in Providence, R.I.; is intended largely for use by snowshoeing parties. (Rebuilt in 1929.) Soon Sleeper Trail is cut across Sleeper Ridge to Mt. Tripyramid.

1902–07: Woodbury Trail built from Waterville Valley to summit by W. R. Woodbury, Paul R. Jenks and Charles W. Blood. Long route climbs over SW spur of Sleeper Ridge.

1912: Camp Heermance built near south summit, under direction of Edgar Laing Heermance, a trail-building minister, who pioneered Blue Trails system in Connecticut. Rebuilt in 1933.

1914: The Bowl is added to WMNF through efforts of Kate Sleeper and WODC; virgin forest is saved from logging. Land is acquired from Louis S. Tainter of Publishers Paper Co.

ca. 1916: Logging disrupts Sleeper and Woodbury Trails.

1917: Beebe River logging railroad begins operation, is eventually extended past Flat Mountain Pond to Camp 12 at SW base of Whiteface.

1920: Ashes of lumber baron Louis S. Tainter are cemented in ledge at S summit and marked by plaque, still present today.

1920s: Downes Brook Trail opened by WMNF. Large slides fall off N ridge of Whiteface into Downes Brook.

1923: Fire sparked by Beebe River logging railroad burns 3,500 acres in Flat Mountain Pond region and on lower SW slopes of Whiteface.

1931: The Bowl is designated as Research Natural Area by Forest Service.

1938: Hurricane obliterates part of Sleeper Trail.

1950s: Woodbury Trail abandoned.

1984: Congress creates 25,000 acre Sandwich Range Wilderness, includes Mt. Whiteface.

1987: Bottom section of McCrillis Trail is closed, new connector opened from Flat Mountain Pond Trail.

TRAIL APPROACHES

SOUTHEAST APPROACH from Wonalancet

Blueberry Ledge Trail, Rollins Trail
8.4 mi. round trip, 3050-ft. elevation gain

TRAILHEAD (1140 ft.): Hiker's parking area beside Ferncroft Rd., 0.5 mi. from NH 113A at corner in Wonalancet village.

This is the shortest and most popular approach to Whiteface, following a bold SE ridge. The upper part is steep and difficult with several rock scrambles. It can be dangerous if wet or icy. There are several fine viewpoints. From hiker's parking, walk 0.3 mi. up Ferncroft Road, turn L across Squirrel Bridge and follow another road into woods. Enter WMNF at 0.7 mi. Easy to moderate grades, mostly in spruces, lead to gentle, semi-open Blueberry Ledges at 1.6 mi.; at top of ledges is view S to Ossipee Range, at 2.0 mi./2150 ft. Ascend easily through hardwoods, then more steeply past restricted Wonalancet Outlook. After long, steady climb, level out on shoulder and dip to jct. R with Tom Wiggin Trail at 3.2 mi./3350 ft. (This steep trail, nicknamed "The Fire Escape," provides alternate 3.0 mi. approach to this point via lower Dicey's Mill Trail. Wiggin Trail ascends 1450 ft. up side of ridge in 1.1 mi.)

Above, tackle steep upper ridge; beginning at 3.6 mi. views R and L are interspersed with winding ledge scrambles. One ledge on L looks across S cliff to Sandwich Dome and Flat Mountain Pond beyond. Look for exceptional flat ledge viewpoint on R, looking N into The Bowl, at 3.8 mi./3900 ft.; see view description below. Reach ledgy S summit, with excellent views, at 3.9 mi./3990 ft. For true summit, continue N on Rollins Trail, dipping to col and jct. L with Kate Sleeper Trail at 4.0 mi. Pass dilapidated Camp Shehadi (may be removed) and climb fairly steeply to wooded summit at 4.2 mi./4020 ft.

SOUTHWEST APPROACH from Whiteface Intervale

Flat Mountain Pond Trail, McCrillis Trail, Rollins Trail
10.4 mi. round trip, 3200-ft. elevation gain.

TRAILHEAD (968 ft.): Start at E trailhead for Flat Mountain Pond Trail off Whiteface Intervale Rd., 0.4 mi. from NH 113A.

This is a longer and less-used approach, with a couple of good outlooks en route. Follow gravel road past beaver meadow L with view of Sandwich Mtn. After several turns, path runs through hemlocks along bank above Whiteface River, passing view up to Mt. Whiteface at 0.9 mi. Descend to cross river (bridge out in 2000) at 1.6 mi., entering Sandwich Range Wilderness. Turn L here, then R onto McCrillis Trail at 1.7 mi. After traverse, bear L at 2.1 mi. and climb easily through gently sloping hardwood forest. Climb steepens at 3.7 mi. into spruce-fir forest. At 4.3 mi./3300 ft. pass first of several ledgy, scrubby outlooks, first on L towards Lakes Region and Sandwich Dome, then on R looking up to S cliff of Whiteface. Trail plunges into deep fir woods for steady climb to S summit, ending with traverse of ledges with views SW to Flat Mt. Pond and Sandwich Dome. At 4.9 mi. McCrillis Trail meets Blueberry Ledge and Rollins Trails behind S summit ledges. Continue 0.3 mi. N on Rollins Trail for true summit.

NORTHEAST APPROACH via Rollins Trail

The Rollins Trail runs along the long, rough N ridge of Whiteface, allowing a loop trip with Dicey's Mill Trail and a two-peak day with a side trip to Mt. Passaconaway. There are several good outlooks down into the Bowl. From point 3.7 mi. up Dicey's Mill Trail, head W on Rollins Trail (elevation 3300 ft.). Descend briefly and traverse broad col, then start climbing first hump on N ridge of Whiteface at 0.8 mi. Fairly steep climb leads to fine view L into Bowl and out to SE at 1.1 mi./3600 ft. Continue up ridge over several wooded humps, with occasional outlooks, to summit of Whiteface at 2.2 mi. Good views at S summit are 0.3 mi. farther S on Rollins Trail. Loop over Whiteface via Dicey's Mill, Rollins and Blueberry Ledge Trails: 10.1 mi., 3100-ft. elevation gain. With side trip to Mt. Passaconaway: 11.9 mi., 3850-ft. elevation gain.

NORTH APPROACH from Kancamagus Highway

Downes Brook Trail, Kate Sleeper Trail, Rollins Trail
12.8 mi. round trip, 2800-ft. elevation gain

TRAILHEAD (1250 ft.): Parking area off short side road from Kancamagus Highway (NH 112) across from Passaconaway Campground, 2 mi. W of Bear Notch Rd.

This is a long, lesser-used approach up the isolated valley of Downes Brook. It's a pretty woods walk through remote country; with 10 brook crossings it should be avoided in high water. Trail starts up road for 100 yards, turns R at top of bank, then turns L onto original route of trail at 0.3 mi. In short distance Mt. Potash Trail diverges R. Easy walking leads to first crossing at 0.7 mi., with three more in next mile. Cross slide outwash at 2.2 mi./1840 ft. After three more crossings, trail stays on W side for long stretch. Make two more crossings, then at 4.3 mi./2850 ft. there are views L across valley to large slides on side of N ridge of Whiteface. Ascent steepens to 10th crossing, above which you reach swampy plateau and jct. with Kate Sleeper Trail at 5.2 mi./3400 ft. Turn L (SE) and follow Kate Sleeper Trail on moderate climb to junction with Rollins Trail in col at 6.0 mi/3900 ft. True summit is 0.2 mi. L (N); view ledges on S summit are 0.1 mi. R (S).

Another possible ascent route from the Kancamagus Highway, this one entailing a loop hike over Whiteface and Passaconaway, can be made via Downes Brook, Kate Sleeper, Rollins, Dicey's Mill, Walden, Square Ledge, Passaconaway Cutoff, and Oliverian Brook Trails. The round-trip distance is 15.6 mi. (including 1.0 mi. road walk), with a 3700-ft. elevation gain.

WINTER

Blueberry Ledge Trail is the most popular approach; a small parking area is plowed beside Ferncroft Rd. The upper section of this trail is very challenging and possibly dangerous if icy; crampons are required. Many winter peakbaggers make the long loop over both Whiteface and Passaconway. Rollins Trail may be hard to follow along the N ridge; expect many slaps in the face from fir branches.

VIEW GUIDE

South Summit: The open S summit of Whiteface presents several tiers of ledges with a 180-degree view S over the broad, low-lying Lakes Region. The best loafing and viewing spot is a few yards SW on the McCrillis Trail.

On the far L (E) is the distinctive rocky cone of Mt. Chocoura, rising above the S knob of Mt. Paugus and Paugus's crumbling SW cliffs. Part of Maine's Pleasant Mtn. can be seen beyond Chocorua, with Conway Lake to the R. Below Paugus and close by is Hibbard Mtn., with the rounded hump of Mt. Wonalancet jutting out on the R. Chocorua Lake is seen over the latter peak and Silver Lake is beyond to the R.

To the SE, past a shoulder of Whiteface, are the fields of Wonalancet, with Great Hill Pond, Great Hill and parts of Tamworth village beyond. Shining in the distance is Ossipee Lake with Green Mtn. in Effingham behind on the L. To the R, looking SSE, are the long, jumbled ridges of the Ossipee Range, with Mt. Shaw, the highest peak, in the center.

Due S and below are the fields of Whiteface Intervale and far beyond, 22 miles away, is the great spread of Lake Winnipesaukee, unfolding between the Ossipee Range on the L and Red Hill, bearing a fire tower, on the R. The twin peaks of the Belknap Range are behind the right-center of Winnipesaukee. Squam Lake stretches to the R of Red Hill, with double-peaked Mt. Israel flanking it on the R. Mt. Kearsarge is seen over the R shoulder of Israel. On very clear days, the dim, broad-shouldered peak of Mt. Monadnock may be espied to the L of Kearsarge. To the R of Israel are the long wooded ridges of the Squam Range. Farther R and nearby to the SW is the wooded cone of Flat Mtn., the southern of two adjacent peaks bearing that name. On the far R is the SE ridge of Sandwich Mtn., with Mt. Cardigan far away over its L shoulder.

By standing on the topmost ledge, the view can be extended to include nearby Mt. Passaconaway and the more distant Moats, Kearsarge North and the Green Hills on the L (NE), and all of Sandwich Dome to the R (WSW). A few yards SW on the McCrillis Trail is an interesting view of Flat Mountain Pond and Sandwich Dome.

Upper Outlook on Blueberry Ledge Trail: This flat-topped crag at 3900 ft. offers an extended view NE and E across the deep ravine of The Bowl to Mt. Passaconaway and many distant peaks. To the L, looking N, a jumble of mountains is seen through the gap between the N ridge of Whiteface and the summit cone of Passaconaway. On the L Mt. Bemis rises beyond the E end of Green's Cliff, with Mt. Deception (L) and Mt. Jackson (R) in the distance. The Southern Presidentials rise from Jackson up to Mt. Washington, soaring above the gaping Oakes Gulf, just E of N and 24 miles away. Mt. Jefferson peers over to the L of Monroe and Boott Spur juts out to the R of Washington. In front of Washington are Owl's Cliff, ledgy Mt. Tremont, Giant Stairs and Mt. Resolution, and Rocky Branch Ridge. Bartlett Haystack is to the R of Tremont, with Mt. Parker to the L and Wildcats E and D in the distance. Wildcat A and Carter Dome rise far beyond the Haystack.

Two miles NE across the beautiful, hardwood-draped Bowl is the shapely wooded dome of Passaconaway. A great slab of rock shines near The Bowl's headwall. Over the R shoulder of Passaconaway are West Moat and North Moat, with Kearsarge North rising above and behind. Middle and South Moat are seen above nearby Nanamocomuck Peak, with the Green Hills behind to the R. Paugus and Chocorua are viewed above Wonalancet Hedgehog. From here the view extends SE and S around to the Ossipee Range and Lake Winnipesaukee, as described above.

NO. OF 4000-FOOTERS VISIBLE: 40 (combined for S summit, Blueberry Ledge Trail upper outlook, and through trees around true summit).

Mount Cabot

ELEVATION: 4170 ft./1271 m ORDER OF HEIGHT: 33
LOCATION: Pilot Range, Township of Kilkenny
USGS MAPS: 7½′ × 15′ Pliny Range, 7½′ Stark

GEOGRAPHY

Bulky, whale-shaped Mt. Cabot and its train of Pilot Range peaks stand guard on the northern fringe of the White Mountains, looming over the town of Lancaster on the W and the Kilkenny region and the headwaters of the Upper Ammonoosuc River to the E. It's the major peak of the wild Pilot Range. This northernmost of the 4000-footers has a real North Country feel to it, with fern-filled fir forests and far fewer hikers than the more popular ranges to the S.

On the S, remote Bunnell Notch (3041 ft.) separates Cabot's slightly lower SE summit from the 3638-ft. North Peak of neighboring Terrace Mtn. Cabot's upper S face features a broad band of talus (broken rock), a distinctive landmark from afar. A high ridge runs NE from Cabot over The Bulge (3950 ft., wooded with no views) and The Horn (3905 ft., a wild and spectacular open viewpoint). From The Bulge the long, trailless Pilot Ridge extends NW over a series of peaks culminating in Hutchins Mtn. (3730 ft., also known as Pilot Mtn.). The secluded upper valley of Mill Brook drains the E slopes of this ridge and the N slopes of the Bulge and The Horn. To the NE of The Horn is a highland plateau cradling Unknown Pond (3177 ft.). This picturesque tarn is guarded on the E by 3510-ft. Unknown Pond Ridge and drains SE via Unknown Pond Brook. Just to the S the West Branch of the Upper Ammonoosuc River rises in the SE-facing ravine enclosed by Cabot, The Bulge, The Horn and the latter's long SE ridge.

A long ridge runs W from the summit of Cabot; between it and the Pilot Ridge is the deep valley of Fox Brook. Bunnell Brook (which drains from Bunnell Notch) and Bone Brook flow off the SW slopes of the mountain to the flatlands of Lancaster.

Though Cabot's broad summit is wooded with no views, good vistas are found on the way up the Mt. Cabot Trail at Bunnell Rock and from a clearing at the site of a former fire tower.

NOMENCLATURE

The mountain was named "Mt. Sebastian Cabot" about 1886 by William H. Peek, an enthusiastic explorer of the White Mountains, in honor of an English sea captain who was the grand pilot of Henry VII. Cabot explored along the coast of New England in the 16th century. The peak was also known as "Grand Pilot," "Pilot Dome," and "Kilkenny Peak." Peek also applied the name "Mons Ovium" to the lower SE summit of Cabot, and dubbed the great talus slope as the "Sheep-Fold," for the resemblance of the boulders to sheep huddled in an enclosure. He also named "The Bulge" (sometimes called "Turtle-Back") and called The Horn, "South Peak."

The Pilot Range was named by early visitors to the upper Connecticut River valley, who used the mountains as landmarks and called them the "Land Pilot Hills." The range was also called "Little Moosehillock" by Timothy Dwight, who twice traveled through this area around 1800.

HISTORICAL HIGHLIGHTS

First Ascent: Unknown

1876: Moses Sweetser's guide includes section on Pilot Mtn., focusing on Pilot (Hutchins) Mtn.

1885: AMC group traverses Pilot Range, including Pilot Mtn. and Mt. Cabot. William H. Peek publishes account and sketches of views in March 1886 *Appalachia*.

1886: The Peek group visits the "Sheep-Fold" talus slope, Bunnell Notch, The Horn, The Bulge and Mt. Cabot; another account appears in Dec. 1887 *Appalachia*.

1892–1903: Upper Ammonoosuc Lumber Company builds logging railroad and conducts intensive timbering operations in Kilkenny region on E side of Cabot.

1903: In wake of logging, huge fire in May scorches 25,000 acres in Kilkenny region, lapping up E slopes of Pilot Range. Present birch forest in area is legacy of fire.

1906: AMC group climbs Cabot in winter, account published in May 1906 *Appalachia*.

1916: AMC guide notes that "of the little-known mountain ranges in New Hampshire, perhaps none have received such scant attention in the public prints as the Pilot Range. . . . The range . . . is included in that vague title, now seldom heard, the Kilkenny Mountains." As for Cabot, guide describes "excellent path, traversed by horses its entire length," from Terrence White farm in East Lancaster (largely the route of today's Mt. Cabot Trail). On S slope of mountain, trail passes view into "bare, fire-swept Bunnell Notch." Guide notes observation tower and firewarden's cabin near summit; camp is connected by telephone with Lancaster. Warden is F. C. Leavitt; water source near summit is later named "Bishop-Leavitt Spring" in honor of this and another fire warden.

1925: New trail from York Pond through Bunnell Notch opens route to Cabot from E.

1960: Short-lived trail is cut across Terrace Mtn.

1965: Tower removed in November.

Late 1980s: Kilkenny Ridge Trail built N from Cabot over The Bulge, The Horn (side trail) and past Unknown Pond to Rogers Ledge and South Pond, and S across Terrace Mtn., Willard Notch, Mt. Weeks to Mt. Waumbek.

TRAIL APPROACHES

East Approach from York Pond Rd. and Berlin Fish Hatchery

York Pond Trail, Bunnell Notch Trail, Kilkenny Ridge Trail, Mt. Cabot Trail

9.6 mi. round trip, 2500-ft. elevation gain

TRAILHEAD (1670 ft.): At end of York Pond Rd., 2.1 mi. beyond gate at Berlin Fish Hatchery; park on R at 2.0 mi., just past Unknown Pond Trail. This is 6.8 mi. from NH 110; York Pond Rd. leaves NH 110 on L (S) 7.1 mi. from NH 16 in Berlin. (In summer and fall, this gate is closed from 4 pm to 8 am; in winter the gate has been kept open all the time. For info call the hatchery at 603–449–3412.)

With the W approach closed (see below), this is the shortest approach to Cabot. From parking area, walk 0.1 mi. SW up York Pond Rd. and turn L onto York Pond Trail. Follow York Pond Trail for 0.2 mi. to clearing with view of Mt. Cabot. Bear R here on Bunnell Notch Trail, obscure and very wet in places. Follow roads through logged areas, then climb moderately W up valley to Bunnell Notch, with several stream crossings. Trail is minimally marked—follow arrows carefully at doubtful points. At 3.0 mi./3040 ft. southbound Kilkenny Ridge Trail departs on L. At 3.1 mi. turn R on northbound Kilkenny Ridge Trail and traverse to jct. with Mt. Cabot Trail at 3.4 mi./3150 ft. Climb through firs into scrubby area with partial view back to SW, and at 3.8 mi./3350 ft. pass short spur R to Bunnell Rock—sunny ledge perch with good view S over Bunnell Notch to North Peak of Terrace Mtn. Steady climb with switchbacks leads to old firewarden's cabin, open to public for overnight use, at 4.4 mi./4070 ft. Just beyond is clearing at site of former firetower with good views NE and SW. Dip into small col and ascend easily to wooded summit at 4.8 mi./4170 ft.

Loop Option

Descent via Kilkenny Ridge, Unknown Pond Trails
11.5 mi. loop, 3000-ft. elevation gain

A long and very scenic loop can be made from end of York Pond Rd. including Mt. Cabot, The Horn and Unknown Pond. From Cabot summit (4.8 mi.), follow Kilkenny Ridge Trail N for 460-ft. descent to col, climb 240 ft. over The Bulge in deep fir forest (no views), then dip to jct. with side trail R to The Horn, at 5.9 mi./3650 ft. Upper part of side trail is steep, rocky scramble, and climb to topmost rock requires use of hands. Panoramic views of Kilkenny region and many distant peaks make the 0.6 mi. round trip, with 255-ft. elevation gain, a must in good weather. Of particular note are views NW along wild, trailless Pilot Ridge; N to mountains of Nash Stream State Forest; SSW to nearby looming masses of Cabot and The Bulge; S to Terrace, Weeks, and Waumbek, with the jagged Presidentials beyond and Carters to L; and E to the Mahoosucs. See panorama in *Scudder's White Mountain Viewing Guide*.

Back on Kilkenny Ridge Trail (6.5 mi.), descend moderately through ferny birch forest, with some meanderings, to picturesque Unknown Pond at 8.2 mi./3177 ft. Here there is beautiful view across water to Horn. Turn R on S link of Unknown Pond Trail for steady descent down valley through birch forest, with several stream crossings. At bottom of downgrade trail follows old logging RR grade past view of Terrace Mtn. Final stretch through logged areas leads to York Pond Rd., 3.3 mi. from Unknown Pond. Turn R to reach parking area at 11.5 mi.

NORTH APPROACH from Mill Brook Rd. in Stark

Unknown Pond Trail, Kilkenny Ridge Trail
12.2 mi. round trip, 3300-ft. elevation gain

TRAILHEAD (1630 ft.): From NH 110 in Stark drive S on Mill Brook Rd. (FR 11) for 3.7 mi. and park off road just before gate.

This out-and-back option includes Unknown Pond, The Horn and Mt. Cabot without the worry of the fish hatchery gate closing at 4 pm. Walk 0.8 mi. up road and turn L on Unknown Pond Trail for steady climb through hardwoods, then lovely birches to Unknown Pond and jct. with southbound Kilkenny Ridge Trail at 3.0 mi./3177 ft. Turn R on Kilkenny Ridge Trail and meander up through birches to side trail L to Horn at 4.7 mi./3650 ft. (Visit to open summit of Horn is 0.6 mi. round trip with 255-ft. elevation gain.) Continue on main trail another 1.1 mi., climbing 300 ft. over The Bulge and up 460-ft. climb to summit of Cabot. Round trip mileage includes side trip to Horn.

WEST APPROACH from Arthur White Road in East Lancaster

Mt. Cabot Trail
7.8 mi. round trip, 2750-ft. elevation gain

TRAILHEAD (1510 ft.): Small parking area near end of Arthur White Rd. in East Lancaster. See AMC guide for detailed driving directions from US 2.

This has been the shortest and by far the most popular approach to Cabot, but *access was closed by landowner along trail as of February 2000. This approach should not be used until the issue is resolved.* For current status, check with WMNF Androscoggin District at 603–466–2713. From parking area, trail follows logging road through old clearcut. At 0.4 mile York Pond Trail splits R on bed of old Kilkenny logging railroad. Continue straight on Mt. Cabot Trail at moderate grade on logging road, eroded in places. Trail becomes more of a footpath and enters WMNF at 1.3 mi. Continue at easy grades through hardwoods to crossing of Bunnell Brook and jct. R with Bunnell Notch Trail at 2.2 mi./2650 ft. Bear L and zigzag up through birches; Kilkenny Ridge Trail joins from R at 2.5 mi. Climb into firs and through scrubby area with partial views back to SW, and at 2.9 mi./3350 ft. pass short spur R to Bunnell Rock—sunny ledge perch with good view S. Steady climb with switchbacks leads to old firewarden's cabin, open to public for overnight use, at 3.5 mi./4070 ft. Just beyond is clearing at site of former firetower with good views NE and SW. Dip into small col and ascend easily to wooded summit at 3.9 mi./4170 ft.

WINTER

Cabot is a wonderful climb in winter, with reliably deep snow and moderate grades ideal for snowshoeing. If open, the W approach has a small parking area plowed near end of Arthur White Rd. For the E approach, a parking area is plowed on the R near end of York Pond Rd; gate at fish hatchery has been kept open throughout winter. The Bunnell Notch Trail can be very hard to find and follow as it nears Bunnell Notch. Mill Brook Rd. is not plowed, making the N approach as described above impractical as a winter day hike.

VIEW GUIDE

Bunnell Rock: This great S-facing ledge perch soaks up the sun and looks across Bunnell Notch to the North Peak of Terrace Mtn., with Mt. Moriah far off to the L (SE) and Mt. Waumbek, the Twins, Mts. Liberty, Lincoln and Lafayette, the Kinsmans and Cannon Mtn. off to the R (SW). In this direction there's also a distant view out towards Vermont, with Killington and Pico Peaks visible on clear days.

Clearing at Firetower Site: This opening, 0.3 mi. below the true summit of Cabot, provides good views NE and SW. The NE view, quite different from any other NH 4000-footer vista, looks over the Kilkenny region and far beyond into Maine. The beautiful pyramid of The Horn rises close by to the NNE, with many unfamiliar ridges and peaks in the North Country beyond. To the R of The Horn the top of the cliff of Rogers Ledge peers over the L shoulder of the gentle mountain called Unknown Pond Ridge. Over the R shoulder of that ridge is the cliff of Greens Ledge. In this direction one can spot several of the high peaks in the Rangeley, Maine area on the horizon.

To the R of and behind Unknown Pond Ridge, looking NE, is the long, low Deer Ridge with a prominent old clearcut patch on its R end, below the knob of Deer Mtn. Maine's Baldpate Mtn. rises beyond Deer Mtn., with bulky Old Speck to the R. Looking E, the Mahoosuc Range runs in a long chain to the R from Old Speck with the broad Androscoggin River valley in the foreground. The sharp peak of Goose Eye is prominent midway along the Mahoosucs. Jericho Lake is seen under Mt. Carlo, the rounded peak just to the R of Goose Eye. Part of the city of Berlin can be seen behind to the R.

The SW view includes some of the central White Mountains and a wide lowland sweep. On the far L, looking SSE, the Presidentials can be seen over the trees, above the rounded dome of South Weeks. To the S is the long, level ridge of Mt. Waumbek, with Mts. Willey, Field and Carrigain appearing above its summit knobs and Mt. Tom to the R. Farther R the ridge leads from Waumbek across to Starr King, with the Hancocks and Osceolas in the distance. Zealand Ridge and Mt. Bond are above the summit of Starr King.

South and North Twin are farther R, with Cherry Mtn. in front. The ridge of Starr King descends R to the spur of Haystack Mtn., revealing more peaks in the distance: Flume and Liberty, Garfield, and Lincoln and Lafayette. Farther R, looking SSW, are the Kinsmans with Moosilauke behind and Cannon in front. Swinging around to the SW and W, the view opens out across a vast expanse of lower country in the Lancaster-Whitefield area and beyond the Connecticut River valley into Vermont, a landscape quilted with fields and woods and dotted with houses. Green Mountain ridges, including Killington, Camel's Hump and Mt. Mansfield, can be picked out on the horizon.

NO. OF 4000-FOOTERS VISIBLE: 39 (including 5 visible only through trees at summit).

Mount Waumbek

ELEVATION: 4006 ft./1221 m ORDER OF HEIGHT: 46
LOCATION: Pliny Range, Township of Kilkenny and Town of Jefferson
USGS MAP: 7½′ × 15′ Pliny Range

GEOGRAPHY

Poking barely above the 4000-ft. mark, the wooded summit of Mt. Waumbek is the culminating point of the Pliny Range, an arc of North Country ridges overlooking the Israel River valley and town of Jefferson to the S and the wild Kilkenny region to the N. The climb up Waumbek via the Starr King Trail is one of the mellowest hikes in the high peaks. The open, lichen-draped fir forest that cloaks the ridgecrest is especially enchanting. The tree cover on Waumbek's summit allows only limited views, but its close neighbor to the W, Mt. Starr King (3907 ft.) affords an excellent view SE to the Presidentials.

The semicircular Pliny Range is noted by geologists as a unique "ring-dike" created when molten magma welled up into a circular crack in the earth's crust and later cooled and solidified into resistant rock. The range begins on the NW with trailless Haystack Mtn. (3330 ft.), then runs SE over Starr King and, with only a slight dip, on to Waumbek. A long, nearly level ridge runs about two miles E from Waumbek, then the range swings N over the rounded summits of South Weeks (3885 ft.), Middle Weeks (3684 ft.) and North Weeks (3901 ft.) before ending at Willard Notch. On the N the Pliny Range encloses a broad hardwood valley known as Willard Basin, drained by Garland and Great Brooks. Willard Notch and Willard Basin are bordered on the N by Terrace Mtn. (3655 ft.) in the Pilot Range.

Mt. Pliny (3606 ft.) is a symmetrical spur peak projecting S from the E ridge of Waumbek. To the S and SW are the expansive lowlands of Jefferson, from which the high ridge of Starr King and Waumbek dominates the landscape. The Waumbek Slide, in a S-facing ravine between the peaks, is a prominent landmark. Crawford Brook flows S through this deep basin between the S ridges of Waumbek and Starr King. Priscilla Brook drains the valley between Mt. Waumbek and Mt. Pliny.

NOMENCLATURE

As the highest peak in the Pliny Range, Waumbek was originally known as "Pliny Major." The Pliny name may have been in use as early as 1784 and appeared on Philip Carrigain's 1816 map. It commemorates a Roman poet and naturalist of the first century.

The Native American terms "waumbekket-methna," meaning "white or snowy mountains," and "waumbik," or "white rocks," were originally associated with the Mt. Washington Range. Sometime in the late 1800s the name "Mt. Waumbek" came to replace "Pliny Major," and "Mt. Pliny" slid down to the SE spur. In 1861 the peak W of the main summit was named in honor of the Rev. Thomas Starr King, a Unitarian minister from Boston whose classic 1859 book, *The White Hills: Their Legends, Landscape and Poetry*, introduced thousands of readers to the beauties of the White Mountains.

HISTORICAL HIGHLIGHTS

First Ascent: Unknown.

1773: Col. Joseph Whipple establishes settlement at Jefferson (then known as Dartmouth).

1860: Waumbek House hotel built at S base of mountain.

1864: Samuel Eastman's guidebook notes that Mt. Starr King is "easily ascended" from Waumbek House, suggesting trail had been built up mountain.

1876: Moses Sweetser's guidebook describes well-trodden path up Starr King and gives elaborate description of view. Recommends visiting in afternoon "when the great ravines are filled with light."

1885: Nathan Matthews of Boston blazes route from Starr King to Waumbek.

1887: Kilkenny logging railroad extended E from Lancaster into Willard Basin on N side of Waumbek. Engineer is killed in 1890 when engine jumps tracks. Operation ends in 1897.

1916: 2nd edition of AMC guide describes obscure trail leading from Starr King to Waumbek.

Mid-1930s: Through trail from Jefferson to York Pond in Kilkenny opened, passing over col between Waumbek and Pliny. This is later named Keenan Brook Trail, then Priscilla Brook Trail. Path abandoned in 1980s.

1940s: Shelter built near summit of Starr King. Rebuilt 1968, removed ca. 1980. Remnants of fireplace are still visible today.

1948: AMC guide reports trail to Waumbek "extremely obscure."

1957: Waumbek Slide falls on S slope during July rainstorm.

1960: With recent founding of 4000-Footer Club, trail to Waumbek is "clear and well-marked," says guidebook.

Early 1960s: Major ski development, "Willard Basin Ski Area," proposed for N slopes of Waumbek. Field surveys begin, open house held Jan. 1965 is attended by 1,300, but lack of financing scuttles project.

Early 1970s: Path between Starr King and Waumbek becomes officially maintained trail as extension of Starr King Trail.

Late 1980s: Kilkenny Ridge Trail opened from Waumbek across E ridge and over Mt. Weeks to Willard Notch and beyond to Terrace Mtn., Mt. Cabot, Rogers Ledge and South Pond.

TRAIL APPROACHES

Southwest Approach off US 2 in Jefferson

Starr King Trail

7.2 mi. round trip, 2750-ft. elevation gain

Trailhead (1550 ft.): Park in lot at end of 0.2-mi. side road, marked by hiker sign, off N side of US 2, 0.2 mi. E of jct. with NH 115A.

The vast majority of hikers climb Waumbek via the Starr King Trail, enjoying moderate grades and attractive forests. Trail follows old logging roads, bearing R at 0.4 and 0.8 mi., then climbs up broad SW ridge of Starr King through fine hardwoods. Swing L at 1.5 mi./2900 ft. for long traverse through shady conifer forest on W side of ridge. Pass spring on L at 2.1 mi./3400 ft. Swing R and up at 2.5 mi., reaching summit of Starr King at 2.6 mi./3907 ft., with glimpse of peaks to N. Beyond high point is ledge with fine view S to Presidentials and beyond. Bear L to clearing at site of former shelter, with more restricted view.

Trail to Waumbek leaves back of clearing behind fireplace of old shelter. Swing E for easy descent and meander along gentle ridge through beautiful, moss-draped open fir forest. Moderate 0.2 mi. climb leads to summit of Waumbek at 3.6 mi/4006 ft.; limited views N and S around summit area.

East Approach via York Pond Trail and Kilkenny Ridge Trail.

Though seldom used for day hikes, the Kilkenny Ridge Trail can be followed from Willard Notch over the three humps of Mt. Weeks and across the long, flat E ridge of Waumbek to the summit. Starting at E end of York Pond Trail at end of York Pond Rd., the one-way distance to Waumbek is 8.7 mi. with 3700-ft. elevation gain. Retracing over this route adds another 800-ft. elevation gain on return (total 17.4 mi./4500 ft.). Point-to-point from York Pond Rd. to US 2 in Jefferson is 12.3 mi./3850 ft. (long car spot required). Open fir forest on ridge E of Waumbek is beautiful. About 0.2 mi. E of summit trail passes over lesser knob with restricted view N.

WINTER

Starr King Trail is excellent for snowshoeing and frequently packed out. The road to the trailhead is not plowed; park at a plowed pulloff on S side of US 2 just E of jct. with NH 115A. This adds 0.3 mi. each way to hike. Deep snow improves views on Starr King and Waumbek; the ridge between is a delightful snowshoe ramble through the firs.

VIEW GUIDE

Mt. Starr King View: The 180-degree S view from the summit of Mt. Starr King includes one of the most impressive vistas of the Presidential Range. On the far L, due E through the trees, is the wooded summit of Mt. Waumbek a mile up the ridge. Shelburne Moriah and Middle Moriah are seen to the R, with Mt. Crescent below. Mts. Moriah, Imp and the sharply rising North Carter hover over the nearby cone of Mt. Pliny, with Middle and South Carter to the R. Looking SE the Presidentials take center stage—a long line of craggy peaks filling the sky. On the L, Howker Ridge leads up to Mt. Madison. Next to the R is lofty Mt. Adams, with King Ravine in front and a long ridge running R down to Edmands Col., at the head of Castle Ravine. Nelson Crag is seen through the col. Next comes Mt. Jefferson, with lowly Mt. Bowman crouching at its foot. Behind and R of Jefferson is Mt. Washington, with Mt. Clay beneath. Mt. Monroe rises beyond Jefferson Notch; to the R Eisenhower's bald dome looms over the nearer Mt. Dartmouth. Mts. Pierce and Jackson are above the broad saddle in the Dartmouth Range between Mts. Dartmouth and Deception. Over Deception are Mt.Webster and Mts. Bemis and Nancy, with Mts. Passaconaway and Whiteface between the latter two. Farther R is the Willey Range—Willey, Field and Tom—with Mt. Carrigain popping up between the last two peaks.

Here the view extends out into the Pemigewasset Wilderness, framed by the broad Cherry Mtn. Notch (between Mt. Deception and Cherry Mtn.). The Rosebrook Range extends R from Mt. Tom, with the ridges of Hancock beyond. Zealand Ridge is a bit farther R, with the Osceolas back on the L and Mt. Bond above. Mt. Guyot is to the R of Bond, with Mt. Hale in front. Farther R South and North Twin are seen above and beyond the long, graceful ridge of Cherry Mtn. Mt. Garfield is to the R of North Twin, with Mt. Liberty rising behind and between them. Mts. Lincoln and Lafayette cut the skyline to the R of Garfield. Farther R are Cannon Mtn., South and North Kinsman, and Mt. Moosilauke.

The view SW and W sweeps over the sprawling lowlands of Jefferson and Whitefield with many distant ridges beyond. Cherry Pond and Little Cherry Pond are prominent to the SW. The twin hills of Mt. Cleveland and

Mt. Agassiz, and Black Mtn. in the Benton Range, are seen beyond Cherry Pond. On the distant horizon are many of Vermont's Green Mountains, including Camel's Hump and Mt. Mansfield.

Mt. Waumbek View: A short side path leads to a limited vista SE to the Presidentials, with Mt. Pliny close by on the L and more distant peaks from the Moriahs on L to the Franconia Range on R. Glimpses can be found on the N side of the summit to Terrace Mtn., marked by a slide on its S face.

NO. OF 4000-FOOTERS VISIBLE: 36 (from Waumbek, through the trees).

Appendices

4000-Footer Feats and Oddities

Over the years a number of unusual twists have been put on the goal of climbing all the high peaks in the White Mountains. Those that we know of are listed below; we're sure there are more we have not heard of, and some we probably don't want to know. These are presented not to encourage compulsive/obsessive readers to duplicate these feats, but to show to what lengths mountain-lovers and devoted peakbaggers will go to pursue their passion.

"DIRETISSIMA"

In the summer of 1970 the Rev. Henry Folsom of Old Saybrook, Conn., worked out the shortest continuous route of walking on trails and roads to climb all the peaks "diretissima"—in the most direct manner. In 19 days (not consecutive) and 244.05 miles (including 22.8 miles on roads and an inadvertent one-mile bushwhack on Kinsman Ridge) he bagged them all, starting with Cabot on the N and finishing with Moosilauke to the SW. His tale is told in the December 1971 issue of *Appalachia*.

EVERY MONTH OF THE YEAR

Gene Daniell, longtime editor of the *AMC White Mountain Guide* and Secretary of the Four Thousand Footer Club, was the first to climb each peak in every month of the year—12 rounds of the 48. He deemed April, with its deep, rotten snow and high water crossings, the toughest month. Several others have since completed this goal or are closing in.

AT NIGHT IN WINTER

In the 1990s, Fred Hunt, a noted Adirondack peakbagger, completed his goal of climbing all the White Mountain peaks at night in winter. On the night of March 6–7, 1999 Mike Bromberg, the cartographer who created the wonderful Wonalancet Out Door Club trail map of the Sandwich Range, achieved his goal of standing atop the summit of every 4000-footer at midnight in winter. Mt. Garfield was the final summit in his quest.

ALL THE PEAKS IN EIGHT DAYS

In the summer of 1991 three crazies named Doug, Al and Bill, fueled by Oreos, jumbo Milky Ways, Pop-Tarts, bananas and Gatorade, went on an eight-day rampage in the Whites. By the time the dust had cleared the quirky trio had hiked 250 miles and nabbed all 48 4000-footers. You can read about their knee-shattering adventure in the June 1992 issue of *Appalachia*.

ALL THE PEAKS IN ONE WINTER

In the winter of 1995–96, Cindy DiSanto, Cathy Goodwin and Steve Martin became the first to scale all the high peaks in one calendar winter—a feat which requires favorable weather and snow conditions and an understanding boss. They made it even though it took them three tries to reach the summit of Mt. Isolation.

THE DARTMOUTH OUTING CLUB 75TH ANNIVERSARY PEAK BAG

To celebrate its 75th Anniversary, the Dartmouth Outing Club synchronized ascents of all 48 peaks on October 6, 1984, with some 350 club members taking part. All reached their respective summits by noon.

ASCENT FROM ALL FOUR POINTS OF THE COMPASS, IN WINTER

The late Guy Waterman, a well-known writer, climber and peakbagger, crafted what may rank as the most amazing winter peakbagging feat ever in the White Mountains. Sometimes accompanied by his wife Laura or hiking friends, at other times alone, he climbed each peak from all four compass directions—east, south, west and north—no matter what obstacles loomed en route. This involved some of the most difficult bushwhack routes one could conceive of in the Whites, a maelstrom of spruce traps, blowdown, cliffs, slides, scrub and bottomless snow. We remember a chance encounter with Guy one summer day atop Mt. Garfield. As we stood and gazed at the Twin Mtns. to the east, Guy matter-of-factly pointed out the route he had navigated on Christmas Eve up the impossibly steep and tangled west slope of North Twin. Look at a trail map and you'll see dozens of equally astounding off-trail routes up the various 4000-footers. Amazing! We believe Guy also once climbed the 4000-footers in alphabetical order.

YOUNGEST AND OLDEST

According to Gene Daniell, record-keeper for the 4000-Footer Club, the youngest to complete the peaks was a 4½-year-old boy, while the oldest were two 79-year-old gentlemen.

OTHER ODDITIES

We have heard of others who have attempted to climb the 4000-footers barefoot, on skis, and walking backwards, but can't say whether they succeeded. If you know of any unusual peakbagging ventures involving the 4000-footers, please let us know so that we may include them in future editions.

How Many 4000-Footers Can You See?

It's a question often asked when standing atop an open White Mountain summit, gazing out at a panoramic view. Once the peaks become familiar, it's great fun to identify them from different perspectives near and far.

A few years ago I began tabulating the 4000-footers visible from some of the better White Mountain viewpoints. When I read in *Adirondac* magazine that Joe Coughlin, an ardent peakbagger from Watertown, N.Y., was surveying the views from the "Adirondack 46" 4000-footers, I was inspired to do the same for the "White Mountain 48."

For "viewbagging" purposes, the New Hampshire 4000-footers fall into five categories:

1. Those with an open summit, a tower, or viewpoints in each necessary direction. On these 23 peaks, all visible 4000-footers can be seen with no trouble on a clear day.
2. Those seven peaks with partial open views in several directions, sufficient to spot all visible 4000-footers with a little walking around.
3. Those with an open view in one direction. To see in all directions from these eight summits, you have to bushwhack around to find openings through the trees.
4. Summits with severely restricted views. You have to work harder on these four.
5. Those that are completely wooded. On these six summits, you must be ready to search diligently for even the slightest view.

The views listed here represent what could be seen if each summit was open. Thus the views for the wooded summits are somewhat theoretical, though with patient bushwhacking nearly all the potentially visible 4000-footers can be spotted.

One peak being visible from another is taken to mean from true summit to true summit, even if it's only the thinnest slice. Secondary summits and other portions of the summit ridge don't count. For mountains with ill-defined summits (e.g. Zealand, Owl's Head), this can be somewhat of a judgment call, especially since it's so hard to see from these "peaks."

This was a project that required clear, crisp days, for distances between mutually visible peaks range up to about 40 miles (e.g. Mts. Whiteface and

Cabot). I enjoyed many glorious days on the finer viewpoints, mixed in with some thrashing through the firs and peering between branches and tree trunks on the wooded summits. In some cases the deep snows of winter gave a welcome lift for seeing over the trees.

The most spectacular view was from Mt. Carrigain on a crystal September day. The most frustrating viewless mountain was Owl's Head—its level crest yielded no satisfactory openings through the trees near the marked summit.

There's no peak from which you can see all of the other 47 New Hampshire 4000-footers, though some come reasonably close. Sharing top honors are Mts. Washington and Carrigain with 43 peaks visible. Low mountain on the totem pole is Mt. Moriah, tucked away up behind the Presidentials in the northeast corner of the Whites, with only eight 4000-footers visible.

One thing is apparent: location is far more important than height. Of the 20 highest White Mountain summits, only eight are in the top 20 in number of 4000-footers visible. The peaks in the south-central area of the Whites are more favorably positioned in this regard than those in the eastern and western ranges. Thus lowly Mt. Tecumseh reveals 36 peaks to the viewbagger, while lofty Mt. Adams yields only 31 because of its towering Presidential neighbors.

NUMBER OF N.H. 4000-FOOTERS VISIBLE FROM . . .

Carrigain	43[a]
Washington	43[b]
Osceola	41
East Osceola	41
North Hancock	41
Passaconaway	40
Whiteface	40
Jefferson	40
Cabot	39
Lafayette	38
Lincoln	38
Bond	38
South Hancock	37
North Tripyramid	36
Tecumseh	36
Middle Tripyramid	36
Waumbek	36
South Twin	35
Moosilauke	34
Flume	33
Willey	33
Liberty	32
Eisenhower	32
Monroe	32
Adams	31
Jackson	30
Garfield	30
Pierce	30
Isolation	29
Carter Dome	29
Bondcliff	28
Field	28
North Twin	27
Wildcat	26
Wildcat D	24
Hale	23
West Bond	23
Middle Carter	22
Owl's Head	22
North Kinsman	22
South Kinsman	21
Tom	21
Zealand	20
South Carter	19
Cannon	16
Galehead	11
Madison	10
Moriah	8

[a]Peaks not visible from Carrigain include: Moriah, Madison, Cannon, Galehead.

[b]Peaks not visible from Washington include: Cannon, North Kinsman, South Kinsman, Galehead. Cannon Tramway building is visible from Washington, but the true summit of Cannon, slightly higher, is not. Only the very tip of West Bond is visible from Washington, in good light.

4000-FOOTER SUMMITS—VIEW TYPES

Open Summit or Tower with 360-Degree View

Adams
Bond
Bondcliff
West Bond
Cannon
Carrigain
Eisenhower
Flume
Garfield
Isolation
Jackson
Jefferson
South Kinsman
Lafayette
Liberty
Lincoln
Madison
Monroe
Moosilauke
Moriah
South Twin
Washington
Wildcat D

Summit with Open Views in Several Directions

Carter Dome
Hale
Middle Carter
Osceola
Pierce
Middle Tripyramid
North Twin
Willey

Summit with Open View in One Direction

North Hancock
South Hancock
North Kinsman
Passaconaway
Tecumseh
Tom
Wildcat

Summit with Restricted View

Field
Galehead
North Tripyramid
Waumbek

Summit with No View

Cabot*
South Carter
East Osceola*
Owl's Head**
Whiteface*
Zealand**

*Views available near, but not at summit
**Views available on approach trail

4000-Footer Checklist

Order	Peak	Height	Date Hiked
1	Washington	6288 ft. / 1916.6 m	07/16/16
2	Adams	5799 ft. / 1768 m	
3	Jefferson	5716 ft. / 1742 m	
4	Monroe	5372 ft. / 1637 m	
5	Madison	5366 ft. / 1636 m	
6	Lafayette	5260 ft. / 1603 m	10/01/16
7	Lincoln	5089 ft. / 1551 m	10/01/16
8	South Twin	4902 ft. / 1494 m	
9	Carter Dome	4832 ft. / 1473 m	
10	Moosilauke	4802 ft. / 1464 m	
11	North Twin	4761 ft. / 1451 m	
12	Eisenhower	4760 ft. / 1451 m	08/21/16
13	Carrigain	4700 ft. / 1433 m	
14	Bond	4698 ft. / 1432 m	
15	Middle Carter	4610 ft. / 1405 m	
16	West Bond	4540 ft. / 1384 m	
17	Garfield	4500 ft. / 1372 m	11/05/16
18	Liberty	4459 ft. / 1359 m	
19	South Carter	4430 ft. / 1350 m	
20	Wildcat	4422 ft. / 1348 m	
21	North Hancock	4420 ft. / 1347 m	
22	South Kinsman	4358 ft. / 1328 m	
23 (T)	Field	4340 ft. / 1323 m	11/12/16

ORDER	PEAK	HEIGHT	DATE HIKED
23 (T)	Osceola	4340 ft. / 1323 m	09/11/16
25	Flume	4328 ft. / 1319 m	
26	South Hancock	4319 ft. / 1316 m	
27	Pierce	4312 ft. / 1314 m	10/23/16
28	North Kinsman	4293 ft. / 1309 m	
29	Willey	4285 ft. / 1306 m	
30	Bondcliff	4265 ft. / 1300 m	
31	Zealand	4260 ft. / 1298 m	
32	North Tripyramid	4180 ft. / 1274 m	
33	Cabot	4170 ft. / 1271 m	
34	East Osceola	4156 ft. / 1267 m	
35	Middle Tripyramid	4140 ft. / 1262 m	
36	Cannon	4100 ft. / 1250 m	
37	Wildcat D	4062 ft. / 1238 m	
38	Hale	4054 ft. / 1236 m	10/29/16
39	Jackson	4052 ft. / 1235 m	10/15/16
40	Tom	4051 ft. / 1235 m	
41	Moriah	4049 ft. / 1234 m	
42	Passaconaway	4043 ft. / 1232 m	
43	Owl's Head	4025 ft. / 1227 m	
44	Galehead	4024 ft. / 1227 m	
45	Whiteface	4020 ft. / 1225 m	
46	Waumbek	4006 ft. / 1221 m	
47 (T)	Isolation	4003 ft. / 1220 m	
47 (T)	Tecumseh	4003 ft. / 1220 m	10/02/16

Bedrock Types of the 4000-Footers

Adams: *Metamorphic*—interbedded mica schist and quartzite
Bond, Bondcliff and West Bond: *Igneous*—Mt. Lafayette granite porphyry
Cabot: *Igneous*—Hastingite and riebeckite granite (The Bulge and The Horn—syenite)
Cannon: *Igneous*—Conway granite, including Cannon Cliffs
Carrigain: *Igneous*—Carrigain syenite porphyry on upper mountain, including summit and crest of Signal Ridge; Mt. Osceola granite on lower W slopes; Conway granite on lower N slopes and in Carrigain Notch; Moat volcanics on S and E slopes of Signal Ridge
Carter Dome, Middle Carter and South Carter: *Metamorphic*—gray paragneiss
Eisenhower: *Metamorphic*—Littleton gray gneiss
Field: *Igneous*—Conway granite on W side, Albany porphyritic quartz syenite on E side, Moat volcanics on N ridge
Flume: *Igneous*—Mt. Lafayette granite porphyry at summit; three other granitic rocks on W slopes
Galehead: *Metamorphic*—Talford schist at summit and on S ridge; *Igneous*—Mt. Lafayette granite porphyry at Galehead Hut
Garfield: *Igneous*—Mt. Garfield porphyritic quartz syenite at summit, part of a ring-dike; Kinsman quartz monzonite on NW and SE slopes; Mt. Lafayette granite porphyry on NE slopes
Hale: *Igneous*—Moat volcanics at summit; rest of mountain is a mix of various igneous and *metamorphic* rocks; Sugarloaves are Conway granite
North and South Hancock: *Igneous*—Mt. Osceola granite
Isolation: *Metamorphic*—Littleton gray gniess on W side, interbedded mica schist and micaceous quartzite on E side
Jackson: *Metamorphic*—Littleton gray gneiss
Jefferson: *Metamorphic*—interbedded mica schist and quartzite
North and South Kinsman: *Igneous*—Kinsman quartz monzonite
Lafayette: *Igneous*—Mt. Lafayette granite porphyry at summit; Mt. Garfield porphyritic syenite on upper E slopes; Kinsman quartz monzonite on lower E slopes and W slopes, including Greenleaf Hut and Old Bridle Path
Liberty: *Igneous*—Mt. Lafayette granite porphyry at summit and on upper W slopes; Kinsman quartz monzonite and Mt. Garfield porphyritic quartz syenite on upper E slopes; Conway granite at The Flume
Lincoln: *Igneous*—Mt. Lafayette granite porphyry at summit and along ridge S to Little Haystack; other granitic rocks as on Lafayette
Madison: *Metamorphic*—interbedded mica schist and quartzite

Monroe: *Metamorphic*—Littleton gray gneiss at summit and on N and W slopes; interbedded mica schist and quartzite at Lakes of Clouds and to E; between Monroe and hut is a narrow band of metamorphic rock known as the Boott member, formed from limestone

Moosilauke: *Metamorphic*—mica schist and micaceous quartzite

Moriah: *Metamorphic*—gray paragneiss on E slopes, along ridgecrest and on upper W slopes; mica schist and quartzite along NW ridge, including Mt. Surprise

Osceola and East Osceola: *Igneous*—Mt. Osceola granite

Owl's Head: Primarily *igneous*—Kinsman quartz monzonite on N and W, Mt. Lafayette granite porphyry on S and E; small circular area of Moat volcanics on SE spur; *metamorphic* band of Talford schist slices across ridge, including summit

Passaconaway: *Igneous*—Passaconaway syenite at summit and on S slopes; Conway granite on lower N and E slopes, including Square Ledge and Albany Hedgehog; small areas of *metamorphic* schist NW and NE of summit

Pierce: *Metamorphic*—Littleton gray gneiss

Tecumseh: *Metamorphic*—schist at summit and West Peak; *Igneous*—Conway granite on E side and S down ridge to Dickey and Welch Mtns.

Tom: *Igneous*—Moat volcanics on summit ridge, Conway granite on W slopes; three bands of igneous rock and one band of *metamorphic* rock on E slopes

North and Middle Tripyramid: *Igneous*—quartz syenite along ridge, exposed at top of North and South Slides; surrounded by several circular bands of other igneous rocks; part of a ring-dike

North and South Twin: *Igneous*—Mt. Lafayette granite porphyry

Washington: *Metamorphic*—interbedded mica schist and quartzite

Waumbek: *Igneous*—quartz syenite; part of a ring-dike

Whiteface: *Igneous*—Passaconaway syenite on main ridge and upper S ledges; Conway granite on SE slopes, including Blueberry Ledges; Kinsman quartz monzoite on SW slopes

Wildcat and Wildcat D: *Metamorphic*—mostly gray paragneiss; at summit of "A" Peak is intrebedded mica schist and micaceous quartzite

Willey: *Metamorphic*—andalusite schist and micaceous quartzite on N and NE part of mountain; *Igneous*—Conway granite on W, S and SE slopes; boundary between rock types is just W of summit

Zealand: *Igneous*—Mt. Lafayette granite porphyry W of Zeacliff Pond, Conway granite E to Zeacliffs and Zealand Notch

Useful Websites and Phone Numbers

TRAIL INFORMATION

Views from the Top—Northeast. *www.lexicomm.com/whites/index.html*
The "Trail Conditions—New Hampshire" section carries reports submitted by hikers—a great way in winter to check up on snow depth and conditions.

White Mountains Info Server. *www.cs.dartmouth.edu/whites*
David Metsky's site is a terrific resource for White Mountain hiking.

Hiking in the Mountains of New England. *http://home.earthlink.net/~ellozy/*
Excellent site with emphasis on peakbagging in the Northeast.

WEATHER

Mt. Washington Observatory. *www.mountwashington.org*
Excellent site includes weather report, live summit camera, avalanche danger, snow depths and conditions at Pinkham Notch, Crawford Notch and other locations.

National Weather Service. *iwin.nws.noaa.gov/iwin/nh/zone.html*
Gives zone forecasts for New Hampshire.
iwin.nws.noaa.gov/iwin/nh/public.html
Gives forecasts for higher summits of White Mountains.

GENERAL INFORMATION

White Mountain National Forest. *www.fs.fed.us/r9/white*

WMNF Supervisor's Office, Laconia, N.H.	603–528–8721
Ammonoosuc Ranger District, Bethlehem, N.H.	603–869–2626
Androscoggin Ranger District, Gorham, N.H.	603–466–2713
Pemigewasset Ranger District, Plymouth, N.H.	603–536–1310
Saco Ranger District, Conway, N.H.	603–447–5448

Appalachian Mountain Club. *www.outdoors.org*

Pinkham Notch Visitor Center, Gorham, N.H.	603–466–2721

Randolph Mountain Club. *www.randolphmountainclub.org*

Wonalancet Out Door Club. *www.wodc.org*

Selected Bibliography

Abbott, Karl P. *Open for the Season*. Garden City, N.Y.: Doubleday & Company, Inc., 1950.

Allen, Dan H. *Don't Die on the Mountain*. New London, N.H.: Diapensia Press, 1998.

Among the Clouds. Mount Washington, N.H.

Appalachia. Journal of the Appalachian Mountain Club, Boston.

Averill, Robert E., ed. *The Moosilaukee Reader, Vol. I & Vol. II*. Warren, NH: Moose Country Press, 1999.

Beals, Charles Edward, Jr. *Passaconaway in the White Mountains*. Boston: Richard G. Badger, 1916.

Bean, Grace H. *The Town at the End of the Road: A History of Waterville Valley*. Canaan, N.H.: Phoenix Publishing, 1983.

Belcher, C. Francis. *Logging Railroads of the White Mountains*. Boston: Appalachian Mountain Club Books, 1980.

Belknap, Jeremy. *The History of New Hampshire, Vol. III*. Boston, 1792.

Bliss, L. C. *Alpine Zone of the Presidential Range*. Edmonton, Canada, 1963.

Bolles, Frank. *At the North of Bearcamp Water: Chronicles of a Stroller in New England From July to December*. Boston: Houghton Mifflin Company, 1893.

Bolnick, Bruce and Doreen. *Waterfalls of the White Mountains*. Woodstock, Vt.: Countryman Press, 2nd edition, 1999.

Burt, F. Allen. *The Story of Mount Washington*. Hanover, N.H.: Dartmouth Publications, 1960.

Burt, Frank H. *Mount Washington: A Handbook for Travellers*. Boston, 1904.

Crawford, Lucy. *The History of the White Mountains, From the First Settlement of Upper Coos and Pequaket*. Portland, Maine: B. Thurston & Company, 1886.

Cross, George N. *Dolly Copp and the Pioneers of the Glen*. 1927.

Cross, George N. *Randolph: Old and New*. Randolph, N.H.: Town of Randolph, 1924.

Daniell, Eugene S., III, and Burroughs, Jon, ed. *AMC White Mountain Guide*. Boston: Appalachian Mountain Club, 26th edition, 1998. All previous editions used back to 1st Edition, 1907.

Dartmouth Outing Club. *A Trail Guide to Mount Moosilauke*. Hanover, N.H., 1978.

Dickerman, Mike et alia. *A Guide to Crawford Notch*. Littleton, N.H.: Bondcliff Books, 1997.

Dickerman, Mike, ed. *Mount Washington: Narratives and Perspectives*. Littleton, N.H.: Bondcliff Books, 1999.

Dickerman, Mike, ed. *The White Mountain Reader*. Littleton, N.H.: Bondcliff Books, 2000.

Doan, Daniel and MacDougall, Ruth Doan. *50 Hikes in the White Mountains*. Woodstock, Vt.: Countryman Press, 5th edition, 1997.

Doan, Daniel and MacDougall, Ruth Doan. *50 More Hikes in New Hampshire*. Woodstock, Vt.: Countryman Press, 4th edition, 1998.

Drake, Samuel A. *The Heart of the White Mountains, Their Legend and Scenery*. New York: Harper and Brothers, 1881.

Eastman, Samuel C. *The White Mountain Guidebook*. Boston: Lee and Shepard, 7th edition, 1867.

Evans, George. *Jefferson, New Hampshire, 1773–1927*. Jefferson, N.H., 1927.

Federal Writers' Project. *Skiing in the East*. New York: M. Barrows & Company, 1939.

Geology Quadrangle Series published by N.H. Department of Resources and Economic Development, Concord, N.H.

Geology of the Crawford Notch Quadrangle, by Donald M. Henderson et alia, 1977.

Geology of the Franconia Quadrangle, by Marland P. Billings and Charles R. Williams, 1935.

Geology of the Gorham Quadrangle, by Marland P. Billings and Katharine Fowler-Billings, 1975.

Geology of the Mt. Chocorua Quadrangle, by Althea Page Smith et alia, 1939.

Geology of the Mt. Washington Quadrangle, by Marland P. Billings et alia, 1979.

Geology of the Percy Quadrangle, by Randolph W. Chapman, 1949.

Geology of the Plymouth Quadrangle, by Charles B. Moke, 1946.

Goodman, David. *Backcountry Skiing Adventures: Maine and New Hampshire*. Boston: Appalachian Mountain Club Books, 2nd edition, 1999.

Goodrich, Nathaniel L. *The Waterville Valley*. Lunenburg, Vt.: North Country Press, 1952.

Gove, Bill. *J. E. Henry's Logging Railroads: The History of the East Branch & Lincoln and Zealand Valley Railroads*. Littleton, N.H.: Bondcliff Books, 1998.

Granite Monthly (The). Concord, N.H.

Hitchcock, C. H., and Huntington, Joshua. *The Geology of New Hampshire*. Concord, N.H.: Vol. I, 1874 and Vol. II, 1877.

Hooke, David O. *Reaching That Peak: 75 Years of the Dartmouth Outing Club*. Canaan, N.H.: Phoenix Publishing, 1987.

Howe, Nicholas. *Not Without Peril*. Boston: Appalachian Mountain Club Books, 2000.

Julyan, Robert and Mary. *Place Names of the White Mountains*. Hanover, N.H.: University Press of New England, revised edition, 1993.

Kidder, Glenn M. *Railway to the Moon*. Littleton, N.H., 1969.

Kilbourne, Frederick W. *Chronicles of the White Mountains*. Boston: Houghton Mifflin Company, 1916.

King, Thomas Starr. *The White Hills: Their Legends, Landscape and Poetry*. Boston: Crosby and Ainsworth, 1859.

Kostecke, Diane M., ed. *Franconia Notch: An In-Depth Guide*. Concord, N.H.: Society for the Protection of N.H. Forests, 1975.

Little, William. *The History of Warren: A Mountain Hamlet Located Among the White Hills of New Hampshire*. Manchester, N.H., 1870.

Littleton Courier (The). Littleton, N.H.

Marchand, Peter. *North Woods*. Boston: Appalachian Mountain Club Books, 1987.

McAvoy, George E. *And Then There Was One*. Littleton, N.H.: The Crawford Press, 1988.

Mount Washington Observatory News Bulletin. North Conway, N.H.

Mudge, John T. B. *The White Mountains: Names, Places & Legends*. Etna, N.H.: The Durand Press, 1992.

Putnam, William Lowell. *Joe Dodge: One New Hampshire Institution*. Canaan, N.H.: Phoenix Publishing, 1986.

Putnam, William Lowell. *The Worst Weather on Earth*. Gorham, N.H.: Mount Washington Observatory, 1991.

Ramsey, Floyd W. *Shrouded Memories: True Stories from the White Mountains of New Hampshire*. Littleton, N.H., 1994.

Randall, Peter E. *Mount Washington: A Guide and Short History*. Woodstock, Vt.: Countryman Press, 3rd edition, 1992.

Randolph Mountain Club. *Randolph Paths*. 6th edition. 1997.

Reifsnyder, William E. *High Huts of the White Mountains*. Boston: Appalachian Mountain Club Books, 1993.

Rowan, Peter and June Hammond. *Mountain Summers*. Gorham, N.H.: Gulfside Press, 1995.

Scudder, Brent E. *Scudder's White Mountain Viewing Guide*. Littleton, N.H.: Bondcliff Books, 2000.

Slack, Nancy B. and Bell, Allison W. *A Field Guide to the New England Alpine Summits*. Boston: Appalachian Mountain Club Books, 1995.

Smith, Steven D. *Ponds and Lakes of the White Mountains: A Four-Season Guide for Hikers and Anglers*. Second Edition. Woodstock, Vt.: Backcountry Publications, 1998.

Spaulding, John H. *Historical Relics of the White Mountains, Also a Concise White Mountain Guide*. Boston, 1855.

Stier, Maggie and McAdow, Ron. *Into the Mountains*. Boston: Appalachian Mountain Club Books, 1995.

Sweetser, Moses F. *The White Mountains: A Handbook for Travellers*. Boston: James R. Osgood and Company, 1876 (and various subsequent editions).

Sweetser, Moses F. *Chisholm's White Mountain Guide*. Portland, Maine: Chisholm Brothers, 1902 edition.

Tolles, Bryant F., Jr. *The Grand Resort Hotels of the White Mountains: A Vanishing Architectural Legacy*. Boston: David R. Godine, 1998.

Underhill, Miriam. *Give Me the Hills*. Riverside, Conn.: Chatham Press, Inc., 1971.

Van Diver, Bradford B. *Roadside Geology of Vermont and New Hampshire*. Missoula, Mont.: Mountain Press, 1987.

Ward, Julius H. *The White Mountains: A Guide to Their Interpretation*. New York: D. Appleton and Co., 1890.

Waterman, Laura and Guy. *Forest and Crag: A History of Hiking, Trail Blazing and Adventure in the Northeast Mountains*. Boston: Appalachian Mountain Club Books, 1989.

Waterman, Laura and Guy. *Backwoods Ethics: Environmental Issues for Hikers and Campers*. Woodstock, Vt.: The Countryman Press, 2nd edition, 1993.

Waterman, Laura and Guy. *Wilderness Ethics: Preserving the Spirit of Wildness*. Woodstock, Vt.: The Countryman Press, 1993.

Waterman, Laura and Guy. *Yankee Rock and Ice: A History of Climbing in the Northeastern United States*. Harrisburg, Pa.: Stackpole Books, 1993.

Welch, Sarah N. *A History of Franconia, New Hampshire*. Franconia, N.H., 1972.

Willey, Benjamin G. *Incidents in White Mountain History*. Boston: Nathaniel Noyes, 1856.

Wight, D. B. *The Wild River Wilderness*. Littleton, N.H., 1971.

Wonalancet Out Door Club Newsletter. Wonalancet, N.H.

About the Authors

STEVEN D. SMITH has been exploring northern New England trails for over 20 years, has nearly completed his fifth round of the White Mountain 4000-Footer list (including once in winter), and is a member of the Appalachian Mountain Club's Four Thousand Footer Committee. He is the author of two previously published White Mountain guidebooks, *Snowshoe Hikes in the White Mountains* and *Ponds and Lakes of the White Mountains*. He has also co-authored two other hiking guides. He owns The Mountain Wanderer Map and Book Store in Lincoln, New Hampshire, specializing in New England outdoors and travel. Steve and his wife, Carol, reside in Lincoln.

MIKE DICKERMAN is an award-winning journalist whose popular hiking column, "The Beaten Path," appears regularly in several northern New Hampshire newspapers. He has successfully climbed all the White Mountain 4000-Footers in both summer and winter. He is the author and/or editor of five previously published books, *Along the Beaten Path*, *A Guide to Crawford Notch*, *Why I'll Never Hike the Appalachian Trail*, *Mount Washington: Narratives and Perspectives*, and *The White Mountain Reader*. He and his wife, Jeanne, live and work year-round in Littleton, New Hampshire.